Women with Disabilities

ESSAYS IN PSYCHOLOGY, CULTURE, AND POLITICS

HEALTH, SOCIETY, AND POLICY
a series edited by
Sheryl Ruzek and Irving Kenneth Zola

Women with Disabilities

ESSAYS IN PSYCHOLOGY, CULTURE, AND POLITICS

**Edited by Michelle Fine
and Adrienne Asch**

Temple University Press
Philadelphia

Temple University Press, Philadelphia 19122
Copyright © 1988 by Temple University. All rights reserved
Published 1988
Printed in the United States of America

Library of Congress Cataloging-in-Publication Data

Women with disabilities.

  (Health, society, and policy)
  Includes bibliographies and index.
  1. Physically handicapped women.   2. Sex
discrimination against women.   3. Physically
handicapped women—Psychology.   I. Fine, Michelle.
II. Asch, Adrienne.   III. Series.
HV3021.W66W68   1988   362.4'088042   87-10099
ISBN 0-87722-474-9   (alk. paper)

OCLC 15696394

Contents

Foreword

By JEFFREY Z. RUBIN, President, Society for the Psychological Study of Social Issues Division of APA

This is a book about edges, margins, and rocky perches. It is the story of survival in these outposts, as told by the residents: disabled girls and women.

Disabled girls and women, you say? Why should I, the reader—a reasonably healthy, affluent Western man or woman—possibly be interested in so arcane, even perverse a topic? The answer is simple: because we are each marginal in some way, and because this book therefore addresses all our lives.

Western society places a premium on wealth, youth, physical strength, and attractiveness. To be at the center of this universe is—or so it would appear—to be precisely where all good Westerners aspire to be. And yet, as this collection of essays culled by Michelle Fine and Adrienne Asch makes clear, no matter how central we may seem to be, all of us are marginal in some way, standing on the outside looking in, excluded from certain experiences even as we are included in others. Centrality is illusory, in that we each are far less pivotal than we fancy ourselves to be. And it is evanescent, constantly shifting with the passage of time and the vagaries of health and experience.

Because of their chronically lesser power in society, women are perennial outsiders. Despite the profound societal changes and advances in the latter part of this century, women remain marginal in many ways, too often relying for their success on the qualities of youth and attractiveness. For sure, to be a young and attractive woman is to have some modicum of control over at least certain aspects of one's life. But to be older, to be unattractive, and, most important, to be disabled or disfigured in some way is be out on the margins of a margin of a margin.

Disabled girls and women, then, are the denizens of this apparently worst-of-both-worlds combination of being female and being quintessentially unattractive through disability. And this powerful book by

Fine and Asch brings the lives of these people before our eyes to observe, to learn from, to share in their joy and optimism, and to cringe at the pain that society—"nice folks" like each of us—continues to inflict upon them.

The numbers are surprisingly large: more than eleven million disabled women in the United States alone. A look at this world is thus far more than a look at the hypothetical end of a theoretical continuum. These are real lives, and lots of them, that Fine and Asch have brought before us. To understand the ability of stigmatized women to create productive and caring lives for themselves—in the shadow of society's imposed disgrace and revulsion—is to understand the reason for continuing optimism about the human condition, and to understand how transparent and silly is the sense that many of us may have of ever really being at the center of anything.

As SPSSI's President, I am immensely proud and privileged to introduce this fine book to you. Read and enjoy!

Foreword

By VIRGINIA E. O'LEARY, President, Psychology of Women
Division of APA

As stated in the bylaws of the American Psychological Association, one of the goals of Division 35, that of the Psychology of Women, is to encourage the integration of information about women with current psychological knowledge and beliefs in order to apply gained knowledge to the society and institutions. *Women with Disabilities* offers an exciting opportunity to reflect on the life experiences of a segment of the population of women about which relatively little is known or understood—women who are disabled.

In the last fifteen years, social and behavioral scientists have learned more about girls and women than they had in the previous sixty. However, the picture is skewed by an emphasis on white, middle to upper-middle class, young, educated, able-bodied women. Fine and Asch offer us a look into the lives of a hitherto neglected population. Their contribution to the rapidly accumulating knowledge about women's diversities (as well as their commonalities) moves us one step closer to understanding the varieties of the female experience. Of equal, perhaps greater, importance is the fact that in documenting what is known about women who are disabled, we are able to identify some of the myriad questions that remain to be answered.

A careful reading of the material presented in the chapters comprising *Women with Disabilities* allows the identification of a comprehensive research agenda worthy of the immediate attention of both researchers and policy makers. It is with pride that Division 35 acknowledges the privilege of having the opportunity to cosponsor this exceptional addition to our collective understanding of women's psychological and social realities.

Preface and Acknowledgments

This book grows out of our personal friendship and our political commitments to feminism and to disability rights. In this volume, we have collected a body of knowledge from varied academic disciplines and from activists. We have tried to piece together a new understanding of the disabled woman and to respect the variety of bodies and minds we found among them. In writing, we have sought to expand the image of girls and women with disabilities from one of passivity and weakness to one also incorporating passion and strength.

This book continues an interdisciplinary conversation about disability, gender, and their interaction. The authors represented in this collection, women with and without disabilities, take seriously the complexities of discrimination by gender and disability status, race, age, and sexual orientation. They also acknowledge the ways in which the social contexts of friendship, political work, and personal forms of resistance affect girls and women with disabilities. Rather than merely lamenting the economic and social disadvantages of today's disabled women, they explore the origins of their situation and challenge its inevitability.

As we bring this book to completion after nearly five years, we have the pleasure of expressing our appreciation to all those who have had a part in its creation. As psychologists, we enjoyed the support of the Society for the Psychological Study of Social Issues (Division 9 of the American Psychological Association) and the Division of Psychology of Women (Division 35 of the American Psychological Association). Their commitment to our enterprise testifies to the increasing recognition of both disability and gender as matters worthy of serious scholarly attention.

This book would not have been possible without the involvement of many friends, strangers, girls, and women willing to talk. We were fortunate to attend Access to Equality: The First National Conference on Educational Equity for Disabled Women and Girls in June 1982 and to try out many ideas on the more than 100 women there. From that conference emerged the Women and Disability Awareness Project, a group of ten disabled and non-disabled women who met together for more than two years to think about infusing disability into feminism, feminism into disability rights, and forging links between the women's and disability rights movements. To our colleagues and friends in this project—Merle Froschl, Liz Phillips, Susan Quinby, Carol Roberson, Harilyn Rousso, Sandy Weinbaum, Sharon Wigutoff, Deborah Yager— our warmest thanks. The girls and women with disabilities we have met over the past five years at a host of conferences and formal and informal gatherings provided us not only with their stories and their hopes but also with their encouragement and enthusiasm for our work. We needed the sense that what we were doing was valuable, and they continually gave it to us. Although we cannot name them all, we especially thank Beth, Frances, Gina, Mary, and Michelle.

Temple University Press has been wonderful to work with. They took a chance on a novel idea, believing in us and our work and its potential contribution. Sheryl Ruzek and Irv Zola, editors of the series, took enormous interest and time. Not only did they carefully comment on drafts of chapters, but they counseled us as somewhat novice editors in the psychological, logistical, and interpersonal management of all those involved in the process. Janet Francendese started out as a colleague and through the long process of editing (and waiting), she became our friend. Jennifer French, Kathleen Glenn-Lewin, Irene Glynn, and Joan Vidal provided patient, meticulous, and sensitive copy-editing that has markedly improved this collection.

Each of us has some particular people to recognize for their friendship and support throughout this process. Michelle is especially indebted to Linda Brodkey, Sam Finesurrey, Dana Kaminstein, Louise Kidder, Rayna Rapp, Theresa Singleton, and David Surrey, and wishes to express appreciation to the University of Pennsylvania Faculty Fellowship Program for its support of this work.

Adrienne would like to thank two groups of people; first, the many readers who taped thousands of pages of manuscripts, correspondence, articles, and books that went into this book. First among these is everyone at Recording for the Blind, staff and volunteer, whose taped books were used in research and whose library was expanded by at least two dozen books—sometimes in a rush—so that the work could get done.

Adrienne's staff of readers came to know this book intimately, often providing useful insights and suggestions as well as clear recording of draft manuscripts in many incarnations. Thanks go to Kevin Coleman, John Fousek, Mark Isaac, Elizabeth Lopez, Kate McReynolds, Alex Treitler, and Tina Trudel for outstanding work, great patience, and warm friendship.

Adrienne also wishes to acknowledge those people who have helped (sometimes forced) her to think about what it means to live in this society as a woman who also has a disability: Ann, Debbie, Ellen, Harilyn, Joyce, Kate, Michelle, Tina, and Valentine. They have done more than help in this struggle; they have struggled with her, and in so doing, have made that struggle much easier, far more interesting, and more enjoyable than it would otherwise have been. In some important ways, they are in these pages.

Last, we cannot say enough to thank the authors in this volume. They were generous with their ideas, enthusiastic about the project, by turns critical and patient with us when we needed it. We were warned that an edited volume would give us untold grief and might not reward us for our effort. Work, frustration, and sometimes grief there was, but working with everyone whose contributions make up this volume has been deeply satisfying and extremely rewarding. As editors, we are fortunate indeed.

A.A.
M.F.
New York City
1987

Introduction: Beyond Pedestals

ADRIENNE ASCH AND MICHELLE FINE

CONTEXT OF THIS VOLUME: "DISCOVERING" THE DISABLED WOMAN

Despite the prevalence of disability in this society, disabled persons tend to be invisible. Reliable estimates indicate that most people's lives will be touched by disability, but the community avoids the topic in much the same way as it avoids encounters with individuals who have disabling conditions. Indeed, public reluctance to deal with disability as a potential for one's own life or those of loved ones is reflected in the lack of information about it. Despite the penchant for data collection, the community and its major institutions know relatively little about the extent and experience of disability in the population.

In 1980 it was estimated that some thirty-six million citizens of the United States had disabilities: 10 percent of the population under age 21; somewhere between 9 and 17 percent, depending upon studies, of all people of working age; and nearly half of all people over age 65 (Bowe 1980; Haber and McNeil 1983). In December 1986 the *New York Times* reported that one in five adults between the ages of 16 and 64 indicated having a disabling condition that affected life activities (*New York Times* 1986). Of the 51 percent of the nation that is female, we can estimate that perhaps one-sixth have disabilities. How do being female and having a disability interact? How do women with disabilities view their experience? These are a few of the questions that spawned this volume. What can we learn about disability from literature, folklore, social science, law, and public policy? Does it matter at what age or stage in life disability occurs? How do race, social class, social circumstances, and sexual orientation influence the lives of women with disabilities?

In 1981 we wrote "Disabled Women: Sexism Without the Pedestal," which appeared in a special issue of the *Journal of Sociology and Social Welfare* (Fine and Asch 1981). We reviewed what was then known about the economic, social, and psychological circumstances of women with

1

disabilities and suggested some explanations for why these women found themselves significantly more disadvantaged than either non-disabled women or disabled men. Disabled women, we found, experience much the same oppression as non-disabled women, without receiving the ostensible rewards of the "pedestal" upon which some (white) women traditionally have been placed. We concluded by proposing directions for research, policy, and politics.

The passage of half a decade has seen growth in the new genre of writing on and by disabled women. Jo Campling (1981) brought to public discourse the private lives and stories of British women with disabilities; her book was hailed here, too, because it spoke for long-silent U.S. women. That same year Duffy (1981) offered a valuable discussion of sexuality as a key arena of both oppression and expression for women with disabilities. More recent works include a report of interviews with forty-five disabled Canadian women (Matthews 1983); the collected essays of an outspoken feminist and disability rights activist (Hannaford 1985); an important collection of research-based chapters on varied spheres of disabled women's experiences (Deegan and Brooks 1985); rich and diverse collections of essays, prose, poetry, and imaginative writing by women, representing a broad range of disabilities and life experiences (Browne et al. 1985; Saxton and Howe 1987). One feminist journal, *off our backs* (1981), and one professional disability publication, *Journal of Visual Impairment and Blindness* (1983), have produced special issues on the situation of disabled women. *The New Our Bodies, Ourselves* (Boston Women's Health Book Collective 1985) attends sensitively and in detail to the concerns of girls and women with disabilities.

Now, six years after the *Journal of Sociology and Social Welfare*'s special issue on disabled women, we present the essays collected in this volume. These writings cross disciplines and politics. They chronicle the intellectual and political odyssey of feminism and disability rights through a more advanced scholarship, a more complicated discussion of political struggles, and a more ambitious attempt to infuse from the margins the reclaimed voices of the "pitied" disabled woman. Recognizing that research in this area is relatively new and that this volume cannot claim to be comprehensive or conclusive, we have attempted to address questions of broad significance within a socialist-feminist framework that acknowledges the importance of class, race, sexual orientation, and disability in understanding and shaping the lives of women. Topics in this essay and throughout the volume relate to disabled women's experiences in the "productive," or paid, work worlds;

in the reproductive, or motherhood, realm; and in the areas of sexuality, family, friendship, community, and politics. Here we discuss the emergence of disabled women as a group for particular attention; we present data about and interpretation of their economic, social, and psychological circumstances; and we discuss what thinking about disabled women contributes to both theory and politics within the movements of disability rights and feminism.

Before examining the data available on girls and women with disabilities, one must note that there is little to be found. To date almost all research on disabled men and women seems simply to assume the irrelevance of gender, race, ethnicity, sexual orientation, or social class. Having a disability presumably eclipses these dimensions of social experience. Even sensitive students of disability (for example, Becker 1980; Davis 1961, 1963; Darling 1979; Gliedman and Roth 1980; Goffman 1963; Higgins 1980; Roskies 1972; Wright 1960, 1983) have focused on disability as a unitary concept and have taken it to be not merely the "master" status but apparently the exclusive status for disabled people. Paralleling what Eisenstein (1983) has described as the "false universalism" of feminist writing of the 1970s, the disability rights literature has chosen to stress commonalities among all disabled people rather than differences based on gender.

Although the meaning of gender for either disabled women or men has been neglected by most rehabilitation and medical professionals, social scientists, and disability rights activists, the attentions of such groups has not focused equally on the two sexes. For many years the thrust of rehabilitation and government study and policy was on the war-wounded or work-injured disabled person, one who was, invariably, a male. Having a disability was seen as synonymous with being dependent, childlike, and helpless—an image fundamentally challenging all that is embodied in the ideal male: virility, autonomy, and independence. Yet this image replicated, if in caricature, all that is embodied in the ideal female: emotionality, passivity, and dependence (Broverman, Vogel, Broverman, Clarkson, and Rosenkrantz 1972). Concerns with "emasculation" may promote efforts directed toward those at the locus of the *masculinity/dependence* contradiction, not toward those at the redundant intersection of *femininity* and *dependence*. Certainly the social imperative seems to have been to study and rehabilitate the "wounded male" (Rose 1984).

Women with disabilities traditionally have been ignored not only by those concerned about disability but also by those examining women's experiences. Even the feminist scholars to whom we owe great intellectual and political debts have perpetuated this neglect. The popular view of women with disabilities has been one mixed with repugnance. Perceiving disabled women as childlike, helpless, and victimized, non-disabled feminists have severed them from the sisterhood in an effort to advance more powerful, competent, and appealing female icons. As one feminist academic said to the non-disabled coauthor of this essay: "Why study women with disabilities? They reinforce traditional stereotypes of women being dependent, passive, and needy."

Feminist anthologies, including key works that mindfully integrate racial and minority group concerns with gender analyses, continue to exclude women with disabilities (Cox 1981; Eisenstein and Jardine 1985; Freeman 1984; Sargent 1981; Snitow, Stansell, and Thompson 1983). In 1983, Hester Eisenstein chronicled major feminist thought since 1970, noting how feminist writings and politics sought to learn from and unite women of the working and middle classes, married women and single women, mothers and non-mothers, lesbians and heterosexual women, women of color and white women, women of all ages. Yet, her otherwise excellent book completely omits comment on the absence of women with disabilities from women's groups and women's writing. Her call for renewed attention to differences among women nowhere recognizes disabled women as a group whose voice needs to be heard. Such omissions by feminists in the mid-1980s are especially distressing when one recalls that disabled women have appeared at political gatherings such as the 1977 Houston conference, the Copenhagen conference on women, and conferences on women and the law since at least 1983. Moreover, despite their presence in anthologies, scholarly publications, and the feminist popular press (in addition to works mentioned above, see Fine and Asch 1982; Finger 1983, 1984; Saxton 1984), non-disabled women scholars have joined men in relegating disabled women to a realm beneath their intellectual and political ken.

Non-disabled academics and activists who have fought hard for women's right to autonomy may fear disability in parents, friends, children, or themselves. Accepting the widespread, if inaccurate, belief that disability inevitably threatens independence, women know that it is they, as women, who will be called upon to care for the disabled individual. As Miller (1976) brought home, it is women who do the culture's nurturing work. Perhaps the conviction that disabled people are inevitably burdensome and that women will be so burdened accounts for feminist resistance to involvement in the disability rights movement.

DISABLED WOMEN: FACT AND SOCIAL CONSTRUCT

Over the past twenty years feminist researchers have unhooked notions of gender from those of sex. The socially acquired aspects of the female—presumably the loving, caretaking, and cooperative work of women—have been separated from the biological aspects. The maternal instinct, along with women's ostensible inabilities to compete effectively or to be sexually assertive, has been demystified and tracked to socially constructed origins (Chodorow 1978; Ruddick 1980).

Likewise, in the past twenty years both the study and the politics of disability have undergone transformation. Activists and scholars have insisted that the *disability* (the *biological* condition) be conceptually disentangled from the *handicap* (the *social* ramifications) of the condition. Obstacles to education, community and political participation, independent living, employment, and personal relationships derived not from the incapacities, for example, of individuals in wheelchairs to walk stairs but in the existence of the stairs themselves. If people with mobility impairments could not enter buildings without ramps or ride inaccessible buses, the fault was in the structures and the transportation system, not in their bodies. If people who wished to work could not because of medical standards that barred anyone with a history of heart disease, cancer, epilepsy, or obesity, or anyone with diabetes or visual or hearing impairments, the problem might be one of arbitrary medical standards and not of a person's inherent incapacity to perform specific job tasks. If young adults with sensory, motor, or learning disabilities were not attaining a postsecondary education, perhaps the problem lay not in their biology but in the institution's architecture, testing requirements, or admissions standards. If disabled people lived with their parents or in institutions long after their non-disabled age-peers had set up households, perhaps the reason lay not with fears for their independence or their physical well-being, but with the lack of *accessible buildings in which to live, of affordable support services such as attendants to help with hygiene, or of transporation to nearby stores.* If men and women with disabilities suffered social isolation or discovered that former friends no longer had time for them, perhaps the problem was not in their psychology but in others' attitudes toward disability and expectations of friendship.

During the 1970s grass-roots groups of disabled people organized along single- and cross-disability lines, formed statewide and national membership organizations and coalitions, founded legal advocacy centers, and published newsletters. They worked along with parents of disabled children and with non-disabled advocates to obtain laws guaranteeing rights of access to education, employment, government services, and community life. By the end of the decade, although disabled people still had far fewer civil rights than those available to people fighting race or sex discrimination, their situation had begun to improve. (For discussions of civil rights legislation, see Bowe 1980, Funk 1987; for disabled people as a minority group see Funk 1987, Hahn 1987; and for the disability rights and independent living movements, see Asch 1986a, Crewe and Zola 1983, Scotch 1984.)

Scholars and activists within feminism and disability rights, then, have demonstrated that the experiences of being female or of having a disability are socially constructed; that the biological cannot be understood outside of those contexts and relationships that shape and give meaning to femaleness and to disability. In what follows, we use the tools of feminist and disability scholarship and politics to explore the situation of women who have disabilities. Finding, as we did earlier, that disabled women still are more disadvantaged than either non-disabled women or disabled men, we discuss the relative impacts of sexism and of disability discrimination, and examine their interaction.

It is ironic to note that the very category that integrates this text, "disabled girls and women," exists wholly as a social construct. Why should a limb-deficient girl, a teenager with mental retardation, or a blind girl have anything in common with each other, or with a woman with breast cancer or another woman who is recovering from a stroke? What they share is similar treatment by a sexist and disability-phobic society. This is what makes it likely that they will be thrown together in school, in the unemployment line, in segregated recreation programs, in rehabilitation centers, and in legislation.

As defined in the Rehabilitation Act of 1973, PL 93-112, as amended by PL 95-602, Section 7, the term "handicapped individual" means

1. any person whose physical or mental impairment substantially limits one or more of the person's major life activities;
2. has a record of such impairment; or
3. is regarded as having such an impairment.

This definition is broad, encompassing conditions not commonly thought of as disabilities but rather as chronic illnesses, health problems, or the like. Disabilities both readily apparent and invisible can interfere with daily activities: mobility, for example, can be affected not only by polio or amputation but by arthritis, a heart condition, or respiratory or back problems. Reading print may be difficult because of vision impairment or the perceptual problems of some types of learning disabilities. People with histories of institutionalization for mental illness or mental retardation may in fact not be hindered in any life task but may carry records that haunt them and impede their access to education and employment. People with cancer in remission, with epilepsy, with cosmetic disfigurements, or with obesity, along with all other people with disabilities, may find themselves regarded as impaired when they can perform in any social role. Thus, the social construction of disability, like that of gender, underscores this fact: it is the attitudes and institutions of the non-disabled, even more than the biological characteristics of the disabled, that turn characteristics into handicaps.

The following data must be preceded by an acknowledgment that throughout, biology is confounded by the social constructions of disability, gender, and their interaction. If twice as many boys as girls are classified in need of special-education services (Gillespie and Fink 1974; Hobbs 1975), the causes cannot be attributed solely to more frequent incidence of biological limitation in boys. Similarly, although it may appear straightforward to determine the numbers of working-age women and men with disabilities, the difficulties in obtaining reliable data are manifold (Asch 1984; *Disability Rag* 1984; Haber and McNeil 1983; Roth 1983).

Obtaining sensitive, accurate data on persons with disabilities requires asking questions that do not confound health status with social role performance. Yet the U.S. Census Bureau continues to assess disability in the following way: "Does this person have a physical, mental, or other health condition which has lasted for six or more months and which (1) limits the kind or amount of work this person can do at a job? (2) prevents this person from working at a job?" (Haber and McNeil 1983: 6). Not only does such questioning fail to pick up those who do not perceive themselves to be limited in work because of a health condition, but it fails to obtain any information about people with health impairments who, for whatever reason, do not choose to work. The Health Interview Survey, another often-used source of disability data, asks about "usual activities" in the past twelve months. As Haber and McNeil (1983) point out, "The 'usual activity' screen reduces disability reporting for women whose "usual activity" was keeping house, but should not affect reporting by men" (p. 3). Do women tend not to report themselves as disabled if they can perform what they consider their primary social roles of homemaker and caretaker? Do women overreport because they, more so than men, traditionally are more willing to admit health problems and are more likely to consult health professionals? Notwithstanding these serious qualifications, there is value in outlining the situation of today's disabled female.

The disabled girl in family and school

Growing up in families where they are usually the only one with a disability, disabled girls stand out from peers and even from their intimates. In that disabled youngsters are of all races, cultures, and economic strata, they might be expected to feel connected to others of their class and race rather than to disabled people of another class or race. Yet they may be barred from the intimacy, security, and place that define community. Within what they consider to be their own group, they may feel ostracized, and they may turn to others with disabilities as their only source of acceptance, affirmation, companionship, and strength (Johnson 1987). Disabled boys and young men may appreciate such contact as well, but we suspect that socialization differs somewhat between disabled boys and girls. Accounts of the lives of disabled women and men reveal that boys are more often encouraged to meet the world, whereas girls are more often kept from it. (See Asch and Sacks 1983; Brightman 1984; Hahn 1983b; Heinrich and Kriegel 1961; Roth 1981.) Reactions of the disabled women we have interviewed confirm this.[1]

Maria, age 15, testifies: "My brother has the same hearing problem as I do. Growing up, he was encouraged in school, sports, and to learn to work. I was protected and kept at home." We know less than we would like about the familial, educational, and social experiences of today's girls and young women with disabilities. Are Maria's parents typical in sheltering their disabled daughter? Certainly disability will not have the same meaning for all parents, and thus it will differ for their daughters. Class, race, ethnicity, and values of particular parents and the medical professionals with whom they interact powerfully influence parental response to the disabled girl; hanging in the balance are her life chances.

Sara, whose parents were middle-class, was born with cerebral palsy in 1950. Physicians told her parents, "Your daughter has an empty hole in her head." Undaunted, the parents persisted in search of doctors familiar with the mythologies, uncertainties, and possibilities for someone with the condition. Through their efforts, Sara was educated in public schools with non-disabled students before mainstreaming was common. She had access to etiquette and speech lessons, and she enjoyed a climate in which she was encouraged to believe in herself. Today her life as an accomplished economist departs dramatically from that of Patrice, who also was born with cerebral palsy that same year. Patrice now lives in an institution because her welfare mother—having neither the education nor the financial resources to question authority—gave her up on the recommendation of physicians.

Social class, then, can alleviate or exacerbate the impact of a disability, just as class and race influence access to decent housing, schooling, cultural activities, and recreational opportunities for the non-disabled. For the educated and economically comfortable parent willing to assist a disabled youngster, these resources may reduce what could otherwise be serious deprivations. Yet Darling's (1979) literature review of the impact of disabled children on family life, as well as interviews conducted by Rapp (1987), caution against assuming that the disabled child born to middle-class parents will have an easier time in life. Cultures and classes that place high value on autonomy, intellect, or appearance may thwart their disabled child or reject the child altogether. Rapp corroborates the finding of Darling's earlier review, that middle-class and educated parents are more likely to reject cognitive or intellectual disabilities in their children, whereas working-class people and poor people may be more hostile to one whose physical condition may render the child vulnerable. Such findings do not differentiate parental response based on the child's gender. Future research on disabled children and their families needs to examine what it means for a mother or father, rich or poor, to have a son or daughter with a disability.

A decade after the passage of the Education for All Handicapped Children Act mandated access to a free, appropriate public education in the most integrated setting possible, many disabled children still spend far more time in special classes than they do alongside non-disabled students. When parents and teachers create individualized educational plans (IEP's) as required by the act, are girls and boys with comparable impairments equally likely to be given the optimal supplemental services or the greatest opportunity for integrated classroom and social activity? We know that disabled young people still do not benefit from equal opportunities in school (U.S. Department of Education 1987), but we cannot yet say whether and how gender influences the education of disabled youths.

Disabled women of working age
Because the government's efforts in behalf of disabled people historically have been aimed at economic productivity and self-support, more is known about disabled women of working age, and better comparisons can be made with both non-disabled women and disabled men. One must be wary of comparisons between women with and without disabilities, however, because age is a confounding variable. For both sexes, disability increases dramatically with age. Whereas 26.7 percent of all non-disabled women are between the ages of 16 and 24, for example, only 10 percent of all disabled women fall in that category. More than 70

percent of non-disabled women are under 44 years of age, but only 38 percent of disabled women are between the ages of 16 and 44. The average age of disabled women is 51, whereas the average age of her non-disabled female counterpart is 33 (Bowe 1984; all data not otherwise noted derive from this source, a summary of 1981 and 1982 data obtained from Current Population Surveys conducted by the Census Bureau in March of both years). Thus, until we learn far more about disabled women by age, we can only speculate that comparisons between disabled and non-disabled women may understate disparities between age-peers. Because the average ages of women and men with disabilities are closer—51 versus 49—such disability/gender comparisons are likely to be more fruitful.

Work disability has been reported by 9 percent of white males, 7.8 percent of white females, 12.9 percent of black males, 13.9 percent of black females, 7.5 percent of Hispanic males, and 8.5 percent of Hispanic females aged 16–64. Disabled men are much more likely than disabled females to participate in the labor force, especially if white or Hispanic. White disabled men participate at almost twice the rate of white disabled women (44 percent of men, only 24 percent of women). Ninety percent of non-disabled white males and 64 percent of non-disabled white females participate in the labor force, meaning that they either work or are actively seeking work. For whites, then, disabled men are about half as likely as non-disabled men to work, whereas for white disabled women the gap is even greater, with disabled white women only three-eights as likely to participate as non-disabled white women. For blacks, the gender difference is far less significant: 26 percent of disabled men participate, as compared to 20 percent of disabled women. Across groups, fewer than 25 percent of women with disabilities participate in the labor force, and they are unemployed consistently more often than are disabled men.

Employed disabled women tend to be tracked in low-wage, service-sector positions. As of 1981, the mean earnings of disabled women fell far below those of disabled men. Including all workers, disabled males averaged $13,863 annually, compared to disabled females, who averaged $5,835. For the disabled person who secured full-time work, her or his earnings approximated those of non-disabled women and men, although in both instances they earned less than their non-disabled counterparts. Whatever comfort can be taken from this discovery, however, is small considering that only 22.3 percent of disabled males and 7.4 percent of disabled females worked year-round, full-time in 1981. This is despite the findings of a recent survey of disabled Americans, which showed that of the three-fourths of all disabled adults out of the labor force, more than two-thirds would prefer to be employed and believe they are capable of doing so (Hill et al. 1986). Thus, we must conclude that relatively few disabled men or women perceive their disabilities as precluding economically productive activity.

Disabled men and women are poorer than those without disabilities. Again, disabled women are at the bottom of the ladder, with black disabled women having less income than any other race/gender/disability category. Income figures are as follows: for *all* white males, $15,832; for white males with work disabilities, $9,394; for white females, $5,912; and for white females with work disabilities, $3,658. For *all* black males, $9,621; for black males with disabilities, $4,245; for all black females, $5,639; for black females with work disabilities, $3,520. Using these figures, the median income for black disabled females is twenty-two cents to the white non-disabled male dollar (Bowe 1984).

The relationship between disability, unemployment or underemployment, and poverty for disabled women is far from clear, however. We know that regardless of age or educational attainment, women with disabilities are employed far less than are either non-disabled women or disabled men (Bowe 1984; U.S. Census Bureau 1983). Bowe (1984) reports that even for disabled women between 16 and 34, only one-third have jobs, and only slightly more than one-third of disabled women with college educations work. Disabled women are also slightly less likely than disabled men to have college educations. College-educated men with disabilities and women without are considerably more successful than disabled women in obtaining employment. Gender and disability discrimination must interact somehow to exclude these women.

Disabled women's generally low levels of education (five times as likely as non-disabled women to have fewer than eight years of schooling) cannot be ascribed to disability factors, whether inherent in biology or in institutional discrimination. Most women become disabled only *after* education and training have been completed. In fact, it is likely that the women's predisability work and living arrangements contribute to disability. Unskilled manual labor, substandard living conditions, poor nutrition, and inadequate medical care all take a toll.

We noted that more blacks than whites or Hispanics report work disability. Without ascribing cause, Alexander (1985) notes that black women confront higher rates of some disabilities than do whites. One in four black women will have high blood pressure during her life; rates of cancer for blacks have gone up by 34 percent, as compared to 9 percent over the same period of time for whites.

Unfortunately, once she has a disability, a woman is likely to discover that such factors as age, gender, predisability education, occupation, and income work to deny her the help she needs. Established to reduce the economic burdens of disabled people, the rehabilitation system disproportionately aids society's haves: those who are male, under 45, white, better-educated, middle-class, articulate, aggressive, "motivated" (Kirchner 1987; Stone 1986; U.S. Dept. of HEW 1975). Rehabilitated women's cases are substantially more likely to be closed in a non-wage-earning capacity (Vash 1982). Women are more likely to be denied such services entirely (Nagi 1969); they are less likely to be referred to vocational training or on-the-job training, more likely to be trained as homemakers, and more likely to be channeled into traditionally female occupations than are men with equivalent skills and aptitudes (Packer 1983).

Given that disabled women are more likely than disabled men to live in poverty and to rely on government income support, it must be noted that allocation of public resources provides little relief for either disabled men or women; still, it does exacerbate gender disparities in that the amount of a Social Security recipient's benefits under the Disability Insurance program is tied to predisability earnings. Mudrick (1983 and this volume) further elaborates upon how gender bias and sex stereotyping work against the woman with a disability whose subsistence depends upon the Supplemental Security Income program, an "income support" based on need rather than entitlement.

In this context of extreme educational and economic disadvantage, worsened for women of color, women with disabilities not only are systematically cut off from productive work but also are denied access to the traditional (if now disputed) responsibilities of women: to nurture and reproduce. In what follows, we offer some hypotheses about the disabled woman's exclusion from either the productive role of paid work or the nurturant, reproductive role. To do so, we discuss the meanings of nurturance, attractiveness and sexuality, and reproduction as they affect women in the spheres of work and love.

NURTURANCE, SEXUALITY, AND REPRODUCTION: THE EXEMPT WOMAN

"Each time I announced I was pregnant, everyone in the family looked shocked, dropped their forks at the dinnertable—not exactly a celebration" (35-year-old, white married woman, mother of two, who contracted polio at age 5).

Disabled women as partners

The income-earning opportunities of women with disabilities are severely constrained. So, too, are their opportunities to be nurtured and to nurture, to be lovers and be loved, to be mothers if they desire. Women with disabilities are less likely than non-disabled women or disabled men to fulfill roles customarily reserved for their respective sexes. Exempted from the "male" productive role and the "female" nurturing one, having the glory of neither, disabled women are arguably doubly oppressed—or, perhaps, "freer" to be nontraditional. Should they pursue what has been thought nontraditional, however, the decision to work, to be a single mother, to be involved in a lesbian relationship, or to enter politics may be regarded as a default rather than a preference. We recognize that many women have no desire to marry, mother, or be sexual with men, and that marriage and childbearing statistics must not be used to measure "social success." Nonetheless, while many non-disabled and disabled women are choosing nontraditional lifestyles, other disabled women go other routes not by choice alone.

Franklin (1977) reported that disabled women were less likely than non-disabled women to be married, more likely to marry later, and more likely to be divorced. Bowe (1984) and Hanna and Rogovsky (1986) report similar findings from the Current Population Survey's data of the early 1980s. Whereas 60 percent of men with disabilities and women without them are married, only 49 percent of disabled women are married. As with employment and earnings data, actual disparities between disabled and non-disabled women may be greater when the age factor previously cited is taken into account. Seventy percent of non-disabled women are under 44 years of age, 26 percent under age 24. It can be expected that many of these non-disabled younger women who show up in census data as unmarried will at some time marry. These data alone do not reveal how much the presence of a woman's disability affects her choices, chances, or inclinations to marry or be involved in a loving relationship with a woman or a man. That more disabled women are unmarried than non-disabled women might be explained by demographic differences alone: being older they have had more time for their marriages to sour just as have millions of others whose relationships dissolve. Many are widowed, as are women of comparable age without disabilities.

When disabled women are compared with non-disabled women and disabled men on rates of divorce and separation, glaring differences again surface between the situation of disabled women and either comparison group. The New York City Affiliate of the National Council on Alcoholism has documented that 90 percent of women alcoholics versus 10 percent of male alcoholics are left by their spouses (Natl. Council on Alcoholism 1980). Hanna and Rogovsky (1986) analyzed 1985 Current Population Survey data on marital status, dividing a subsample of ever-married but not widowed men and women into three categories: non-disabled, mildly disabled, and severely disabled. They found that of this group, more women than men in all categories were divorced, but that significant differences emerged between "severely disabled women" and other groups. Only 14 percent of men termed "severely disabled" were divorced, but 26 percent of severely disabled women were. While men's rates of separation were 3 percent, 5 percent, and 7 percent for each category of disability status, women's rates of separation were 4 percent, 6 percent, and 11 percent. Thirty-seven percent of "severely disabled" women, as contrasted with 22 percent of "severely disabled" men who were once married, are no longer married, for reasons *other* than death of a spouse.

Anecdote, interview, and autobiography corroborate the census data and the stereotype of the disabled woman as alone. For both men and women whose disabilities occur before marriage, literature reveals considerable apprehension about finding a mate. Hahn (1983b) and Asch and Sacks (1983) reviewed large numbers of published autobiographies and noted how little could be found about intimate relationships; of those who did live with adult partners, nearly all were men.

In personal accounts and interviews reported in Bowe (1981), Brightman (1984), Duffy (1981), Heinrich and Kriegel (1961), Matthews (1983), and Roth (1981), we discover how relatively difficult it is for disabled men or women to find a partner relationship. Nonetheless, many more men than women eventually established relationships they found satisfying. Matthews (1983) found that only five of the forty-five women she interviewed were married, and more than half reported no sexual relationship since becoming disabled. Only half of the seventy-five orthopedically disabled women who responded to Duffy's (1981) questionnaire had ever been married. Bonwich (1985) recounts that twenty-nine of the thirty-six rural, spinal-cord-injured women she interviewed had been romantically involved or married prior to their becoming disabled; of these twenty-nine, fifteen saw the end of these relationships soon after onset of disability. Only one of the more than sixty pieces in Browne, Connors, and Stern's (1985) collection of disabled women's writing mentions marriage. Although many of the women represented are lesbians, none discusses an ongoing intimate relationship or provides a glimpse of the trials and pleasures of meeting a lover and maintaining a valued partnership.

In conferences of disabled girls and women in which the topic of relationships comes up at all, discussion centers around the difficulty of meeting men who pay them any notice. The only group of disabled adults in which women are *more* likely than men to be married is women who are labeled retarded. Safilios-Rothschild (1977) has suggested that the retarded wife may fit all too well the criteria of the "good wife": one who is docile, passive, loyal, and dependent, not likely to show her husband up.

How can we explain these data? If disability is thought to reinforce the customary female characteristics of passivity, compliance, and good nature, why should women with disabilities frequently be without partners?

A look at the literature on the views of the non-disabled toward persons with disabilities reveals that the attitudes of non-disabled women and men are overwhelmingly negative. Men's attitudes, however, are the more extreme (Siller, Ferguson, Vann, Holland 1976). These researchers found that disabled children and adults were more likely to be rejected as family members than as acquaintances or workmates by both men and women, but rates of rejection were greater for non-disabled men. Hanna and Rogovsky (1986) suggest that the disabled woman may be more negatively viewed by both women and men than the similarly disabled man. In surveying non-disabled college students at an Eastern public university, they found that images of "disabled woman," "disabled man," and "woman," differed markedly. When asked how women and men using wheelchairs became disabled, non-disabled students attributed male disability to external situations such as war, work injury, or accident. They attributed female disability to internal causes, such as disease. The authors suggest that attributing disability to disease may foster more negative attitudes because disease stimulates primitive fears of contagion or of the person's inherent moral badness. Thus, the disabled woman may be viewed as more dangerous than a similarly disabled male, more morally suspect, or more deserving of her fate.

When these same students were asked to draw associations for "woman," and "disabled woman," the associations cited for the two could not have been more different. "Woman" drew associations of worker (intelligent, leader, career); of sexuality (soft, lovable, orgasm); of mother or wife (wife, mother, mom, married, childbearer). When asked to associate to "disabled woman," students described her in terms of dependence and impairment (crippled, almost lifeless); of age (gray, old, white hair); of despair (someone to feel sorry for, pity, sorry, lonely, ugly). She was virtually never depicted as wife, mother, or worker by the more than one hundred students questioned.

Attractiveness and nurturance

To understand these phenomena and their consequences for disabled women, we speculate about the implications for disabled women of cultural views of attractiveness and of nurturance. First, it is important to note that a pervasive "attractiveness stereotype" enables people to believe that those who are attractive are also "more sensitive, kind, interesting, strong, poised, modest, sociable, outgoing, and exciting, sexually warm and responsive," and will "hold better jobs, have more successful marriages, and happier and more fulfilling lives" (Berscheid and Walster 1972: 46, 74). In short, attractiveness is linked to virtue, to all that is desired, especially by men of women. In the cultural imagination, beauty is linked to goodness and nurturance, the traits most sought after in women both as lovers and as workers. Ample evidence substantiates that perceptions of women's attractiveness influence women's educational and work opportunities (Unger 1985; Unger, Hilderbrand, and Marder 1982). Unfortunately for the disabled woman, only a few attributes count toward attractiveness in the United States, and a woman's bodily integrity is one such requirement (Hahn 1983a; Lakoff and Scherr 1984). Furthermore, a woman's beauty is seen as a reflection of a male partner's social status. As Lakoff and Scherr (1984) note in *Face Value: The Politics of Beauty:* "The message we are given daily by the myriad images of beauty is that women must look a certain way to be loved and admired, to be worth anything" (p. 114).

In a discussion of male notions of attractiveness, these authors note that physical grace and ease are also important in the assessment of what is desirable in women. The woman with a disability, whether apparent or invisible, may display less than the norm or the fantasied ideal of bodily integrity, grace, and ease. The very devices she values for enhancing free movement and communication (braces, crutches, hearing aids, or canes) may repel men seeking the fantasied flawlessness. Even those with "intact" bodies, such as Mary, a woman with a severe perceptual/motor problem stemming from a learning disability, can find themselves deemed clumsy and therefore unattractive. Given that disabled women are found unattractive by college students as well as by clinicians (Hanna and Rogovsky 1986; Unger 1985; Unger, Hilderbrand, and Mardor 1982), and given that men value physical attractiveness in a partner significantly more than women do, it is little wonder that heterosexual women with disabilities are more likely than disabled men to be alone.

The argument of women's attractiveness as a display of male status is not sufficient, however, to explain the underinvolvement of disabled women in intimate relationships with men (and women). To pursue the heterosexual question first and more extensively, it appears that men's unacknowledged needs and dependencies—satisfied often in relationships with women—reduce men's desire to become connected in work or in love with disabled women. Drawing on the writing of Miller (1976), we contend that if a woman's role in heterosexual relationships has been to accommodate a man emotionally while not exposing his vulnerabilities, the disabled woman may be thought unfit. If men desired only the passive, doll-like female of the stereotype, disabled women might do, but the doll must be functional as well as decorative. Feminist theorists such as Hartmann (1981) and Zillah Eisenstein (1984) have argued that the smooth functioning of advanced capitalism requires the illusion, if not the reality, of a heterosexual nuclear home warmed and nurtured by an all-giving and all-comforting woman.

Brownmiller (1984) characterizes nurturance when applied to women as "warmth, tenderness, compassion, sustained emotional involvement in the welfare of others, and a weak or nonexistent competitive drive. Nurturant labor includes child care, spouse care, cooking and feeding, soothing and patching, straightening out disorder and cleaning up dirt, little considerations like sewing a button on a grown man's raincoat, major considerations like nursing relationships and mending rifts, putting the demands of family and others before one's own, and dropping one's work to minister to the sick, the troubled, and the lonely in their time of need" (pp. 221–22). Men may assume incorrectly that a disabled woman could not contribute either physical or emotional housekeeping to a spouse and children. If a woman cannot sew on a button because she cannot use her hands, she may be thought unfit to help with the mending of emotional fences as well.

Disabled persons (men and women) often elicit in non-disabled others powerful existential anxieties about their own helplessness, needs, and dependencies (Hahn 1983a). For a man who may have such emotional residues well-buried, their activation in the presence of a disabled woman may stimulate reflexively his rejection of her. Even if a man believed that a particular disabled woman could manage to run her own life and master the details of helping him with his, how could he accept help from an unwhole, "sick" woman? How can she minister to his needs when a disabled woman epitomizes all that is needy herself? Might it be that taking help from such a presumably helpless woman arouses guilt or shame in any man who might consider it? If men can accept emotional sustenance only from women who can provide the maximum in physical caretaking, the woman with limitations may be viewed as inadequate to give the warmth, companionship, and shelter men traditionally expect from their mates. If men fear both their own and another's dependency and intimacy to the extent that Chodorow (1978) and Gilligan (1982) have argued, if disabled persons awaken such feelings, and if men desire women who can satiate their own emotional needs without either publicly acknowledging them or requiring reciprocity, disabled women are likely to be rejected forcefully as lovers/partners.

Disabled women who have partners, especially if they are non-disabled men, are likely to discover that they and their partners are subjected to curiosity, scrutiny, and public misunderstanding. Ubiquitously perceived as a social burden, the disabled woman evokes pity that spreads to her partner. "Whenever my husband and I are shopping, and he is pushing my wheelchair, people stop us and say [to him], 'You must be a saint.' What about me? Do you think it's easy to live with him?" The public assumption is that this woman is a burden and her husband is either saintly or a loser himself.

The view of the disabled woman as limited emotionally because she may be limited physically may account for the acknowledged preference of disabled men for non-disabled partners. In their review of the autobiographies of blind women and men, Asch and Sacks (1983) discovered that the men sought sighted wives to complement them; to confer upon them a status of normal, successful, integrated; and to ensure their smooth navigation literally and figuratively through the world. In a study of the coping strategies of disabled scientists, a group that was overwhelmingly male, many reported that one major strategy was acquisition of a woman/wife (Redden, personal communication, 1980). In a *New York Times* article enshrining negative stereotypes about non-disabled women who marry disabled men and the men they marry, Rose (1984) postulated that the disabled man is the perfect outlet for nurturance and competence for non-disabled women who could not fulfill themselves or demonstrate their full capacity in a relationship with a truly competent male. Here, disabled men are perceived as lacking all capacities for self-direction merely because they cannot walk or see; non-disabled women are pictured as dominating their disabled spouses. The reverse situation of a disabled woman with a non-disabled male partner is omitted altogether from the discussion.

Male commitment to narrow conceptions of attractiveness and nurturance also may illuminate the rejection of disabled women as workers. The presumed costs of hiring disabled workers have been refuted elsewhere (Hill et al. 1987; U.S. Dept. of Labor 1982); the resistance to hiring women with disabilities stems from sources more primitive and unrecognized than either fiscal conservatism or esthetic and existential anxiety (Hahn 1983a). To the extent that women are employed in ways that sustain male domination, the "neutered" disabled woman fails to fill the bill (Rich 1980). We assert that the resistance to employing disabled women derives in part from the unacknowledged forms of heterosexual male privilege sustained in the workplace. Sheehy (1984) reminds us that male judges sometimes have awarded workers' compensation benefits to women with disabilities deemed so unattractive that future employment was highly unlikely!

We contend that men spurn disabled women as workers and partners because they fail to measure up on grounds of appearance or of perceived abilities in physical and emotional caretaking. Although this argument aids understanding of her marginality in the arenas of heterosexual love and male-controlled work, it fails to fully explain the situation of disabled lesbians. We have found no data on the numbers of lesbians with disabilities or on their acceptance by non-disabled lesbians as partners, but comments made by many disabled lesbians indicate that within the community of lesbians the disabled woman is still in search of love. Disabled lesbians have described being dismissed, shunned, or relegated to the status of friend and confidante rather than lover, just as have heterosexual disabled women.

Chodorow (1978) and Gilligan (1982) have much to say about women's capacity for relatedness. At its best, that relational potential renders women well-suited to cooperate, empathize, affiliate, examine the interpersonal dimensions of moral questions, anticipate others' needs—all those qualities current feminists at once struggle against and delight in. Cultivated by the culture to perpetuate male dominance and now seen as the source of women's potential strength for our own and the world's betterment (H. Eisenstein 1983; Miller 1976), these very qualities may be stimulated when a woman confronts a disabled woman as a potential lover. If the dark, problematic side of a capacity for relatedness is a too-ready potential for merger with another, stereotypes about the presumed dependency and neediness of a disabled woman could easily send women scurrying in the other direction. So long as non-disabled women hold the stereotypes that the disability rights movement fights against, the thought of a disabled woman as a lover may engender fears of merger, exaggerate lack of boundaries, and spawn fantasies of endless responsibility, of unremitting and unreciprocated care. Until non-disabled men and women recognize that disabled people can contribute to others' well-being, contemplating "taking on" such a woman as friend or lover will tend to activate such fears.

These arguments, admittedly, are speculative. Whether or not these dynamics operate in intimate heterosexual or lesbian couples involving a disabled partner remains to be explored. Whether or not heterosexual and lesbian relationships are characterized by similar patterns must be discovered. So, too, must we inquire about interdependence, reciprocity, and gender roles in couples where both partners have disabilities. Although many disabled people shun other disabled people as intimates, not all do. From our interviews, observations at disability conferences, and conversations with scores of women, we suspect that disabled women who marry *after* onset of disability are more likely than similarly disabled men to have a disabled spouse. Becker (1980) reports that 75 percent of deaf women marry deaf men. Because disability, unlike race or ethnicity, has not created natural cultures or communities wherein people customarily look to one another to create intimacy and family, one wonders whether those women whose partners are also disabled consider this a positive choice, a default option, or an irrelevant characteristic. What is crucial is that readers understand that *why* disabled women encounter difficulty in establishing nurturing relations is a significant question and not one with an "obvious answer."

Why disabled women are alone is an important question. That they are has complicated consequences. For example, Kutner and Gray (1985) and Kutner (1985) have specified how the condition of "aloneness" interacts with access to medical care and social support. In their investigations of people with renal failure who used various forms of dialysis, Kutner and Gray learned that maintainance of a home dialysis regimen (which is considered optimal for people with this condition) was substantially affected by marital status. Home dialysis requires a partner ready to assist the user for four to six hours three times a week. As a consequence of gender-stratified aloneness, men are more likely than women to receive home dialysis (and white women are more likely to receive it than black women). Supportive people, of course, need not be spouses, but for those Kutner and Gray surveyed, lack of such a spouse often resulted in less than the best medical care.

When Kutner surveyed 332 Atlanta-area residents with cardiac, kidney, and mobility disabilities regarding their perceptions of social support, she found that married people received help from more sources than did their never-married or formerly-married peers. However, the gap in help received between married and nonmarried was greater for women than for men. As is all too often true, the woman getting the least help was the one most likely to need it: she was more likely than an unmarried man to head a household with dependent children and thus to face the combined stresses of single parenthood and disability.

Sexuality and motherhood

Often deprived of the chance for long-term intimacy, disabled women also are commonly considered unfit as sexual partners and as mothers. Many women speak angrily of the unavailability of adequate counseling on sexuality, birth control, pregnancy, and childbirth from either gynecologists or rehabilitation professionals. Ignorant of the adverse consequences of some birth control devices for women with particular conditions, many gynecologists prescribe unsafe methods. Safilios-Rothschild (1977) notes that since coronary research has been conducted almost exclusively on men, it has produced data relevant only to men. Women who seek information about resuming sexual activity after a heart attack have been provided with male standards or with no answers at all. So astonishing is it to some physicians that disabled women might be sexual that Galler (1984) reports completely unnecessary abdominal surgery for one woman because no one believed that someone with cerebral palsy could have the symptoms of venereal disease.

One woman with spina bifida described a preadolescent encounter with her gynecologist this way:

"Will I be able to have satisfying sexual relations with a man?"

"Don't worry, honey, your vagina will be tight enough to satisfy any man."

Her satisfaction probably didn't cross his mind.

Motherhood, the institution and experience that perhaps has dominated all cultural conceptions of women—eclipsing even expectations of beauty, softness, or ever-present sexuality—often has been proscribed for a woman with a disability. Many states have had laws forbidding people with histories of epilepsy, mental retardation, and psychiatric disability from marrying. Fears that disabled women would produce children with similar conditions (nearly always groundless since the vast majority of disability is not hereditary) have mingled with convictions that they would harm, deprive, or burden children they attempted to rear. As a result, many medical professionals still urge or coerce women into being sterilized (Finger 1984; Macklin and Gaylin 1981; U. S. Comm. on Civil Rights 1983). Women in interviews cite recent sessions with gynecologists who urged them not to bother with birth control by saying, "Get your tubes tied. You couldn't take care of a child yourself." Women with diabetes, epilepsy, and spinal cord injuries report difficulty in finding obstetricians or midwives willing to help them through what they view as "high-risk" pregnancies (Asrael 1982; Collins 1983).

Problems in mothering for disabled women are not limited to the medical aspects of reproduction. Regardless of marital status or the disability status of any partners, disabled women report discrimination in adopting, in being permitted to provide foster care, and in winning child custody after divorce. Sadly and perversely, Gold (1985) reports, a 1978 amendment to the California welfare and institutions code intended to prevent discrimination against disabled parents has, in fact, been used to sanction unannounced home visits and the removal of children simply on the grounds that mothers were blind. In 1986 a Colorado social service agency took custody of a 13-month girl, alleging that the underweight child was malnourished because her blind single mother could not feed her properly. Even after two doctors testified that the child, though small, was not malnourished, the social service agency would not permit the child to be returned to her mother (*Braille Monitor* 1986).

Exemption or exclusion from voluntary sexuality and reproduction has not exempted disabled females from sexual abuse and victimization. Perhaps even more than non-disabled women, disabled women confront serious psychological and social problems in ending abusive or exploitative relationships. Galler (1984) and *Disability Rag* (1986) relate instances in which women with cerebral palsy or mental retardation have been ignored by professionals when they report rape. If women without disabilities hesitate to give up abusive relationships because they cannot imagine how they will survive economically, disabled women in abusive homes may feel even more trapped. Melling (1984) discusses the problem of wife abuse in the deaf community, noting a battery of factors that conspire against deaf women standing up for themselves in degrading or even dangerous situations. Even more than the non-disabled girl, a disabled girl is an easy victim of abuse by male relatives. Unfortunately, even personal care attendants employed by the disabled woman are not infrequently reported to abuse the women they have been hired to assist. One counselor of disabled women in a Denver domestic violence project has commented that many disabled women, like their non-disabled counterparts, return to the abusive relationships because "it is the only thing they have had. As bad as it is, for many it is better than living in an institution or going back to their families" (*Disability Rag* 1986: 9–10).

Disabled girls and women, in numbers hard to estimate, are raped at home, in institutions, or on the streets. We know of women whose stay in long-term care institutions or rehabilitation facilities included sterilization with official approval because, they were told, there was danger of molestation in the institution. An inquiry into California's community care facilities for the mentally and physically disabled and for the elderly found that "daily, throughout this state, residents of community care facilities are being sexually abused, beaten, fed spoiled food, forced to live with toilets that don't work" (New York Times 1984). We wonder how many of these same women have been sterilized to keep the effects of rape from the public eye. That such exploitation frequently occurs outside of institutions as well is demonstrated by one study conducted by the Seattle Rape Relief Center. The center found that between May 1977 and December 1979, more than three hundred cases of sexual exploitation of physically or mentally disabled women came to its attention (Bellone and Waxman 1983). Extrapolating to the state of Washington, the center estimated that perhaps thirty thousand rapes of such women occur annually.

Self-esteem, resistance, and identity
If our culture views being female and disabled as "redundant," whereas being male and disabled is a contradiction, we must ponder on the effects of such role definitions and social options on the self-concept of the disabled woman. Some women accommodate societal projections, becoming the dependent creatures their parents, teachers, and others expected. In fact, the psychological literature suggests this response to be the norm. Consider this in relation to findings that disabled girls and women perceive themselves and are perceived by others more negatively than is the case with disabled boys and men. They report more negative self-images (Weinberg 1976), are viewed in less favorable ways (Miller 1970), and are more likely to be victims of hostility than are disabled men (Titley and Viney 1969). The Asch and Sacks (1983) analysis of autobiographies of blind women and men indicated that the women internalized negative messages much more than did the men, seeing themselves as burdensome, unwanted, and unlovable, whereas men rarely did.

Weinberg's (1976) self-concept research found that negative self-concept was less related to one's level of disability than to one's gender—with women reporting more negative feelings than either disabled or non-disabled males. In a review of the self-esteem literature on disability, Darling (1979) found that—contrary to predictions of much psychoanalytic and labeling theory discussions—disabled children and adolescents demonstrated levels of self-esteem not substantially different from those of their non-disabled counterparts. Nonetheless, she reports, disabled girls evidence lower self-esteem than disabled boys and either non-disabled girls and boys.

Such findings about self-esteem need to be analyzed. It may be that males with disabilities can escape some of the trap of the disability role by aspiring to male characteristics of mastery, competence, and autonomy; disabled women and girls, however, forsake their gender role if they seek to escape from disability-imposed dependence by such means. We believe that such role contradictions can plague the female seeking to affirm her identity in the presence of a disability. Particularly for the disabled girl (and the self-esteem literature generally concentrates on children and adolescents) becoming socialized in a family and school unclear about what norms to suggest or what hopes to give her for her future, self-esteem may be a serious problem.

A look at current discussions of male and female paths of development suggests ideas about the sense of self and of socialization of the disabled girl. Many of these are elaborated upon by Harris and Wideman in this volume. What happens to a disabled girl growing up in a family where her mother perceives that, because the daughter is disabled, she is fundamentally different from the mother and thus is not expected to develop into the kind of woman the mother aspired to be? Friedman (1980) suggests that a mother's major task is to "hand down the legacy of womanhood . . . to share it and be an example of it" (p. 90). If the mother's definition of womanhood is based upon being attractive to and caring for a mate, she may inculcate in her daughter the belief that disability renders such a life impossible.

Thus, the disabled girl's best hope may be to turn to the traditionally male norms of achievement for establishing a sense of herself. Although she may acquire many skills and psychological resources to assist her in the productive world, she is not becoming the typical girl and young woman for whom establishing affiliative ties is of paramount importance (Person 1982). Autobiographies of many disabled women emphasize their quest for independence, work, and escape out of the stereotype of disability as helplessness. As one disabled woman put it to us: "I was raised to be a non-disabled son." However proud she may be of her accomplishments, the disabled girl knows she is not becoming like other women. Unless she likes that difference, it may lead to the lowered self-esteem found in psychological studies and in the autobiographical literature (Asch and Sacks 1983).

We have said that her "best" hope is to turn toward male standards of achievement. Like the 15-year-old Maria quoted earlier, however, many disabled girls are sheltered, kept from activities and opportunities where they might manage mastery of skills or acquiring of friends. In such a sad and too-common situation, the disabled girl may have no sense of identity with her mother or other girls and women, and no validation for accomplishments beyond the home. Little wonder, then, that there are trapped and demoralized girls and women.

At the other end of the spectrum are disabled females who resist all the gender-based and disability-based stereotypes and take pride in the identities they forge. Because of or despite their parents, they get an education and a job. They live independently, enjoy sex with men or women, become pregnant and carry to term if they choose, or abort if they prefer. They relish their friendships, intimacies, lovers, activities. Some determine that they will play by the rules of achievement and succeed at meeting standards that are often deemed inaccessible to them. Some accept societal norms of attractiveness and enjoy the challenge of living up to them, disability notwithstanding. Others choose to disregard anything that seems like "passing" (Goffman 1963). Like Sarah in *Children of a Lesser God,* they demand that the world accept them on their terms, whether those terms be insisting upon signing rather than speaking, not covering their burn scars, not wearing clothing to hide parts of their bodies others may see as "ugly" or "deformed," or rejecting prostheses that inhibit and do not help.

Following her mastectomy, Lorde (1980) refused to wear a prosthetic breast: "On the day after the stitches came out . . . I got so furious with the nurse who told me I was bad for the morale of the office because I did not wear a prosthesis. . . ." (p. 52). Diane, a quadri-amputee interviewed by Gelya Frank, refused her prostheses because "I knew it was going on my body. And that would add more sweat, and more asthma, because I would have to work harder with it. So I always saw my body as something that was mine, and something that was free, and I hated anything kind of binding . . ." (Frank 1981:84). Michele, a 17-year-old Hispanic high school student, told us that she wore her prosthetic arms only to her doctor's appointments. They are clumsy, she said, and she could manage to do things much more easily without them; she was perfectly comfortable having people see her short and "deformed" arms.

Having, as a child, incorporated her disability into her identity, Harilyn Rousso (1984) resisted her mother's attempts to make her appear more typical. She explains: "She [her mother] made numerous attempts over the years of my childhood to have me go for physical therapy and to practice walking more 'normally' at home. I vehemently refused all her efforts. She could not understand why I would not walk straight. . . . My disability, with my different walk and talk and my involuntary movements, having been with me all of my life, was part of me, part of my identity. With these disability features, I felt complete and whole. My mother's attempt to change my walk, strange as it may seem, felt like an assault on myself, an incomplete acceptance of all of me, an attempt to make me over" (p. 9).

From these and many other examples, we know that some disabled girls and women flourish in spite of the pressures from family and the distortions and discrimination meted out by society. We need to know much more than we do about what helps some disabled girls and women resist, but this volume testifies to both the travails and the victories of these women.

DISABLED WOMEN: IMPLICATIONS FOR DISABILITY RIGHTS AND FEMINISM

The struggles of feminism and of disability rights have much in common. In order to pursue gender and disability equality, activists have argued for the elimination of laws, institutional structures and practices, and social attitudes that have reduced women or disabled people to one biological characteristic. Although both movements have borrowed and profited from the black civil rights movement, these later movements share the indisputable fact that in some situations biology *does* and *should* count. However, feminism and disability rights advocates insist that instances where biology matters are extremely rare, and such cases can be minimized by changing society to better incorporate all its citizens.

In the writings of such socialist-feminists as Hester Eisenstein (1983, 1985), one discovers a fine understanding of the differences among women. Also present are continued commitment to economic and political freedom as well as to psychological liberation, and a balanced appreciation of women's attributes of nurturance and cooperation that neither glorifies women nor denigrates men. She and others, such as many of the contributors to the Sargent (1981) discussion of the "unhappy marriage" of Marxism and feminism, maintain that women's situation will not and cannot improve substantially until they gain full economic, political, sexual, reproductive, and psychological recognition. Recognition in their terms includes appreciation of both sameness *and* difference, and it entails social transformation in order for diversity to be tolerated and not punished. They understand that some differences, even if culturally created, are acceptable and perhaps even valuable, not only for women but for men and for social and political institutions.

We believe such an analysis can readily incorporate the particular issues of disability rights and of disabled women. That portion of the disability rights movement calling for societal change along with equality of opportunity should also be able to address concerns particular to disabled women. We suggest that progress for disabled people will not be achieved through stress on equality of opportunity alone, no matter how crucial such equality is, and we believe that disability rights theorists and activists can borrow from socialist-feminists who call for societal transformation in addition to equality of opportunity within existing arrangements.

Although we would not now assess the relative contributions of race, sex, or disability discrimination to any one woman's life experience or to that of disabled women in general, we can cite areas of theory and politics in disability rights and feminism that will benefit from specific attention to the concerns of today's disabled women. In thinking about the barriers to disabled women's full social, economic, and political participation, we also seek to recognize which ones are most amenable to work through disability rights activity, which ones through feminism, and which ones through both.

Omolade (1985) and Joseph (1981) have argued that in certain instances black women share more commonalities with black men than they do with white women. To ignore that fact and look to white feminists to embrace all of black women's concerns violates political and psychological reality. The same can be said for women with disabilities—including racial/ethnic minority women with disabilities—who may need to look to feminists, to their ethnic or racial group, and to the disability rights movement for support. One must recall the crucial difference between relations of disabled women and men and relations of women and men of color commented upon earlier: many disabled men reject disabled women as intimates based on their own feelings about nurturance and attractiveness. Black men, however, may be intimate with black women even if sexism persists within family and community relations. While we in no way suggest that disabled women and men should look only to one another for intimacy, that disabled people often reject one another for such intimacy may make genuine political struggle together for all disabled people's rights especially difficult.

Nonetheless, access to transportation, to housing, and to public places is a concern of all disabled people in which disabled women's best hope probably hinges on their joining and broadening the existing disability rights movement. As we have said, independent living for disabled women may raise special problems in the training and supervision of personal care attendants and assistants. Independent living centers will need to pay attention to reports of abuse and domestic violence, perhaps modifying recruitment, training, and supervision of attendants; assisting disabled women with assertiveness training and self-defense classes; and pressuring domestic violence projects and battered women's shelters to reach out to disabled women.

Disabled girls and women confronting the separate, nearly always inferior special-education and vocational rehabilitation systems must ally themselves with the disability rights movement to improve (or abolish) these bureaucracies that so profoundly affect disabled people's access to knowledge and employment. To make these systems less biased against disabled people—the very people they purport to serve—and less perpetuating of disability stigma and stereotype, disabled women must act in consort with the disability rights movement. Some sectors of that movement are male-dominated and may, without persistent pressure from women, ignore the gender and racial biases pervading these institutions. The mission of compelling regular educational, vocational training, and employment services to properly assist disabled people—thus abolishing or circumscribing the need for special services altogether—is one for the disability rights movement as a whole.

If we can generalize from our interviews, conference participation, and reading of the stories of disabled women, disability dominates gender in their discussions about education and employment opportunity, notwithstanding the disparities between disabled women and men noted earlier. Although they may object to being channeled into traditionally female occupations by the vocational rehabilitation system, or to being kept from sports and adventures by parents and schools, disabled women focus on how their disability affects their access to education and jobs. Whether disabilities are apparent or invisible, they focus on fielding the humiliating and non-job-related disability questions of the employment interviewer or the medical examiner, and not on questions about marital status, dependents, or sexual harassment on the job. Perhaps this lack of concern stems from their awareness that they are not viewed as sexual beings, or perhaps from an accurate assessment that their disability obscures everything else about them to the employer or the college admissions officer. (We wonder, though, if 40-year-old disabled men are asked if they live with their parents, as 40-year-old disabled women are asked by men and women who should know better.)

While getting jobs for disabled women may be a disability problem impeded only secondarily by sexism, what happens on the job is as likely to be influenced by gender as by disability. Earnings and benefits for disabled women are far less than for disabled men, and thus disabled women must join with other women workers in struggles for comparable worth, for an end to job segregation by sex, and for an end to tying disability, pension, and Social Security benefits exclusively to earnings. Thus, for disabled women, equal access to education, to jobs, and to economic security depends on work with both disability rights and feminist groups.

The task of broadening the horizons of disabled girls and women awaits feminist commitment to showing disabled women how much they have in common with other women. Disabled women need to know that they are faring less well than disabled men in education and employment, in getting a range of jobs, in receiving the economic security and social support they need, and in their access to sexuality and intimacy. Harilyn Rousso, founder of the pioneer Networking Project for Disabled Women and Girls now being replicated throughout the country, comments that many young disabled women look to the most conventional of women's jobs simply to assert their sisterhood with non-disabled women, from whom they otherwise feel separate and different (Rousso 1987). The desire to be "normal" and "like other women" may actually foster disabled women's tolerance of sexism within the specialized service systems they encounter, as well as within disability rights groups and within marriages to disabled men. Disabled women will never fight such sexism until they are enabled to discover their commonalities with non-disabled women.

Women with disabilities have not been "trapped" by many of the social expectations feminists have challenged. They have not been forced to get married or to subordinate paid work to childrearing or housekeeping. Instead, they have been warned by parents that men only "take advantage"; they have been sterilized by force or "choice," rejected by disabled and non-disabled heterosexual and lesbian partners, abandoned by spouses after onset of disability, and thwarted when they seek to mother.

Such contradictions and tensions emerged at the First National Conference on Disabled Women and Girls in Baltimore in 1982. As such, they demonstrate disabled women's challenge to feminism. In a keynote dialogue between a major feminist speaker and a major disability rights activist, non-disabled and disabled women witnessed gaps as well as similarities:

Letty Cottin Pogrebin: "The concerns about sexual harassment affect all women."

Judy Heumann: "You know, I use a wheelchair, and when I go down the street I do not get to be sexually harassed. I hear non-disabled women complaining about it, but I don't ever get treated as an sexual object."

Pogrebin: "You would hate it."

Throughout that weekend, and running through all our interviews, conversations, and conferences since that time, has been the response of disabled women: "Try two weeks or thirty years without that sexual attention. Then tell us if you would hate getting some, even in the form of harassment!" Denied the basic, if oppressive, gender-role prescriptions and offered nothing to replace them but often the worst of dead-end jobs, disabled women have been without social role or gender-based value. Their anger at such deprivation uncomfortably reminds non-disabled women that sexual objectification is one vehicle by which at least heterosexual confirmation may be conveyed—a vehicle about which these women may feel more ambivalence than they choose to admit.

Indeed, a valuable effort to begin such conversations among women (disabled and not) and among disabled persons (women and men), to introduce women with disabilities into feminism, and to incorporate a feminist perspective into disability rights is *Building Community* (1984), a book of discussion, questions, readings, and exercises produced by the Women and Disability Awareness Project, New York City.

More recently, disabled women have challenged feminism on yet another bedrock position: that of the alleged contradictions between women's rights to reproductive freedom and parental autonomy over the lives of disabled newborns. Not only do disabled women confront non-disabled women with that they prize about themselves in the areas of beauty and nurturance, but they compel these same women to examine what they expect of mothering and of the kind of children they choose to bear, rear, and love. What are women saying to disabled people when they choose to abort fetuses with Down's syndrome or spina bifida because "it would be better for the fetus. It would have been a vegetable"? If some disabled women challenge such decisions as based on inaccurate information available about the potential of such people, are they eroding women's fragile reproductive freedoms currently under severe attack? If women do not wish to mother such a child, are they expressing realistic concerns that such children will drain them financially or emotionally? Are they responding to fears about what would await such a child in the larger world or to fears that they will not receive what they prize about being mothers? Does a woman's right not to bear a child known to be disabled extend to her right to end medical treatment to an infant born with a disability?

Feminists struggling to maintain reproductive choice and disabled people struggling to assert their rights to existence, support, and opportunity have been confronting one another about these issues in the past five years. These tangled questions of women's reproductive rights versus disabled newborns' rights to treatment, of women's rights to decide what types of children they will mother versus disabled women's conviction that they deserve to be mothered and to mother, have sparked passionate and soul-searching panels and writings. (In addition to Asch and Fine, this volume, see Asch 1986b, 1986c; Fine and Asch 1982; Finger 1984; Harrison 1986; Rapp 1984; Rothman 1986; Saxton 1984.) This continuing dialogue promises an enriched feminism. Feminism will be strengthened by appreciation of disabled women and by a recognition that feminist commitments to nurturance, diversity, and inclusiveness can be used to create a society that provides opportunity for all people, without consigning certain people to the role of unending caretakers to others.

In these pages and in the following chapters, we have taken a risk in trying to unearth the complexities of gender and disability. Our goal has been to introduce the former into disability scholarship, the latter into feminist thought, and both into the mainstream of social science. Beyond this, we demand attention to the lives and experiences of women with disabilities, be it on the streets, at work, in bed, in maternity wards, at feminist rallies, within the ranks of the disability rights movement, or across progressive grass-roots movements. We further seek it in psychology and sociology texts, legal casebooks, folklore, popular literature, and film. We demand that the images of helplessness, passivity, need, and longings for care be projected no longer onto disabled women, but be redistributed throughout all of society, rich in fear, need, desire, and hope.

Notes

Acknowledgments: We would like to thank Richard K. Scotch and Irving Kenneth Zola for comments that have assisted us in developing this chapter, and Janet Francendese and Tina Trudel for thorough reading, suggestions, and wording that have clarified and sharpened our ideas.

1. Since 1982 and the First National Conference on Disabled Women and Girls, the authors have participated in more than twenty conferences in the Northeast and Midwest on disabled women and girls. Many have been sponsored by the Networking Project for Disabled Women and Girls or by the Women and Disability Awareness Project. Others have been held by colleges and universities, state or local offices for the handicapped, independent living centers, feminist groups, disability organizations, professional rehabilitation or service organizations, the National Women's Studies Association, and the Association for Women and Psychology. We have heard the stories of hundreds of women with a range of disabilities, including many whose disabilities occurred before

adulthood and others who have discovered its meaning during adulthood. Unless otherwise cited, our examples come from conversations at these conferences, from formal interviews, or from our participation in many meetings with the Women and Disability Awareness Project.

References

Alexander, V. 1985. Black women's health concerns. *National Campaign to Restore Abortion Funding* (Fall), 8–9.

Asch, A. 1984. The experience of disability: A challenge for psychology. *American Psychologist* 39(5):529–36.

———. 1986a. Will populism empower disabled people? In *The new populism: The politics of empowerment*, ed. H. C. Boyte and F. Riessman. Philadelphia: Temple University Press.

———. 1986b. Real moral dilemmas. *Christianity and Crisis* 46(10):237–40.

———. 1986c. On the question of Baby Doe. *Health/PAC Bulletin* 16(6):6–10.

Asch, A., and L. Sacks. 1983. Lives without, lives within: The autobiographies of blind women and men. *Journal of Visual Impairment and Blindness* 77(6):242–47.

Asrael, W. 1982. An approach to motherhood for disabled women. *Rehabilitation Literature* 43(7–8):214–18.

Becker, G. 1980. *Growing old in silence*. Berkeley, Calif.: University of California Press.

Bellone, E., and B. Waxman. 1983. *Sexual assault and women with disabilities: An overview*. Los Angeles: Planned Parenthood. (Monograph.)

Berscheid, E., and E. Walster. 1972. Beauty and the beast. *Psychology Today* (March), 42–46, 74.

Bonwich, E. 1985. Sex role attitudes and role reorganization in spinal cord injured women. In *Women and disability: The double handicap*, ed. M. J. Deegan and N. A. Brooks. New Brunswick, N.J.: Transaction.

Boston Women's Health Book Collective. 1985. *The New Our Bodies, Ourselves.* 2d ed., revised. New York: Simon and Schuster.

Bowe, F. 1980. *Rehabilitating America*. New York: Harper and Row.

———. 1981. *Comeback: Six remarkable people who triumphed over disability.* New York: Harper and Row.

———. 1984. *Disabled women in America*. Washington, D.C.: President's Committee on Employment of the Handicapped.

Braille Monitor. 1986. Legalized kidnapping: State takes child away from blind mother (August–September), 432–35.

Brightman, A. J., ed. 1984. *Ordinary moments: The disabled experience.* Baltimore, Md.: University Park Press.

Broverman, I., S. Vogel, D. Broverman, F. Clarkson, and S. Rosenkrantz. 1972. Sex-role stereotypes: A current appraisal. *Journal of Social Issues* 28: 59–78.

Browne, S., D. Connors, and N. Stern, eds. 1985. *With the power of each breath.* Pittsburgh, Pa.: Cleis Press.

Brownmiller, S. 1984. *Femininity*. New York: Simon and Schuster.

Campling, J., ed. 1981. *Images of ourselves: Disabled women talking*. Boston: Routledge and Kegan Paul.

Chodorow, N. J. 1978. *The reproduction of mothering*. Berkeley, Calif.: University of California Press.

Collins, G. 1983. The success story of a disabled mother. *New York Times,* October 12, cdd1–2.

Cox, S., ed. 1981. *Female psychology: The emerging self.* New York: St. Martin's Press.

Crewe, N., and I. K. Zola, eds. 1983. *Independent living for physically disabled people.* San Francisco: Jossey-Bass.

Darling, R. B. 1979. *Families against society: A study of reactions to children with birth defects.* Beverly Hills, Calif.: Sage.

Davis, F. 1961. Deviance disavowal: The management of strained interaction by the visibly handicapped. *Social Problems* 9:120–32.

———. 1963. *Passage through crisis: Polio victims and their families.* Bloomington, Ind.: Bobbs-Merrill.

Deegan, M. J., and N. A. Brooks, eds. 1985. *Women and disability: The double handicap.* New Brunswick, N.J.: Transaction.

Disability Rag. 1984. Special issue. June.

———. 1986. Care that kills. 7(6):9–10.

Duffy, Y. 1981. *. . . All things are possible.* Ann Arbor, Mich.: A. J. Garvin Associates.

Eisenstein, H. 1983. *Contemporary feminist thought.* Boston: G. K. Hall.

Eisenstein, H., and A. Jardine, eds. 1985 (1981). *The future of difference.* New Brunswick, N.J.: Rutgers University Press.

Eisenstein, Z. 1984. *Feminism and sexual equality: Crisis in liberal America.* New York: Monthly Review Press.

Fine, M., and A. Asch. 1981. Disabled women: Sexism without the pedestal. *Journal of Sociology and Social Welfare* 8(2):233–48.

———. 1982. The question of disability: No easy answers for the women's movement. *Reproductive Rights Newsletter* 4(3):19–20.

Finger, A. 1983. Disability and reproductive rights. *off our backs* 13(9).

———. 1984. Claiming all of our bodies: Reproductive rights and disabilities. In *Test-tube women: What future for motherhood?* ed. R. Arditti, R. Duelli-Klein, and S. Minden. Boston: Pandora.

Frank, G. 1981. *Venus on wheels: The life history of a congenital amputee.* Unpublished doctoral diss., Anthropology Department, University of California, Los Angeles.

Franklin, P. 1977. Impact of disability on the family structure. *Social Security Bulletin* 40:3–18.

Freeman, J., ed. 1984. *Women: A feminist perspective.* Palo Alto, Calif.: Mayfield.

Friedman, G. 1980. The mother-daughter bond. *Contemporary Psychoanalysis* 16(1):90–97.

Funk, R. 1987. Disability rights: From caste to class in the context of civil rights. In *Images of the disabled: Disabling images,* ed. A. Gartner and T. Joe. New York: Praeger.

Galler, R. 1984. The myth of the perfect body. In *Pleasure and danger,* ed. C. S. Vance. Boston: Routledge and Kegan Paul.

Gillespie, P., and A. Fink. 1974. The influence of sexism on the education of handicapped children. *Exceptional Children* 5:155–62.

Gilligan, C. 1982. *In a different voice: Psychological theory and women's development.* Cambridge, Mass.: Harvard University Press.

Gliedman, J., and W. Roth. 1980. *The unexpected minority: Handicapped children in America.* New York: Harcourt Brace Jovanovich.

Goffman, E. 1963. *Stigma: Notes on the management of spoiled identity.* Englewood Cliffs, N.J.: Prentice-Hall.

Gold, S. 1985. A year of accomplishment: Sharon Gold reports to the blind of California. *Braille Monitor* (November), 629–40.

Haber, L., and McNeil, J. 1983. *Methodological questions in the estimation of disability prevalence.* Available from Population Division, Bureau of the Census. Washington, D.C.: Government Printing Office.

Hahn, H. 1983a. Paternalism and public policy. *Society* (March–April), 36–44.

———. 1983b. "The good parts": Interpersonal relationships in the autobiographies of physically disabled persons. *Wenner-Gren Foundation Working Papers in Anthropology* (December), 1–38.

———. 1987. Civil rights for disabled Americans: The foundation of a political agenda. In *Images of the disabled: Disabling images,* ed. A. Gartner and T. Joe. New York: Praeger.

Hanna, W. J., and B. Rogovsky. 1986. Women and disability: Stigma and "the third factor." Unpublished paper, Department of Family and Community Development, College of Human Ecology, University of Maryland, College Park.

Hannaford, S. 1985. *Living outside inside: A disabled woman's experience: Towards a social and political perspective.* Berkeley, Calif.: Canterbury Press.

Harrison, B. W. 1986. Feminist realism. *Christianity and crisis* 46(10):233–36.

Hartmann, H. 1981. The unhappy marriage of Marxism and feminism: Towards a more progressive union. In *Women and revolution: A discussion of the unhappy marriage of Marxism and feminism,* ed. L. Sargent. Boston: South End Press.

Heinrich, E., and L. Kriegel. 1961. *Experiments in survival.* New York: Association for the Aid of Crippled Children.

Higgs, P. 1980. *Outsiders in a hearing world.* Beverly Hills, Calif.: Sage.

Hill, N., T. Mehnert, H. Taylor, M. Kagey, S. Leizhenko, et al. 1986. *The ICD survey of disabled Americans: Bringing disabled Americans into the mainstream.* Study no. 854009. New York: International Center for the Disabled.

Hill, N., T. Mehnert, M. Boyd, H. Taylor, S. Leizhenko, et al. 1987. *The ICD survey II: Employing disabled Americans.* Study no. 864009. New York: International Center for the Disabled.

Hobbs, N. 1975. *The futures of children: Categories, labels, and their consequences.* San Francisco, Calif.: Jossey-Bass.

Johnson, M. 1987. Emotion and pride. *Disability Rag* 8(1):1, 4–6.

Joseph, G. 1981. The incompatible ménage à trois: Marxism, feminism, and racism. In *Women and revolution: A discussion of the unhappy marriage of Marxism and feminism,* ed. L. Sargent. Boston: South End Press.

Journal of Sociology and Social Welfare. 1981. Women and disability: The double handicap. 8(2). Entire issue.

Journal of Visual Impairment and Blindness. 1983. Being blind, being a woman. 77(6). Entire issue.

Kirchner, C. 1987. Assessing the effects of vocational rehabilitation on disadvantaged persons: Theoretical perspectives and issues for research. In *Proceedings of the Annual Meeting of the Society for the Study of Chronic Illness, Impairment and Disability, 1984–1985.* Salem, Ore.: Willamette University Press. (Forthcoming.)

Kutner, N. G. 1985. Gender, social class, and social support to disabled persons. Paper delivered at the Society for the Study of Social Problems, August, American Sociological Association, Washington, D.C.

Kutner, N. G., and H. L. Gray. 1985. Women and chronic renal failure: Some neglected issues. In *Women and disability: The double handicap,* ed. M. J. Deegan and N. A. Brooks. New Brunswick, N.J.: Transaction.

Lakoff, R., and R. L. Scherr. 1984. *Face value: The politics of beauty.* Boston: Routledge and Kegan Paul.

Lorde, A. 1980. *The cancer journals.* Argyle, N.Y.: Spinsters, Ink.

Macklin, R., and W. Gaylin. 1981. *Mental retardation and sterilization: A problem of competency and paternalism.* New York: Plenum.

Matthews, G. F. 1983. *Voices from the shadows: Women with disabilities speak out.* Toronto: Women's Educational Press.

Melling, L. 1984. Wife abuse in the deaf community. *Response to Family Violence and Sexual Assault* 9(1):1–2, 12.

Miller, A. 1970. Role of physical attractiveness in impression formation. *Psychonomic Science* 19:241–43.

Miller, J. B. 1976. *Toward a new psychology of women.* Boston: Beacon.

Mudrick, N. R. 1983. Disabled women. *Society* (March), 51–55.

Nagi, S. 1969. *Disability and rehabilitation.* Columbus, Ohio: Ohio University Press.

National Council on Alcoholism. 1980. *Facts on alcoholism and women.* New York: Affiliate.

New York Times. 1984. Panel details "abusive conditions" in California care facilities. January 16, B11.

New York Times. 1986. Census study reports one in five adults suffers from disability. December 23, B7.

off our backs, 1981. *Women with disabilities.* 11(5) Entire issue.

Omolade, B. 1985 (1981). Black women and feminism. In *The future of difference,* ed. H. Eisenstein and A. Jardine. New Brunswick, N.J.: Rutgers University Press.

Packer, J. 1983. Sex stereotyping in vocational counseling of blind/visually impaired persons: A national study of counselor choices. *Journal of Visual Impairment and Blindness* 77(6):261–68.

Person, E. S. 1982. Women working: Fears of failure, deviance, and success. *Journal of the American Academy of Psychoanalysis* 10(1):67–84.

Rapp, R. 1984. XYLO: A true story. In *Test-tube women: What future for motherhood?* ed. R. Arditti, R. Duelli-Klein, and S. Minden. Boston: Pandora Press.

———. 1987. Chromosomes and communication: The discourse of genetic counseling. *Medical Anthropology Quarterly* (forthcoming).

Rehab Group. 1979. *Digest of data on persons with disabilities.* Falls Church, Va.: May.

Rich, A. 1980. Compulsory heterosexuality and lesbian existence. *Signs* 5(4):631–60.

Rose, P. 1984. Hers. *New York Times,* April 5, C2.

Roskies, E. 1972. *Abnormality and normality: The mothering of thalidomide children.* Ithaca, N.Y.: Cornell University Press.

Roth, W. 1981. *The handicapped speak.* Jefferson, N.C.: McFarland and Co.

———. 1983. Handicap as a social construct. *Society* (March–April), 56–61.

Rothman, B. K. 1986. On the question of Baby Doe. *Health/PAC Bulletin* 16(6):7, 11–13.

Rousso, H. 1984. Fostering healthy self-esteem. *The Exceptional Parent* (December), 9–14.

———. 1987. Positive images for disabled women. Conference Presentation at Moving Up and Out Together: Women and Disability, April 11, Southern Connecticut State University. New Haven, Conn.

Ruddick, S. 1980. Maternal thinking. *Feminist Studies* 6(3):343–67.

Safilios-Rothschild, C. 1977. Discrimination against disabled women. *International Rehabilitation Review* (February), 4.

Sargent, L. 1981. *Women and revolution: A discussion of the unhappy marriage of Marxism and feminism.* Boston: South End Press.

Saxton, M. 1984. Born and unborn: The implications of reproductive technologies for people with disabilities. In *Test-tube women: What future for motherhood?* ed. R. Arditti, R. Duelli-Klein, and S. Minden. Boston: Pandora.

Saxton, M., and F. Howe, eds. 1987. *With wings: An anthology of literature by and about women with disabilities.* New York: The Feminist Press.

Scotch, R. K. 1984. *From good will to civil rights: Transforming federal disability policy.* Philadelphia: Temple University Press.

Sheehy, L. 1984. *Women and disability.* Unpublished thesis for LL.M., Columbia University Law School, October 2.

Siller, J., L. Ferguson, D. H. Vann, and B. Holland. 1976. *Structure of attitudes toward the physically disabled.* New York: New York University School of Education.

Snitow, A., C. E. Stansell, and S. Thompson. 1983. *Powers of desire: The politics of sexuality.* New York: Monthly Review Press.

Stone, D. 1986. Policy case: Selecting clients for rehabilitation. Paper presented at the Hastings Center for Society, Ethics, and the Life Sciences, Hastings-On-Hudson, New York, May.

Titley, R., and W. Viney. 1969. Expression of aggression toward the physically handicapped. *Perceptual and Motor Skills* 29:51–56.

Unger, R. 1985. Personal appearance and social control. In *Women's World: A new scholarship,* ed. M. Safire, M. Mednick, D. Izraeli, J. Bernard. New York: Praeger.

Unger, R., M. Hilderbrand, and T. Mardor. 1982. Physical attractiveness and assumptions about social deviance: Some sex-by-sex comparison. *Personality and Social Psychology Bulletin* 8:293–301.

U.S. Census Bureau. 1983. *Labor force status and other characteristics of persons with a work disability: 1982.* Current Population Reports, Series P-23, no. 127. Washington, D.C.: GPO.

U.S. Commission on Civil Rights. 1983. *Accommodating the spectrum of individual abilities.* Washington, D.C.: GPO.

U.S. Department of Education. 1987. *Ninth annual report to Congress on the implementation of the Education of the Handicapped Act.* Washington, D.C.: U.S. Department of Education.

U.S. Department of Health, Education, and Welfare. 1975. *Report of a comprehensive service needs study.* Contract no. 100-74-03-09. Washington, D.C.: GPO.

U.S. Department of Labor, Employment Standards Administration. 1982. *A study of accommodations provided to handicapped employees by federal contractors. Washington, D.C.: GPO.

Vash, C. 1982. Employment issues for women with disabilities. *Rehabilitation Literature* 43(7–8):198–207.

Weinberg, N. 1976. The effect of physical disability on self-perception. *Rehabilitation Counseling Bulletin* (September), 15–20.

Women and Disability Awareness Project. 1984. *Building community: A manual exploring issues of women and disability.* New York: Educational Equity Concepts.

Wright, B. A. 1960. *Physical disability: A psychological approach.* New York: Harper and Row.

———. 1983. *Physical disability: A psycho-social approach.* New York: Harper and Row.

I: Bodies and Images

All of us develop images of our bodies and attempt to understand and accept our physical selves. In Western culture particularly, with its emphasis on and proscriptions for attractiveness, body understanding and acceptance is problematic for women. How much more problematic and important acceptance is for disabled women is the focus of this section. The chapters discuss disabled women's experience of their bodies as well as their attempts to reconcile their senses of themselves with cultural models of acceptable bodies and stereotypes of disability.

We need not cite the numerous examples of academic works that link disability to psychological disorders to make the points that disabled people are regarded as impaired people, and that disabled women are regarded as damaged and asexual.[1] The remarkable resurgence of concern with health, fitness, and physical beauty in the 1970s and 1980s has prompted feminists to reiterate or reframe questions about the cultural meaning of femininity and beauty.[2] Lakoff and Scher (1985), for example, discuss appearance as the last taboo and great divide among women. Even in the women's movement, women avoid acknowledging their attractiveness or feelings of competitiveness about appearance; they do not admit to themselves or to others that appearance matters in this culture. The feminist discussions of self-image or competitiveness among women are not related to disabled women. How do women with disabilities come to terms with bodies that depart from cultural norms of acceptability and attractiveness? The silence in the literature seems to imply that the implications are obvious.

Like some recently published accounts of disabled women's lives,[3] the following chapters contradict much of the prevailing widsom by testifying to women's capacity to integrate experiences that are conventionally associated with drastic and adverse psychological consequences. Gelya Frank presents an anthropological reconstruction of Diane DeVries' life experience; DeVries, a woman with congenital absence of arms and legs, challenges preconceived notions about identity and appearance. Beth Meyerowitz, Shelly Chaiken, and Laura Clark explore the meaning of breast cancer to women who were socialized as

39

non-disabled women and who experience this body-altering disability in adulthood. The section closes with Deborah Kent's childhood and adult responses to literary portrayals of disabled women within the framework of her own search for identity. She contrasts negative and devalued stereotypes with depictions of disabled women forging positive self-images and leading rich lives. Because no one develops a sense of self apart from others, these chapters open the discussion of relationships that occupies the following section.

Notes

1. For classics of psychoanalysis on body image with bearing on the mental health of people with disabilities, see S. Freud, "Some Character-Types Met With in Psycho-analytic Work," *Standard Edition of the Complete Psychological Works* (1916), vol. 14 (London: Hogarth, 1953–1974); E. Jacobson, "The 'Exceptions': An Elaboration of Freud's Character Study," *Psychoanalytic Study of the Child* 14 (1959), pp. 135–54; A. Lussier, "The Physical Handicap and the Body Ego," *International Journal of Psycho-Analysis* 61 (1980), pp. 179–85; W. Niederland, "Narcissistic Ego Impairment in Patients with Early Physical Malformations," *Psychoanalytic Study of the Child* 20 (1965), pp. 518–34. For a critique of psychoanalytic writing on people with disabilities, see A. Asch and H. Rousso, "Therapists with Disabilities: Theoretical and Clinical Issues," *Psychiatry* 48, no. 1 (1985), pp. 1–12. For a discussion of the implications for life chances of physical appearance for women and men, see E. Berscheid and E. Walster, "Physical Attractiveness," in L. Berkowitz, ed., *Advances in Experimental Social Psychology,* vol. 3, (New York: Academic Press, 1974); R. K. Unger, M. Hilderbrand, T. Madar, "Physical Attractiveness and Assumptions about Social Deviance: Some Sex-by-Sex Comparisons," *Personality and Social Psychology Bulletin* 8, no. 2 (June 1982), pp. 293–301.

2. For feminist discussions of the role of beauty in women's lives, see L. C. Pogrebin, "Of Beauty," *Ms* (December 1983), pp. 73–78, 109; S. Brownmiller, *Femininity* (New York: Simon and Schuster, 1984); R. T. Lakoff and R. L. Scherr, *Face Value: The Politics of Beauty* (Boston: Routledge and Kegan Paul, 1984).

3. Writings of and interviews with British, U.S., and Canadian women with disabilities can be found in J. Campling, *Images of Ourselves: Disabled Women Talking* (Boston: Routledge and Kegan Paul, 1981); S. Browne, D. Connors, and N. Stern, *With the Power of Each Breath* (Pittsburgh: Cleis Press, 1985); and G. F. Matthews, *Voices from the Shadows: Women with Disabilities Speak Out* (Toronto: Women's Educational Press, 1983), respectively.

1. On Embodiment: A Case Study of Congenital Limb Deficiency in American Culture

GELYA FRANK

The use of the body for most people has a culturally prescribed, developmental, and finally habitual character. The individual with physical disabilities, however, must learn to integrate identity and function anew—to accept a variant body image and to learn to use the body automatically and unself-consciously in culturally acceptable ways. The purpose of this paper is to describe and interpret the manner in which Diane DeVries, an American woman, now in her thirties and born with quadrilateral limb deficiencies, views her body and uses it to accomplish everyday activities. The rubric will be "embodiment," a concept taken from the phenomenological movement in philosophy (Spiegelberg 1976). A goal of phenomenological investigations has been to identify and describe the essential forms of human experience, beginning with the body as a locus for sensation, perception, and interaction (Merleau-Ponty 1962; Sartre 1957; Schilder 1950). In a recent article I drew on the life history of Diane DeVries to develop a theory of the phenomenon of empathy (Frank 1985). But here my purpose is applied, hence my reference to the phenomenon of embodiment as a "rubric" to frame a discourse on the experience of disability in American culture.

Experiences of the world presuppose an embodied consciousness habituated to the biological endowments of the species; these in turn constitute the way that the environment is perceived and experienced (Von Uexküll 1957). It is distinctive of human beings that they inhabit cultural worlds, each a selection and elaboration of elements with the capacities of our species (Hallowell 1956). The parameters of a world-view are time and space as defined by the culture (Kearney 1984). In Henry's (1971) ethnography of American families with schizophrenic children, attention to these highly abstract parameters helped make even the most mundane behaviors comprehensible: a father's usual failure to provide a flashlight on hikes while exhorting his frightened sons to keep their pace in the dark, an absent mother's sudden attention and display of physical affection when her infant strays close to traffic could be seen to promote patterns of dysfunctional behavior in the children given the cultural constitution of their environment. The concept of "embodiment" might well cover a broad range of traditional anthropological topics such as the effect on personality of weaning and toilet-training practices, the coding of voice and gesture for communication, and the ritual elaboration of life cycle events as expressions of the social body or the body politic (Scheper-Hughes and Lock 1987). A phenomenological treatment of such topics, as in the work by Henry, would emphasize the experience of the individual as the sensory and productive unit of the species. This paper addresses the embodiment of one individual, Diane DeVries, a woman with disabilities, in order to mark its features as an American case for this and future discourse.

To what other concepts might the rubric of embodiment stand in contrast? In the United States, the embodiment of persons with disabilities has been the target of research in social psychology on "adjustment" to physical handicap and illness (Barker 1977).[1] The approach holds that persons with disabilities experience inner conflicts because of a loss of body function or appearance that is culturally valued (Wright 1983).[2] The negative emotions accompanying loss and stigma may be managed through unconscious psychological defenses such as denial or through such conscious attitudes as the favorable reevaluation of one's intact features and capabilities relative to those impaired. Management of inner conflicts leads to active engagement in social life, a sense of achievement, and satisfaction. While this theory does explain the adjustment of Diane DeVries to her disabilities, it glosses over some areas of her experience, such as the cultural problem of interpreting when adjustment was indeed taking place. Diane rejected the use of prostheses for upper extremity function. Using Wright's terminology, it could be said that this represented an adjustment to the lack of arms and legs since Diane stressed instead her "asset values"—e.g., her womanly figure and her ability to write better with her stumps when unencumbered by artificial arms. At the time, however, Diane's rejection of prostheses was judged by clinicians to reflect poor adjustment and to auger a life of dependence. Looking back over Diane's life history, an active and essentially normal pattern for her age, gender, and class is revealed (Frank 1984), which suggests that Diane did "adjust" to her disability as a participant in American culture. The embodiment of Diane DeVries—her view of her body and use of it—came into conflict, then, with the special culture of rehabilitation[3] as represented by her clinical team.

There are other dimensions of experience that the more inclusive rubric of "embodiment" may illuminate better than the concept of "adjustment." In addition to managing internal conflict and social interactions, a person with disabilities may face a heightened ambiguity[4] in living a conventional American life. For example, the interdependence with others in daily tasks of dressing and toileting can engender an intimacy and identification that defies cultural definitions of the boundaries of the physical self. Consider Diane's expression of participation in the embodied experiences of her younger sister:

It's true that there is a Diane within this Diane who can dance which enabled me to teach my younger sister Debbie, but there's another reason I could coach her so well. It's hard to explain. Ever since Deb could walk she was taking care of me. I saw her body move from childhood's awkwardness to adult gracefulness and strength. But not only did I *see* this, I felt her movements. In a sense, part of her body (the part I lacked on the exterior) was mine too. So, since I *knew* how her body moved, I could coach her in dancing.[5]

The problem of ambiguity further arises in forming a realistic body image on which function can be based. Diane grappled with the implications of being diagnosed as someone who does or doesn't have legs. Through adolescence and early adulthood she believed, in disagreement with her clinical team, that she could walk with prostheses if an appropriate pair were fabricated. In 1981, Diane expressed a vision in which she was "restored" arms and legs:

"There's a woman minister in the church. She's highly annointed and has the gift of healing, and she's been promised a miracle," Diane told me. "I had a vision that God promised to restore my arms and legs. That minister was standing at the foot of my bed." "That's great!" I said. Perhaps wickedly, I added, "Did you ask Him when?" Diane laughed, and replied most reasonably, "In His own eternal time."

Such an image represents a reservoir of latent powers, powers that belong to Diane by birthright. With her Christian faith, Diane still believes that she may one day walk. From the standpoint of embodiment, it would be an error to dismiss such experiences of the body as irrelevant to Diane's functioning or as evidence of faulty adjustment.

There is an intactness to Diane's descriptions of her body. She is native to it; she knows it from the inside. Persons with disabilities like Diane are presently living out a dialectical problem in defining themselves as "disabled." By accepting this label, they are attempting to deal with their variance in straightforward ways that include accepting tax-supported services for independent living, engaging in collective action to extend legal protection for their rights, and even publicizing their lives in studies such as this one to promote understanding and social responsibility. At the same time, they are insisting upon their intactness and wholeness as individuals facing essentially the same challenges as other members of society—work, sexuality, family, play, and so on. Ultimately, they wish to be seen as "persons," not as "patients." For them, it is "being-in-the-world" that is important, as indicated by the response of the mother of a ten-year-old girl born without arms and legs to an article I had sent her on the life history of Diane DeVries:

I found it a little difficult to write a response to your paper because it was so very academic and it is *so different* to be living it day to day with someone like Diane or our Robin—we take for granted so much!!, presuming I guess that other people know what limb-deficient people *can* do. The adjustments we make in helping Robin are constants in our lives and therefore "normal"—for example, toileting and dressing. And we have tried to have Robin see herself as "normal"—and have found that her peers accept her as such in so many (or most) ways. Lots of day to day and living experiences of Diane are similar to Robin's, and adaptations are commonly made by Robin to get things—the things she gets into and out of are wonderful. The enclosed article was done by the city editor of our local newspaper after several people had suggested Robin as a subject—he spent quite a lot of time on it and we think it's pretty nice. The hardest part is "being under the microscope" again, but we felt it might help educate a few people . . . there is no guarantee that anyone will not become handicapped at some time in their life, and everyone deserves as much freedom as possible. Maybe your work and our reality will help in this direction.[6]

If medicine aims at being not only curative but restorative, its goal must be to relate back to the world of the patient. We must therefore have conceptual structures—languages—that let us mediate our understanding across settings, from the clinic, to the academy, to the community. It is proposed that the very highly abstract concept of "embodiment" can give us a vantage to see the experiences of persons with disabilities across the boundaries of those settings. Finally, there is the temporal dimension. As the historical context in which persons with disabilities live is ever-changing, the cultural meaning of disability changes. People once regarded in Western cultures as "freaks" (Fielder 1978) or "paupers and beggars" (Stone 1984) are now defined as "persons with disabilities." Concrete descriptions will always be necessary to comprehend the fit between theories of their embodied life and their lived experiences.

CLARITY AND AMBIGUITY IN LIVING AS A "CONGENITAL AMPUTEE"

Diane Fields DeVries was born on March 20, 1950, in a small town north of Dallas, Texas. She was the first child of Kenneth and Irene Fields, each 20 years old, white, nominally Christian, and the product of working-class homes. Another child, Debbie, was born two years later, after the family had moved to southern California. After several years, two more children—a boy and girl—were added to the family. Diane's father worked as a carpenter. At age 5, Diane was referred to the new Child Amputee Prosthetics Project (CAPP), at the University of California at Los Angeles, where she began a program of wearing artificial arms and legs. She was given a three-wheeled cart for ease of mobility. As a result of growth in her stumps, she underwent numerous surgeries during childhood to remove painful bone spurs. She also suffered from attacks of constipation, heat prostration, rhinitis, and asthma.

Until junior high school, Diane attended the Benjamin F. Tucker School for Handicapped Children and spent summers at the Los Angeles County Crippled Children's Society Camp. Beginning about the time of puberty, she lived for intermittent periods at Rancho Los Amigos Hospital, a Los Angeles County rehabilitation facility. There she gave up using her artificial arms, replaced the three-wheeled cart with an electric wheelchair, and eventually began wearing a pair of nonfunctional cosmetic legs, which she later abandoned. Diane attended a "normal" high school in Long Beach, and her first active sexual encounter occurred at graduation. The following years were marked by independent living in an apartment with her own attendant, the social use of "pills and weed," sexual experimentation, and frequent changes of residence. In 1969, Diane began living with Jim DeVries. In the turbulent years that followed, Diane and Jim split up. Diane bounced in and out of convalescent homes, her father was diagnosed with cancer, and her parents were divorced. Diane returned to Rancho, where she experienced an important love affair with a man with quadriplegia. Concurrent with the breakup of that relationship and the death of her father, Diane was motivated to leave Rancho and begin studies at UCLA. It was there, in 1976, that our collaboration began on her life history.

In 1977, Diane transferred to the University of California at Berkeley, partly to be at the pulse of the Independent Living Movement. Diane and Jim were married there. It was a year marked by Jim's struggle with alcoholism and a tense adjustment to the responsibilities of married life. The couple returned to Los Angeles, filed for divorce, and Diane moved to a convalescent home. There, in 1980, she was "saved" at a Christian church and "healed" of asthma. In 1981, Diane was seriously injured in a car accident. Jim returned and was introduced by Diane to the church, where he was baptized by immersion and "delivered" of alcohol. Subsequently, Diane and Jim attended Bible college and their life, until recently, has been centered almost entirely around the church community. Despite rather frequent changes in residence and a minimal level of financial security, this has been a period of stability and peace for them. Their recent disenchantment with the "hypocrisy" of their church in integrating the disabled into full participation, and with other practices, has led them to break away. While Diane remains committed to a self-consciously Christian life, she has decided to return to UCLA to finish her undergraduate degree in sociology. Currently, she works on a part-time basis as a peer counselor at a transitional living center for persons with mainly traumatic disabilities. She presently plans to make a career in social work after graduation.

The events just recounted summarize and up-date the life history of Diane DeVries (Frank 1984). The synopsis is intended to provide background to questions of embodiment raised by Diane's having been born a "quadruple amputee," missing both legs almost completely and having above-elbow stumps of about equal length. At birth, Diane weighed 5 pounds 3 ounces and measured 17 inches. Labor lasted 48 to 60 hours and culminated in a breech presentation. Diane's mother remembered having a case of the "flu," which lasted three days near the end of the second trimester of pregnancy but was not severe enough nor early enough during the pregnancy to account for Diane's having been born without limbs. The lack of a known etiology leaves an open field for interpretation. Diane has taken the point of view that "it was just something that happened." This was Diane's father's response to her childhood inquiries. Diane argues strongly against any association of her limb deficiencies with thalidomide: not only are her "amputations" symmetrical and neat, but there are no other malformations. Compared to people having complex disabilities, Diane feels *really* lucky."

> D: When Mom was pregnant with me, they had no idea that anything was wrong, because I kicked and the whole bit, you know. And they couldn't take X rays. It was too far past that to take X rays. So they had no idea. The doctor, when I was delivered, the doctor fainted.
> G: Literally?
> D: Literally. The nurse had to finish it. He was just out, you know. So they

got me out. And I guess they probably took some test to find out, but they never did.

G: Did your mother take any drugs while she was pregnant?

D: No. Well, see, I asked after, you know, when they were divorced. That's when I started asking a lot of questions, and first I asked *her*. And she kinda, every time I asked her she gets real quiet and looks away and doesn't say too much. You know, Yes, or No, and that's about it. So I finally got ahold of my Dad, and I tried to get him, and he says, "All I can tell you is what *I* know. *I* know that when I saw your mother, she wasn't taking anything. And there's never been anything else like this in the rest of the family, going back." So, he doesn't know. *He* believes, my Dad believes, it's just something that happened. And I do, too. I don't believe she took pills. That's not like her.

G: No, but around the time you were born or a little bit later, there was a thing with thalidomide.

D: That was later. Yeah.

G: That was later.

D: That was about '56 or something.

G: Right.

D: But, uh, Dad believed and I do, too, that it was just something that happened. Because that's the only thing that's wrong with me, is just that I don't have no arms and legs. And they're nice and neat, too. I didn't have any weird fingers hanging off or any feet, you know. A lot of them have that.

G: Yeah, you were lucky.

D: Yeah, I think I'm *really* lucky, 'cause I've seen kids like that, and I just, I couldn't stand it. At least I can dress how I want and look how I want, and I've been pretty lucky. So . . . but that was it. There was no other defects. Like my lungs weren't crooked, or my heart wasn't, you know, up in the wrong place or something. You know. So probably it was just something that happened, I would think.

From childhood Diane DeVries' attitude toward her body when healthy and free of devices has been remarkably positive. This sense of her body has persisted despite surgeries beginning at age 7 for painful neuromas and cysts at the ends of her stumps, attacks of asthma perhaps at first self-induced but later involuntary, and discomfort from heat due to her high ratio of body volume to skin area. While Diane was always aware of the differences between herself and others, they might often be taken for granted:

G: How old were you when you first realized that you looked different from most other people?

D: I realized that right away.

G: So you always had that awareness.

D: Oh yeah. It never hit me one day.

G: You never had a special awareness that outside your family people were looking at you differently?

D: I always knew it. It was always there because my body was *so* different.

G: How did you feel about that differentness? How did you understand it?
D: I just knew I was different. Certain things could happen during the day to make me sad or mad, 'cause I could go . . . weeks without it bothering me at all, because nothing happened. But something *could* happen, like once when I was a little kid. I was in the wagon and we were in this trailer park, and some kid came up to me with a knife. He said, "Aw, you ain't got no arms, you ain't got no legs, and now you're not gonna have no head." He held me right here, by the neck, and had a little knife. It was one of those bratty kids that did weird things. So that day, I really. . . . You know, certain times, certain things happened. Otherwise, I didn't notice it.

If Diane has moments of alienation from herself or feelings of regret about her body, she has not conveyed them to me. A more relevant focus for an individual like Diane may be to protect herself from the attitude so easily taken by the non-disabled that her body is flawed and unacceptable. In an interview, for example, I sensed a defensiveness in Diane's response to questions meant to elicit a global assessment about her body. "Do you feel like you're crippled?" I asked her. "Do you feel handicapped?" Diane answered, "Yeah. Lately."[7] Her back had been giving her trouble. There was pain when she moved and difficulty in moving gracefully. She felt lucky that her arms were still strong enough to pull her up as she transfers from place to place. Taking her unexpected response as a cue, I asked Diane not to assess her body as a whole but to tell me how she feels about the parts she has.

G: What's your strongest point?
D: My arms.
G: Your weakest?
D: You mean physically? It's a toss-up between my back and my hips. Now it's my back. But that's fucking up my hips, too. My lungs are probably weaker than my back.
G: What parts do you feel affectionate towards?
D: My arms. I love them. My boobs. That's about it.
G: What parts make you feel the reverse?
D: My back. My lungs. My chest cavity. I hate them.
G: How about your face?
D: I don't know. I don't like my mouth. That area. I've always wished I could change that. My teeth and everything. It's weird.
G: What's wrong with them?
D: My lips—the top one—which is it? I haven't even looked at myself for days. Anyway, one of my lips is bigger. The bottom one goes in. I don't like it. If I could, I'd . . . [gestures][8]
G: Have your chin pushed down?
D: Make it even. When I was young I never smiled. I hated my picture taken anyway. But when I had to have it, I never smiled, because I thought I looked dumb smiling. I got over it, but I don't remember at

what age. I let it all out. Started showing my teeth because I wanted to laugh and smile.

G: What about the rest of your face?

D: It's all right except the acne. That's because I'm Aries and I worry. The rest is all right.

G: How do you like your eyes? Your nose?

D: They're not extraordinary, but I like them.

G: What kind of ears do you have?

D: My left ear sticks out. I've got my Dad's left ear. The right one's normal. It just goes back. So I always keep my hair cut over my ears, 'cause I don't like this left ear to stick out. They look all right.

G: What does your back look like?

D: . . . I don't know. I mean, I haven't seen my back in so long. Um. I know it's starting to look like . . . I noticed one day in the other apartment . . . I was getting out of the bathroom and I went over to the bed. The mirror was there standing against the wall. I looked at myself—hadn't done it in a while, didn't have no clothes on—and I could see that it was "going" . . .

Diane traced an "S" in the air with her stump to indicate scoliosis. Like us all, then, Diane scrutinizes her body and evaluates it according to normative standards of appearance and function. Expecting her to praise or damn her body as a whole is to force an alien perspective. Judging her body on its own terms, neither more nor less, she appears to judge well.

There are fundamental ambiguities concerning Diane DeVries' body, however, that she has had to live with and resolve. Paramount is the question of whether Diane does or doesn't have legs. The term "congenital amputee" is a misnomer. Diane supports the distinction between her congenital limb deficiencies and true amputations in part on the basis of never having had phantom pains, although she knows what they are through vicarious experiences at Rancho.

G: Are you considered an amputee?

D: Congenital amputee.

G: That's a strange idea.

D: Yeah, 'cause amputees you think of being amputated. I freaked out when they put me on the amputee ward. I don't have phantom pains— never had any of those.

G: Do you ever have the feeling that you have limbs?

D: Oh no.

G: Never?

D: No. But I can understand how you would move certain parts of you to do certain things. Like dancing I can really get into. That's why I think I could show my sister Debbie a lot—she dances like a snake—because I could understand which leg you move this way and that. Which I think is kind of weird since I've never done it. And I learned to walk really quick in my legs, get my balance, and use my arms really quick. But I never feel like I have them. It's just that I know because I think about it a lot.

G: You talk with your hands.

D: But I never feel it like they do. I never get phantom pains.

G: Do they have the pains their whole life or just after the operation?

D: Some get it for quite a while. A guy at Rancho explained it better than anyone. He lost his leg ten years ago. They gave him an artificial leg. It's like putting a leg into a very tight cast. I could imagine what that could feel like—just awful. It's really painful, like your leg is in another thing, all cramped. It was really bad, so he would hardly wear it.

To call up an image of Diane in the company of people who have had an arm or leg cut off leaves something to be desired. Her "arms" and "legs" can only be postulated. They exist in a state of potential as much as in a state of loss. This is clearest with respect to Diane's arms. She does in fact have arms, in the form of two upper stumps of about equal length.

Diane's legs are more problematical. For all practical purposes, she was considered to be lacking legs. At CAPP she was diagnosed as having "congenital absence of both legs at the hips." In an early clinical description, however, Diane was reported to "ambulate" by swinging the left and right sides of the pelvis alternately forward. Diane would call this "walking." Six months after coming to CAPP, she received her first pair of artificial legs, two stubby pylons set into a pelvic platform. In them, Diane continued to walk by means of pelvic rotation. Even at this early date, the CAPP staff anticipated that for Diane walking would be achieved only with much difficulty because she lacked stumps to which artificial legs might be independently attached.

The language used to describe Diane's lower limb deficiencies itself evokes the presence of limbs. Notes at Diane's admitting examination at CAPP state: "There appears clinically and by x-ray to be a femoral head only on the right, and no bony components on the left lower extremity." Thus there is the suggestion that Diane has at least a rudimentary right lower extremity. Over the years other statements appear in the reports, such as: "The legs are represented only by soft tender nodules in the anterio-inferior aspect of the groin-buttocks area. There's good anterior and posterior flexion of this tissue mass." While the word "stump" is never used to describe this area, the possibility of attaching prostheses independently to each buttock was considered. Diane's physical therapy at age 11, for example, included mat exercises to improve the strength in her gluteal muscles.

Today Diane thinks of herself as having the ability to walk and in some sense as having legs. She reports: "They discovered I had hip bones when the doctors were standing around in preparation for my first surgery. I was walking already."

G: Walking?
D: Walking. On the floor. Scooting around.
G: How?
D: I just moved my hips back and forth. I still do it when I have to.
G: Give it to me in more detail.
D: I sit on the floor on my butt, and I move each . . . Well, these, I call them legs, 'cause they *are* in a way. Just move each one with your hip. Just like anyone else would. Just move the top of their leg. And I got around like that. You know, around the house, not outside.
G: Walking on the front part? What would be your thigh? Or on the point of it?
D: Just like I'm sitting right now. Except walking.
G: It's hard for me to visualize exactly what you have there.
D: When I was younger, it was just my butt. But then I realized I could move each and they were separate. So they were legs, you know. I walked on them. When I was younger and thinner it was easier. I could bounce around. I used to be able to stand on my head! That amazes me when I think about it. I was really *light* then. They discovered I had hips and that surprised me, because I figured that if I'm walking, of course I had them.

Diane feels she does have independent legs, to the extent that she could move each hip in the prosthesis and "one leg would go out and then the other." But she does not concur with CAPP that "I don't have long separate legs. You know, stumps."

The ambiguous presence/absence of Diane's legs is exaggerated in the more symbolic and disembodied modes of being. Diane sometimes has legs in dreams and visions. She has referred to the battery for her electric wheelchair as "my legs" and to the mobility she gains in her wheelchair as "walking." Since she tells me that, given legs, her proportions would be tall, I am certain that she has imagined herself that way. She is familiar enough with what legs do and how they feel to coach her sister in dancing and to empathize with the phantom pains of a true amputee. And there are the jokes that are shared among friends and the banter in which Diane's legs are made conspicuous by their absence. At a birthday party, her friend Alice announced as we entered, "Hey, don't nobody step on Diane's toes." Later she threatened, "Diane, if you don't have a drink, I'm going to sit on your legs." Preparing me for the sight of a black eye, Diane once mentioned that she had "walked into a fist." Is it just Diane and her friend who joke this way? "Everyone I know says things like that. It's only natural, I guess, 'cause I've always done it, so they pick up on it." Diane's mother is the only one, she says, who "freaks out" when Diane talks that way. "Debbie's always teasing Ma.

She's always saying, 'Yeah, when I was born, God gave Diane the boobs and gave me the arms and legs!' "

FUNCTIONING WITH AND WITHOUT ARTIFICIAL LIMBS

When Diane DeVries was brought in 1955, at age 5, to the Child Amputee Prosthetics Project, she was immediately fitted with a pair of artificial arms. Six months later she was fitted on an experimental basis for ambulation with a pelvic platform, a bucket with stubby feet. The goal of treatment at CAPP was "to provide limb deficient or amputee children with the means and motivation to lead as nearly normal, productive and satisfying lives as possible." In an interview with Diane's parents in 1959, her future was presented by the CAPP staff as a choice between being a *dependent person* with institutional type care or being an *independent person* with limited but attainable employment skills and capacity to take care of herself. To be "independent" would require prosthesis use. Thus Diane was trained to use prostheses—both upper and lower—from roughly age 4 to 18 to "increase her functioning," although it was felt that Diane would always be very dependent on others.

The clinical ideals for normalizing Diane's life conflicted with the choices she made for herself. Over time, she rejected the use of artificial arms. What she wanted passionately, however, was to walk. When Diane was 12, her occupational therapist wrote: "Diane's non-wearing at home and at school, her pleas for freedom from anything which tends to be heavy, her limited, but perhaps impressive ability with her stumps, her overgrowth problems and her frequent absences make it difficult to carry out a well-ordered therapy. But we do feel," the report continued, "that a substitute which will provide reach, firm grasp and motions which resemble those of the normal arm is advantageous and that the advantage will be more obvious in the future."

It was apparent from the very beginning that no matter how competently Diane learned to use her artificial arms, she would always need to have someone place things in her reach, pre-position her terminal hooks, or prearrange objects that she needed to handle. What advantage she might gain in reach and grasp using these complex devices was canceled by the restrictions imposed by the confining equipment. Many of the tasks she learned to perform slowly and with great effort using upper prostheses—writing, reading a book, or holding a cup—were ones she could perform with her stumps. It should be kept in mind that the pattern of Diane's childhood was a constant round of surgeries, brief periods of healing, physical and occupational therapy with and without prostheses, enforced wearing of prostheses at school, adjustment to new prostheses as old ones were outgrown or mastered, growth of the bones in her stumps, consequent tenderness and irritation, and more surgeries. Punctuating this cycle were the bouts with respiratory illnesses and constipation. Wearing artificial arms complicated Diane's life and forced her to choose between her native capabilities and a questionable substitute. Artificial legs did not pose these problems.

In an interview about her various prostheses, Diane talked exclusively about the lower, and distinguished them with names of her own. First were "the little legs" (the pelvic platform)—straight, about a foot high off the ground, with feet that were "normal shaped." The tone of her recollection of them is casual:

The bucket top was a little bit of plaster on the butt and then when it came up to the waist it had leather going all around the waist. And then it just buckled in the front. Then coming down from this bucket thing were the two legs. They were made of, at that time, the plaster also. The skin-colored plaster. And then two little feet. So I could move around. And the legs, since they were so short, they had no knees or anything. Like two sticks, almost, with feet on them. So I could walk around. That's all I really needed them for, was just to reach tables—school tables. They weren't that useful to me. I could walk around in them. But I could walk around without them at that time. It didn't matter.

Diane was successful enough with the pelvic platform to be graduated within a year to a new prosthesis. This was a Canadian hip disarticulation type, modified over time to have rocker feet, locking knees, and solid functional feet.

Concurrently, she was given a three-wheeled scooter. The scooter was positively exciting. It was "like a tripod thing," Diane recalls. "It had three wheels. Two in the front and one in the back. And it stands on something like a pole, this bucket goody. You sit in it. First they gave me two crutches, because they were convinced I wouldn't give my arms up—no crip does." She described the joy of a 5-year-old suddenly able to propel herself across the room:

D: I put my arms on and used the two crutches they designed and they put me in the scooter. And I came across the room and I *dug* it, 'cause it was so *easy.* And I thought, "Wow. Far out." I just tripped around the room, and they didn't want me to take it home that day, 'cause they had a few repairs and all. And I was mad. I was crying when I went home, 'cause I wanted it. But I got it a couple of days later. It was all finished. I had it until I was about 12.
G: What did it enable you to do that you couldn't do before?
D: Go outside by myself when I was home. Get around by myself. I did give the arms up. Then I needed only a crutch. I did it with my right arm perfectly, since it's the longest one. So I used it, and could go see my neighbor friends by myself.

G: What about stairs?

D: I was so light, I'd go over my friend's house and whoever was there would just carry me up the stairs.

G: What about stairs at your house?

D: Yeah. I'd have to go out the den. I always stayed in the den or in our room—Debbie's and mine. From our bedroom there's a little porch thing, then one stair and a den. I got down that stair by holding onto the door on one side, and put my crutch on the other.

G: How did you get back up?

D: I'd just go over and hold the door with my left arm. Then I'd push up with the crutch just enough to get the right wheel up and then I'd push on up. I had good balance. I had to. I fell over several times, at school, going too fast, and there were bumps.

G: So you could go outside.

D: I could visit friends outside by myself. Get around school by myself. Didn't have to wait for someone to help me out of my desk or anything. I was already up, because I was in that thing all the time. I could reach things better because it was a more normal height for someone my age. It was really neat. The reason they took it away, at 12 you start realizing how you look to other people.

Diane gave up wearing artificial arms sometime after the tenth or twelfth pair. They were "more of a hassle than a help," she recalls. "Anything took longer. Turning pages. I can remember turning pages. For therapy they'd make me hold the book down for someone else. I used to hate that." It felt unnatural to practice using both arms equally, "which I'd hate because I was right-handed, so I'd always use this arm [gestures]. They made me use them all the time. I hated it." Using just her stumps, Diane could color, simulate eating and drinking, and handle doll dishes, according to a diagnostic examination at age 9. Except for bilateral lifting, the right stump was used almost exclusively. Her range of "reach" (quotation marks in the original report) was limited and she asked to have objects put into her range so they might be skillfully manipulated with her stumps. She frequently used her head as a holding assist, requiring her to lean over the table, making her field of vision and posture poor. While her trunk stability was extremely good, and the lower extremity prosthesis was "used well" for ambulation, the first appearance of Diane's scoliosis is noted. The evaluation resulted in a decision "to solve" Diane's upper extremity prosthesis problems before initiating changes in the lower. CAPP's goal now was to add length and grasp to the artificial arms, with the anticipation of making Diane's field of vision more normal, enhancing her balance, and preventing further scoliosis.

Despite the mixed results with artificial arms, and the contrasting picture of Diane's strength and coordination in her artificial legs, a decision was made when she was 12 years old to end her training with lower extremity prostheses:

This child has had a five to six-year program during which she used experimental legs of various types. This program was not successful. It is felt that a significant part of her present enthusiasm for the use of the upper extremities is due to her release from the ordeal of struggling with lower extremity legs which gave her such limited function and satisfaction. Therefore, it is recommended that her visits to physical therapy be discontinued and her time more profitably spent in Occupational Therapy.

From a layperson's point of view, this conclusion seems difficult to understand when the earlier evaluations are taken into consideration. One physical therapy report from the period 1957 to 1959 states that in her prostheses with rocker feet Diane "never complains of her lower extremities and walks around school a great deal. Although it is slow she has mastered the use of them very well." She was never seen by the therapist to lose her balance on them. She was adept at walking in them by pelvic rotation and also the hip-hiking method. CAPP's decision in 1962 to abandon training with the artificial legs must have been both puzzling and frustrating to Diane. It was, in any event, a decision she later struggled unsuccessfully to reverse.

According to the CAPP files, Irene Fields reported in 1963 that her daughter wanted to be fitted with functional legs. It was then that Rancho Los Amigos Hospital was first mentioned as a resource, with the possibility of Diane's placement in residence there. She was admitted there as an in-patient in 1964, at the age of 14, and a decision to fit her with functional legs was made based on evaluations by the psychiatry and orthopedic departments. She spent most of her days in her scooter, with only about 20 minutes of independent ambulation "hopping on gluteal mass with axillary crutches" on level ground, stairs of standard size, and ramps. The weight of standard lower prostheses and the instability of full-height components were considered too difficult for Diane to manage. The staff at Rancho agreed to work with the prosthetics department of CAPP. They would use simple, lightweight components at first, graduated in height. Diane was sent home until such time as CAPP would be ready to start.

In 1966, Diane's mother reported to CAPP that Rancho's staff decided against the lower extremity prosthesis. Making legs that Diane could walk on was "impossible." Now grown too big to fit the bucket of her cart, Diane used a standard electric wheelchair and a manual junior-size wheelchair to fit under the desks at school. According to her mother, Diane accepted the fact that she could not have functional legs.

Nevertheless, when asked in a psychological interview, at age 16, what she hoped to gain by being at Rancho, Diane responded: "Artificial legs—walk!" According to her mother's report, however, Diane wanted CAPP's help to obtain cosmetic legs to wear in the wheelchair. It was emphasized to Diane that cosmetic legs would make it harder for her to be transported during transfers and that she had to lose weight, particularly in the area of her hips. Months later, she received a ready-made pair no longer needed by another patient. Although Diane described these legs to me as "stupid" and insisted that she hated them, her feelings toward them appear ambivalent:

> D: They had . . . the plaster wasn't a bucket. It was just a piece in the front. It took up my whole front and went around the other side.
> G: From where to where? Around your waist?
> D: It went around my waist down to the end of my leg and around to the sides. The legs were coming off the front of this thing. The legs looked really nice. They were real-looking, if you put nylons on them. I used to put five pairs of nylons on to cover up the wooden marks.
> G: Really?
> D: Yeah, and those were just the plain-colored ones. And in those times, when I had those legs, the colored nylons were in. It was good for me, 'cause I could hide a lot of weird things on my legs—screws and shit. And they were a great shape. They were long. But everyone tells me if I had legs I would be tall. But I don't know if I'd have been *that* tall. They were pretty long. Anyway, then I would sit on the two straps. There were these straps and they would come across each hip up to the front end strap. And you pulled it tight as hell. I mean *tight*. Because after you get them on—when I was wearing them, then, you'd put them on me and the taxi driver would come to take me to school. By the time he picks me up and puts me in the cab, they're loose. So you got to put them on *really* tight to last all day—four transfers. I hated them. I just hated them because they were clumsy and they'd get loose. One time at school, the cab driver picked me up out of the cab and the legs just landed on the floor. Dumb things.

In the following year, physical and family crises resulted in Diane's hospitalization and living away from home. She was eventually readmitted as an in-patient at Rancho until she completed her high school education. She was graduated in 1968, while living there. That fall, Diane was discharged from Rancho into her own apartment in the care of a full-time attendant. Diane was on her own and 18 years of age.

In 1973, Diane contacted her old surgeon friend, Dr. Cameron Hall, at CAPP for help in obtaining functional legs. The persistence of her desire to walk was expressed fully and urgently in a letter carefully handwritten by Diane on 16 pages of lined notebook paper. Diane explained that she was in crisis in her relationship with a man with whom she had been living and who had left town for a year. He returned to tell Diane that her handicap was, for him, the obstacle to their marriage. Diane asked for the surgeon's help:

He has finally admitted our problem was my handicap. He said he lied about it because he didn't want me to think it made him love me less. He said we just can't go on this way because we are destroying ourselves as well as each other.

Dr. Hall. I told you our story in such detail because I want you to know how much Jim and I love each other and to show you how much we have gone through for five years. I have made up my mind this time I have to *try* something for Jim and I. I have had many "boyfriends" but all of them, except for 2 just wanted to see what it was like to have sexual intercourse with a girl without arms and legs. God has been good to me. Not many people which are handicapped have such an exciting life as I do and not many are lucky enough to find a man to love me as much as Jim does.

I was brought from Texas when I was 3 years old to UCLA. They trained me completely. They taught me everything I would need to know. They never thought of what I might do if I got married. I love UCLA and all the doctors, therapists, and surgeons connected with it. I know I was more or less their "guinea pig," but in order for me to survive I had to be. Now, I am asking for their help.

They must have something which can help me *do* for my man. Even if they have to transplant arms and legs on me. No matter what they come up with, I'll try. I'll train for as long as I have to, but I guarantee I'll learn sooner than they expect me to, just as I did when they were first training me.

When I was going to Benjamin F. Tucker Handicap School, I had a pair of legs where I could actually walk in, and they looked fairly real. I also had crutches and my artificial arms. In therapy, I was learning to walk in the parallel bars *without* my crutches. Then I gave up my arms because "they" realized I could do more without them. I was then sent to Rancho, for 2 years, to get *functional legs* and I designed a pair of crutches I could use without artificial arms. They made the crutches and I had therapy. They made the "bucket" and told me to get my shoes. On rounds one day, after two years of hard work, Dr. Perry told me I couldn't have legs to walk in because I had no leg stumps. Dr. Hall, I know I can walk if someone would take the time to help me.

Although CAPP was a children's facility, Diane was accepted because of her "extremely poor family situation." As she was now reportedly obese, with all muscular tissues soft and flabby, CAPP's medical director characterized Diane's desire to walk as totally unrealistic. Nevertheless, some possible methods were discussed. The following year, the request was again evaluated: "In terms of lower extremities, Diane would like very much to try to walk on legs to whatever extent she can. Legs for cosmesis have no meaning to her as her friends know her and accept her without legs, and she feels no need to 'cover up' when she goes out. However, the wish to try to walk is long-standing and strong." The report continues: "The expenditure of energy as opposed to the amount of function she would actually get does not seem to matter to her, as her fantasy is of standing on her own, on legs, and moving however far she can, even if only a few feet." Diane was told she would have to start with an upper extremity prosthesis, with which she began working again. Reports of low back, right hip, and stump pain appear. A corset was recommended for the low back pain but it interfered with the trunk movements Diane needed to make in transfers and nearly all other activities. Surgical fusion of the spine was suggested by CAPP but rejected by Diane. In the fall 1975, Diane began her first quarter as a student at UCLA and moved to an apartment with an attendant in the area of Westwood. The Department of Rehabilitation provided Diane with a van for transportation to and from campus. A new upper extremity prosthesis was checked out for her the following summer. The CAPP files on Diane DeVries end here. Diane's request for functional legs and decision to enroll in college reflected her wish, as reported at the time, not to be "simply sitting in her wheelchair doing nothing" in another ten years. While she was successful in fulfilling that wish, it was not with functional legs but in her wheelchair that she did so.

SELF-IMAGE AND IMPRESSION MANAGEMENT

Diane DeVries has always been aware of looking different, but her conscious management of the impression she makes on other people has evolved over time. It is largely the result of her experience in the company of peers with disabilities at Benjamin F. Tucker School for Handicapped Children, then at the Los Angeles County Crippled Children's Society Camp, and later in a teenage ward at Rancho Los Amigos Hospital. In a sense, Diane grew up to be bicultural, adapting to settings geared to disability and to ones that are not (Frank 1984). Diane's present body image and style of self-presentation seem to have been established at least by age 15, when a psychiatrist wrote: "She has formed a fairly rigid self-concept that does not include the attachment of 'mechanical devices.' Before she will at all consider the use of prostheses, especially for the upper extremities, she will need to see clearly the advantage of learning to use such devices. Even then, she will resist altering her body image." Diane's description of herself prior to entering Rancho supports this picture:

G: What image did you have of your body before Rancho?
D: . . . It's hard to say because I still had more or less the same . . . I always liked my body when I had nothing connected with it.
G: What about clothes?
D: I hated clothes. We have home movies of a childhood friend and I, movies of us doing things together. I never had any clothes on. I always

had underwear on. I think that used to embarrass everybody, because I never had any on. My Dad was the one that started getting me to dress. It didn't bother him until I started "growing." Then he said, "You'd better start wearing clothes." He understood, just that along with asthma and the heat I just hated anything binding me, close to me. I think I just saw my body as a leave-me-alone kind of thing. Most handicapped kids, when they hear they're going to get a new arm or a new leg, get really excited. It's going to be a neat thing to use. And still, now, I go over to CAPP sometimes and listen to all the kids. They're the same as when I was a kid. They're all excited about a new arm, new leg, you know. But I never could get excited about it because I knew it was going on my body. And that would add more sweat, and more asthma, because I'd have to work harder with it. So I always saw my body as something that was mine, and that was free, and I hated anything kind of binding anything. And I guess it stayed, 'cause I'm still the same way. I could never get excited about the appliances they gave me—arms and legs, those kinds of things. The wheelchair—yeah. Anything that gave me more freedom.

A description of Diane at age 11 corroborates these recollections. A cheerful, adaptable, and compensatory attitude toward her body is revealed in this report from summer camp:

She used a device for ambulation and one crutch which took her most any place she wanted to go. She loved and was able to participate actively in crafts, swimming, and horseback riding. . . . She would talk freely about her disability and seemed to want to show everyone that she could do things as well as anyone. The first day as I was carrying her, Diane remarked, "You know I'm not very heavy because I don't have arms and legs and stuff like that." Carrying articles under her chin from the table after meals was a favorite task; and she could dust bed tops in the cabin very well.

Even earlier, Diane was participating in swimming classes for handicapped children in Long Beach. She was agile, quick to learn, and eager to show off her achievements.

While at age 12 or 13 Diane was referred to in a CAPP report as "very much of an exhibitionist," her attitude may be as easily seen as an acceptance of her body in its natural state:

It was felt by all that Diane is very much of an exhibitionist and is possibly "happiest" and freest when she is unencumbered. She had derived great satisfaction from "starring" in the swim shows. She expresses no observable concern about going among strangers or into new situations without her prostheses.

At Rancho, too, an issue was made of Diane's emerging style of self-presentation. Sleeveless garments were her preference. In her scooter, she liked to wear dresses with narrow straps she could slip into by herself and that allowed her the greatest freedom of movement. Some members of Diane's clinical team felt uncomfortable, however, with seeing her naked stumps. In attempting to assess the appropriateness of Diane's appearance, personal and professional reactions blur:

Diane prefers wearing spaghetti strap or other low cut sun dresses because she feels less encumbered and can also undress more easily. Those present felt that this is somewhat unattractive and possibly disturbing. It had been suggested to the family that she wear unbuttoned bolero jackets over the dresses but this has not been carried through. The subject of Diane's appearance to those present and to those around her was discussed at length. This seems to be a definite problem. Some felt that the cart is disturbing to behold. Some felt that they prefer seeing her with the prosthesis and others dissented. This area might be explored further as this seems to be a somewhat problematic area.

There seems to be general uncertainty as to what approach should be taken when Diane is without her prostheses. It was felt that she couldn't be excluded particularly since she is without her arms so often. She is given praise for what she achieves without, and this may only give her more encouragement not to use them. This would be an area of further exploration with CAPP.

Being placed on a teenage ward at Rancho affected Diane's self-presentation. Her peers were very critical of their own and others' appearance. Here Diane abandoned the three-wheeled cart because it looked "weird" and began to use an electric wheelchair for mobility instead:

D: The reason they took the scooter away, at 12 you start realizing how you look to other people, too. So it came into my head, "Hey, this is kinda weird, just flippin' down the hall on 3 wheels. All the other kids had electric wheelchairs and I knew I could have one. Then my whole body. . . . To me, it was always as though they were trying to cover up my body. Like, "Here's legs, here's a scooter, some arms," you know. Add all this junk to my body. And I never liked it. I always liked my body to be completely free. I didn't need all that *shit*. So I thought, "Well, I could get a chair. And I'd just have me and the chair. It'd be just like this thing, the scooter, except it wouldn't look half as weird." So that's when I started looking forward to getting a chair.
G: When did you become aware that it might be weird to people?
D: When I went to Rancho. Around 12. That was the first time I was around crips that much. Many. Real true crips. And I saw that *they* cared about how they looked. That's when I started to realize it.
G: Were they more critical of the way you might look than "norms"?
D: Yeah.

Diane's present code of dress and comportment was formulated during her Rancho stay and can be summed up as "looking together." In describing how to look "together" while eating, Diane also reveals the sometimes scathing, sometimes deeply supportive regard of peers for others with disabilities. "Looking together" means:

D: . . . to go around in whatever you're in, your wheelchair, on your braces, or whatever, and not look clumsy. It's not looking "self-assured" either. I keep wanting to say that, but I don't think that's the word. I mean, people are already looking at you. You know, any crip's going to be looked at. But at least if they look at you, at least they'll say: "Wow, look at that person in the wheelchair. Hey, but you know, not too bad!" Because after they get over the fact that you're in a wheelchair, then they look at you. And as long as you're not hanging over your wheelchair and drooling out of your mouth, not doing something you don't have to do, that to me is looking "together."

G: What are some of the other things?

D: Like when I was kid, I hated wearing skirts and dresses, because with a skirt you could notice even more that there are legs missing than when you wore shorts and a top. Shorts and a top fitted your body and that made the fact that no legs were there not look so bad. You didn't have loose material hanging around. And whatever I did, like feed myself, drink, I was able to do it without any sloppiness. You know, I've even seen a girl at camp with no arms that bent down and lapped her food up like a dog.

G: You saw someone like this?

D: Yeah. That pissed me off. And I knew her. And I went up to her and says: "Why in the hell do you do that?" And I said, "They asked if you wanted a feeder or your arms on. You could have done either one, but you had to do that." She said, "Well, it was easy for me." To me that was gross. She finally started wearing arms, and she started feeding herself. But to me that was just stupid, because people wouldn't even want to eat at the same table as her. They'd get sick to see someone lapping up their food. Like I remember Vicki, this friend of mine, one of the nicest things I ever heard anyone tell me . . . one time, we were still at Rancho, and we were eating dinner, and she once told me: "For someone with no hands, you sure are neat." I said, "Oh!" It made me feel good, because I hate dropping things and all this, so you have to be super careful in the beginning, when you're learning how to do it. And then it gets to be very natural, if you can do it good.

"Looking together" is important for making contacts that can develop into sexual intimacy, long-term commitments, and marriage. Diane was not inhibited in learning how to flirt:

I've always been really in tune with my body. I can remember when I was younger seeing crips that didn't know how to carry themselves or hold themselves right. Not because they couldn't but because they didn't realize they weren't doing it. So I've always watched myself. When I was little I knew how to hold myself and look right, look "together," or whatever you want to say. So growing older, I just became even more aware. Just like when you get older and girls start noticing boys, well, they learn to flirt. Well, I learned to flirt—obviously—but I learned as I grew older how to move my body with the flirting because I have to do it differently. Because my body's different. I mean, I know my body perfectly—every movement, everything, because I notice it all the time. And I always did. I never . . . They should teach crips that, I think, because not enough of them are aware of it. You are, at Rancho, but they force you to be. And that's what's good. But a lot of these kids now don't and it's too bad.

In cultivating a "together" look, it was important to Diane and her friends to resist taking on the stereotypic image of "crip":

G: What are some of the things that people do when they don't look "together?"

D: It depends on your handicap. Like me, I would never wear a skirt, a long skirt, like they used to. I've even seen some people with no arms wearing long sleeves pinned up or rolled up clumsily so they're *this* fat. You can find a lot of clothes that fit you. It's not hard. If they have someone take care of them, they won't tell them: "No. I want my hair this way." They'll just let them do it. That's dumb. It's *your* body. They're helping *you* out. And just the way you sit, too.

G: What do you mean?

D: You can sit so that they really notice your wheelchair—mold yourself to the chair—that's bad. Or you could just sit in it like you sit in any chair. And when you talk, talk. Don't just sit there stiff so they can still notice just your chair. You got to let them see *you*. I mean they're going to look at you anyway, so you might as well give them something to look at. That's how my best friend, Christy, was. I think I just molded myself a little bit after her, 'cause she was that way. She figured: "Hell, if they're going to look, they can have something to look *at*." She knew her good points, and she used them. And that's what I did.

Diane developed a distinctive style of dress suited to her shape and needs. Her wardrobe consists of ready-made items with occasional minor alterations. In the warm climate and casual lifestyle of southern California, her style is appropriate.

D: You try to wear things that fit your body, like shorts and stuff. I mean that I don't have arms and legs, and I don't mind *now*—well, I never did, I guess—showing that I didn't have arms and legs. That didn't bother me, if it looked good and compact. You know, there's some amputees that have little fingers hanging off, or little feet down there, and I thought I was lucky that I came out nice and together. The only thing that's different is the lengths of my arms, which isn't *too* bad. But if you just wear, I don't know, I mean, I always wore what I liked. It still fitted me well and, well, except when I was a kid, I had to do what *she*, my mother said. So it didn't look too good. I don't think . . . I didn't look good to myself until I got to go to Rancho.

G: What did you start doing for yourself then?

D: I started dressing the way I felt like dressing. Like in the scooter, on weekends, when I wasn't at school, and was still living at home, my Dad let me wear shorts, just as long as I wasn't going to the show or nothing. But wearing shorts in a scooter looked dumb to me, because I'm sitting in a bucket with shorts and a blouse on. Well, the bucket itself looks like a butt. So it looks like I was naked on the outside anyway, because you wouldn't see the shorts. But I always wanted to wear a shift. But they said, "Naw, you don't want to play in a shift." So when I started going to Rancho, and the surfer scene was out and all this, there was a lot of neat shifts, and I, and I'd wear them over the bucket so it would cover it and wouldn't look dumb. I only wore shorts if I was going to be in my wheelchair. I started doing what I wanted to, dressing the way I wanted to.

G: How do you think you look best?

D: [Laughs.] I don't know. Shorts, or body shirt and shorts. Because you've got to show off what's best. My best thing is my boobs, you know, 'cause that's big and they look nice. That's all I got that looks real good. And when I'm thin, my shape's all right, for someone with no legs. You know, looks like a time thing—whatever that thing's called.

G: An hourglass.

D: So you shouldn't cover up what you got. But if you're shy, that's a problem.

Given Diane's preference for being unencumbered by devices, her acceptance at all of cosmetic legs in high school is difficult to understand. When she talks now about the cosmetic legs, it is with disgust:

G: How long did you have them?

D: I don't know. I had them when I started high school, so I had them in the 10th grade. Then I went to Rancho. At Rancho, they just kind of laid there for two years, hanging around on the side. I didn't wear them. Then I got out of Rancho when I was 18 and I took them with me. And I never wore them. And then Jim and I left that apartment—the first apartment I lived in—and we left them there in the window, all dressed up real sexy: Nylons and pantaloons. High heels. [We laugh.] They were really weird. I hated them.

G: Why did you wear them so long?

D: Well, I didn't really. I just had them around.

G: Who encouraged you to wear them?

D: Rancho. The original reason I went to Rancho was to get a pair of legs that I could walk in without my arms. That's why I was at Rancho. Well, they seemed to have lost that reason in the two years I was there. So one day rounds comes—that's when all the doctors come around and look at you—and I asked them where my legs were. I'd been there a year and a half. Well, they told me, "Go get your shoes." So I did. They said, "We're not making you those legs. We decided you wouldn't be able to walk." I blew it. That's another story. But anyway, they said, "But we have a pair of cosmetic legs for you." I said, "Cosmetic? You mean to help me look better?" He says, "Yeah." I said, "I don't really need any cosmetic legs. If I can't walk in them, I don't want them." You know, they put the pressure on you. So Mom came and got me one day, and they didn't have those legs at Rancho. This woman used to walk in those legs that I had. [Laughs.] They were going to buy them from this woman, because she didn't want them no more. So we went to the house and picked up the legs that I was going to wear—supposedly—for the rest of my life. So we went back to Rancho and they fixed it up to that plaster thing and all this. And then they even tried to teach me to transfer from car to chair, from chair to bed, with these legs on. It was hopeless. There was no way the legs would stay on. They knew they made a bad choice, but they just kept pushing me to wear them. I said, "This is crazy." And the people at school complained. They'd call the hospital and say, "Hey, this is just too much. She needs to keep coming in and getting her straps tightened."

G: Were you disappointed when you found out that you had to go and get them from somebody?

D: Yeah. [Let-down voice.] It was like they were cheap old hand-me downs. I didn't like that at all. I remember the lady coming out and bringing them. What almost freaked me out was she walks out to give me these legs and I say, "God, she walks good." She had a new pair of artificial legs. And I said, "Why can't they make me something like that?" It really pissed me off, but then I knew she had stumps, and all that. So, but yet, it kind of upset me that they couldn't even make a pair. They just got hers.

While the cosmetic legs could not substitute for the functional legs Diane wanted, they did offer her some pleasure: On the night of Diane's senior prom, her date forgot she was wearing them and stroked her leg sensuously on the way to the dance. The legs provided Diane with an archetypically female opportunity for self-expression in our culture, that of shopping for shoes. In this she had all the enjoyment without any of the discomfort—her foot was a perfect fit:

G: How did you shop for the shoes?

D: When I first got the legs, they told me the size. They measured it for me. So I just went out to the store with Debbie and Mom and bought shoes. I bought a pair of boots. Debbie just killed me for it, because it was real hard. They were real tall boots and at that time they had those boots that were real shiny and, you know, vinyl leather, and they stuck to your leg. And she had a hell of a time getting those things on. I'd have to wear them a good four days before she'd want to take them off to change them. And they were bright orange. I had to really be careful what I wore, I had those, and sandals, and all kinds of shoes. Oh, I had more shoes. . . .

G: Did it ever occur to you that by buying bright orange boots you were buying the most visible shoes possible?

D: I don't think so, at the time. I just, I *liked* them, so I got them. I know I always liked bright things. I was always like that. So I just got them. They were a bitch to put on, though.

G: Why did you like shoes so much?

D: I don't know. Maybe 'cause I couldn't have them normally. [Laughs.] But when I got my new legs, I'd always go out and get some shoes.

G: Can you describe the feeling for me?

D: God. I don't know. It's just . . . It was exciting going in and picking out new styles. It was like Christmas, 'cause I always knew when I was getting my legs, I'd say, "Ah ha, got to get me some shoes."

G: Now you don't like shoes anymore.
D: I know I'll never have legs anymore.

"The only thing that's wrong with me," Diane has said, "is just that I don't have any arms and legs." Over the course of research, it gradually became clear to me that Diane DeVries' self-image was really very positive. But it was only through a leap of communication, a metaphor, that I was able to grasp an essential feature of her self-concept—the fact that she conceived of her body as lovely. Why I may have doubted this has more to do with my preconceptions about disability than with Diane DeVries herself, as I have elsewhere discussed (Frank 1985). The following dialogue, then, came as a surprise to me even though I had initiated it with a visionary perception. Sitting with Diane, talking in the half-light of her apartment, I relaxed my gaze and let my eyes fill with light. This dissolved the image of Diane before me into a pale, pretty haze. In that moment I saw that her form resembled the famous statue of the Venus de Milo. I told her what I saw and her response came back with the force of an epiphany.

G: I got a weird image, letting my eyes flood with light. You got pale and looked like the Venus de Milo.
D: My mother's friend one time gave her a candle of the Venus de Milo. And I came home and they lit it. I thought there was something symbolic there. That was terrible.
G: Did you identify with it?
D: Oh yeah! I was going with a black guy named Rico and I gave him a big statue of the Venus de Milo for his birthday. He loved it. His wife got mad and broke it over his head. He reglued it. It was pretty, too.
G: She's an image of you, really. She doesn't have legs.
D: And also the one arm is shorter than the other. That's what's so weird, too. Also, Diane is Greek. Or Roman. Diane is the other name for Venus.[9]

In talking further, we discovered that for each of us the image of the Venus de Milo did not seem intended to have arms or legs, but was beautiful in its own right. The perspective reflected in our conversation permanently altered my conception of Diane as "disabled." Her body need not be seen from the point of view of its deficits but, rather, as integrated and complete. This is, I believe, the dominant mode in which Diane experiences her embodiment.

CONCLUSION
This paper presented a discussion of the embodiment of a woman with quadrilateral limb deficiencies in the United States. Through her account of her life and with the help of supporting records, it has been

possible to examine the development of Diane DeVries' positive self-image, her ability to perform culturally prescribed activities, and her capacity to present herself as a member of the mainstream society. What has been documented here is the manner in which these abstractions have been experienced as acts for a person whose appearance and functioning are quite different from the expected. I have argued elsewhere that the profile of Diane's life, viewed at the level of social structure, looks quite "healthy" with respect to her integration in a wide variety of institutions and social networks (Frank 1984). Diane has a keen ability to grasp the cultural rules appropriate to settings and situations, as well as a strong drive to perform and excel in accomplishing life's everyday tasks, which she does in a manner consistent with her physical capabilities. The adaptable and compensatory attitude she displayed in childhood remains a resource in her adult years, as does her persistence in accepting the image of her body as natural and fundamentally normal.

In our society, as in any, one method for understanding the "rules of the game" is to observe where the action is. What acts are people motivated to perform? With what do they concern themselves? How do they spend their time? What goals or values are they promoting? From the perspective of Diane's embodiment in American culture, it appears that mobility and independence of self-care are central values, ends to be striven for in themselves. Anything that gave her more mobility, more independence, was accepted and incorporated into her body scheme. Her account brings out the importance, again and again, of being able to do things for oneself, not losing time fumbling with prostheses, and not having to wait around for help. It also reveals the power of mainstream standards of beauty. The use of cosmetic legs in teenage years reflects an experiment in meeting the requirements for acceptable appearance. A more enduring solution for Diane has been to wear clothes that emphasize rather than disguise her shape and that highlight her assets. In Diane's description of her body as it could only appear in a mirror, there is the implicit comparison to a more perfect body, to "perfect" ears that don't stick out, and "perfect" teeth that meet evenly. Her account implies that, in the inventory of body parts, ample breasts can serve to overcome a deficit of arms and legs. In all, the body is an object to be groomed and outfitted, to be made ready for particular kinds of social actions.

For the Child Amputee Prosthetics Project, it was important to promote artificial limbs as a means to enhance Diane's functioning and "normalize" her appearance. The dubious benefits of prosthesis use for Diane point out the cultural biases of the CAPP program, funded by

federal grants during the 1950s, the period after World War II characterized by an ideology of rehabilitation and faith in technology. Since
that time, the clinical staff at CAPP has come to recognize that severely
limb-deficient children like Diane will most frequently reject the use of
prostheses. The medical approach to Diane's body, with its technical
vocabularly geared to classification and denotation, failed to reckon
with the "presence/absence" of Diane's legs. Adjustment to her disability was measured by the degree to which Diane accepted the prescription of artificial arms, which were seen as the key to increasing her
chances for "independence." The phenomenological implications of
Diane's ambiguous lower limb structure were virtually ignored, including her interpretation of her early experiences in lower extremity prostheses as setting up the possibility that she could walk. In this, Diane's
own faith in technology is revealed.

Within the special cultures of disability, interesting "ethnic"
boundaries also appear. From the standpoint of the culture of rehabilitation the projection by CAPP of a future life for Diane of "dependence"
versus a life of "independence" overlooks a great deal. The fact is that
social life for everyone is a matter of interdependence. The "independence" that Americans with disabilities achieve in the community
frequently involves the assistance of attendants or family members,
special equipment requiring servicing, and a structure of social supports
as part of that "self-sufficiency." Independence, then, is very much a
matter of definition and degree. Diane's characterization of the "crip"
peer culture reveals, too, a set of special social relations. In the hierarchy of disability, to lack limbs is to be on a higher level of acceptability than to be incontinent or to lack muscle control ("looking
together means not hanging over your chair, drooling, doing something
you don't have to"). It is clear that control over body functions and body
boundaries are very much at stake.

Fiedler (1978) writes that truly physically variant human beings
challenge the conventional boundaries between male and female, sexed
and sexless, animal and human, large and small, and self and other.
Such boundaries maintain the basic categories elaborated by cultures
for the survival over time of the group. For me, the encounter with
Diane challenged my adherence to the conventional linkages among
physical normalcy, beauty, sexuality, and social integration. In addition,
it evoked for me a heightened awareness of issues beyond the elementary forms of social order, such as my own anxious feelings of helplessness and immobility, and of lack and loss (Frank 1985). The
encounter with Diane further evoked an image of mythic beauty, the
Venus de Milo, which, it should be remembered, is the portrait of a

goddess. My field experiences support Fiedler's argument that physically variant members of the culture, simply as a consequence of their appearance, serve as metaphors for fundamental issues of human consciousness and evoke powerful feelings. In addition to the accounts of people with disabilities, our presumably able-bodied reactions can reveal much about our culture's formulation of embodiment.—What, after all, is a little boy doing, gleefully threatening with a penknife to take off the head of a limb-deficient little girl?—Conversely, understanding the culture's formulation of embodiment makes us more cognizant of what physically variant individuals must accomplish in order to live fully in society at a given time.

Notes

1. Spiegelberg (1976:524) points out that Merleau-Ponty's phenomenology strikes chords of resonance with the work of such Anglo-American philosophers as Whitehead, Dewey, Lovejoy, and Mead. G. H. Mead (1934) was particularly important in the development of the field of social psychology, which concerns itself with the relationship among self-awareness, the responses of others to behavior, and identity. The work on illness and disability in social psychology, with its attention to "somatopsychological" problems, resembles closely the phenomenological approach based on "embodiment" suggested here. The former tends toward the measurement of population variables, the latter toward the interpretation of experience. For interpreting experiences related to disability the rubric of "embodiment" is more abstract, and therefore more inclusive, than the concept of "adjustment."

2. Another important concept in the study of disability is that of "stigma." Goffman's (1963) work in sociology on this topic, with its attention to face-to-face relations, shows the influence of the phenomenologist Alfred Schutz's work on intersubjectivity. In this and earlier writings on "impression management" (1959), Goffman points out practices used to present or withhold information about oneself to others for strategic advantage in face-to-face encounters. Again, "embodiment" is a more inclusive rubric that includes, for example, behaviors relating to function that have nothing to do with cosmesis.

3. According to Berkowitz (1980), rehabilitation medicine was a product of World War II. New surgical procedures that prolonged the life expectancies of paraplegics created the medical problem of restoring their bodily functions as well. "Rehabilitation," as developed by military doctor Howard Rusk and others, had the goal of "the restoration of a disabled person to his highest functional level" (p. 112) and was intended to address all aspects of the person. A large grant by Bernard Baruch financed programs at Columbia and other universities to promote research and training in physical medicine. The concept of rehabilitation centers based on interdisciplinary teams providing interrelated services was endorsed by the federal government. The Child Amputee Prosthetics Project is a center on that model. From its inception in 1955 to 1959, it was financed with funds made available to the State of California from the United States Children's Bureau and later received support from other federal agencies (Blakeslee 1963:xii).

4. Spiegelberg (1976:525–526) writes: "Merleau-Ponty's thought has been

called a 'Philosophy of Ambiguity'. . . . However, the term "ambiguity" has a much more pejorative meaning in English than in French. . . . In fact, in his inaugural lecture at the Collège de France he characterized the true philosopher by his equal taste for clarity (*évidence*) and ambiguity. . . . Here he also distinguishes a positive sense of ambiguity, i.e., the repudiation of absolute knowledge, from the bad sense of mere equivocation." In her study of the rearing of children with limb deficiencies as a result of thalidomide, Roskies (1972) carefully notes the ambiguity and uncertainty of mothers' experiences.

5. The quotes by Diane DeVries are drawn from tape-recorded interviews conducted mainly in 1976, which along with her extensive medical file at the Child Amputee Prosthetics Project formed the data base for a doctoral thesis (Frank 1981a). Additional data and comments are taken from subsequent research. A detailed life chart, discussion of life history methods, and interpretation of adaptations made by Diane DeVries appear in Frank (1984). A method for clarifying the impact of observer bias in this and other biographical research is presented in Frank (1985). An ethnographic short story about a crisis in Diane's life while living in a convalescent hopsital has also been published (Frank 1981b). The life history as a collaborative method with living subjects is discussed in Frank (1979) and Langness and Frank (1981). A draft of the present article was published in the Wenner-Gren Working Paper Series on the Anthropology of the Handicapped, sponsored by the Wenner-Gren Foundation for Anthropological Research in October 1984. In 1987, Diane objected that I failed to inform her about the publication of the Wenner-Gren paper in *Culture, Medicine and Psychiatry* until it was already in print. She no longer wanted to publish transcripts of her speech that make it appear ungrammatical. This concern was prompted in part by Diane's seeking admission at this time to graduate schools in social work. She felt that people she might meet in her future professional life might think her uneducated if they read these articles. I argued against revising any of the original transcripts, but offered instead to add a note in future publications about my strong methodological interest, at the dissertation stage of this study, in using an exact transcription rather than a "smoothed-out" narrative. Naturally it can be as much of a shock to read one's unedited speech as to be caught in a candid photo. Diane's sensitivity here reflects a change in her identity, as she aspires—with confidence sprinkled with the normal doubts—to success in a professional career.

6. These comments by Kathleen Tovey, dated June 3, 1985, were sent in response to the article on "Life History Model of Adaptation to Disability" (Frank 1984). The newspaper article she enclosed, "Robin: A 'One-in-a-Million' Child Breezes through Life and into the Hearts of Her Classmates," was published in the Bend, Oregon *Bulletin*, Section C, p. 1, May 12, 1985.

7. Diane sees herself as someone who could *become* handicapped. "I'm proud of and grateful to have 2 upper stumps," she wrote to me after reading a draft of this study in which it was suggested that she has no limbs whatsoever. "If I didn't have them, then I would be *crippled*. I do have limbs—2 uppers!"

8. Diane uses gestures a great deal, inscribing a circle in the air to indicate the totality of something, or drawing a graceful line to indicate the trailing off of an idea. When getting a serious point across, she might make repeated jabs at the air. If discussing something negative, she might wag her arm from side to side, indicating "No." When talking about others, she might indicate their relative location by jerking her arm. "Over there." When excited, she might raise

both arms at once and bring them down together on her lapboard. For emphasis, Diane's gestures are completely and immediately comprehensible as a version of standard body language in this society. As such, they are part of the normal flow of conversation.

9. In Roman mythology, Venus was the goddess of spring, bloom, beauty, and, later, love. Her Greek name is not Diana but Aphrodite. (Diana, whose Greek name is Artemis, was goddess of the chase, chastity, and the moon.) Factual discrepancies, such as in Diane's recall of dates, have been reconciled as much as possible by cross-checking sources. What is important for understanding Diane, however, is her interpretation of events, including her adoption of a powerful metaphor by which she identifies with a goddess.

References

Barker, Roger G. 1977. *Adjustment to physical handicap and illness: A survey of the social psychology of physique and disability.* Milwood, N.Y: Kraus Reprint Co. [Original 1953]

Berkowitz, Edward David. 1980. *Rehabilitation: The federal government's response to disability, 1935–1954.* New York: Arno Press. [Original 1976]

Blakeslee, Berton, ed. 1963. *The limb-deficient child.* Berkeley: University of California Press.

Fiedler, Leslie. 1978. *Freaks: Myths and images of the secret self.* New York: Simon and Schuster.

Frank, Gelya. 1979. Finding the common denominator: A phenomenological critique of life history method. *Ethos* 7(1):68–94.

———. 1981a. *Venus on wheels: The life history of a congential amputee.* Ph.D. Dissertation, Department of Anthropology, University of California, Los Angeles. (Copies available from UMI, 300 N. Zeeb Road, Ann Arbor, Mi. 48106).

———. 1981b. Mercy's children. *Anthropology and Humanism Quarterly* 6(4):8–12.

———. 1984. Life history model of adaptation to disability: The case of a "congenital amputee." *Social Science and Medicine* 19(6):639–645.

———. 1985. "Becoming the other": Empathy and biographical interpretation. *Biography* 8(3):189–210.

Goffman, Erving. 1959. *The presentation of self in everyday life.* Garden City, N.Y.: Doubleday.

———. 1963. *Stigma: Notes on the management of spoiled identity.* Englewood Cliffs, N.J.: Prentice-Hall.

Hallowell, A. I. 1956. The self and its behavioral environment. *Culture and experience*, pp. 75–110. Philadelphia: University of Pennsylvania Press.

Henry, Jules. 1971. *Pathways to madness.* New York: Random House. [Original 1965]

Kearney, Michael. 1984. *World View.* Novato, Cal.: Chandler & Sharp.

Langness, L. L. and Gelya Frank, 1981. *Lives: An anthropological approach to biography.* Novato, Cal.: Chandler & Sharp.

Mead, George Herbert. 1934. *Mind, self, and society: From the standpoint of a social behaviorist.* Chicago: The University of Chicago Press.

Merleau-Ponty, Maurice. 1962. *Phenomenology of perception.* Colin Smith, trans. London: Routledge and Kegan Paul. [Original 1945]

Roskies, Ethel. 1972. *Abnormality and normality: The mothering of thalidomide children.* Ithaca: Cornell University Press.

Sartre, Jean-Paul. 1957. *Being and nothingness: An essay on phenomenological ontology.* H. E. Barnes, trans. New York: Washington Square Press. [Original 1943]

Scheper-Hughes, Nancy, and Margaret M. Lock. 1987. The mindful body: A prolegomenon to future work in medical anthropology. *Medical Anthropology Quarterly* 1(1):6–41.

Schilder, Paul. 1950. *The image and appearance of the human body: Studies in the constructive energies of the psyche.* New York: International Universities Press. [Original 1935]

Spiegelberg, Herbert. 1976. *The phenomenological movement: A historical introduction,* vol II. The Hague: Martinus Nijhoff.

Stone, Deborah A. 1984. *The disabled state.* Philadelphia: Temple University Press.

Von Uexküll, Jakob. 1957. A stroll through the worlds of animals and men: A picture book of invisible worlds. In C. H. Schiller, trans., *Instinctive behavior: The development of a modern concept.* New York: International Universities Press [Original 1934], pp. 5–80.

Wright, Beatrice A. 1983. *Physical disabilities—A psychosocial approach,* 2nd ed. New York: Harper & Row.

2. Sex Roles and Culture: Social and Personal Reactions To Breast Cancer

BETH E. MEYEROWITZ, SHELLY CHAIKEN, and LAURA K. CLARK

For many people, the word "disability" calls to mind the image of a person disabled since birth, of an adult who has become disabled through serious injury, or of an older adult who has become disabled later in life. Nevertheless, people in middle age are not immune to disability. Instead of a marked decrease in the incidence of disability in mid-life, there is a shift from primary causes such as infections, birth complications, and accidents to chronic disease. For example, cardiovascular disease and cancer account for approximately 70 percent of all deaths (Michael 1982), and the onset of these diseases frequently occurs in mid-life.

With a chronic disease (that is, one that continues over a long time) many patients are not in imminent danger of death but must learn to live with the disabling effects of the disease. Of the three in ten Americans who are expected to develop cancer, nearly 40 percent will live for at least five years after they are diagnosed (American Cancer Society 1983). Many of them will need to adjust to disabilities caused by cancer and its treatment.

This chapter focuses on aspects of the experience of a chronic illness in middle age that may affect, and be affected by, sex roles and sex-role stereotypes. Disabilities that begin in mid-life disrupt ongoing behavior in people who have well-established roles and who do not have ready access to support from similarly disabled peers. Moreover, some patients may hold the stigmatizing, stereotypic attitudes toward people with disabilities that are held by many non-disabled individuals (Dembo 1982). These attitudes might intensify the emotional impact of the disease and could lead patients to disavow the similarities between their own situations and those of persons with other forms of disability, thus failing to take advantage of potential legal rights and social support networks. By drawing on sex-role conceptualizations to examine the influence of the disability, it may be possible to elucidate how the disability is experienced by patients and how it is viewed by family members, health care providers, employers, and others.

The psychosocial impact of chronic illness on a patient depends on a number of variables, including the nature of the disability, the extent to which the person has ascribed to traditional roles, and the reactions of others to the newly acquired disability. Because this book focuses on the impact of disabilities on women, we have chosen to discuss breast cancer, a disease that affects the lives of millions of American women and that involves changes in a body part that may be most strongly associated with femininity in our culture.

CHRONIC DISEASE AND WOMEN IN MID-LIFE
Disabilities may have a particularly aversive impact when they disrupt a woman's actual or perceived abilities to perform important, self-defining social roles. Not only must the person deal with the immediate fears, emotional reactions, and physical impairments that typically accompany a life-threatening, disabling disease; she may also face an unexpected sense of rolelessness and a sudden assault to self-esteem. The specific nature of the disability in conjunction with the particular social roles that the woman is committed to will influence the extent to which this impact is felt. Clearly, many people experience distress when unwanted changes in lifestyle are required. Moreover, such distress may be exacerbated when the illness disrupts the performance of behaviors in roles that are most central to the individual's sense of self.

The performance of behaviors consistent with the traditional female role can be disrupted in a number of ways by a chronic illness. For example, if the illness is decremental to physical appearance, some women's self-identity might be seriously threatened because of the great importance that our culture places on physical attractiveness in evaluating the worth of women (Centers 1972; Harrison and Saeed 1977; Safilios-Rothschild 1977).

Given our society's youth-oriented standards, the negative impact of such visible disabilities may be exacerbated by the fact that middle-aged women already may have begun to label themselves, and be labeled by others, as less attractive and as sexually unappealing. Nevertheless, for the middle-aged woman who has adjusted to the fact that age-related changes may have reduced her desirability as an object of sexual attention (Bell 1975), or for the woman for whom physical attractiveness has never represented a major source of self-esteem, the impact of illness-induced decrements on self-image may not be marked. In addition, disruption in other functions that are central to the traditional female role, such as nurturance or childrearing responsibilities, may exert a particularly dramatic impact on women who are traditional in their sex-role orientation. Thus, some women may experience a loss of "woman-hood" in addition to the other possible losses accompanying chronic illness.[1]

The impact of a chronic illness on others' perceptions of, and interactions with, the chronically ill woman also may be influenced by sex-role stereotypes. Even patients whose self-concepts are not strongly influenced by traditional role conceptions may have difficulties when others display their own stereotypic attitudes. Family members or friends may find it particularly difficult to accept a physically disfigured woman who at times may be unable, or unwilling to provide nurturance. Individuals who had been important sources of social support may devalue the newly disabled woman or may ignore her present needs in order to maintain an image of the patient as an "appropriately" functioning adult. Some may withdraw from the chronically ill in order to avoid being reminded that they, too, could become disabled. In an attempt to maintain a belief in a just world (Lerner and Miller 1978), these people may prefer to believe that persons with disabilities are different from "the rest of us" in some intrinsic way.

Finally, the attitudes of health care providers toward the chronically ill woman may influence the quality of care she receives. It has been argued that mental and medical health professionals hold beliefs about the personalities and behaviors of women that may result in women receiving less adequate treatment than men (Fidell 1980, Howell 1974). For example, stereotypic views of women may predispose physicians to overattribute their symptoms to psychogenic causes, thus delaying correct diagnosis and treatment of diseases of physiological origin (Fidell 1980). Once correctly diagnosed, women may be subjected to excessive use of surgical procedures and mood-modifying drugs (Fejer and Smart 1973; Fidell 1973). Such procedures, combined with physicians' expectancies that women may be "difficult" patients whose physical complaints and medical concerns can be largely ignored (Cooperstock 1971; Millman 1977), may adversely affect women's abilities to adjust medically and emotionally to disabilities caused by chronic illness.

To summarize, we have suggested that the performance of behaviors associated with traditional female sex roles may be disrupted by the onset of a chronic illness in mid-life. For women whose adherence to traditional sex roles is central to their self-identities, disruptions in sex-role behaviors may create problems over and above the direct impact of the illness. Sex-role stereotypes also may affect the ways in which chronically ill women are perceived and treated by others, perhaps exacerbating the impact of the illness. The rest of this chapter explores the impact of breast cancer on women, with special attention to the possible ways in which sex roles and sex-role stereotypes may influence adjustment to, and coping with, the disease.

BREAST CANCER AND THE FEMALE SEX ROLE

Every year in the United States, well over 100 thousand women, half of whom are under 60 years of age, are diagnosed as having breast cancer.[2] Nine percent of American women are expected to develop the disease at some time in their lives (American Cancer Society 1983), and 73 percent of these women will live for at least five years after being diagnosed (Anon., "NCI Releases," 1984). Clearly, many women in mid-life face living with breast cancer and its treatment.

Breast cancer has received more attention in the psychosocial literature than any other kind of cancer. A review of recent *Psychological Abstracts* revealed that only brain tumors approached receiving the number of citations that breast cancer did, and many brain tumor studies focus on the neurological, rather than the psychosocial, effects of cancer. There are several possible explanations for the disproportionate interest that psychological researchers have shown in breast cancer. For example, practical research considerations may play a role in the degree to which breast cancer is studied. The prevalence and survival rates associated with breast cancer suggest that many patients are available for study and would continue to be available for follow-up. Moreover, the nature of the disease and its treatment rarely interferes with patients' abilities to participate in research. These logistic advantages are not unique to breast cancer, however, and thus do not seem to account entirely for the interest that mental health professionals have shown in this disease.

In addition to practical research considerations, the sex-role–specific nature of breast cancer and its most common treatment, breast amputation, has led to a concern for the well-being of patients that has stimulated psychological research. Derogatis (1980) summarizes this concern when he states that "breast and gynecologic cancers possess the capacity for being particularly catastrophic experiences by virtue of the direct impact they have on essential components of the women's identity" (p. 2). He goes on to describe studies predicated on the hypothesis that "the fundamental female role is seriously threatened by breast cancer" (p. 6).

Clearly, issues of sex role and gender identity are central to conceptualizations about the psychosocial impact of breast cancer and are probably responsible, in part, for the widespread research and clinical interest in the disease. Our cultural focus on breasts is mirrored in the scientific literature. This attention has led to an increased sensitivity to the major impact that breast cancer can have on quality of life. Unfortunately, at times there has also been a tendency to draw conclusions that may be founded more in stereotypes of women than in sound data (see Meyerowitz 1981a).

The influence of sex roles and sex-role stereotypes is not limited to the scientific literature. Sociocultural views of women and of the role of the breasts in female identity may affect the reactions of physicians, nurses, friends, and family members, as well as those of the patient herself. In the following pages we examine the empirical evidence for some widely held beliefs regarding the psychosocial impact of breast cancer on women.

General Reactions to Breast Cancer

That the diagnosis and treatment of breast cancer can have a major impact on the physical, emotional, and interpersonal lives of the women who contract it is well known. Most women with breast cancer experience marked physical symptomatology and lifestyle disruption. Some of the more commonly reported physical symptoms are direct surgical effects of the mastectomy, such as pain and arm weakness (Silberfarb, Maurer, and Crouthamel 1980), lymphedema (Burdick 1975), and phantom breast sensations (Bressler, Cohen, and Magnussen 1956; Jamison, Wellisch, and Pasnau 1978). For women who have had mastectomies—still the majority of women with breast cancer—there can be discomfort associated with wearing a prosthesis and difficulties in finding well-fitted clothing. The possibility of changed body image, concerns about femininity, and changes in sexuality can accompany breast loss, as discussed more fully later. More general physical symptoms not associated with the breast surgery per se are common. In one study (Meyerowitz 1981b), more than half the patients reported experiencing one or more of the following problems up to three years following mastectomy: fatigue, irritability, nervousness, sleep difficulties, and loss of strength. Perhaps in part as a result of these physical impairments, patients may find that their day-to-day activities are disrupted (e.g., Eisenberg and Goldenberg 1966). Silberfarb, Maurer, and Crouthamel (1980) found that patients questioned four months after treatment reported changes in job status and a need for help with housework chores. Recreational activities, particularly those requiring use of the homolateral arm, can be disrupted (Maguire 1975).

In addition to the physical symptoms associated with breast cancer, women experience emotional distress. Morris, Greer, and White (1977) found that 46 percent of a sample of mastectomy patients reported emotional distress three months postoperatively. Similarly, Maguire and co-workers (1980) indicate that many mastectomy patients who had not received counseling reported being anxious (48 percent) and/or depressed (51 percent) at some point during the year and a half following surgery. These findings are consistent with studies and anecdotal reports that describe temporary depression and anxiety as normal reactions to breast cancer and mastectomy (see Meyerowitz 1980 for a review).[3] In addition, it is typical for breast cancer patients to express considerable fear and concern regarding their current and future health, the possibility of mastectomy complications, and changes in their physical appearance (Meyerowitz 1981b). Every ache and pain can lead to fears of recurrence and death (Quint 1963). These fears are not unique to the patient but are common among loved ones (Grandstaff 1976), perhaps leading some women to conceal their concerns in order to protect family and friends.

Interpersonal relationships can be affected in other ways as a result of changes in the patient and in those with whom she interacts. The patient's emotional distress, fearfulness, and physical disability may lead her to withdraw or to become dependent and demanding (e.g. Bard 1952). Family and friends may have such strong negative reactions to breast cancer and mastectomy that their social interactions with the patient decrease or change (Wortman and Dunkel-Schetter 1979). Silberfarb, Maurer, and Crouthamel (1980) found that marital difficulties, reported by 22 percent of early-stage breast cancer patients, were the most common source of "serious emotional disturbance" (p. 452). Other authors (for example, Lee and Maguire 1975; Wellisch, Jamison, and Pasnau 1978) have identified increased marital discord among breast cancer patients, although some investigators (Lichtman, Wood, and Taylor 1982) do not report frequent disturbance in this area. Relationships with children may be influenced as well (Grandstaff 1976). Mothers may be unable to maintain their typical levels of nurturance and involvement; children may become fearful, withdrawn, and hostile toward their mothers (Lichtman, et al. 1984). Work and other social relationships may be disrupted, although these areas have received little empirical attention to date.

Other sources of distress and disruption for breast cancer patients can include employment discrimination (McCharen and Earp 1981; Anon., "Cancer Patients" 1980) and possible termination of health insurance (Schain 1976). This discrimination, in conjunction with the possible need for assistance at home and the expense of treatment and follow-up, can create serious financial difficulties for patients and their families.

The extent of physical symptomatology and the intensity of distress associated with early-stage breast cancer typically diminish over time. Several investigators have reported that most women who do not receive follow-up treatments and who do not experience a recurrence of cancer are likely to return to preoperative functioning within two years of surgery (for example, Eisenberg and Goldenberg 1966; Meyerowitz 1983; Morris, Greer, and White 1977; Schottenfeld and Robbins 1970). Nevertheless, some women—and estimates are as high as 15 percent— do not report improvements in quality of life (see Meyerowitz 1980; Weisman, Worden, and Sobel 1980). Even women who report improvements following the immediate stressors of diagnosis and treatment are likely to experience lifelong psychological effects from having had cancer (Mages and Mendelsohn 1979). Patients may have recurrent fears, moments of deep sadness over past losses and future threats, and an ongoing sense of vulnerability. For women who have lost one or both breasts, the changes resulting from amputation of a major body part are, of course, permanent; they can result in altered self-image, physical discomfort, and changes in daily activities.

Although the aversive effects of breast cancer are by far the more commonly documented by researchers, many women report positive changes as well. For example, Meyerowitz, Sparks, and Spears (1979) found that interpersonal relationships can improve as family and friends make special efforts to spend more time with the patient. In that study, 17 percent of the patients described improvements in their family relationships, compared to 23 percent who reported increased difficulties with family. Some women also reported that they gained a greater appreciation for life and an increased resistance to being bothered by minor daily problems (Grandstaff 1976).

Much of the literature on the psychosocial impact of breast cancer has been retrospective and lacking in appropriate controls. The nature of the questions asked and the constraints of clinical research make it very difficult to determine the extent to which the emotional distress and lifestyle disruption experienced by many patients actually are *caused* by cancer and its treatment. Many women do report behavioral, emotional, cognitive, and/or social changes following the diagnosis and treatment of breast cancer. Those changes are not unique to breast cancer, however. The general reactions described also are commonly reported by patients with other forms of cancer (for example, Craig and Abeloff 1974; Holland 1973). Why, then, is breast cancer regarded as a particularly stressful disease, causing special problems for patients and meriting intense psychological investigation?

Do Breast Cancer Patients Experience Special Problems?
In a recent review, Streltzer (1983) claimed that "cancer of the breast continues to receive more attention than other forms of cancer because of special problems associated with adjustment" (p. 719). There are several possible explanations for this assertion. First, women with breast cancer may have reactions similar to those of other cancer patients and yet react with greater intensity or for longer duration. This explanation could be valid if either women in general or breast cancer patients specifically had particularly strong reactions to their cancer. Second, breast cancer patients, as a result of the presumed meaning and importance of the breast to female identity, may have specific kinds of problems over and above those observed in other cancer patients. Finally, another potential contributor to the commonly held view that breast cancer has a special impact may involve the reactions of others toward breast cancer and mastectomy. People with whom the patient interacts may exhibit their own fears and negative attitudes toward breast cancer and, consequently, may cause special concerns for the patient.

With reference to the first explanation, there is scant evidence to suggest that women have more extreme emotional reactions to cancer than men do. Sobel and Worden (1979) found no sex difference in the frequencies of male and female cancer patients experiencing high emotional distress following treatment. Fox and co-workers (1982) examined the suicide rates of cancer patients and found that male patients had significantly higher suicide rates than same-age men in the general population. Female cancer patients, in contrast, did not commit suicide more frequently than did other women. These statistics fail to suggest that women generally react more negatively than men to cancer.

The related issue—whether women react more strongly to breast cancer than either men or women do to other diseases—has been more controversial. Many writers have assumed that such an intensified reaction occurs on the part of breast cancer patients for the reasons alluded to earlier. Supporters of this position point to research in which breast cancer patients have been compared to women who have received breast biopsies for benign lumps (for example, Maguire 1978; Morris, Greer, and White 1977; Polivy 1977) and women in general surgery clinics (Gottesman and Lewis 1982; Lee and Maguire 1975; Ray 1978). In almost every case, breast cancer patients have reported significantly greater distress for months and even years postoperatively. Nevertheless, when breast cancer patients are compared to other *cancer* patients, the findings are not so clear-cut. For example, Gordon and co-workers (1980) found that lung cancer patients experienced more difficulties than did breast or melanoma patients, and Krouse and Krouse (1981) reported that hysterectomy patients reported more distress than did breast cancer patients. Worden and Weisman (1977) measured depression and self-esteem in women with breast cancer, Hodgkin's disease, melanoma, and colon cancer and reported no significant differences (on either self-reports or clinical ratings) between the breast cancer patients and the patients with other forms of cancer. They concluded that their data do not support the belief that breast loss is the primary cause of psychosocial problems for breast cancer patients. Levine, Silberfarb, and Lipowski (1978) reported, however, that breast cancer patients are referred for psychiatric consultation at a significantly higher rate than other cancer patients, and Louhivuori and Hakama (1979) found that breast cancer was associated with an increased risk of suicide among Finnish women, although the increase in risk was not as high as it was for some other groups of cancer patients.

Whether or not breast cancer is associated with a particularly negative emotional aspect, it is frequently assumed to produce special problems over and above those experienced by other cancer patients—specifically, difficulties in the realm of sexuality and body image. Regarding this second explanation, many authors believe that the impact on "femininity" is responsible for the special distress presumed to accompany breast cancer and mastectomy. Numerous anecdotal reports describe breast cancer patients as tremendously concerned about their physical appearance and their worth as women. Kent (1975) states that the first concern for a mastectomy patient is her image to the world, since the operation may often produce a "sexual identity crisis." Anstice (1970) claims that many patients feel that they are "no longer of any value as women" (p. 882), and Byrd (1975) describes patients as needing professional advice regarding their image to the world, their image to their mates, and, especially, their sexual self-image.

This view of breast cancer patients is widely held and has led to a number of recommendations for helping patients. Many writers have recommended that women be fitted as soon as possible for breast prostheses so that external appearance can be restored (for example, Akehurst 1972; Ervin 1973; Kent 1975). Similarly, the literature contains numerous suggestions regarding the importance of helping women look "feminine" and attractive. For example, nurses are told to help women fix their hair and apply makeup during the hospital stay (Anstice 1970; Byrd 1975).

Certainly some women, perhaps those for whom physical appearance is central to self-identity (cf. Woods 1975) experience intense concerns about body image and femininity and would benefit from physical appearance counseling following their mastectomies. Moreover, most may want to be informed of the options available for restoring external appearance, including reconstructive surgery. Data suggest that patients who choose breast reconstruction do so for a variety of reasons, including expectations for changes in daily living, discomfort with external prostheses, and desires for improvements in feminine self-image (Freeman, Cash, and Winstead 1984; Rowland and Holland 1984). Women who have had such surgery report overwhelmingly that they were satisfied with the results of the operation (Rowland and Holland 1984). In addition, retrospective studies have reported positive changes in daily functioning (Rowland and Holland 1984) and feminine self-image (Freeman et al. 1984) following breast reconstruction. These studies suggest that there is some validity to the view that breast cancer can be associated with at least temporary concerns about feminine self-image for some women.

It is, of course, important that breast cancer patients' possible concerns about body image and appearance receive attention and understanding by health care professionals (see Meyerowitz 1981a). Nonetheless, little empirical evidence exists to support either the primacy of body image concerns for most breast cancer patients (Hendrick 1984) or the psychological importance of helping women "look feminine" as quickly as possible. At times and without adequate data, the tendency has been to view these recommendations as meeting universal needs among patients, despite several studies that have called into question the belief that breast loss is the most important concern of patients. For example, Peters-Golden (1982) found that only 6 percent of breast cancer patients "thought that the breast was a uniquely sensitive or troubling site for cancer" (p. 487). Meyerowitz (1981b), who asked 112 breast cancer patients to list their most important concerns, found that "future health" was listed more frequently than physical attractiveness and that concerns about health were by far the more upsetting to patients.

Recommendations for focusing on physical appearance may be irrelevant, or even angering, for women for whom this aspect of the traditional female sex role is not a central determinant of self-esteem. In describing her personal experiences following mastectomy, Lorde (1980) comments that most prostheses restore lost functioning, whereas breast prostheses are designed solely to restore appearance as perceived by others. She tells of the tremendous pressure she received to wear a prosthesis immediately following her mastectomy and of the difficulties she faced when she refused to do so. In her view, "This emphasis on the cosmetic after surgery reinforces this society's stereotype of women, that we are only what we look or appear, so this is the only aspect of our existence we need to address" (p. 57). Clearly, clinicians and researchers must learn to attend to sex-role issues without falling prey to sex-role stereotypes.

While extreme statements about loss of femininity are often anecdotal, and, to date, without firm empirical bases, reports of changes in sexual functioning and satisfaction among breast cancer patients are fairly well documented empirically.[4] Several studies have reported that slightly under half of early-stage breast cancer patients report sexual difficulties three to four months following mastectomy (for example, Derogatis 1980; Maguire 1978). Whether these rates of reported sexual difficulties surpass those reported by patients with cancer at other sites is difficult to determine, however. For example, a review of the literature led Derogatis and Kourlesis (1981) to conclude that sexual problems are common among many cancer patients, even some patients whose cancer is not associated with sexual organs. Gynecologic cancer patients, understandably, report high rates of dysfunction, approaching 100 percent for operations such as pelvic exenteration (Derogatis and Kourlesis, 1981). Curiously, and perhaps because of prevailing sex-role stereotypes, relatively little has been written about sexual problems among men with genital cancers, and most of what is available focuses on functional problems per se with very little mention of feelings, body image, self-esteem, or perceived loss of masculinity (Gorzynski and Holland 1979; vonEschenbach 1980). Patients with ostomies (a surgical procedure whereby an opening is created in the abdominal wall for the excretion of bodily wastes) also have been found to report high levels of sexual dysfunction and dissatisfaction. Rolstad, Wilson, and Rothenberger (1983) found that 32 percent of a sample of patients with ostomies said that surgery had made intercourse more difficult, and 60 percent of the women and 52 percent of the men stated that they felt less sexually attractive after surgery. From these data it seems that sexuality can be affected in patients with a wide range of cancers, including but not restricted to breast cancer.

With changes in sexual functioning, as well as with most other reactions to breast cancer (or any other disability), it is difficult to determine the extent to which patients' emotional distress and lifestyle disruption are influenced by other people's reactions to the disease. Evidence that breast cancer patients' psychosocial reactions may be partially determined by the attitudes and behaviors of others is generally indirect. Considerable data suggest that many people have strong reactions to cancer and that such reactions may influence the ways they treat patients (for example, Wortman and Dunkel-Schetter 1979); it is possible that such disruptions are more likely to occur for patients whose disease has effects related to traditional sex roles. For example, one study investigated the adjustment of young adults who had had cancer as children (Gogan, et al. 1979). Females who had visible physical impairments and limitations tended to be unmarried, whereas visible disabilities in men did not affect marital status. The presumed importance of physical appearance in making women attractive to men may also account for the fears that some women without steady partners express regarding their abilities to develop relationships following mastectomy (Holland and Mastrovito 1980). In some cases, these fears are founded on experiences with men who have difficulties accepting a woman who has lost a breast. Married women also may experience the adverse reactions of spouses to their breast amputation (for example, Jamison and Pasnau 1978). Meyerowitz (1981b) found that 45 percent of a sample of breast cancer patients reported difficulty in showing the postoperative site to their spouses; this difficulty was significantly correlated with anxiety and depression. One woman reported that she never went to bed without her prosthesis because of the distress her mastectomy caused her husband. Interestingly, difficulty in looking at the site *oneself* was less frequent and was not associated with emotional distress or with difficulty in showing the site to the spouse.

Given the importance of the emotional aspects of relationships for some women (Wills, Weiss, and Patterson 1974), disruptions in social support systems may be particularly disturbing. Peters-Golden (1982) found that breast cancer patients often attributed ineffective social support to the fact that friends and loved ones incorrectly assumed that breast loss, not cancer, was the primary concern for the patient. Based on responses from breast cancer patients and from disease-free men and women, she concluded that "there appears to be a continuum formed by three perspectives: men (who distinguish cancer from breast cancer quite strongly, and focus on breast loss); women (who make less of a distinction, and emphasize breast loss less); and women with breast cancer (who make a distinction between breast cancer and cancer at other sites, but who do so mainly on a medical basis, and who feel that breast loss is a matter of secondary concern)" (p. 490). These data suggest that breast cancer patients are likely to encounter reactions from others based on assumptions about breast cancer and its emotional impact that differ from their own experiences.

Reactions of others also may play a role in affecting patients' distress in areas other than body image and sexuality. McCharen and Earp (1981) found that employers' decisions to hire women who had had breast cancer are associated with company-related variables (for example, size of company, employers' experiences with breast cancer) rather than variables specifically related to the patient and her health status. There is also a curious finding, reported by more than one author (Polivy 1977; Worden and Weisman 1977), that the period of peak distress for breast cancer patients occurs several weeks or months later than for patients with other kinds of cancer. While this finding is only suggestive, it does make one wonder if something happens specifically in the social relationships of breast cancer patients that leads to an increase in distress following surgery. Even the finding, on the high psychiatric referral rate for breast cancer patients compared to other cancer patients (Levine, Silberfarb, and Lipowski 1978) may reflect not only the level of distress experienced by patients but also physicians' greater propensities to perceive psychiatric problems in women (Fidell 1980). In this instance, such a propensity on the part of the physicians may lead women to receive better, rather than worse, treatment, since there is some evidence that psychological distress in cancer patients in general may be underestimated by physicians (Derogatis, Abeloff, and McBeth 1976).

As the preceding review demonstrates, there are a number of possible explanations for women's reactions to breast cancer and mastectomy. The literature suggests that feminine self-identity may be an important area of concern for some women, though not all. The belief that some authors have expressed, however, that decrements in feminine self-image as a result of breast loss will lead to severe emotional distress for most women, over and above that experienced by cancer patients in general, is not supported by existing studies. Indeed, comparisons of breast cancer patients to other cancer patients indicate that most breast cancer patients report moderate, not extreme, levels of distress. Moreover, patients report that health concerns, rather than changes in physical image, are the primary source of their distress. Areas that seem to be disrupted by the experience of breast cancer primarily involve interpersonal relationships, particularly sexual and marital relations. Although these problems are not unique to breast cancer patients, they may be particularly upsetting for some women because success in such relations traditionally has been viewed as central to the female sex role.

Nonetheless, disruption in these roles should not be attributed exclusively to *intrapersonal* concerns. These difficulties may be as much, or more, a product of the expectations and sex-role stereotypes held by those with whom the patient interacts. In fact, similar stereotypes may be held by clinicians and researchers and may partially underlie their contentions regarding the special intrapsychic problems facing breast cancer patients. These stereotypic views may lead to overestimates of the problems faced by breast cancer patients (and to a relative inattention to the coping resources of breast cancer patients) and, perhaps, to underestimates of the problems faced by patients with some other forms of cancer.

Notes

1. Although we are not undertaking a comparative gender analysis, it is worth noting that the performance of behaviors associated with the traditional male role also may be disrupted by mid-life chronic illness. For example, reductions in work-related activities, loss of physical ability (Pleck 1976), and loss of independence resulting from chronic illness (Schaffer 1981)—changes that would have a highly negative impact on most men and women—may be particularly disruptive for those men who have adhered strictly to the traditional male role. Such individuals may perceive that they have lost their "masculinity" and are no longer "whole men."

2. Although breast cancer does occur in men, women account for more than 99 percent of the diagnoses.

3. It is difficult to separate the effects of breast cancer from those of mastectomy, because at the time this review was written some form of mastectomy was the treatment of choice for early-stage breast cancer patients.

4. It is important to note that these data on sexual dysfunction pertain exclusively to behaviors in a heterosexual relationship. Whether or not one's personal sexual behaviors (such as masturbation) or sexual interactions with other women would be equally affected by breast cancer is unknown.

References

Akehurst, A. C. 1972. Post-mastectomy morale. *Lancet* 2:181–82.

American Cancer Society. 1983. *Cancer facts and figures.* New York: Author.

Anonymous. 1980. Cancer patients cite widespread job discrimination. *Oncology Times* 2(7):12.

———. 1984. NCI releases new SEER data on cancer patient survival. *Oncology Times* 1(1):3–22.

Anstice, E. 1970. Coping after a mastectomy. *Nursing Times* 66:882–83.

Bard, M. 1952. The sequence of emotional reactions in radical mastectomy patients. *Public Health Reports* 67:1144–48.

Bell, I. 1975. The double standard: Age. In *Women: A feminist perspective*, ed. J. Freeman. Palo Alto, Calif.: Mayfield.

Bressler, B., S. F. Cohen, and F. Magnussen. 1956. The problem of phantom breast and phantom pain. *Journal of Nervous and Mental Disease* 123:181–87.

Burdick, D. 1975. Rehabilitation of the breast cancer patient. *Cancer* 36:645–48.

Byrd, B. F. 1975. Sex after mastectomy. *Medical Aspects of Human Sexuality* 9(4):53–54.

Centers, R. 1972. The completion hypothesis and the compensatory dynamic of intersexual attraction and love. *Journal of Psychology* 82:111–26.

Cooperstock, R. 1971. Sex differences in the use of mood-modifying drugs: An exploratory model. *Journal of Health and Social Behavior* 12:238–44.

Craig, T. J., and M. D. Abeloff. 1974. Psychiatric symptomatology among hospitalized cancer patients. *American Journal of Psychiatry* 131:1323–27.

Dembo, T. 1982. Some problems in rehabilitation as seen by a Lewinian. *Journal of Social Issues* 38:131–39.

Derogatis, L. R. 1980. Breast and gynecologic cancers: Their unique impact on body image and sexual identity in women. *Frontiers of Radiation Therapy and Oncology* 14:1–11.

Derogatis, L. R., and S. M. Kourlesis. 1981. An approach to evaluation of sexual problems in the cancer patient. *CA: A Cancer Journal for Clinicians* 31:46–50.

Derogatis, L. R., M. D. Abeloff, and C. D. McBeth. 1976. Cancer patients and their physicians in the perception of psychological symptoms. *Psychosomatics* 17:197–201.

Eisenberg, H. S., and I. S. Goldenberg. 1966. A measurement of quality of survival of breast cancer patients. In *Clinical evaluation of breast cancer*, ed. J. L. Hayward and R. D. Bulbrook. London: Academic Press.

Ervin, C. V. 1973. Psychologic adjustment to mastectomy. *Medical Aspects of Human Sexuality* 7(2):42–65.

Fejer, D., and R. Smart. 1973. The use of psychoactive drugs by adults. *Canadian Psychiatric Association Journal* 18:313–19.

Fidell, L. 1973. Put her down on drugs: Prescribed drug usage in women. Paper presented at the Western Psychological Association meeting, Anaheim, California, April.

———. 1980. Sex role stereotypes and the American physician. *Psychology of Women Quarterly* 4:313–30.

Fox, B. H., E. J. Stanek, S. C. Boyd,and J. T. Flannery. 1982. Suicide rates among cancer patients in Connecticut. *Journal of Chronic Disease* 35:89–100.

Freeman, E. L., T. Cash, and B. Winstead. 1984. Perceived changes in physical self-concept and marital and sexual relations in patients who have had mastectomy and breast reconstruction surgery. Paper presented at the annual meeting of the Society of Behavioral Medicine, Philadelphia, May.

Gogan, J. L., G. P. Koocher, W. E. Fine, D. J. Foster, and J. E. O'Malley. 1979. Pediatric cancer survival and marriage: Issues affecting adult adjustment. *American Journal of Orthopsychiatry* 49:423–35.

Gordon, W. A., I. Freidenbergs, L. Diller, M. Hibbard, C. Wolf, L. Levine, R. Lipkens, O. Ezrachi, and D. Lucido. 1980. Efficacy of psychosocial intervention with cancer patients. *Journal of Consulting and Clinical Psychology* 48:743–59.

Gorzynski, J. G., and J. C. Holland. 1979. Psychological aspects of testicular cancer. *Seminars in Oncology* 6:125–29.

Gottesman, D., and M. S. Lewis. 1982. Differences in crisis reactions among cancer and surgery patients. *Journal of Consulting and Clinical Psychology* 50:381–88.

Grandstaff, N. W. 1976. The impact of breast cancer on the family. *Frontiers of Radiation Therapy and Oncology* 11:145–56.

Harrison, A. A., and L. Saeed. 1977. Let's make a deal: An analysis of revelations and stipulations in lonely heart advertisements. *Journal of Personality and Social Psychology* 35:257–64.

Hendrick, S. S. 1984. Working with breast cancer patients. Paper presented at the Society of Behavioral Medicine, Philadelphia, April.

Holland, J. 1973. Psychologic aspects of cancer. In *Cancer medicine,* ed. J. F. Holland and E. Frei. Philadelphia: Lea and Febiger.

Holland, J. C., and R. Mastrovito. 1980. Psychologic adaptation to breast cancer. *Cancer* 46:1045–52.

Howell, M. 1974. What medical schools teach about women. *New England Journal of Medicine* 291:304–7.

Jamison, K., D. K. Wellisch, and R. O. Pasnau. 1978. Psychosocial aspects of mastectomy: I. The woman's perspective. *American Journal of Psychiatry.* 135:432–36.

Kent, S. 1975. Coping with sexual identity crises after mastectomy. *Geriatrics* 30(10):145–46.

Krouse, H. J., and J. H. Krouse. 1981. Psychological factors in postmastectomy adjustment. *Psychological Reports* 48:275–78.

Lee, E. C. G., and G. P. Maguire. 1975. Emotional distress in patients attending a breast clinic. *British Journal of Surgery* 62:162.

Lerner, M. J., and D. T. Miller. 1978. Just world research and the attribution process: Looking back and ahead. *Psychological Bulletin* 85:1030–51.

Levine, P. M., P. M. Silberfarb, and Z. J. Lipowski. 1978. Mental disorders in cancer patients: A study of 100 psychiatric referrals. *Cancer* 42:1385–91.

Lichtman, R. R., S. E. Taylor, J. V. Wood, A. Z. Bluming, G. M. Dosik, and R. L. Leibowitz. 1984. Relations with children after breast cancer: The mother-daughter relationship at risk. *Journal of Psychosocial Oncology* 2:1–19.

Lichtman, R. R., J. V. Wood, and S. E. Taylor. 1982. Close relationships after breast cancer. Paper presented at the annual meeting of the American Psychological Association, Washington, D.C., August.

Lorde, A. 1980. *The cancer journals.* Argyle, N.Y.: Spinsters, Ink.

Louhivuori, K. A., and M. Hakama. 1979. Risk of suicide among cancer patients. *American Journal of Epidemiology* 109:59–65.

Mages, N. L., and G. A. Mendelsohn. 1979. Effects of cancer on patients' lives: A personalogical approach. In *Health psychology—a handbook: Theories, applications, and challenges of a psychological approach to the health care system,* ed. G. C. Stone, F. Cohen, and N. E. Adler. San Francisco: Jossey-Bass.

Maguire, P. 1975. The psychological and social consequences of breast cancer. *Nursing Mirror* 140(14):54–57.

———. 1978. Psychiatric problems after mastectomy. *Breast cancer: Psychosocial aspects of early detection and treatment,* ed. P. C. Brand, P. A. vanKeep. Baltimore: University Park Press.

Maguire, P., A. Tait, M. Brooke, C. Thomas, and R. Sellwood. 1980. Effect of counseling on the psychiatric morbidity associated with mastectomy. *British Medical Journal* 281:1454–56.

McCharen, N., and J. A. L. Earp. 1981. Toward a model of factors influencing the hiring of women with a history of breast cancer. *Journal of Sociology and Social Welfare* 8:346–63.

Meyerowitz, B. E. 1980. Psychosocial correlates of breast cancer and its treatment. *Psychological Bulletin* 87:108–31.

———. 1981a. The impact of mastectomy on the lives of women. *Professional Psychology* 12:118–27.

———. 1981b. Postmastectomy physical concerns of breast cancer patients. Paper presented at the American Psychological Association. Los Angeles, August.

———. 1983. Postmastectomy coping strategies and quality of life. *Health Psychology* 2:117–32.

Meyerowitz, B. E., F. C. Sparks, and I. K. Spears 1979. Adjuvant chemotherapy for breast carcinoma: Psychological implications. *Cancer* 43:1613–18.

Michael, J. M. 1982. The second revolution in health: Health promotion and its environmental base. *American Psychologist* 37:936–41.

Millman, M. 1977. *The unkindest cut.* New York: Morrow.

Morris, T., H. S. Greer, and P. White. 1977. Psychological and social adjustment to mastectomy: A two-year follow-up study. *Cancer* 40:2381–87.

Peters-Golden, H. 1982. Breast cancer: Varied perceptions of social support in the illness experience. *Social Science and Medicine* 16:482–91.

Pleck, J. H. 1976. The male sex role: Definitions, problems, and sources of change. *Journal of Social Issues* 32:155–64.

Polivy, J. 1977. Psychological effects of mastectomy on a woman's feminine self-concept. *Journal of Nervous and Mental Disease* 164:77–87.

Quint, J. C. 1963. The impact of mastectomy. *American Journal of Nursing* 63(11):88–92.

Ray, C. 1978. Adjustment to mastectomy: The psychological impact of disfigurement. In *Breast cancer: Psychosocial aspects of early detection and treatment,* ed. P. C. Brand and P. A. van Keep. Baltimore: University Park Press.

Rolstad, B. S., G. Wilson, and D. A. Rothenberger. 1983. Sexual concerns in the patients with an ileostomy. *Diseases of the Colon and Rectum* 26:170–71.

Rowland, J. H., and J. Holland. 1984. Women with cancer: Psychologic and immunologic perspectives. Paper presented at Society of Behavioral Medicine meeting, Philadelphia, May.

Safilios-Rothschild, C. 1977. *Love, sex, and sex roles.* Englewood Cliffs, N.J.: Prentice-Hall.

Schaffer, K. F. 1981. *Sex roles and human behavior.* Cambridge, Mass.: Winthrop.

Schain, W. 1976. Psychological impact of the diagnosis of breast cancer on the patient. *Frontiers of Radiation and Oncology* 11:68–89.

Schottenfeld, D., and G. F. Robbins. 1970. Quality of survival among patients who have had radical mastectomy. *Cancer* 26:650–54.

Silberfarb, P. M., L. H. Maurer, and C. S. Crouthamel. 1980. Psychosocial aspects of neoplastic disease: I. Functional status of breast cancer patients during different treatment regimens. *American Journal of Psychiatry* 137:450–55.

Sobel, H. J., and J. W. Worden. 1979. The MMPI as a predictor of psychological adaptation to cancer. *Journal of Consulting and Clinical Psychology.* 47:716–24.

Streltzer, J. 1983. Psychiatric aspects of oncology: A review of recent research.

Hospital and Community Psychiatry 34:716–24.

vonEschenbach, A. C. 1980. Sexual dysfunction following therapy for cancer of the prostate, testis, and penis. *Frontiers of Radiation Therapy and Oncology* 14:42–50.

Weisman, A. D., J. W. Worden, and H. J. Sobel. 1980. *Psychosocial screening and intervention with cancer patients.* Boston: Harvard Medical School, Department of Psychiatry.

Wellisch, D. K., K. R. Jamison, and R. O. Pasnau. 1978. Psychological aspects of mastectomy: II. The man's perspective. *American Journal of Psychiatry* 135:543–46.

Wills, T. A., R. L. Weiss, and G. R. Patterson. 1974. A behavioral analysis of the determinants of marital satisfaction. *Journal of Consulting and Clinical Psychology* 42:802–11.

Woods, N. F. 1975. Influence on sexual adaptation to mastectomy. *JOGN Nursing* 4(3):33–37.

Worden, J. W., and A. D. Weisman. 1977. The fallacy of postmastectomy depression. *American Journal of the Medical Sciences* 273:169–75.

Wortman, C.B., and C. Dunkel-Schetter. 1979. Interpersonal relationships and cancer: A theoretical analysis. *Journal of Social Issues* 35:120–55.

3. In Search of a Heroine: Images of Women with Disabilities in Fiction and Drama

DEBORAH KENT

I was 15 when I discovered *The Barretts of Wimpole Street*, Rudolf Besier's (1930) play about Elizabeth Barrett and Robert Browning. I read it with exhilaration. Never before had I encountered a woman like Elizabeth—intelligent, sophisticated, and unable to walk—who was loved and courted by a man. For Robert, her disability seemed almost irrelevant. He fell in love with her through reading her poetry, the purest expression of her soul.

I can't remember a time when I wasn't aware that I was different from most other people, and that my differentness was a judgment against me. By the dawn of adolescence I had absorbed enough innuendoes to suspect that, no matter what social graces I managed to cultivate, no matter how I dressed or wore my hair, I would never be the kind of girl boys wanted to flirt with or to ask on dates. My reading heightened my apprehensions about the future. In books, it seemed, the only way a woman could be fulfilled was through the love of a man; and the only women worthy of that love were lithe and lovely, unblemished, physically perfect. The smallest flaw—an uneven gait, a malformed hand, a squint—was enough to disqualify a woman from romance, from all hope for happiness. If even a trifling imperfection could loom as such an insurmountable obstacle to fulfillment, what chance was there for a girl who was totally blind, as I was?

And then suddenly there was Elizabeth Barrett. Perhaps there was a Robert Browning for me somewhere, too. Perhaps my disability did not, after all, sentence me to the isolation and loneliness of a social outcast.

After the first flush of elation, even Elizabeth Barrett began to trouble me. It was true that Robert continued to love her, even when he learned that she hadn't left her couch in ten years. But her disability was

90

not quite so irrelevant to him as I tried to believe. Though he never rejected her because she was disabled, he never accepted her as a disabled woman, either. From their first meeting he was convinced that through the sheer power of his love she would somehow walk again—and Elizabeth did not disappoint him. What would have happened, I pondered, if she had never risen from her couch and made her triumphant journey across the room? Would Robert have gone on loving her if she couldn't be rescued, if she failed to make him the hero he meant to be? How would the play have ended if she continued writing sensitive, witty, elegant verse, propped upon her pillows?

It was beyond imagining. *The Barretts of Wimpole Street* required a happy ending, and a happy ending was possible only if Elizabeth were cured. Only if she became physically whole at last could she be granted lifelong happiness.

My disability, I knew, would never yield, not even to the power of love. I had to conclude that Robert Browning was not the man for me after all. I could never aspire to become a woman like his Elizabeth.

IN SEARCH OF A HEROINE
According to Rachel Brownstein (1982), identification with female characters in literature has tremendous importance in the emotional development of young women.

Girls, enjoined from thinking about becoming generals and emperors, tend to live more in novels than boys do, and to live longer in them. . . . To suspect that one can be significant only in the fantasy of fiction, to look for significance in a concentrated essence of character, in an image of oneself rather than in action or achievement, is historically only feminine, or mostly. (p. XV)

In career opportunities and personal goals, women with disabilities have been even more restricted than their non-disabled peers. If non-disabled women feel a need to look for significance through identification, to become the heroines they read about, this need may be even more intense among women who are disabled.

Identification with female characters in books can have a profound impact upon a woman's emerging sense of herself. Brownstein explains:

To want to become a heroine, to have a sense of the possibility of being one, is to develop the beginnings of what feminists call a 'raised consciousness.' It liberates a woman from feeling, and therefore perhaps from being, a victim or a dependent or a drudge, someone of no account. (p. XIX)

The young woman with a disability has, more than likely, internalized substantial portions of just such a view of herself. Terms such as "victim," "dependent," and "person of no account," comply with the most

widely held stereotypes of the disabled woman, stereotypes she is generally taught to accept as definitions of herself. The need to find heroines
in literature, therefore, may be even more crucial for the disabled
woman than it is for the woman who lacks such "double minority"
status. I know that in my adolescent quest for identity—a quest that
lasted well into adulthood—I sought in fiction and drama the heroines
who eluded me in real life.

Though strangers and even many who considered themselves
friends defined me exclusively in terms of my blindness, I think I
always had a strong enough sense of myself to know that it was only one
aspect of the person I was. Why then, in my search for role models, was
it so essential to find women with disabilities? Why couldn't I identify
fully with Jo March or Jane Eyre, with Austen's Elizabeth Bennett or
Shakespeare's Viola? Though none of these characters were disabled,
they all possessed traits that I recognized and understood. In some sense
their sufferings and triumphs sounded echoes in my own experience
and exemplified the life I hoped to live some day.

All of these women, and nearly every other potential heroine I
encountered in fiction or drama, ultimately find fulfillment because
they are attractive and desirable to men. Even clumsy, tomboyish Jo
March and plain, shy Jane Eyre are chosen for marriage by men who love
them. Brownstein writes:

The marriage plot most novels depend on is about finding validation of one's
uniqueness and importance by being singled out among all other women by a
man. The man's love is proof of the girl's value and payment for it. (p. XV)

Nearly everything I read confirmed that, for a woman, true validation
was a gift that could be bestowed only by a man.

I longed to believe that I, too, might somehow find the love and
fulfillment that other women regarded as their birthright. Yet I was
afraid to hope too much, to try too hard, lest I should appear pathetic
and ridiculous to the people around me. One disabled woman,
Catherine Butler Hathaway (1943), describes this feeling eloquently in
her autobiography:

I had heard people laugh and talk about grotesquely unbeautiful women who had
the absurd effrontery to imagine that men were in love with them. . . . There
was a curious and baffling law of nature (or human nature) which was very hard
on them, and on me. If a girl or woman was pretty, her function of loving and
being loved was treated seriously and sympathetically by everyone. But if she
were awkward and homely, and nevertheless eager for love, that function seemed
to be changed into something mysteriously comic and shameful. (p. 55)

Like Catherine Hathaway, I tried to conceal my youthful infatuations for boys who might regard me at best with condescending pity. Painful as it was, I endeavored to be "realistic." I observed the flirtations of other girls with awe and envy, and I dared not identify too closely with the women I met in the pages of books.

TARNISHED IMAGES

Considering the importance of the marriage theme in literature, and the widely held consensus that disabled women are disqualified from this supreme feminine fulfillment, it is not surprising that few playwrights or novelists have chosen to depict women with disabilities. Even when a disabled woman does appear, she is rarely the heroine I yearned for when I was growing up. It would have been wonderful to discover a blind woman or a girl with facial scars being courted by an eligible man. But if love and marriage were out of the question, I would have been thrilled simply to read of a disabled woman who found other forms of fulfillment—through friendships, work, appreciation of nature and art. The heroine I sought needed only to feel good about herself, to express this positive feeling in the way she lived her life.

In preparing to write this paper, I have examined more than thirty novels and plays that portray disabled women. They vary from light popular fiction (du Maurier's *The King's General*) to the most serious literature (Joyce's *Ulysses*). Some works were written in Victorian England, while others reflect the mores of the United States today. As radically as these pieces differ in other respects, they are remarkably alike in their presentations of disabled women. Whether she is blind or deaf, facially disfigured or paraplegic, the disabled woman is typically shown to be incomplete not only in body, but in the basic expression of her womanhood. Frequently she is a victim—her disability the lingering reminder of some hideous accident or vicious act of violence. Generally she is both physically and economically dependent upon others, constantly draining their resources and giving little in return. Where men are concerned, she is nearly always "someone of no account." Most of these characters, at one point or another in their histories, express bitterness, despair, and self-loathing. Their anguish is generally seen as the inevitable outgrowth of the disability itself. Social stigma, which is in fact responsible for so much of the pain endured by disabled women in real life, is seldom explored or even acknowledged. The girl with a clubfoot is miserable because she cannot dance; the blind girl longs for the sunsets she will never see. They do not rebel against the world's view that they are helpless, useless, pitiable, and undesirable.

It would be impossible to describe all of these works in detail or to chart them according to some arbitrary scheme of differences and similarities. A more effective way to convey the essence of these novels and plays may be to examine a few salient examples, and to share my personal responses to them.

Approaching the topic from the point of view of a disabled woman seeking a heroine with whom to identify, I have selected four pieces for detailed description and analysis. The first two works embody some of the most negative stereotypes in their portrayals of women with disabilities. They present these characters as objects of pity or contempt, who give little to others and whose lack of self-respect is never questioned. The remaining two works offer the most positive images of disabled women I have found. They depict independent, vital women who are not defined in terms of disability alone—women who value themselves and are esteemed by the people around them.

Deciding which were the most devastating portrayals of disabled women was no easy task. Among the contenders were Sontag's (1967) *Death Kit*, in which a young woman's blindness becomes a metaphor for the insidious forces of death and destruction—the ideal prescription for her suicidal lover. Then there was Kata's (1961) *A Patch of Blue*, the tale of a blind girl who sits all day in the park stringing beads, and who hates everything black (including black people) because there is too much blackness in her life already. Another runner-up was Wharton's (1970) *Ethan Frome*. In this novella, generally hailed as a minor masterpiece by critics, Mattie Silver's paraplegia is seen as the punishment meted out by a stern, impartial deity to three people who have broken His commandments.

In these and many comparable works, writers have used disabled women more as metaphors than as fully drawn characters. In my search for a heroine I wasn't looking for a metaphor; I needed a true-to-life woman whom I could care about and believe in.

Furthermore, I found a distinct tendency for some writers to categorize disabled women as either saints or sinners. Gide's (1931) Gertrude in *Pastoral Symphony* and Dickens' (1845) Bertha Plummer in "Cricket on the Hearth" are the essence of sweetness and purity, while Trollope's (1857) Mme. Neroni uses her privileged invalid status to lure men as a spider lures flies to its web. In either case, the disability is perceived as the determining factor in the characterization.

In all fairness, many of the disabled women in the works I considered are fully developed and thoroughly sympathetic. Yet they are scarcely characters I or most other young women would choose as role models. Trevor's (1973) portrayal of Miss Sampson in *Elizabeth Alone*, for example, is wrenchingly powerful. Miss Sampson, disfigured since birth, concludes at the age of 13 that romance will never have a place in her life. For years she is sustained by her religious faith, a faith that is shattered as the novel runs its course. Wracked by doubt, she agonizes not only over her own wasted life but also over the meaningless suffering intrinsic to human existence. Through the depth of her compassion Miss Sampson emerges as a truly heroic figure. Yet in her isolation and torment, she is not the heroine I would wish to become.

Ultimately the works I found most disturbing were those that seemed on the surface to portray the disabled woman with sensitivity and awareness, while actually furthering some of the most destructive stereotypes. For reasons I shall explain, my final choices as examples of negative images of disabled women are Laura Wingfield in Tennessee Williams' (1945) play *The Glass Menagerie*, and Edith Morrisey in *The Bleeding Heart*, a novel by Marilyn French (1980).

"BUT MOTHER, I'M CRIPPLED!"

I was thoroughly familiar with *The Glass Menagerie* when, with a group of other students, I was assigned to produce its opening scenes in a college drama workshop. When roles were handed out, I assumed without a second thought that I would play the part of Laura Wingfield—introverted, brittle Laura, who walks with a limp and waits eternally for the gentlemen callers who never come. It wasn't that I admired her, or saw the role as a challenge. Somewhere in my secret heart I felt that Laura was part of me, a part held in abeyance, to be sure, but one that might some day rise to submerge everything I had struggled for and achieved in my life. She was with me when I sat alone in the dorm on Saturday nights. I remembered her whenever I fantasized about some boy who had offered a passing hint of friendliness. Sometimes, clattering into class with my white cane, I felt as conspicuous as Laura, listening to the resounding *clump, clump!* of her leg brace.

Nearly everyone else in the group seemed to perceive the connection between Laura and me. I didn't argue when the boy who was serving as director told me to learn Laura's lines. Then, to my astonishment, another girl in the cast spoke up. "Why don't I play Laura?" she suggested to me. "You can be Amanda instead. You shouldn't have to be the one to stand up there and say, 'But Mother, I'm crippled.'"

It was a moment of revelation. Laura had become so entangled in my image of myself that I had never dreamed of playing a different part. I can't say that those simple words liberated me from her forever. But for the first time I dared to believe that she did not have an absolute hold upon me, that if I could find another way of viewing myself I might perhaps put some distance between us at last.

"A childhood illness has left her crippled, one leg shorter than the other and held in a brace," Williams explains in his stage directions. "Stemming from this Laura's separation (from the outside world) increases until she is like a piece of her own glass collection, too exquisitely fragile to move from the shelf" (Williams 1945:5). Later he prescribes that "the light upon Laura should be distinct from the others, having a peculiar pristine clarity such as light used in early religious portraits of female saints or madonnas" (p. 9). Laura is too ethereal to be tainted by the raw sexuality of the women in so many other Williams plays. Her disability sets her apart from most worldly concerns, destining her for the "saint" stereotype. Her saintliness is not a matter of choice; she has never decided to relinquish the gritty scramble for mates that preoccupies women in the outside world. Rather, she has assumed the world's view of her as asexual, dependent, a perennial child.

"Girls who aren't cut out for business careers usually wind up married to some nice young man," exclaims Laura's mother, Amanda. "Sister, that's what you'll do!" "But Mother," Laura protests, "I'm crippled!" (p. 35). To be "crippled" does not merely mean to walk with an awkward gait. As Laura tries to remind her mother, when it comes to courtship and marriage she is automatically disqualified.

Amanda is deeply self-involved, endlessly reliving and embellishing her memories of her southern girlhood. All her life Laura has heard about the Sunday afternoon when her mother entertained seventeen gentleman callers. Laura, growing up in a depression-era St. Louis, could never aspire to a career of balls and moonlit drives under the best of circumstances. As Amanda chatters on about her own glorious past, exhorting Laura to follow in her footsteps, she seems oblivious to the pain she must cause her daughter.

When Amanda does give Laura her full attention, it is with deep concern about her daughter's future. As Laura is almost totally passive, making no move on her own, Amanda attempts to bring her out of herself. She takes her to church socials where she might make some friends. She enrolls Laura in business college, hoping that she may some day be able to support herself. Always looming before her is the specter of impoverished spinsterhood. "I know so well what becomes of unmarried women who aren't prepared to occupy a position," she laments. "I've seen such pitiful cases in the South—barely tolerated spinsters living on the grudging patronage of sister's husband or brother's wife, stuck away in some little mousetrap of a room, encouraged by one inlaw to visit another—little birdlike women without any nest, eating the crust of humility all their lives" (p. 34). Though her harping becomes intolerable, Amanda does have a point. At a time when jobs are scarce and women have few alternatives to marriage, her apprehension about Laura is well-founded.

Amanda insists that the word "crippled" must never be spoken, refusing to let Laura stereotype herself as handicapped. But her extreme reaction whenever the word is uttered indicates a more insidious attitude. For Amanda there is something unspeakable about Laura's condition, something that must be denied and hidden away. To be "crippled" is somehow shameful, a disgrace. Laura has never been allowed to acknowledge her lameness as a part of herself. Instead she has been driven into retreat, turning more and more inward with the passing years until, at the age of 24, her world revolves around her collection of tiny glass animals.

Angry and rebellious, Laura's younger brother Tom fantasizes about becoming a writer and breaking free of his dreary job and home life. Only guilt over Laura's plight holds him back. Amanda promises she will let him leave once the question of Laura's future is resolved, and she implores him to introduce his sister to some nice young man from the plant where he works.

Laura is so withdrawn that her dialogue reveals little of her inner life, but she does admit to her mother that back in high school she liked a boy named Jim. He was one of the most popular boys in her class, and he hardly noticed her at all. But he teasingly nicknamed her "Blue Roses," and she has cherished that memory of being singled out for his special attention. By sheer coincidence, the nice young man Tom eventually brings home for his sister to meet proves to be the same Jim O'Connor she has dreamed of for seven years.

The action of the play crystallizes around Jim's visit, surely the most stirring event of Laura's entire life. At the sight of him Laura becomes so distraught that she flees the room. But when they are finally alone together Jim's gentleness and sincerity rapidly win her confidence. His advice that she overcome her inferiority complex by thinking of herself as superior in some way has the ring of pop psychology. Still, he is moved by her vulnerability, recognizing her as a woman worthy of a man's affection. For a few tremulous moments it almost seems that romance has entered Laura's life at last. Jim tells her she is pretty, he leads her into a dance, and in a moment of tenderness, he kisses her.

Laura's rapture is snatched away almost before she can catch her breath. "I shouldn't have done that. That was way off the beam," Jim exclaims, pulling away from her (p. 106). He tells her that, much as he'd like to say he will see her again, he is already engaged to a really wonderful girl. Too devastated to utter a word, Laura mutely offers him her treasured glass unicorn as a parting gift.

The glass menagerie, and the unicorn in particular, symbolize Laura's exquisite fragility. Like Laura, the unicorn has no place in the modern world. Williams suggests that it is not Laura's physical disability per se, but the way she has come to feel about herself that has brought her life to a dead end. The fact remains, however, that Laura Wingfield conforms precisely to the stereotype of the disabled woman as helpless, pathetic, and unqualified as a prize for males to pursue. She is a constant worry to her family; her life is a morass of loneliness and monotony.

Regrettably, I cannot argue that Williams' portrayal of Laura is wholly unrealistic. A distressing number of women with disabilities (as well as men and women who are not disabled), convinced that they can never compete, do abandon the struggle. *The Glass Menagerie* is the heartbreakingly vivid story of a woman's wasted life—a story that deserves to be told. Williams, however, implies that Laura's tragedy is inevitable. He fails to convey that, born into a different family, encouraged to feel more positive about herself, she might have found love and happiness in spite of the brace on her leg. For most spectators, the play evokes no sense of outrage against the forces that have kept Laura from living fully. It is the image of the poor crippled girl—forever a child playing with her glass animals—that lingers on.

I could have lived with Laura in those crucial growing-up years if only I hadn't felt doomed to follow the road she traveled. But literature and life hadn't offered many alternatives. It came to me as a shock when I realized I need not be the one to declare, "But Mother, I'm crippled!"

"THE INDOMITABLE POWER OF WEAKNESS"

For millions of modern women, groping toward identity in a world of shifting demands and social values, the literature of feminism has offered heroines of a new breed. The protagonist of the contemporary women's novel is intelligent, sensitive, and often ambitious. In her struggle to balance her priorities, home and family are frequently sacrificed to make way for a profession and that ever-elusive goal known as self-realization. The feminist heroine may suffer, she may be ill-used and disillusioned, but in the end she discovers her own strength and power.

Though feminist literature chiefly reflects the experiences of middle- and upper-class white women, women from most minority groups have added their voices to the chorus. A number of authors have given their readers glimpses of life as a woman who is black, Hispanic, native American, or lesbian. Disabled women, however, have been strangely reticent about shaping their life experiences into fiction, and feminist literature as a whole has given little space to women with disabilities.

Marilyn French is one of the few feminist writers who has chosen a disabled women to be a character in one of her major novels. French is widely read and respected as a champion of women's social and intellectual equality with men. Yet, in her depiction of a woman with a disability, she clings to the same stereotypes cherished by writers since Dickens and Trollope. Perhaps the image of Edith Morrisey is no more negative than the images of a dozen other disabled women in novels and plays, but when I consider French's otherwise elevated consciousness, I feel that I and all disabled women have been betrayed.

Edith Morrisey is a minor character in *The Bleeding Heart*, and an offstage character at that. She appears only through her husband Victor's account of her, and in the fantasies of Victor's lover, Dolores. Dolores is the novel's protagonist, a true feminist heroine: intellectually supple, a tireless seeker after truth. She has endured the anguish of a destructive marriage and a daughter's suicide, and she has the strength of steel that has been forged in fire.

While on a year's sabbatical in England, Dolores is passionately drawn to Victor Morrisey, a fellow American, a businessman who also is temporarily stationed abroad. She is attracted first by the deep pain she reads in his face, by the sense that, unlike most men she has known, he is vulnerable, open to profound emotion. Not until they have been lovers for several months does she hear the story behind that look of anguish. He reveals at last the history of his relationship to Edith, the wife who will claim him in the end, despite the intense closeness he and Dolores share.

At first it is the typical tale of the suburban housewife, left to the vacuuming and the dirty diapers while her husband pursues the adventure of his rising career. Edith accuses Victor of caring more for his work than he does for her and the children. She leaves him briefly but returns out of a sense of duty (the children need a father, even one who is almost never home). Besides, she has nowhere to go. For a time she settles down with patient resignation, while Victor launches a series of affairs with other women.

Their marriage seems to be holding together until the inevitable night when Edith sees Victor in a restaurant, holding hands across the table with his latest conquest. Later, when he comes home, she confronts him with the suppressed rage and hurt of twenty years. "She looked like a fury," Victor tells Dolores, "and for the first time in all the years I'd known her I saw the Edith who lived underneath that stiff smile, that sweet manner. She was unstoppable" (French 1980:243).

Victor expects Edith's rage to burn itself out; he waits for her to rush to him in tears, ready to patch up their quarrel and start over. Instead, Edith snatches up his most treasured book, tears it to pieces, and dashes out of the house. A few hours later the police call to tell him that she has had an accident.

Tortured by guilt, Victor spends day after day at Edith's bedside. For a time she refuses to speak to him; then she unleashes fresh tirades of pent-up resentment. At last she is spent. "It was pitiful," Victor recalls. "So weak she was, having given up her anger, you felt there was nothing at all to her. . . . She had no energy to cry and protest, but also she had no energy for anything else. It felt as if her soul had atrophied" (p. 257).

At last Edith can go home. She is paralyzed from the waist down. In the course of repairing her scarred face the doctors have given her a facelift, so now she looks almost like a little girl. All of the fight has gone out of her; she smiles gently as Victor waits upon her. One evening she tells him that perhaps her injury has been worth it, proving to them how lucky they really are to have each other. "To bring up the children in a peaceful and orderly and loving home, that was always my ambition," she explains. "And that I have achieved, . . . regardless" (p. 260). It is Victor's turn now to cry like a child, burying his head in her lap.

As Victor sees it, Edith did her duty by him while he was out having fun. "I made a cripple out of her," he concludes, "and it's my turn for duty now" (p. 264). At last he spends his evenings with his wife at home, listening to the incidents of her day, doing what he can to make her comfortable and happy.

One day he runs into one of his former lovers and tells her about his life with Edith. "Oh, how nice!" Alison exclaims. "You have what you've always wanted, a woman with a child's face and a child's dependency. You don't have to worry about her running around because she's numb, and you don't have to worry about her running away because she has no legs. She's utterly housebound, utterly subject, utterly passive. Just what you wanted" (pp. 264–65).

After hearing the story in all its agonizing detail, Dolores is haunted by the image of Edith, the woman she has never met. "She kept seeing the woman with a girl's face and a blue hair ribbon in her yellow hair smiling and nodding. 'Victor says the economy will not improve for a while,' . . . 'Victor says that book is trash.' From across the room the woman smiled at Victor, smiled sweetly, secure at last in the indomitable power of weakness" (p. 267). In this novel, which probes the hidden complexities of the power struggle between the sexes, Edith represents the passive, subjugated woman whom, according to French, men secretly desire. Fighting back earned her nothing but Victor's contempt. She wins him at last only by inspiring his pity and guilt, by asking for nothing and accepting his homage to her helplessness.

Undeniably, French raises a valid issue. She seeks to expose a destructive pattern common to many relationships between men and women, a pattern in which the woman must yield her autonomy and be strong only in secret, behind a veneer of feminine frailty. Yet, to make her point, French exploits the disabled woman as a symbol of everything that is wrong between women and men.

Edith is submissive and asexual. "Even though I feel nothing there now," she tells her husband, "I want you to have what you want" (p. 260). With her sweet smile and her empty hands folded on her lap, murmuring platitudes about how her accident was worth it after all, Edith embodies many of the most debilitating stereotypes behind which disabled women lose their individual identities. When she loses the ability to walk, she also is robbed of her sexuality, her intellect, and her sense of self. French, speaking through Victor and Dolores, never suggests that a woman who becomes paraplegic might lead an active, interesting life, or that her personality could remain unaltered. Like Laura Wingfield, Edith Morrisey is not only physically impaired but emotionally stunted as well. Her disability is equated with complete passive dependency.

If Delores is a contemporary heroine, Edith is her antithesis. The non-disabled reader, identifying closely with Dolores, will be outraged that Victor prefers Edith's helplessness to Dolores' fire. For me, however, and I think for most other disabled readers, Edith exemplifies all of the negative images that have helped to stifle our growth toward equality. From a writer like Marilyn French, so eloquent, so expressive of the struggles of most women, we who are disabled had a right to expect far more.

HEROINES LOST AND FOUND

In my quest for disabled heroines, I found myself seeking women with the traits that make French's Dolores such a powerful figure: wit and intelligence, integrity, passion and strength. As a demonstration of these characteristics, the heroine who is disabled must accept her impairment without apology and find a place for herself in the world. Not surprisingly, therefore, I was confronted with few viable choices as I tried to select two thoroughly positive characters for discussion.

Miss M., the narrator of Walter de la Mare's (1922, 1941) *Memoirs of a Midget*, warranted serious consideration. Like Dolores, she demands utter honesty in her relationships with others and is unflinching as she reveals the truth about herself. Her interests range over poetry, the stars, and the art of tying knots. Although her diminutive stature makes her an object of curiosity and even ridicule, she never regards herself as anything less than a whole person.

Memoirs of a Midget is marred, however, in one significant respect. The book's prologue, attributed to one of Miss M.'s close friends, explains that the memoirs are being published following her uncanny disappearance. By the close of the novel, the mystery is explained by implication. Miss M. has joined her friend Mr. Anon, also a little person, and together they have escaped to the island of their fantasies, where all the people, the houses, and even the forests are of their own size. Throughout the book Miss M. is intensely real, a young woman struggling to find truth and love amid the world's hypocrisy; yet to grant her a happy ending, de la Mare transports her to a land of make-believe. The message is unmistakable: for a woman as different as Miss M., this world can never be a true home.

Like Miss M., Sarah Norman in Medoff's (1980) drama *Children of a Lesser God* manages to hang onto her dignity and self-respect. Profoundly deaf since birth and communicating exclusively in Sign, she is unable (or, according to her teachers, unwilling) to learn to speak. When she marries a hearing man she discovers that he, too, is not satisfied with her as she is; he wants her to speak aloud, to be like everyone else. Like Robert Browning, he wants to be the agent of her miraculous cure. Sarah finally leaves him, recognizing that they can find no common ground. She cannot resolve her existence as a deaf woman with her need to meet the expectations of the hearing world.

Similarly, Janice Ryder in Greenberg's (1970) *In This Sign* and Clare Thompson in Twersky's (1953) *The Face of the Deep* are vivid and moving characters who, in their youth at least, believe that life can be rich and fulfilling, notwithstanding their disabilities. Both of these women, however, are so battered by society's ostracism that they become figures of tragedy. Though each survives with an unquenchable spark of vitality, neither is the sort of heroine one would want to emulate.

Of all of the women with disabilities I have met in plays and novels, only two approach the true heroine I dreamed of as an adolescent. I hope that my brief discussion may convey some part of the excitement and delight I felt when I discovered Wyn Harper in Margaret Kennedy's (1964) *Not in the Calendar* and Liesl of Robertson Davies' (1970, 1972, 1975) *Deptford Trilogy.*

"A VERY RUM LITTLE CUSTOMER"

Not in the Calendar is one of those utterly remarkable novels that, for some unaccountable reason, are overlooked and forgotten by critics and the reading public alike. Published in 1964, just before the women's movement gained momentum, it is in its quiet way a rallying cry for feminism. Among the women in Kennedy's gallery of minor characters are childish, pampered Lallie; Ida the maid, with dreams of rising to a higher station in life; and Daphne, with her unsettling habit of slipping long confessional letters beneath the doors of houseguests. All of them are drawn with affection and understanding, and none relies upon men in her quest for fulfillment.

The protagonist is Carrie Knevett, introduced in 1883 at the age of 8 and followed until her death in 1938. Carrie is the sort of saint who is not to be found in the calendar. She is a woman who never forgets the painful lesson learned in childhood: that she must ignore the dictates of others and follow her own heart instead.

The misfit child of a large upper-class English family, Carrie makes friends with Winsome Harper, the deaf daughter of her father's kennelman. (Winsome, like her sisters Dainty and Dolly, is named for a hound.) The novel revolves around this friendship, which, although almost destroyed by the opposition of Carrie's family, endures for a lifetime.

Winsome is eventually taken into the home of the wealthy Seddon family to be a companion to their deaf daughter, Myra. Myra's tutor, Christine, gives her the more respectable name Wyn, teaches her to read and to write, struggles to instruct her in speech, and discovers her extraordinary talent for painting. Within a few short years, the grimy kennelman's child, once considered an idiot by everyone but Carrie, is studying art at a Paris conservatory.

Christine is at first apprehensive, afraid that Wyn will be overwhelmed by the strain of student life. As Wyn flings herself into this new world, her teacher reflects that she "accepted her affliction, was resigned to its discipline, but she would recognize no stigma of inferiority. . . . The girl had emerged as . . . a very rum little customer, standing valiantly and precariously upon her own two feet" (Kennedy 1964:94).

As a young woman, Wyn accepts Christine's view that "for most decent men, they (Wyn and Myra) are nuns. Their affliction placed a gulf between them and other people in which desire was likely to founder" (p. 83). Wyn realizes that there are men among her fellow art students whom she might sleep with if she chose, but she concludes that "she was never likely to get a man worth having, and she preferred to be a nun" (p. 86).

It is not her deafness alone that makes Wyn an unlikely candidate for marriage. Not conventionally attractive, she is a large woman with "a square, suety face," and a personality that many find abrasive. She is fiercely loyal to those she loves, but she has no patience with shallowness and hypocrisy; she refers to the society ladies who buy her paintings as "cows." Wyn is as strong-willed as Edith Morrisey is compliant—hardly the sort of mate many men would select, especially at the turn of the century.

Yet, unlike Laura Wingfield, Wyn is never portrayed as a figure of pathos because she has no romantic attachment. None of the marriages in the novel are very appealing, and Kennedy conveys the distinct impression that Wyn hasn't missed much. What makes her life rich, and to some even enviable, is her dedication to her work, and the depth of her friendships—especially her friendship with Carrie Knevett.

Carrie was the first human being with whom Wyn could communicate, and throughout their lives she is the only person to whom she can speak clearly and comfortably. At times their awareness of each other's thoughts and feelings leaps beyond the restrictions of speech or Sign to become almost wholly intuitive. Wyn, however, does not allow herself to be dependent upon Carrie as an intermediary between herself and the hearing world. She insists that Carrie must lead her own life, even when separation from her is agony. She hires an interpreter to help her deal in public, and she cultivates a lively assortment of artistic friends who admire her work and appreciate her wry humor.

Like Wyn, Carrie never marries, preferring the freedom of life as a single woman. Wyn is clearly an influence in her professional life when Carrie decides to become a teacher of the deaf. In her relationship with Wyn, however, Carrie is never a martyr. As children they approached one another as equals across the chasm of language and class difference. The love and respect they share grow deeper and stronger with the passing years.

Even after her paintings earn international acclaim, Wyn seeks to conceal from the general public the fact that she is deaf. She fears that she will be categorized as a deaf artist and will never be able to compete with other painters on their own terms. Though Christine and Carrie are fighting to demonstrate that deaf children can benefit from education, that their potential must not be wasted, Wyn refuses to step forward and join in the struggle. She expresses only contempt for "dirty deaf children," a covert loathing for the untaught, unloved child she herself once was.

Wyn and Carrie are in their fifties when they travel together back to the village of their childhood. Wyn is overwhelmed by long-suppressed memories, living once more the misery and aching loneliness of the first years of her life. Yet, once she has confronted the ghosts that have haunted her for so long, she is finally free of them. She recognizes fully that she has left Winsome far behind her. She is now a renowned artist, a woman who has built a life rich and rewarding. At last she is ready to endorse Carrie's school for deaf children. Without feeling compromised or devalued, she can speak for the needs of deaf people everywhere.

In the novels and plays I have examined, Wyn Harper is one of the few disabled women whose life combines professional achievements and the satisfaction of deep and enduring friendship. Furthermore, she is almost alone in her resolution of the conflict between self-acceptance and assimilation into the world of non-disabled people—a conflict few writers even acknowledge. She may be eccentric and lacking in social graces, but Kennedy never paints her as an object of pity or contempt. Wyn demands that the world accept her as she is. In the end she is not merely accepted, but respected and loved.

"AN AFTERMATH OF HEALING TENDERNESS"

I thought I had found all of the novels and plays necessary to prepare for this paper when an acquaintance suggested, with no further explanation, that I shouldn't begin until I read *World of Wonders*, by Robertson Davies (1975). Although it was the third part of Davies' *Deptford Trilogy*, I pounced on it at once in what was by then my obsessive quest for disabled heroines.

From the first I sensed that I lacked a certain background. Not having read the earlier books in the series, I found it difficult to sort out the relationships among the world-famous magician Magnus Eisengrim, his friends Ramsey and Liesl, and the two film producers who are making a movie in which Eisengrim is to star. But as Eisengrim began regaling them with the account of his personal history I read on eagerly, awaiting the appearance of the disabled woman I had been promised.

Sure enough, there she was—Happy Hannah, the fat lady in the World of Wonders Carnival, which Magnus joins at the age of ten. Maternal and tough, a dedicated student of Scripture and a connoisseur of human nature, Hannah is the only nurturing figure in his tormented adolescence. Of course she does display herself as a carnival freak, and she has a core of loneliness and despair that prevents her from assuming proper heroine stature, but overall Hannah manages to project a thoroughly positive impression.

At last Eisengrim leaves World of Wonders and attaches himself to a troupe of traveling players. In amazement and delight, I realized that Davies hadn't been recommended to me because of Hannah after all. The really important disabled woman in *World of Wonders* was clearly Madame Tresize, the aging actress, still performing despite her lameness and the progressive loss of her sight. Magnus becomes her adoring servant, enthralled by her refinement and dignity, deeply moved by her devotion to her actor husband. After the sordid life of the carnival, she is proof that human beings still can be gentle and pure. He cherishes every smile, each kind word she drops his way, and refers to her always as "My Lady."

In some ways even Madame Tresize failed to meet my standards. She goes to elaborate lengths to conceal her impairments from the public, indicating that she has not come to terms with them herself. But, like Hannah, she is a woman of character, worthy of admiration and respect.

I read on, marveling that *World of Wonders* had yielded not one, but two, positive images of disabled women. I had nearly reached the close of the novel when I was seized by the greatest revelation of all. The heroine I awaited was neither Hannah nor My Lady. She had been with me through the entire book, and Davies hadn't given a clue by which I could recognize her. Only in the final thirty pages did I learn at last the story of Liesl—Lieselotte Vitzliputzli.

They are all listening and offering periodic comments as Magnus continues his tale—the two filmmakers, Ramsey, and Liesl herself. Magnus recounts how, in his early twenties, he is employed by an elderly Swiss nobleman to repair a valuable collection of nineteenth-century mechanical toys. They have been smashed, twisted, and trampled to bits, and as he begins the meticulous task of identifying the thousands of tiny springs and wheels, arms and heads, he wonders whose fury could have wrought such savage destruction. As the weeks pass he senses he is being observed, and one day he catches sight of someone peering in through the window. "The watcher was a very odd creature indeed," he explains, "a sort of monkey, I thought. So I waved to it and grinned, as one does at monkeys. . . . I knew that with monkeys the first rule is never to show surprise or alarm. . . . The only thing you can do is to keep still and quiet and ready for anything. I spoke to it in conventional German."

"You spoke in a vulgar Austrian lingo," says Liesl. "And you took the patronizing tone of an animal trainer. Do you have any idea what it is like to be spoke to in the way people speak to animals?" (Davies 1975:279–80).

It was Liesl who, in a whirlwind of rage, had smashed all of those prim, dainty Victorian wind-up dolls, out of "pure bloody-mindedness. For which I had good cause. . . . I looked like an ape. I still look like an ape, but I have made my apishness serve me, and now it doesn't really matter. But it mattered then [at the age of 17]. . . . It mattered more than the European war, more than anybody's happiness" (p. 281).

At this point Liesl becomes the narrator, filling in the details of her past before she proceeds with that explosive first meeting with Magnus. Orphaned at the age of 11, she lived a conventional life with her wealthy grandfather. When she was 14 a doctor determined that she had a rare growth disorder, and that she would become a giant unless she underwent a series of X-ray treatments. The treatments halted her growth at 5 feet 11 inches, but "one cannot hope to escape such an experience wholly unscathed. The side effects were that I had huge feet and hands, a disfiguring thickening of the skull and jaw, and surely one of the ugliest faces anyone has ever seen. But wasn't I lucky not to be a giant as well!" (p. 282). In addition, her speech became hoarse and difficult to control, until it sounded to her like the bark of a dog. "What was I to do? I was young and very strong, and I could rage and destroy" (p. 283).

Liesl's destruction of her grandfather's antique toys is merely one episode of this all-consuming anger. When Magnus catches sight of her and speaks to her in that patronizing tone, she shatters the window of the workshop and leaps upon him, wrestling him to the floor. He is stronger than she expects, and soon he sits astride her chest, pinning her arms at her sides.

From this unlikely beginning, they form a deep and lasting friendship. "I soon realized that he spoke my language," Liesl recalls. "I mean that he asked intelligent questions and expected sensible answers. He was also extremely rude. . . . 'Can't you speak better than that?' he demanded. And when I said I couldn't, he simply said, 'You're not trying. You're making the worst of it in order to seem horrible. You're not horrible, you're just stupid, so cut it out'" (p. 285).

In the weeks that follow, Liesl's feeling for Magnus ripens into an intense attraction, and soon they become lovers. With his help she learns to speak clearly once more. As she watches him rebuild the toys, instilling in them a certain magic they did not possess before, he brings her to a sense of wonder she has never known.

Although Magnus has transformed her life, she does not cling to him out of fear and desperation. She realizes they will remain great friends and lovers, but that they are not destined to settle down as a bourgeois married couple. "When I gained enough confidence to go out into the world again I was happy in a casual physical way with quite a few people," Liesl explains, "and some of the best of them were of my own sex" (p. 293).

Not all of her liaisons are casual, however, I learned when I finally read the first two volumes of the trilogy, *Fifth Business* and *The Manticore*. Not only does she remain close to Magnus throughout her life, but she forms intimate, enduring bonds with two other men—Dunstan Ramsey and David Staunton. In each instance the relationship is forged out of turmoil. But, as Ramsey remembers, thinking back upon the first night they spent together, "Never have I known such deep delight nor such an aftermath of healing tenderness" (Davies 1970:262).

In a sense, Magnus Eisengrim brings about Liesl's rebirth, enabling her to cast aside her ruinous anger and become the wise, capable, sardonic yet loving woman we meet in these three novels. In her turn, Liesl aids in the rebirths of Ramsey and Staunton. She shows Ramsey that in his life of selfless dedication to others he has not allowed himself to be quite human. "There's a whole great piece of your life that is unlived, denied, set aside. . . . Why don't you just for once do something inexplicable, irrational—the Devil's bidding, just for the hell of it? You'd be a different man!" (Davies 1970:260).

The mothering metaphor is especially evident in Liesl's relationship with David Staunton. On a climbing expedition in the Alps she leads him into a deep underground cavern where ancient religious rites were once celebrated. David is terrified of the cave and unmoved by the row of bear skulls along the wall. When she forces him ahead of her half a mile along a tortuous tunnel, he emerges at last into the clean mountain air, touched for the first time in his life by a sense of awe.

Like Magnus, Ramsey and Staunton are initially repulsed by Liesl's physical appearance, but all three soon become accustomed to her face and relate to her without discomfort. As Liesl says herself, by now her disfigurement doesn't really matter.

Davies' Trilogy is immensely complex, and Liesl is imbued with enough flaws and contradictions to make her convincingly human. She assumes many roles, drawing out confidences, imparting acid bits of truth and wisdom, and praying in the Alpine cave at the altar of the ancients. She has a purely practical side as well, serving as manager, or "autocrat," behind the scenes of Magnus's traveling magic show. Although her appearance in each volume of the trilogy is relatively brief, she somehow takes on the dimensions of a major character, a woman who has lived to the fullest and has earned the unqualified love of those around her.

It is significant that so many of the women Davies creates have disabilities: Hannah, Madame Tresize, Liesl, and Magnus's mother, Mary Dempster, who becomes mentally ill after she is struck on the head by a snowball containing a stone. All of them are portrayed as gentle, dignified, tender, and caring. In fact, Ramsey is convinced that Mrs. Dempster is, quite literally, a saint. By contrast, the non-disabled women in the trilogy (with the notable exceptions of Ramsey's former lover Diana and Staunton's female therapist) are shallow, childish, scheming, or generally ineffectual. Is Davies perhaps straying perilously close to the "saint" side of the saint-or-sinner dichotomy? Does he obliquely suggest that a woman who is impaired can achieve a depth of character unnecessary to her non-disabled sisters, or somehow simply beyond their reach?

It is a nettling thought. But when I consider the texture of Liesl's characterization, my confidence in Davies is restored. Whatever his purpose, he has given the world a character whose disability in no way humbles or hampers her, a heroine in the truest sense of the word.

SOME FINAL THOUGHTS

When I think about the images of disabled women in literature, it is tempting to focus on the most negative, to dredge up one deplorable example after another. Fortunately, a few writers such as Kennedy and Davies have helped to balance the account. Wyn Harper and Lieselotte Vitzliputzli are not only unique as disabled characters; they stand out among women in contemporary literature. Never dominated by men, never bowing to social stigma based on disability or sex, they build independent lives enriched by deeply rewarding work and friendship. Without resentment, they live beyond the confines of convention, yet they gain the world's acceptance and respect.

Neither Wyn nor Liesl lives out the marriage plot that, according to Brownstein, is so crucial to most women in novels. They can serve as models for those who seek affirmation beyond being chosen and won by a man. Vital as it is to find characters who so successfully break with tradition, I am still left with a sense that something is missing. Nowhere in my reading have I encountered a disabled woman whose story ends in the usual way, with a happy, conventional marriage. Wonderful though they are, even Wyn and Liesl subtly reinforce the notion that a woman with a disability cannot fit into the traditional female roles of wife and mother.

As women explore an ever wider range of options, we need more characters, disabled or non-disabled, whose lives reflect the array of choices open to us. In order to feel that we can choose to carve out new roles in this changing world, we must know that the option to follow tradition is ours as well. Non-disabled women may, together, be outgrowing the marriage plot; but I, for one, would still warm to the story of a blind woman or a woman with cerebral palsy who falls in love, gets married, and lives happily ever after.

Ironically, of all of the plays and novels I read for this chapter, none was written by a woman who is herself disabled. Though a number of disabled women have written autobiographies, few, if any, have ventured to translate their experiences into fiction and drama. As the struggles of disabled women draw increasing attention through scholarly studies and autobiographical accounts, perhaps women with impairments will feel more free to express themselves in literary forms accessible to the general public. It is my hope that in the decades ahead we will create our own heroines: women whose lives hold meaning not merely for those of us who are disabled, but strike a universal chord with the joys and heartbreaks of women everywhere.

References

Besier, R. 1930. *The Barretts of Wimpole Street.* Boston: Little, Brown.

Brownstein, R. 1982. *Becoming a heroine: Reading about women in novels.* New York: Viking.

Davies, R. 1970. *Fifth business.* New York: Viking.

———. 1972. *The manticore.* New York: Penguin.

———. 1975. *World of wonders.* Middlesex, England: Penguin.

de la Mare, W. 1941 (1922). *Memoirs of a midget.* New York: A. Knopf, The Reader's Club.

Dickens, C. 1971 (1845). Cricket on the hearth, in *Christmas Books.* New York: Collins.

French, M. 1980. *The bleeding heart.* New York: Ballantine.

Gide, A. 1959 (1931). *Pastoral symphony.* New York: Alfred A. Knopf.

Greenberg, J. 1970. *In this sign.* New York: Holt, Rinehart.

Hathaway, K. B. 1943. *The little locksmith.* New York: Coward-McCann.

Kata, E. 1961. *A patch of blue.* New York: Popular Library.

Kennedy, M. 1964. *Not in the calendar.* New York: Macmillan.

Medoff, M. 1980. *Children of a lesser god.* Clifton, N.J.: James T. White and Co.

Sontag, S. 1967. *Death kit.* New York: New American Library.

Trevor, W. 1973. *Elizabeth alone.* New York: Viking.

Trollope, A. 1963 (1857). *Barchester towers.* New York: New American Library.

Twersky, J. 1953. *The face of the deep.* New York, Cleveland: World.

Wharton, E. 1970. *Ethan Frome.* New York: Scribners.

Williams, T. 1945. *The glass menagerie.* New York: New Classics.

II: Disabled Women in Relationships

A major contribution of feminist theory of the past decade has been to demonstrate the centrality of relationships in the lives of women.[1] The chapters in this section are organized around the idea of relationships, addressing hitherto unasked questions about how disabled women fare in and experience their relationships. The first two chapters give glimpses into what growing up with a disability means for a young girl in her relationships with her parents. Although there are personal accounts and social science reports of parenting disabled girls and boys,[2] few mention the gender of the children studied and fewer still suggest that the children's gender made a difference. Perhaps disability overwhelmed every other characteristic of the child, either for the parents or for the social scientists. Perhaps parents of children with disabilities, like most parents of non-disabled children, hold many of the same expectations for their preadolescent children regardless of gender. Parents, school, and society generally allow children a wider latitude to develop until the onset of puberty. Virtually all the accounts of parents and of social researchers into the lives of parents and children with disabilities stop before the children reach puberty.

In studies of the mother-daughter relationship, there has not yet been any examination of whether that relationship is altered in character if the daughter has a disability from birth. Integrating psychoanalytic and disability rights perspectives, Adrienne Harris and Dana Wideman here reexamine existing psychoanalytic data and accounts of parent-child relationships to explore the possible meaning of childhood disability for that most significant early attachment. Harilyn Rousso expands our knowledge of the parent-child relationship by looking at how parental expectations influenced their adolescent daughters' social and sexual lives. Working from a small sample of women with disabilities and from interviews with parents of disabled women, she reports that as adults, the daughters regarded parents' expectations as highly significant psychological factors in adolescence.

111

Several recent books join an extensive literature attesting to the preciousness of friendships among women, regardless of their attachments to men.[3] Just as disability has not been considered in feminist analysis, talk of friendship has been absent from most discussions of the lives of women or men with disabilities. Perhaps this latter omission derives from a research focus on the effect of disability on the lives of non-disabled people, rather than on the lives of disabled people themselves. Redressing this gap in feminist and disability scholarship, Berenice Fisher and Roberta Galler reflect on their own thirty-year friendship and on other pairs of disabled and non-disabled friends to discover the impact of disability on the relationship. This chapter demonstrates that disability in friendship only highlights and dramatizes issues that beset all important personal relationships—issues of interdependence, reciprocity, discrimination in the world, and real differences in life circumstances as obstacles to be overcome.

Addressing the expectations of the community, Marilynn Phillips presents a case study of how one woman's experience of a polio-related disability was shaped by her working-class and Polish-Catholic origins. Like the nuclear family, the ethnic community can exert powerful influences on the development of social and sexual self-confidence. Phillips' subject vividly recalls her attempts to reconcile her self-image with the values of the people among whom she lives.

There is woefully little information on the role of intimate couple relationships in the lives of disabled women.[4] We acknowledge that this volume does not sufficiently address the omission, but we predict that this reticence will not continue much longer. As more disabled people reveal more about their lives (and they are beginning to do so), they will address the conflicts and rewards of building intimate partnerships. This section concludes with a study by Barbara Levy Simon of women who have never been married and who have a disability. Simon writes of disability in women more than 65 years old, a period in life when physical limitation is nearly a majority experience. Disability, she notes, draws these never-married women away from the margins; once estranged from other women because of their single status in a coupled world, they now share a powerful connection with other women in their age group.

Notes

1. Three feminist classics advancing significant views about relationships for women are J. B. Miller, *Toward a New Psychology of Women* (Boston: Beacon, 1976); N. J. Chodorow, *The Reproduction of Mothering* (Berkeley: University of California Press, 1978); C. Gilligan, *In a Different Voice: Psychological Theory and Women's Development* (Boston: Harvard University Press, 1982).

2. Among the best of parent narratives of life with their disabled children are M. Killilea, *Karen* (New York: Dell, 1952); M. Killilea, *With Love from Karen* (New York: Dell, 1960); T. F. Spradley and J. P. Spradley, *Deaf Like Me* (New York: Random House, 1978); M. N. Jablow, *Cara: Grow with a Retarded Child* (Philadelphia: Temple University Press, 1982); R. Massie and S. Massie, *Journey* (New York: Alfred A. Knopf, 1984); H. R. Turnbull III and A. P. Turnbull, *Parents Speak Out*, 2d ed. (Columbus: Charles E. Merrill, 1985). For some representative social science treatments of raising children with disabilities, see R. H. Barsuch, *The Parent of the Handicapped Child: A Study of Child-Rearing Practices* (Springfield, Illinois: Charles C. Thomas, 1968); R. B. Darling, *Families against Society: A Study of Reactions to Children with Birth Defects* (Beverly Hills, California: Sage, 1979); E. Roskies, *Abnormality and Normality: The Mothering of Thalidomide Children* (Ithaca, New York: Cornell University Press, 1972).

3. Recent books on women's friendships are L. B. Rubin, *Just Friends: The Role of Friendship in Our Lives* (New York: Harper and Row, 1985); J. D. Block and D. Greenberg, *Women and Friendship* (New York: Franklin Watts, 1985); J. Raymond, *A Passion for Friends: Towards a Philosophy of Female Affection* (Boston: Beacon, 1986); L. C. Pogrebin, *Among Friends: Who We Like, Why We Like Them and What We Do with Them* (New York: McGraw-Hill, 1987). These and other books are reviewed by C. Heilbrun, "The Future of Friendship," *The Women's Review of Books* 3, no. 9, (June 1986), p. 1, 3–4.

4. For comments on how autobiographies of disabled women and men characterize partner relationships, see A. Asch and L. Sacks, "Lives Without, Lives Within: The Autobiographies of Blind Women and Men," *Journal of Visual Impairment and Blindness* 77, no. 6 (June 1983), pp. 242–47; H. Hahn, "The Good Parts: Interpersonal Relationships in the Autobiographies of Physically Disabled Persons," *Wenner-Gren Foundation Working Papers in Anthropology* (December 1983), pp. 1–38.

4. The Construction of Gender and Disability in Early Attachment

ADRIENNE HARRIS and DANA WIDEMAN

In the first moment of any infant's life, child and culture meet up in the matter of gender. The first *social* task of the surrounding adults, who up to this point have been engaged in the physical aspects of childbirth, is to deliver the child into the sex-gender system. What this means for a female infant is that from the first moments of life she is ushered into and assigned a place in a system of rules, roles, and meanings. This system is perhaps better thought of as a code with one overriding, relentless feature: a woman's position is denigrated, undervalued, and organized around absence and lack.

Infancy studies in child development give a good picture of the intricate and subtle patterns of interaction through which a gender position is communicated to children. Gender is really one of those powerful prisms through which we see and understand our children. There is a stunning example of this in a research study where half the participants were told that the 15-day-old infant seen on a videotape was male and the other half, that the child was female (Condry and Condry 1976). Everyone was asked to rate this child on some simple physical parameters. How active, how irritable, how alert did they find this infant? What is striking is that, from the point of view of adults in our culture, gender assignments *create* major judgments of difference. The label of "boy" or "girl" applied to the same infant produced radically different behavioral ratings. There are different theories to account for how the child comes to understand and experience itself as a gendered person. It is a complex process, never mere passive conditioning, but we must start with an awareness of the power and presence of the sex-gender system in the minds and behavior of parents and of the larger culture.

115

In this chapter we want to think about the particular developmental demands on young female children for whom the absorption and development of gender identity is intertwined with another complex social fact, disability.

This essay proceeds with several crucial presuppositions, about disability, about gender, and about the use of mainstream psychology and psychoanalysis. First, both disability and gender, whatever the material or biological base, are most crucially understood as socially constructed and historically mediated categories of experience (Gliedman and Roth 1980). A disability has a social meaning and it is that indisputable fact that constitutes the major difficulty for disabled people and their families. Second, social stigma, negative labels, and social processes may be internalized and become aspects of intrapsychic life, both conscious and unconscious (Goffman 1963). Third, if internalization occurs, it is not passive nor mere behavioral conditioning, but an active construction of experience. The route from social stigma to internal psychic experience is complex, problematic, not inevitable, and never passive mirroring. The consequences of disability and disability as it interacts with gender will be understood only in the light of careful exploration of the interacting social, historical, and psychodynamic forces.

PSYCHOLOGY IN RELATION TO DISABILITY: THE PUZZLE OF IDEOLOGY

The dilemma in writing this chapter is a familiar one to feminist social scientists. The tools we use must be criticized even as they are brought to bear upon the phenomena that interest us. It is an article of belief in mainstream psychology, and often in orthodox psychoanalysis, that these disciplines are value-neutral, that such theories develop free from the influence of cultural factors, economic and political interests, and other social forces. It is important to demystify psychological theories, to see, that is, that they are loaded with values, interests, and assumptions of normality that derive from the dominant culture.

Psychological theories have an ideological function. This means that in creating norms of behavior and development and insisting that these are scientifically derived norms, social facts and values are transformed into natural and universal facts. In the case of women and other people made marginal by the dominant culture, these theories have been part of the problem, not the solution. Psychological theories have had a history as part of the cultural apparatus that keeps socially devalued persons in place. One of the ways mainstream psychology has functioned as ideological distortion lies in its tendency to locate pathology of personality within the individual. This can mean a subtle or not-so-subtle blaming of the victim when theory is invoked to name the experience of persons or groups at variance with the standard. "Paranoia is the hallmark of black patients," a well-established analyst once assured me, thereby eclipsing several centuries of racism.

Classical psychoanalytic thought treats disability as a precursor to narcissistic disorders, and a compromise to very early primary narcissism. Within a classical framework in psychoanalysis, the individual's experience of disability is viewed only as a negative aspect of self-image, as a defense against genetic weakness, almost inherently and inevitably a feature of the individual's psychic life. History and the social context for experience are washed out. The analytic approach organizes itself almost exclusively around the concept of disability as a symptom. Absence of overt conflict is too often read as denial; the development of strengths and competencies, as avoidance or reaction formation. There is little scope in analytic treatment of disability for any vision of transcendence or empowerment or resistance to normative structures and ideals.

I want to argue later that this use of psychoanalysis is a betrayal of the theory and of the disabled persons it is addressed to. Listening to parents' accounts of analytic interpretations in which the parent always feels excluded, blamed, and manipulated by theory, it is hard not to suspect that many professionals working with disability use theory to distance themselves from the disabled persons and their families, that theory is being used to lull the therapist's anxiety rather than to illuminate (Turnbull and Turnbull 1978).

Another ideological feature within psychology, contributing to the dilemma of understanding individuals within history and society, is the importance ascribed to early experience, indeed to very early experience. In the 1960s, for example, developmental psychology was overtaken by research and writing on what was termed the "competent" infant. There is a clear ideological operation in this work that records and affirms the installation of social control and rationality at earlier and earlier points in the developmental cycle, a process that rationalizes, individualizes, and familiarizes psychological life (Harris, 1987). Donzelot (1980), for example, has argued that this ideological movement, accomplished in pediatrics, education, and social life over the course of the past century, leaves the mother in a curious and contradictory position. Through the mediating activities of the child experts' advice on the conduct of family life, she is empowered to act by the culture but is scapegoated as the primary problem in instances of pathology.

The responses, feelings, and self-understanding of many mothers of handicapped children bear witness to the ready assumption and internalization of these contradictions (Barsch 1968; Darling 1979; Roskies 1972; Turnbull and Turnbull 1978). Roskies' work on the mothers of children exposed to thalidomide early in the mothers' pregnancy documents the imposing demands on women, the mixture of authoritarian advice and lonely isolating alienation. In all these accounts the most punitive and difficult encounters are with members of the "psy" apparatus, educators and doctors and the psychological establishment at whose hands parents feel powerless, out of control, and nonetheless the center of responsibility and blame.

A psychological and psychoanalytic treatment that seeks to illuminate or examine the experience of early attachment of disabled female children and their mothers (for mothers are *practically*, although not essentially, the first primary figures) must negotiate this terrain with a strategy that holds a number of different perspectives simultaneously. We need to ask as deeply and reflectively as possible how early interactions of a disabled female child and her primary caretaker affect development without colluding with the woman-hating aspects of psychological theory. Such theory shears mothers from the social and interpersonal context, leaving certain absences unremarked (in particular that of the father, but also the larger culture through its institutions and social forms) and rendering the mother the often solitary, very often guilty focus of various forms of control and criticism.

The theoretical task is to critique the ideological features of the psychoanalytic focus on early experience while maintaining some commitment to the depth and richness of primary early conscious and unconscious experience. Excavating early trauma or conflict must not be used deterministically to consign any individual to some social or theoretical dead-ended space. Early trauma and the resulting conflicts it can set up do not rule out transcendence, and complex adult evolutions. In thinking of early experience for disabled infants and their parents, two features of this early relationship must be held in mind. First, it is a two-way process, an activity of imagination, projection, fantasy, and identification in which parent and child, with different levels of consciousness and sophistication, participate. Second, this process of attachment, which is the very heart and soul of identity formation, coincides in the case of a congenitally disabled infant with the enormously taxing process of adaptation the parents are making to the diagnosis they have been given and to the child to whom it has been applied.

Reading the accounts of parents (Barsch 1968; Bernheimer et al.

1983; Darling 1979) and the work on infant bonding with disabled children (Klaus and Kinnell 1976), one hears an absolutely human mix of love, grief, sadness, hatred, depression, and hope. Barsch's work on the families of disabled infants indicates that adaptation accompanies the process of childrearing; it does not precede it. Some parents report the first days and months of the disabled infant's life with a strong sense of duality, the fantasy of a non-disabled child alongside the actual infant. Although there are many differences in attachment that we can postulate depending on the type of disability and the social meaning attached to it, a number of sociocultural mechanisms may fail when a disabled child is born. Following the work of Klaus and Kinnell (1976), we can say that the parents' identity may be compromised, their ego threatened. In those trying moments the environment offers them no support; indeed, it may actually withdraw support. There are no rituals associated with the birth of a handicapped baby; rather, there may be confusion and frequently a public and personal silence. Under most circumstances the rituals and celebrations built around childbirth are aimed at enhancing both the parents' ego and the parent-infant relationship. The absence of this public and culturally significant affirmation may contribute to a sense of isolation and loneliness in parents, and especially in the mother, who is often the infant's primary caretaker (Breslau et al. 1982).

The issues of guilt and anger—the two emotional reactions experienced strongly by many parents—seem to be of paramount importance. One may speculate that those feelings, if unresolved or denied, may play an important role in projecting guilt and anger onto the baby. As in the case of any depressed parent, will the child introject that experienced depression in the other person, and to what extent will she use that introject in forming the core part of her early identity?

The process of attachment is just that, a process, with many other features in addition to depression. Klaus and Kinnell (1976) give a detailed account of the development and transitions in a mother's response to her child born with Down's syndrome. It is a rich, complex, emotional history, with implacable despair and terror, with hatred spoken of openly (hatred not of the baby, the mother says, but of what has happened to the baby), a sense of shame and guilt marbled throughout with expressions of love, of connectedness that increases in power as the process of attachment and identification unfolds. All parents must learn to "read" their baby, that is, to note the signals of sociability in their infant. Disability does not wipe out all these signals; they are manifold and subtle. Gaze, hand movement, smiling, cooing, the size of the infant and the appearance of vulnerability: all these signals engage parents in attaching and in assigning a shared identity and humanity to their infant (Lewis and Rosenblum 1976). The documentation of mothers' responses to disabled infants clearly marks both anguish and triumph.

Urwin's study of the language skills of two blind children, although focused on the unfolding of a cognitive skill, also documents the two phases of parental response (Urwin 1978). The parents of the children she observed were variously affected. In both cases there was a degree of depression, some tension in the marriages. Nonetheless, the play activities of these children were a remarkable aid to both social and cognitive development. Jumping games, games of calling and answering, developed in particular by one father who wished to promote independence and exploration in his child, had the triple effect of encouraging physical prowess, social cooperation, and self-esteem through language and vocal play.

Several points should be made at this juncture. First, love and hate, depression, ambivalence, and projected imaginings of one's infant are features of *all* parental responses, though not all features are conscious. Winnicott, among other psychoanalysts, has written frankly and clearly about the scope and depth of maternal ambivalence (Winnicott 1958). It may be that when a child is born with a disability, the disability becomes the focus for parental or maternal ambivalence. Or, it may be that the presence of disability and the combination of introspection and intervention that arises for parents in the wake of bearing a child with a disability means that the normal process of conflicted feelings towards the infant becomes more explicitly part of the parental discourse about that child.

Second, the magnitude of the experience of forming attachment and simultaneously integrating knowledge of the social and personal meaning of disability should be acknowledged. To minimize this process, along with its trauma and its transcendent aspects, is to diminish the large and substantial emotional work of which parents of disabled infants are amply capable. At the same time it must be noted how sparse the record is in considering the attachment experiences of disabled infants. Blachar and Meyers (1983) have reviewed the psychological literature on attachment and disability. They point out an interesting anomaly in the studies they reviewed. More frequently than with non-disabled mother-infant pairs, these studies focus on the mother's attachment, not the infant's. While we know something about the process of adaptation and bonding from the parents perspective, a perspective on the disabled infant is curiously absent from the proceedings. It is possible that this phenomena perpetuates the social experience of disabled people in rendering them less personed, less visible, less privileged in any particular social interaction. The disabled infant is eclipsed and somewhat negated as an intending, attaching being. What can be said, in respect to the disabled infant's attachment processes, is that the social matrix and the parents' intrapsychic, personal, and sometimes relational struggle may place great demands upon the infant.

Another difficulty in using psychological theory as an interpretive tool lies in the conventional social science predilection for generalization, prediction, and control. There is little *predictively* that psychoanalysis and psychological studies of early childhood and early parent-child interaction can fruitfully offer to an understanding of disability and gender development. The theories operate more authentically in the reflexive mode. That is, these theories and conceptual models gain relevance in some particularity. They allow historical reconstruction, they are interpreted and, usually in the clinical setting, interpreted in dialogue. Here, therefore, we can be only speculative and suggestive, imagining in the light of current work on early development, both clinical and empirical, how the social facts of disability and gender might affect parent-child interaction and the development of subjectivity, identity, and sexuality.

Reviewing the work on disability and personality from a psychological perspective, there is another difficulty. Psychoanalytic theory has had a particularly problematic position in work on disability. From direct evidence in the literature (Asch and Russo 1985) and indirect evidence in the reports of parents of disabled children (Turnbull and Turnbull 1978), it can be seen that the impact of a psychoanalytic approach has been primarily punitive. Professionals all too often use the theory as a weapon, reducing every rageful or angry expression to a manifestation of denial or avoidance. The major insight of psychoanalysis, that some forces or pressures on our behavior are unconscious, is too often used to bolster professional authority and undermine a parent's or a disabled child's experience of their own reality. This is a misuse of a powerful and complex theory. An appropriate use of this approach acknowledges unconscious process but must remain close to the person's experience if it is to be helpful in any serious way. In the experience of many disabled persons, psychoanalysis is one of the chief culprits in victim blaming, turning disability into symptom, operating in a reductionist strategy that ties cause and effect, disability and outcome in a simple linear, causal chain. In the Turnbulls' account of parents' experiences at the hands of professionals, you can see psychoanalytic theory used mostly as defense and rarely with the empathic listening that is, in fact, its hallmark. Thinking psychoanalytically, we have to ask what the meaning and experience of the disability is for the non-disabled observers. How much does the disability act as a lightning rod, a crucible for others' anxieties and projections? Feminists, after an initial repudiation of psychoanalysis for its role in the distortion of women's experience, have found that psychoanalysis refreshed and transformed by feminism is a powerful means of understanding the connections between gender, individuality, and consciousness. The same creative encounter of psychoanalytic theory and the radical critique of mainstream understanding of disability also will be important.

In the strategic task of correctly insisting on equal possibilities, and equal rights, a functional approach predominates. There is a decided weighting of studies (and there are many of them) that stress adaptive capacity, functional levels, and the more conscious forms of self-report and self-description. Currently the women's movement is evolving a theory and practice that insists simultaneously on equality and difference. We suggest that such an approach can be powerful for many groups consigned to the margins of social life, including women with disabilities. This approach insists on the commonality of capacities and possibilities for development for all humans but reserves also some place for difference and specificity. The particularity, the lived subjectivity of femininity and disability, need to be elaborated. Psychoanalysis, as a theory that takes seriously fantasy, resistance, the complex *actions* through which an individual internalizes her experience, may play a role in building this picture of difference.

In Darling's (1979) review of studies of disability, a study is reported that claimed significant levels of depression, manifest in the scores on Rorschach tests, for children with polio who required maintenance on iron lungs. Countering the claims of depression were other studies showing self-esteem and high functioning capacities. Perhaps we need to think that both readings of children in such situations may be helpful.

An analytic reading of the intrapsychic experience of such a life experience probes the emotional adaptations, conflicts, and consequences of a dramatic and extreme experience, where it is not hard to imagine that fear, rage at the ordeal of incarceration, and inhibition in contact with that machinery are normal responses. Such a reading entails no particular negative predictions about behavior or levels of functioning.

Analytic listening is a particularly disciplined activity that requires a tension between empathically imagining someone's experience on the basis of projection of a shared humanity and at the same time hearing difference, hearing the specific and unique features of another person's subjectivity. This is a central requirement for any psychoanalytic reading of disability by a therapist or theorist who is not disabled. It requires equality in the sense of imagining a commonality in wishes, aspirations, and fears. It also requires assumptions of difference as well as the ability to listen to the way disability is the lived experience of the individual.

In trying to understand as fully as possible the lived experience of the children stricken with polio and bound to the particular lifesaving machinery their condition demands, perhaps we need to try and imagine ourselves into that experience, the enforced inhibition, the limits on activity and mobility, the physical powerlessness in relation to machinery and to the bodily experience of paralysis. Freed to imagine the intensity of the child's rage or anxiety, we may see, too, the passionate intensity to master the experience, a mastery, which in clinical practice, one often sees having both transcendent and debilitating aspects. It is remarkable, for example, how often children faced with disappointing, disappointed, or malevolent people in powerful positions in their lives internalize these figures as an aspect of self. Badness or malevolence often seems to be less dangerous if it is experienced as contained inside the self, rather than loose in the world. Listening to children or adults recalling the struggle to master difficult, painful, or terrifying experiences, it is striking how variable the subjective understandings and adaptations are, how rich the mixture of fantasy, soaring transcendence, denial, and sadistic rage, attesting to the astonishing power of the individual's imaginative resources. How does a disabled child hear and incorporate the socially experienced and socially generated sense of the disability and its meaning?

We will make a careful and strong brief for the importance of the intrapsychic dimension to any deep understanding of human behavior. The psychological approach at its best—which here means its most dialectical—asks about the consequence of experience for inner life, insists on attention to the level of fantasy and unconscious processes, and asks us to consider that all people use the consequences of their experience, often in the form of internal objects, sometimes parental images, voices, or scripts, to make sense of who they are and to operate in the world. But to use such intentional language is to make an account too focused on conscious processes. Individuals constitute these inner worlds in the very act of social relationships; consciousness is the outcome of the attachment experiences. Children gain their first experience of identity by being mirrored. That is, they experience identity first as reflected identity, feeling about themselves in some relation to how they are treated and seen. These primary figures and primary modes of relating that constitute personality arise in largely unconscious ways. Several clinical examples may illuminate this point.

A woman who contracted polio as a child speaks of the problematic necessity to demonstrate at all times and at all costs capacities and functional competence. She felt that it was impossible to speak or even to think very clearly about difficulty, about the physical demands of functioning, about the gloomier underbelly of human experience and growth. You don't learn easily to know your body, its limits, its pains, its signals of stress. Acknowledging anguish, doubt, pain, or anger leads too easily down the slippery slope to larger domains of feeling, to a depression or rage that may feel debilitating or endless. This is true for many people. It is perhaps doubly dangerous for disabled people. The defenses of splitting and denial in the service of the necessity to demonstrate total functional capability can themselves be costly and energy draining. None of these comments or ruminations need end in victim blaming or scapegoating, or the maintaining of ghettoization or marginality for a disabled person. Rather, these speculations take seriously the impact and psychic cost of a major life experience, be it the trauma of an illness or the socially mirrored understanding and experience of a disability. The danger from an analytic point of view is not in acknowledging the mixture of love, desire, hate, greed, and terror that constitutes (in all the flowering differences of individual subjectivities) personal life at a profound level, but rather in its denial.

The costs of denial can be seen in the following account of clinical work with the younger surviving brother of a man with hemophilia. From early childhood, this man, now in middle age, was told by his family that he had himself avoided the disorder by virtue of being a twin. He describes the central feature of his inner life as a feeling of badness, a feeling that arose before there was language to describe it, an inchoate sense of something badly wrong with him. Two other experiences of self appear: they are early and persistent memories. He is the caretaker, a person with a job, not a life. His job is to watch and care for his siblings, in particular his brother. Second, it is not possible to be sick. Even minor colds evoke terror and a sense of disorganization. His experience of his mother is of someone remote and desperate, someone holding everything together but likely to fall apart in the face of any demand. This man grew up in an economically pressed family that had few social and personal tools for understanding their situation and that was psychologically constituted to avoid any help or intervention. One can indeed imagine the atmosphere of chronic emergency and depressed anxiety that must have characterized family life.

For this man, the experience of maleness and illness are almost inextricably intertwined. At the same time, the connection between body and feelings was denied. His terror of illness and bodily collapse is explicitly connected to memories of his brother's endless physical pain and to the danger of any disruptive physical experience. He remembers being told he could kill his brother if he hit him. The terror and anguish of the experience, as well as the bizarre message of his own aggressive power have left this man split off from the daily experience of the body. Minor aches, bodily manifestations of stress or exhaustion must equally be denied. He has also been deeply self-destructive and abusive of his body. As a child he fought constantly outside his household. No one at home noticed (could notice) the bruises, cuts, blood on his male body. This man has maintained a complex, ambivalent relationship to his own blood throughout his life. There is in his reports of childhood an endless litany of accidents, fights, many instances of bloodletting; at a later stage he poisoned his blood with drugs. All this attests to the powerful meaning attached to the brother's disability. In this man's psychic life, gender and disability are powerfully fused, perhaps inevitable in a disability so specifically gender-linked. His twinship saved him from hemophilia, so healthy masculinity becomes a conception polluted with guilt. This man's life history is an instance of displaced disability where damage, fear of death, the dull experience of depression and pain have been internalized in a physically unaffected sibling.

Think again of the dilemma recorded by the women who contracted polio as a child. She remembers the confusion, the doubled messages of "nothing is wrong but everything is wrong," and the resulting denial. The struggle in disability rights and the lives and aspirations of disabled women is for the right and access to productive work, to loving and vivid relationships and the full experience of subjectivity. It may be strategic to stress the accurate findings of competence, ego-strength, and adaptive functioning. This strategy is like that of the earlier phases of the women's movement where similarity and equality with men, and the eradication of difference, were goals along with the naming of sex differences as arbitrary and socially inscribed distinctions designed to maintain oppression. Current feminist work has moved to a more intricate account of the costs of patriarchy, of the damaging intrapsychic consequences of oppression and exclusion. We have also looked for ways to dismantle this exclusion, routes to transcendence and to empowerment. Psychological theory and, in particular, psychoanalysis have played a crucial role in new assertions of female power, of the specificity and authenticity of a female text. An understanding of femininity and disability can, we believe, grow from careful attention to the needs and rights of all people for equality, and to the privileging of difference in the lives of individuals.

The inclusion of more analytic and intrapsychic work with disabled women meets the demand Asch (1984) has made in her critique of psychological research on disability. Turning some attention to the inner experience of disability, the complexity of the conflict of social forces and individual responses (both parent and child) offers a rich human picture. Such examination is not conducted at the expense of another activity Asch has called for, the process of naming stereotypic cultural attitudes that introduced and maintain disability as a socially constructed phenomenon. These cultural stereotypes lead to the denial of subjectivity to the disabled person, a diminishing of identification, and at times the projection of disowned and negative aspects of self onto the disabled person by non-disabled people.

A perusal of much of the psychological and psychoanalytic work on early attachment and early development does suggest implications for particular forms of interventions, specifically intervention in the service of early affirmation of the basic integrity of the child.

In a recent paper focused on empathic identification and imagining, Turnbull and Turnbull (1985) highlight this point. Rehabilitative intervention—procedures fostering growth and competence—is valuable and necessary, but it can yield an intended but damaging side effect. Rehabilitative efforts carry to parent and child the strong, though covert, message that something is wrong, missing, lacking. The child must be fixed. It is certainly the burden of much of the psychological literature on early experience to confirm that an infant or young child does have exquisite, if not fully conscious, antennae for just these sorts of feelings and assumptions. Deborah Samuelson, in an emotional and pained letter to her disabled daughter, bears witness to the psychic costs for daughter and mother of the relentless requirement to fix up the child with a disability (Samuelson 1986). The psychological and psychoanalytic literature on early development also teaches us that in terms of emotional readiness and psychic organization, a disabled child, like all infants, is quite ready to be experienced as adequate, lovable, and whole. A major insight in the work on early attachment has been realization of how early and how actively infants are prepared to respond to parental attunement. What follows are separate considerations of the problem of attachment and the problem of gender development. While these processes are obviously interconnected, there are some issues specific to attachment and some to gender.

DISABILITY AND ATTACHMENT

The most illuminating, but provocative, theory of early development useful in thinking about the impact of disability upon a child's development is the object relations school, a psychoanalytic theory derived from Freud's later work on the importance of ego functioning, a theory committed to the notion that personality and self are the outcome of interpersonal experience and the internalization of social relations with primary persons in the child's world.

This school of theory sets the development and constitution of self or subjectivity in the matrix of social relationships, in particular the first and primary relationships. Object relations theory focuses on attachment, a two-way process in which the child's internalization of early relations, her fantasies and symbolizations, lead to an inner object world which is the complex reflection of the first social experiences. It is two-way because the parent is also engaged in a mutually reflective process of projection and identification. A central assumption in this work is that subjectivity is social as well as individual, that self is, in part, the outcome of how one experiences oneself as a socially known and apprehended being.

This theory, or rather a range of theoretical approaches encompassing quite divergent concepts, presents a complex and perhaps unsettling set of implications for the development of disabled children, for this approach describes mechanisms for the *internalization* of socially derived experiences (Mahler et al. 1976; Winnicott 1980; 1971). It makes of identity and personality a social and interactional process, which raises, in the case of disability, the question of how being mirrored in the social surrounding could potentially lead to the experiencing of a socially derived sense of damage as inextricably a part of self. Rather than trying to do justice to a broad and complex theory by summarizing the approach, the following describes crucial claims explored and promoted in the theory and relevant and problematic in considering the development of disabled children—disabled girls in particular.

Object relations theory focuses not on conflict or oedipal triangulated struggle but on the intense, mutually constituting experience of mother and child. It is in this dyad, in the first and most intense social relationship, that self arises. Self is first reflected, mirrored in the maternal gaze; one becomes by being seen. The earliest forms of inner psychic life in the child are the internalized objects (that is, social objects, people or aspects of people) as they exist in relation to the infant and to each other. This is not a passive process, certainly not exactly predictable.

Theoretical work and clinical observation, joined now with empirical observation of early interaction (Lewis and Rosenblum 1976; Mahler et al. 1976), illuminate this process of mutual and reciprocal elaboration in microanalytic detail. Winnicott, a major theorist, draws attention to three major phases of early development that can be examined in light of the experience of a disabled infant (Winnicott 1980). His ideas stress paradox, play, and illusion, and a subtle interweaving of personal and interpersonal experience. In the beginning, there is no such thing as an infant, "no external factor; the mother is part of the child" (Winnicott 1980: 6). Winnicott makes the point somewhat dramatically that the infant is initially a unit of infant-maternal care. The ego support of the mother, through her preoccupation and her projective identification with the baby, is an empathic imagining of the child's wishes, needs, and experiences, based on the mother's imagining and identification. This primary stage of dependence and merged identities forms the matrix for a next phase, where the child experiences the necessary illusion of omnipotence. Here the role of the parent is to foster the illusion of omnipotence, to enable the child to experience that subjectively created objects and events in the environment are under her control. The beginning of personhood, or self, arises as the child moves through two interrelated phases. As the body ego, based on sense and movement, develops, a sense of boundaries arises. The child comes to know a distinction between inside and outside. At the same time, the child encounters objects and persons experienced as alien, outside, separate. Here the parental role is to provide some break in the empathic imagining, in a shift from *intuiting* infant need to *reading* the child's signals. In another paradoxical move, the mother provides events or objects in such a way (that is, non-intrusively) that the child experiences the object or event as though she herself created it.

In yet a further development, the child's experience of omnipotence is diminished through encounters with objects or persons that survive the child's aggression or destructiveness. This is actually a profound and important developmental negotiation. The child needs to experience unsuccessful attempts at destruction in which the object survives in an undefended way. What does that mean? The object, and often the object is a person, is robust and flexible enough to contain the child's anger and to survive and limit the aggression, survive it without sadistic retaliation or collapse. In the very act of surviving, a limit is placed on the child's aggression that also marks a limit to the child's feeling of omnipotence. The object is not just an extension of the child. Survival establishes difference and brings to an end the child's illusory omnipotence. Aggression, activity, and autonomy are thus established on a more secure basis. When the illusory experience of omnipotence is broken, the child establishes the realness of the outside world and also her own sense of aliveness, limits, and boundaries. Winnicott calls the psychic arena in which this process is elaborated "transitional space." It is a space where parent and child, through play, symbolization, and communication constitute child-self and self-in-relation. Self comes into being—or ego is integrated, to use another theoretical vocabulary—through the experience of self in encounter with objects found and created by the child, then in the object or person's survival of the child's attempts to destroy it, and subsequently by internalizing the collective or collaborative meaning of play carried in the dialogue between adult and child.

Mahler has been interested in this psychic space between parent and child in a slightly different way (Mahler et al. 1976). Individuation—a sense of a separate self, Winnicott's idea of the capacity to be alone in the presence of another person—arises in a process of separation and return, movement from the ego-support of the parent and return to it (the phase called *rapprochement*). Lest this sound too dauntingly theoretical, we can ground this idea in the clinical and observational insights of many researchers in the everyday life of parents and children, in the games of hide and seek, the creative play of children with their imaginary companions, teddy bears, and precious blankets, and in transitional objects that are part mother, part child, imbued by the child with the special properties and identity of the mother.

These theories bear a considerable relationship to the cognitive constructionist theories of Piaget, where the child actively operates (sensorally, cognitively) upon the world of objects (social and otherwise) to build up internal schemas, patterns of action and expectation. This presumption of activity on the part of the child would mean that disability or damage is not initially self-evident to the child. DeCarie, in her work on infants suffering from the effects of thalidomide, examined their motor development and early reactional and relational development in the context of Piaget's developmental stages (DeCarie 1965). What one might imagine, then, is that the disabled child may develop with a stronger sense of discrepancy between the active, constructing self and the social stigma, communicated to her and internalized, of disability.

This discrepancy is at the heart of what Winnicott described as true and false self, a core self that remains active and creative (if often deferred), and a false self, a defensive carapace that arises in response to the world or the parent's mirroring.

In this model of development, the primary figures' experience and response to the infant is a crucial element in self-constitution. At this point in imagining the impact of disability upon personality development and the construction of a gendered experience of self, disability as a monolithic entity begins to deconstruct. Here is where prediction and generalization fail, for one needs to know the social meaning of the particular disability. This question is only answerable in its particularity. What we can do is pose questions. Starting from the more general and social level, what is the meaning of the particular disability? What aspects of functioning are affected, and how do parents and others understand the implications of disability, as they are socially determined and institutionally communicated (that is, through the diagnosis, the subsequent encounters with schools, etc.)? What is the mother's degree of individuation? What is projected into the infant?

In thinking about this early developmental progress for a disabled infant and her parents, my questions are directed to the three phases Winnicott has described. The infant's dependency depends in part on the parents' capacity to provide ego support, and this depends on identification. If depression is an early, even if transient, aspect of the parental response to their disabled child, how does this affect the merged intersubjectivity of mother and baby? Does the baby experience the maternal depression as an early part of self? With what consequences? Winnicott speaks at some length about maternal depression. In a paper on communication (Winnicott 1980) he notes that the maintenance of a true self—that is, a core feeling of aliveness and ongoingness which is the hallmark of the child—coming into being as a person is dependent on the mother also having an aliveness, a lively inner world. When that is missing, he suggests—and depression is often implicated in such cases—the child's task is to fit in with the mother as a "dead object," or else the child has the daunting task of enlivening the mother; in essence the baby reassures the mother. Is this one of the special dilemmas in early attachment for disabled children and their parents? In Winnicott's view, this disturbance in development occurs at a time of ego integration and demands of the immature infant unusual resources.

What might this mean for disability? There are a number of different alternatives to consider, not solely negative or devastating. One can imagine the development of a sense of resiliency and enterprise in a child taking on quasi-parental roles rather early in life. Precocity may have very positive consequences as well as or instead of psychic costs.

Disruptions or stresses in early attachment leave a mark on subsequent efforts to individuate and experience self as separate. Again, no prediction, but questions: How do the parents permit or foster frustration and independence? Does the disability pull from parents an intrusive managing style of supervision, or does the anxiety about excessive dependency lead to counterdependence, to a pressure on precocious autonomy? Here gender may be important as male and female children appear to have somewhat different routes through the separation and rapprochement phase.

We have set up questions here, not definitive predictions. The clinical and theoretical work on early attachment and early object relations suggests central points in development where the interaction of parent and child has consequences for the child's psychic life. Inherent in this model is identification, the mechanism of projection and introjection, which is interactive. To answer the question of the impact of congenital disability on an infant, one must know who the mother or primary figure imagines her child to be, how alive the mother's inner life is, how individuated she is so the child is not maintained (in the mother's inner life) as a set of maternal projections and fantasies, and, finally, how the parent enables the child to create an inner and outer world through play, activity, and separateness. These answers will be particular, in the subjective experience of children and their families. Social definitions of disability may intrude on this process as they are internalized, transformed, mediated through family members, and communicated to the child through the way the child is seen, experienced, and played with.

To specify the intricacy of the attachment process and then to conclude that it is only negativity and damage that are internalized is really to give up the actual radical insight of psychoanalysis in favor of a rather behaviorist model of simple conditioning. One must simultaneously imagine both the depth of the internalization of early experience and the range of experience in child and parent that may be operative. Pain and guilt and loss will be present, perhaps, but also we may see in parental response a sense of the child's specialness, of the child's power to transcend difficulties and make human contact. Identification and attachment on the part of the parent may come in the wake of admiration for the child's courage. It is crucial to remember the extraordinary capacity of the child to form social bonds, to make the attachment. Therefore, we must see early experience as an intricate and deep encounter of two complex (though differently complex) psychologies.

DISABILITY AND GENDER
It is clear that disabled women suffer a dual discrimination in work force participation, education, and on a variety of economic and social measures (Asch 1984); that is, that disability and being female interact in a profoundly discriminatory and disadvantaging way. Here a slightly

different issue is considered. From the perspective of psychological research on disability, from thinking antiphonally and somewhat combatively both as feminist and psychoanalyst, the question arises as to how disability operates or functions in the process of gender development.

Starting with surface observations, there is evidence that disabled people are less sex-role stereotyped. In Barsch's (1968) work and work on deaf children (Harris 1978), fathers were reported to be more involved in sex-typing than mothers, more concerned that their children manifest appropriate sex roles. A closer look at similar findings among deaf people indicates that most of the difference in sex typing between disabled and non-disabled groups is accounted for by the women; that is, it is deaf women who are the less sex-sterotyped. There are two questions to revise at the onset. What is the impact of the particular meaning and experience of "femininity," constructed and constituted between parent and disabled female child, upon identity? And what is the impact upon sexuality? Is there less sex-typing because the child is not seen as sexed, or not seen as sexual? Our sense of our sexuality is probably never entirely freed from our sense of our gender, though neither are simple unitary of monolithic aspects of self. Hence, questions about gender lead us to questions about sexuality.

Are disabled women less the object of the vast (conscious and unconscious) mechanisms and processes of the sex-gender system than the non-disabled? In Barsch's study of parental reactions, parents were often vague and vaguely uneasy as to the sexual or relational future of their children. From a feminist perspective, we might see the failure of the culture to leave its heavy sex-typing brand on the disabled girl as a liberation. The powerful, willed autonomy of many disabled activists writing and speaking of their experience attests to a level of self-assertion and independence unusual for women. This may be an important part of the truth, but only a part. We need to learn more about this phenomena of a less sex-stereotyped person. Is the independence and self-sufficiency the product of avoidance; is it the outcome of marginalizing the disabled girl, or of repressing her sexuality?

A perspective on the development of gender, using current analytic work from several traditions, is in order here. There is much debate and ferment at this time among feminist psychoanalysts, based on differences of approach, cultural background, and emphasis. The theoretical work that follows bears on the issues of sexuality and gender identity and upon gender identity and individuation. This provides a basis for questions about the experience of disabled women.

In thinking about identification and femininity in the context of disability, one guiding element (perhaps *provoking* is a better word for the mix of antagonism and influence) has been the current work in French psychoanalysis, the work of women both imbedded in the Lacanian tradition and reacting against it. This work is particularly useful for feminists in its conception of the displacement of women from the Symbolic order, that is, their placement as people subjected to the law, or patriarchy, but excluded from its representation. This tradition in psychoanalysis aims to unravel such monolithic categories of experience as "woman," "femininity," and "sexuality." A number of these writers (Irigaray 1985; Kristeva 1980), as well as other American feminists and psychoanalysts (Chodorow 1978; Dinnerstein 1976; Flax 1980), have undertaken a new and careful excavation of the complexities of the relationship of mother and daughter, examining the mixture of envy, identification, and symbiosis in that dynamic interaction.

The relevance of this work for any understanding of disabled women is great. What are the implications for the disabled girl of a relationship with her mother, if we acknowledge that for many women, the gender identity (not inherently, but socially and developmentally) shared with mother is extremely problematic? Does disability act as a break on the symbiotic merging of mother and daughter? Does it act as a focus for the ambivalence and conflict that characterize mother-daughter relations? One could imagine a scenario in which the rupture in the mother-daughter connection frees the girl from messages of deep ambivalence about women's bodies and women's pleasures. There are really two questions. One has to do with the connections and communications made between mother and daughter regarding identity and the meaning of femininity. The second is concerned with the tie between gender identity and sexuality. One aspect of developing confidence and enthusiasm and a sense of entitlement in regard to sexuality is the parental communication to the child about her sexuality.

As with many aspects of development, one avenue towards an articulated and confident sexuality arises in a context in which the child or young person can be imagined as a sexual being. To the degree that parents of disabled children steer clear of imagining or envisioning their disabled child as sexual, one important source of input for the girl may be diminished. This is not, of course, to claim that in terms of inner feeling, fantasy, or sexual excitement, disabled young women are inhibited. We speak specifically of the sense of entitlement to pleasure and to sexual life. As with attachment, the presence and attitude of the father may be crucial. If same-sex identification is problematic for parents of a disabled child, father-daughter connections may be an avenue of clear-cut and less ambivalent identifications. A straightforward identification with the father also may provide particular strengths, assertiveness, and the particular sense of entitlement and authority that in psychoanalytic theory is termed "phallic."

Here the question of language and the particular connections among language, gender, and sexuality come into play. Language sets sexual differences and marks sexuality. Here language carries a large and complex meaning as an embodiment (and also an abstraction) of order, patriarchy, law. In its structure, its codification, and its interpretive power, language establishes certain possibilities for men and women and for their desire, while it silences or proscribes others. At the most obvious level, it establishes sexual difference as an opposition and assigns all the potency, reality, and privilege to one sex, that one representing the phallus. The Phallus, in this conception, can be embodied in the penis, but it is actually more powerfully the idea or idealization of sex, symbolizing the authority to speak about desire.

Some analysts uncritically (Mitchell and Rose 1982) and some critically (Irigaray 1985; Kristeva 1980) examine the implications of this for women. The position of women in this system is that of Other, the object of desire, never its subject. Women cannot begin to claim, to explore, to develop their own desires and sexual selves because there is no way in language as it is structured and managed to speak about feminine desire. Irigaray (p. 93) quotes Freud—"the juxtaposition 'feminine libido' is without any justification"—and she goes on to work out, in great detail, the chain of silences, repression, and convoluted movements proscribed for women in the course of development. The paradox she and other analysts are struggling with is that the naming of "opposite" sexes masks the actual state of things where one sex—women—is silenced in this crucial way in order to take the place of the mirror-mother. This reflects masculine desire, being the *place* (object) to which men return or turn to in following their own desires. The dilemma for women, then, and for feminist discourse on this matter, is to find a way into language, a way to power and speech that would establish, for the first time, difference—heterogeneity against the monolithic construct of the Phallus.

It would seem that a disabled woman may operate under a double silence, excluded or marginalized from the position women take up as passive and receptive and silenced in regard to their own pleasure. If disabled women are not imagined or treated as sexual beings, even within the constrained place women are pressed to occupy, how submerged and silenced is their sexuality? Sexuality and disability has been a tabooed subject in public discourse. In some recent public discussion of sexuality and spinal cord injuries, there is what we might think of as liberating texts, writing and speaking out that struggles to free our sexual-imagination from the exhaustively singleminded and monolithic preoccupation with the Phallus and with genital experience exclusively and obsessively centered on penetration and domination.

Some disabilities may call for or evoke different, unstereotyped relations to the body, a spreading and extending of eroticization of the body in the name of authentic heterogeneity. Disabled women may need to join in the struggle all women are engaged in, to learn, indeed to invent language and ways of speaking about their particular desires and pleasures. The situation of women freed from the oppositional and negative features of sex socialization by further marginalization and silence can be considered as something less than liberated. In regard to sexuality and feminine identity, it seems the task at this point (and it is a demanding and confusing one) is to break the silence.

A related preoccupation in analytic work at the moment (compatible with many of the themes just discussed) is the experience of mothers and daughters. Psychoanalysis considers the earliest relationship and the implications of that first attachment for individuation and, more recently, for sexuality. Dinnerstein (1976) and Chodorow (1978) have done ground-breaking work in examining the implications of the experience of intense merging and symbiosis with the powerful mother of our earliest experience. As they and others have suggested, the early experiences with a primary love object hold not only the memories of pleasure and connectedness but also the complexity of tangled identification and projection. For a variety of reasons, the conjunction of identification and love for young girls in respect to their mother makes the process of separation less dramatically enforced and indeed shakier for the girl. Autonomy and relatedness upon separation are more difficult, less securely achieved for many girls.

One of the implications of the current work on mother-daughter interaction is that "femininity" as it is construed by each woman and elaborated in the context of a mother-daughter relationship, is projected and identified in the other. One would have to ask quite specifically how each partner in this complex, consciously and unconsciously rendered dialogue imagines and sees the other. It is not uncommon for a daughter to experience her mother as depressed, envious, an embodiment of negating, prohibitive forces. What is prohibited: action, growth, separation. There is a more classical analytic interpretation of this in terms of the girls' oedipal guilt, the anxiety and guilt at going beyond the mother. Menaker's (1975) work on female masochism suggests the guilt at separation is often a deep and trenchant experience for women in relationship to the actual mother or to the image of mother they have internalized. Perhaps we should undertake a more historically grounded consideration. Empowerment for contemporary women stands in opposition to the muted ambivalence, the depression and thwarted development of the earlier generation of our mothers.

CONCLUSION

This exploration of the consequences of early attachment and encountering the sex-gender system for disabled girls frames questions, not answers. We come more and more to see that personality, sexual experience, and identity are constructed for any individual through the dynamic processes and interactions with primary figures. It is through such processes that values, proscriptions, and standards flow, and are projected into the interaction. We will need to know in the specific instance of a particular young woman with a particular disability how it is understood, accepted, rejected, interpreted by her family in concert with, against, in spite of the messages and demands of the larger culture, and how she internalizes, makes sense of, transcends the intrapsychic consequences of that interaction.

We have identified what we might call hot spots in development in which to ask particular questions. Do the depression and conflict, the guilt and ambivalences more prevalent in the early responses to disability by parents affect attachment? Does the disability come to figure in the complex projections and identification of mother-daughter experience in a way that adds to the girl's difficulties in separation? What happens between parent and child in families where attachment and gender identity are negotiated? What would happen if, in the interventions in early development for disabled children, the focus was placed on the importance of being seen as whole, as gendered, and as sexual?

These questions offer the avenues to knowing and recognizing the full complexity of the disabled woman's experience. Disabled women are framing their own questions (Asch and Rousso 1985). As with many women, the charting and naming of a full humanity can feel like flying in the teeth of a powerful gale. The questions here insist on the full humanity of all women, forging a connection that respects and does not submerge heterogeneity. For disabled women as for other women, this process will entail the development and sustenance of a language for their particular pains and pleasures.

References

Asch, A. 1984. The experience of disability: A challenge to psychology. *American Psychologist* 39:5.

Asch, A., and H. Rousso. 1985. Therapists with disabilities: Theoretical and clinical issues. *Psychiatry* (February):1–12.

Barsch, N. 1968. *The parent of the handicapped child: A study of childrearing practices.* Springfield, Ill.: Charles Thomas.

Bernheimer, L., M. Young, and P. Winton. 1983. Stress over time: Parents with young handicapped children. *Journal of Developmental and Behavioral Pediatrics* 4 (3):177–81.

Blacher, J., and C. E. Meyers. 1983. A review of attachment formation disorder of handicapped children. *Am. J. Mental Deficiencies* 87 (4):359–71.

Breslau, N., D. Salkever, and K. Stanch. 1982. Women's labor force activity and responsibility for disabled dependents: A study of families with disabled children. *J. Health and Social Behavior* 23:169–83.

Chodorow, N. 1978. *The reproduction of mothering.* Berkeley: California University Press.

Condry, J., and S. Condry. 1978. Sex differences: A study of the eye of the beholder. *Child Development* 47:812–19.

Darling, R. B. 1979. *Families against society: A study on reactions to children with birth defects.* London: Sage.

DeCarie, T. 1965. *Intelligence and affectivity in early childhood.* New York: International Universities Press.

Dinnerstein, D. 1976. *The mermaid and the minotaur.* New York: Harper and Row.

Donzelot, J. 1980. *The policing of families.* New York: Pantheon.

Flax, J. 1980. Mother-daughter relationships: Psychodynamics, politics and philosophy. In *The future of difference,* ed. H. Eisenstein, A. Jardine. New Brunswick, N. J.: Rutgers University Press.

Gliedman, J., and W. Roth. 1980. *The unexpected minority: Handicapped children in America.* New York: Harcourt Brace Jovanovich.

Goffman, E. 1963. *Stigma: Notes on the management of spoiled identity.* Englewood Cliffs, N. J.: Prentice-Hall.

Harris, A. 1987. The rationalization of infancy. In *Critical developmental theory,* ed. J. Broughton.

——. 1978. The development of the deaf individual and the deaf community. In *Deaf children,* ed. Lynn Liben. New York: Academic Press.

Irigaray, L. 1985. *Speculum of the other women.* Ithaca, N. Y.: Cornell University Press.

Klaus, M., and J. Kinnell. 1976. *Mother-infant bonding.* St. Louis: C. Mosby.

Kristeva, J. 1980. *Desire in language.* New York: Columbia University Press.

Lewis, M., and L. Rosenblum. 1976. *The effect of the infant on the caregiver.* New York: Academic Press.

Mahler, M., F. Pine, and A. Bergman. 1976. *The psychological birth of the infant.* New York: Basic Books.

Menaker, E. 1975. *Masochism and the emergent ego: Selected papers of Esther Menaker,* ed. L. Lerner. New York: Human Sciences Press.

Mitchell, J., and J. Rose, eds. 1982. *Feminine sexuality: Jacques Lacan and the école Freudienne.* New York: Norton.

Roskies, E. 1972. *Abnormality and normality: Mothers of thalidomide children.* Ithaca, N. Y.: Cornell University Press.

Samuelson, D. 1986. A letter to my daughter/myself: On facing the collective fear of being different. *Feminist Studies* 12:155–68.

Turnbull, A. P., and H. R. Turnbull III. 1978. *Parents speak out*. Columbus: Charles E. Merrill.

———. 1985. Stepping back from early intervention. Paper presented at the DEC/CEC Early Childhood Conference, Denver, October.

Urwin, C. 1978. The development of communication between blind infants and their parents. In *Action, gesture, and symbol: The emergence of language*, ed. Andrew Lock. New York: Academic Press.

Winnicott, D. D. 1958. Hate in the counter-transference. In *Collected papers: Through paediatrics to psychoanalysis*. London: Tavistock.

———. 1971. *Playing and reality*. London: Tavistock.

———. 1980. Communicating and not communicating leading to a study of certain opposites. In *The maturational processes and the facilitating environment*. New York: International Universities Press.

5. Daughters with Disabilities: Defective Women or Minority Women?

HARILYN ROUSSO

A noted disability rights activist once stated, "Behind every successful disabled woman is a pushy mother." While we may be rightly wary of such a simplistic formulation, this chapter argues that parents, both mothers and fathers, are a powerful influence on the degree of social success, as culturally defined, of adolescent women with disabilities.

The parent-daughter relationship is a complex one, particularly during adolescence. There are the parents' attitudes and expectations, the daughter's perception of those expectations (which may differ from the parents' reality), and the daughter's unique response to those perceived expectations (which may involve agreement, rebellion, struggle, and confusion). The parents, in turn, may be influenced by the daughter's attitudes and behavior.

The intent here is to explore the relationship between parental expectations and disabled adolescent women's degrees of involvement and success in the heterosexual arena. The few existing studies suggest that during adolescence, many women with disabilities have less active heterosexual lives than do their non-disabled counterparts; they have their first dates, steady partners, and sexual encounters later, and they engage in most social activities with less frequency. Both the general topic and these particular findings have not stimulated scholarly curiosity or social concern for a variety of reasons, reflecting biases and stereotypes in the areas of both sexuality and disability. On the one hand, continued societal ambivalence toward the role of sexuality in development results in a major research emphasis being placed on situations in which sexuality seems out of control (for example, out-of-wedlock pregnancies, the spread of venereal disease) (Carrera 1983). Situations that hamper the emergence or expression of sexuality are

139

rarely acknowledged as a problem. On the other hand, there is a myth in our society that disabled people are asexual. It is reflected in our genderless language—paras and quads, the blind, the deaf; in our unsexy associations to disability—sick, helpless, dependent, childlike; and in our pathetic media images—poster children and telethons.

Because so much of female sexuality has focused on physical appearance, disabled women are particularly likely to be misperceived as asexual. Thus, their more limited sexual activities during adolescence may appear to be an inevitable consequence of disability. To the extent that disabled women *are* ever viewed as sexual, they are too often stereotypically assumed to be capable of reproducing only "defective" children, or to be unable to nurture any children (Fine and Asch 1981). From this perspective, their limited heterosexual activities may be perceived as a source of relief, the best form of contraception, not requiring investigation. In addition, civil rights activists frequently state that equal opportunity is hardest to legislate in the social arena. Legal action can require an employer to hire a black or disabled person, but it cannot require a potential partner to date a disabled woman or man. Attitudinal studies suggest that while disability per se is an anxiety-producing topic for many individuals, the prospect of intimate contact with disabled people is far more uncomfortable and distressing than professional or casual interactions (Asch and Rousso 1985).

The intent of this chapter is to begin to address the research gap, building on existing studies. Presented here are the results of a pilot study on the heterosexual interests and experiences of adolescent women with disabilities, and their relationships to parental attitudes and expectations in the heterosexual area. Comparisons are made between disabled and non-disabled women and among disabled women themselves. The focus is on heterosexual activities because we believe these may have particular developmental significance given the biased definitions of womanhood in our culture. By no means is it the intent to devalue other forms of sexual expression; these are expected to become the subject of future research.

THEORETICAL FRAMEWORK

For both women and men, participation in a range of social and sexual activities during adolescence facilitates the completion of a variety of developmental tasks. Blos (1962) and others describe how such participation helps the young person begin to break familial ties and form connections with nonfamilial partners in the outside world. It also provides opportunities to explore budding sexuality, to develop social skills, and to establish the capacity for intimacy. In addition, specifically *heterosexual* involvement offers an important avenue for the development of a sense of identity. For adolescent women in particular, dating, kissing, sexual encounters, and going steady may be a significant component of gender-role identity, contributing to feelings of adequacy as women. Whether or not we agree, the traditional and still widely upheld measure of a woman's success in our culture is her capacity to attract and keep a man, preferably through marriage, and to bear his children. Thompson (1984) acknowledged surprise and distress at the finding of her recent study that for white, working-class teenage girls, their ultimate goal was "true, monogamous, permanent, one-man, one-woman couple love" (p. 355), with career as a distant second, only when love fails. Similarly, Zellman and Goodchilds (1983) reported that more than half the teenagers in their study believed that a woman's most important job remains in the home.

Adolescence is a training ground for adult roles as they are customarily defined. Given these adolescent visions of a woman's role, for the adolescent woman, the flurry of heterosexual activities is assumed a confirmation of womanhood, whereas the absence of such activities is often experienced by the young woman herself and the world of family, friends, and community around her as a sign of failure. Bardwick (1971) writes,

> The sexuality of the adolescent girl fuses with the rewards of dating. Early dating is a testing ground for success in the very new femininity and feminine desirability. As a result, the girl is ready to fall in love again and again and assures herself of her desirability by her collection of broken hearts. (p. 52)

Malmquist (1985) adds, "The self-esteem of most girls is more contingent on success in social relationships than on school grades. In a national survey of adolescents, assets for achieving popularity and social acceptance were mentioned three times more often by girls than by boys as one of their worries" (p. 68).

This is not to say that there are no adolescent women who focus instead on school, career, and other areas. Such women exist and do not necessarily suffer from their choices, but they appear to be the exception rather than the rule. The culture and the literature focus on the heterosexual area as the compulsory workplace for young women. The present study maintains this bias in part to consider its impact on the lives of disabled women.

Despite the proclaimed importance of heterosexual activities in adolescence, few research studies focus on what factors help or hinder social success during the teenage years. This is in sharp contrast to the multitude of studies on academic and vocational success, and on ways to *reduce* heterosexual contact. Again, this gap may reflect a devaluing of sexuality and, more specifically, "women's work." It may alternatively reflect the fact that social success by adolescent women and men is accepted as the norm. Although many people recall their social lives in adolescence with a certain degree of discomfort and distress, it is generally assumed that most adolescents date, eventually find partners, and lead socially active adult lives. Partnerless people are studied only when they are middle-aged and it is clear that they have not met the norm.

While direct studies of social achievement in adolescence are lacking, information on this topic is often included or implied in works on gender-role identity. Although social success and achievement of gender-role identity are by no means identical and at best complexly related, gender-role works have something important to offer our present research. They stress that parental attitudes, expectations, and behaviors play a major role in the sexual development of women (and men). Depending on their theoretical orientation, such works note how children imitate or identify with their parents and how parents foster gender-appropriate behavior (Katz 1979). Significantly, studies of academic success also have emphasized the importance of parental standards and goals for their children's success. For example, parents who encourage academic performance and set high goals for their children are often rewarded by the child's high achievement, although sometimes children rebel and drop out of the academic arena (Malmquist 1985). These works by no means agree on the nature of the parental influence, nor do they claim that parents are the only important factor. They do, however, lay the ground for an investigation of the heterosexual achievements of adolescent disabled women.

The lack of research on the sexual development of disabled women has already been noted. Existing studies include those by Welbourne et al. (1983), which compared the psychosexual development of forty-seven women who had become blind before the age of 10 with thirty-nine women who were sighted; Duffy (1981), which studied the social and sexual experiences of seventy-five orthopedically disabled women, forty-five of whom were disabled before the age of 15; and Landis and Bolles (1942), the oldest and most extensive study, which compared the social and sexual history of 100 women disabled before the age of 13 with epilepsy, rheumatic heart disease, cerebral palsy, and a range of orthopedic disabilities with 100 non-disabled women. In all three studies, the disabled women fared less well socially and sexually during adolescence than their non-disabled peers. The studies suggested some of the obstacles that the disabled women faced: transportation problems, architectural barriers, lack of self-confidence, rejecting peers, pessimistic parents and community, and the lack of role models for social success. Some of the disabled women were successful despite the odds. Limited social achievement was never found to be an inevitable consequence of having a disability. Only the Landis and Bolles study attempted to study factors facilitating social success in a systematic way. Family dynamics were studied in depth and found to be an important factor in psychosexual development.

Although the specific formulation of family dynamics that Landis and Bolles provide, described below, may be less relevant today than in the past, their awareness of the importance of environmental factors is impressive and a major contribution. Until relatively recently, developmentalists have taken the position that disability inevitably alters development, causing a host of psychosocial problems, including problems with id, ego, and superego (Asch and Rousso 1985). Only in the past several years have studies confronted this biological determinism, linking environmental factors and particularly parental attitudes to self-esteem and the body image of disabled children (Darling 1979; Kris Study Group, Beres/Caldor section, 1971; Lussier 1980; Rousso 1984). Several studies suggest that disabled children fare better in their development when parents are able to put the disability in perspective, seeing their disabled children as children first, with disability as only one of many characteristics. Problems appear more likely to arise when parents become preoccupied with and unduly pessimistic about the disability. Such parental preoccupation with disability may reflect individual dynamics, but often it also reflects cultural values— the devaluing and stigmatizing of disabled people, and even more so, of disabled women in our society.

The present study builds on these preliminary findings. It also reflects the author's clinical experience as a psychotherapist and personal experience as a woman with cerebral palsy. It hypothesizes that disabled adolescent women fare better in the heterosexual area when parents view them as women first, capable of meeting typical female role expectations. It also assumes that many parents do not have this perspective; for them, "disabled woman" translates into "defective woman," which drastically alters their vision of who this daughter could or should become. For this altered vision, disabled women pay a price.

RESEARCH FINDINGS AND DISCUSSION

The present research studied the heterosexual experiences and parental expectations during adolescence of forty-three women with physical

Table 5.1. AGE OF FIRST SOCIAL SEXUAL EXPERIENCES

	Age in Years	
Experience	Disabled before Adolescence	Disabled after adolescence
First date	17.7	14.5
First kiss	17.0	14.2
First sexual contact	18.2	16.1
First experience with intercourse	22.0	18.3
First steady relationship	19.2	17.0
First recollection of masturbation	15.9	15.9

and sensory disabilities. The majority of these women were white, heterosexual, and single, in their twenties and thirties with some degree of college education. The range of disabilities included mobility impairments, brain and neurological disabilities, blindness, and deafness. A full description of the sample, the research hypotheses, and the data-gathering instruments for the study appear in the appendix at the end of the chapter.

Thirty-one of these women were disabled at or before the age of 10 and thus they experienced adolescence with a disability. They are the prime focus of the study. The remaining twelve were disabled after age 10, and most of them after adolescence. Thus, for the most part, this latter group went through adolescence as non-disabled young women; they serve as a comparison group for the original thirty-one, enabling us to compare the disabled and non-disabled experience in adolescence. The two groups are referred to throughout as women disabled before adolescence and women disabled after adolescence.

Building on previous research, this study hypothesized that the women disabled before adolescence would be less socially and heterosexually active during their adolescent years than the group disabled after adolescence. The findings supported this hypothesis. More specifically, when the women in the study were asked at what age they had their first date, kiss, sexual contact, experience with intercourse, and steady relationship, the mean age was later in all areas for the women disabled before adolescence in comparison to those disabled after adolescence (see Table 5.1). It is important to note, however, that the mean age for the first recollection of masturbation was about the same for the two groups. Masturbation is to be distinguished from the other categories listed in that it is a sexual activity that does not require the presence of a partner. The fact that women disabled before and after adolescence both recall beginning to masturbate at about the same age suggests that both groups may have had a similar level of interest in and awareness of sexual feelings, but differences in the opportunity to express those feelings.

In comparing themselves to their peers, almost three-fourths of the women disabled before adolescence felt that they had their first social and sexual experiences later than their peers, and more than three-fifths described themselves as less socially active than their peers. In contrast, among the women disabled after adolescence, only one in four felt that they had their first social and sexual experiences later, and only one in three felt they were less socially active than their peers. Interestingly, although the questionnaire did not specify whether the women should draw comparisons with their disabled or non-disabled peers, most of the women disabled before adolescence indicated that they were drawing comparisons from non-disabled peers or offered answers with regard to each peer group separately. Clearly, the majority of women disabled before adolescence perceived themselves as participating less fully and, by implication, less successfully than their non-disabled counterparts in the social area.

In explaining their less active heterosexual lives during adolescence, almost nine out of ten women disabled before adolescence felt that their disability was an important factor, although there were widely varied perceptions on how the disability impeded their social lives. Some women emphasized their inability to "circulate." One woman said, "Planning to go anywhere was so complex. I was exhausted before I got out the door." Another noted, "Having to have my younger sister tell me what boys were saying on the telephone, since I could not hear myself, was not conducive to romance." Others spoke about their lack of self-confidence and lower self-esteem: "I was so shy—I didn't expect anyone to want to go out with me." Or, "No one wanted to deal with a blind girl. It makes me tearful to think of it. All of my successes and failures felt connected to my disability." Still others mentioned architectural and transportation barriers. Many described attitudinal barriers, including the prejudices of friends who excluded them from social activities and of potential partners who were reluctant to be seen with them, as well as discouragement from family, professionals, and the community at large. Comments included, "Boys treated me like a pal rather than a girlfriend, as though my disability disqualified me from being female." Also, "People expected so little of me socially; in retrospect, it is shocking to realize that." Many of the women felt that their disability affected their social lives in more than one way. The direction of the effects was predominantly negative.

Those women disabled before adolescence who felt less active in the heterosexual arena than their non-disabled peers reported a variety of consequences, some of them positive. One woman said, "By the time I got involved with someone, my head was in a better place. I did it [had sex] because I wanted to, not because of peer pressure." However, most women reported harsh negative consequences, including lost opportunities and damage to their self-esteem as lovable, complete women. One respondent reported, "All those lost years can never be recaptured, no matter how active I am now." Another wrote, "I felt so abnormal and defective; it was a hard image to shake even when I became happily sexually involved as an adult." Yet another woman added, "I eventually rushed into bed with the first man who asked me." Still another: "I remember one point in my late adolescence painfully asking myself, 'How can I be a *real* woman if I am 19 years old and have never had a date in my life?'"

All six of the lesbians and bisexual women disabled before adolescence seemed to have had some interest in getting involved in heterosexual activities during adolescence. Most did not become involved with women until well after adolescence. There were no lesbians and only one bisexual woman among those women disabled after adolescence, so cross-group comparisons could not be made. However, we can note that of the six, five felt less heterosexually active and successful than their peers as a result of internal and external barriers rather than choice, and four of the five felt there were negative consequences in terms of both lost opportunities for exploration and lowered self-esteem. One woman stated, "It was difficult enough to be feeling so confused about my sexual identity. Not to be able to experiment with boys only added to my confusion and growing self doubts." Another noted: "Even though I was beginning to think that boys were not for me, I would have felt better about myself if I had had the opportunity to say no."

These comments suggest that for disabled adolescent women, as for non-disabled women, heterosexual activities may be closely linked to feelings of adequacy as women. In a society that devalues disabled women and questions their womanhood by virtue of their disability, the lack of social success may be one more reason not to feel like "true" women.

The findings from the present research corroborate some of the results of the few studies on the topic. Welbourne et al. (1983) found that the blind and sighted women they studied followed the same sociosexual patterns. For the blind women, however, there was a longer, later age range for the age of the first date, and the mean age of first experience with sexual intercourse was significantly later. Duffy (1981), in her study of orthopedically disabled women, found that the average age for the first date was substantially later for women disabled before the age of 15 in comparison to those disabled after age 15; her study also indicated that the early-onset group had a more limited range of social and sexual experiences than those disabled later in life.

Landis and Bolles (1942), in comparing the social and sexual histories of 100 disabled women with those of 100 non-disabled women, found that more of the disabled women had never dated and had no interest in doing so; those who dated began to do so later; more of the disabled women had never been in love in comparison to the non-disabled women; and as a group, the disabled women had less heterosexual contact, less homosexual involvement, and were less likely to have engaged in masturbatory activities. They also found the disabled women to be less knowledgeable about and less interested in sexual matters. They summarized this set of findings by describing disabled women as "hyposexual."

Landis and Bolles also studied the disabled and non-disabled women's relationships with their families of origin. Their findings on this topic offer introduction to the issue of parental role in sexual development and a considerably different formulation from the present study. In particular, in their sample Landis and Bolles found that disabled women were more closely tied to their parents and less involved with the outside world. Combining information on involvement in the sociosexual arena with information on involvement with family, the authors developed an index of psychosexual immaturity and found that disabled women were "psychosexually immature" in comparison to their non-disabled counterparts.

In explaining their findings, Landis and Bolles suggest that biological and environmental factors surrounding a childhood disability may contribute to psychosexual immaturity, which in turn may lead to "hyposexuality." In particular, their view is that having a disability from childhood may necessitate more parental care and attention, exclusion from childhood activities, and interference with strivings toward independence. A pattern of dependency is established that continues throughout adulthood. Because of young disabled women's close family ties and their failure to move out in the world, sexual development is often delayed. The authors make a clear distinction between delayed development and thwarted development. They do not feel that the disabled women were thwarted in their heterosexual development; if they had been, there would have been higher incidences of masturbatory and homosexual activities, which there were not. Instead, they feel the lack of sexual interest can be explained only in terms of a delay.

They note, however, that not all the disabled women developed such dependency patterns, nor were all lacking in social and sexual experience. Some women had greater separateness from their families, and their sexual development proceeded in a more typical fashion.

The particular family dynamics that Landis and Bolles describe—over involvement by disabled women with their families and a reluctance to move out into the world—are not documented by the present study, which occurred more than forty years later. When asked to measure their degree of involvement with their families and friends during adolescence, the women disabled before adolescence were no more involved with their families and no less involved with their friends than the women disabled after adolescence. Despite their more limited direct involvement in social and sexual activities, the early-onset group as a whole was no less *interested* in social life than was the group of women disabled after adolescence. None of the women disabled before adolescence explained their limited involvement in the heterosexual arena in terms of lack of desire and interest—for none of them was it a deliberate choice to abstain. Notably, as indicated previously, in the area of masturbation, the early onset women were on par with the later-onset group, clearly documenting that there was private sexual exploration and sexual interest. What emerges from these findings is a picture, not of complacent dependency on parents and lack of sexual need and interest, but of a strong desire on the part of the disabled adolescent women to move into the heterosexual arena and of major difficulty in doing so.

PARENTAL ATTITUDES AND EXPECTATIONS
The present study hypothesized that parents of women disabled before adolescence would have a different set of expectations for their daughters than parents of daughters disabled afterwards. In particular, it was assumed that parents of women disabled before adolescence would have lower heterosexual expectations and higher educational/vocational expectations compared to parents of the other group because they believed that their daughter, because of her disability, could not meet typical female role expectations. Many of the findings supported this hypothesis.

In an effort to distinguish the parental expectations of the two groups of disabled women, all the women in the sample were asked to recall their middle adolescence, ages 13 to 17, and to evaluate their parents' future expectations for them in three sociosexual areas and three educational/career areas. In particular, they were asked to what extent they believed their parents expected them to have an active sociosexual life, to get married, and to have children, and to what extent their parents expected them to complete high school, complete college, and get a good job.

While the parental expectations for the two groups were not different to a statistically significant degree, there were some important trends. On all three sociosexual goals, both mothers and fathers of the women disabled before adolescence had lower expectations than the parents of the comparison group. In contrast, in two of the three educational/career areas (except completing high school), the parents of the early-onset group had higher expectations than those of the later-onset group. In a related question, the women were asked to determine whether, during adolescence, they thought their parents were more interested in their school life, more interested in their social life, or equally interested in both. While relatively small percentages of both groups felt that their parents were solely interested in their social lives, slightly more than half the women disabled before adolescence felt that their parents were mainly interested in their school lives; only a third of the women in the comparison group felt this way.

There is a possible explanation for the lack of statistically significant differences between the two groups. First, both groups were asked to consider their parents' expectations for them when they were adolescents. The comparison group, consisting of women not disabled until after adolescence, was being asked to recall a time before disability occurred. Their recollections may be colored by the possible change in their parents' expectations of them after they became disabled. Also, many of the women who became disabled before adolescence commented that they did not know what their parents' expectations for them were in the social arena; their parents were noticeably silent about this. When they were adolescents, they interpreted their parents' silence as a confirmation of the societal sterotypes that they did not have much social potential, but in retrospect they were not sure that this is what the parental silence meant; thus, they were reluctant to acknowledge negative parental expectations in the social arena on their questionnaire, although that is what they felt while they were growing up.

Another measure of parental expectations in the social arena is the extent and nature of parent-daughter communication on sexual and social issues. Fox (1980) reports that mother-daughter communication on sexual matters is important because it raises the daughter's awareness of her own sexuality and enables her to make more responsible choices about her sexual behavior. For non-disabled women, this often means taking more contraceptive responsibility. As the present

Table 5.2. PERCENTAGE OF PARENTS WHO TALKED ABOUT THE TOPIC

Topic	Disabled before Adolescence (n = 31)		Disabled after Adolescence (n = 12)	
	(%)	(n)	(%)	(n)
Menstruation	77.4	(24)	83.3	(10)
Female anatomy	41.9	(13)	41.7	(5)
Male anatomy	32.3	(10)	25.0	(3)
Intercourse	32.3	(10)	25.0	(3)
Birth control	22.6	(7)	33.3	(4)
Venereal disease	16.1	(5)	33.3	(4)
Dating	51.6	(16)	83.3	(10)
Marriage	38.7	(12)	66.7	(8)
Children	38.7	(12)	58.3	(7)

author has written elsewhere (Rousso 1981, 1984), for disabled women raised in a society that views them as asexual, parent-child communication about sexuality serves to acknowledge and confirm the young woman's social and sexual potential. Such conversations not only encourage contraceptive responsibility in the heterosexual area but also encourage entrance into the arena.

For both groups of women in the sample, mothers were one of three major sources of sex information, friends and literature being the other two; fathers, in contrast were relatively unimportant. These findings are consistent with other research on the sources of sex information for teenagers in general, as summarized in a recent *Ms.* magazine report on teenage sexuality (Goodman 1983). They also concur with Fox and Inazu (1980), who reported that within the family, mothers, more so than fathers, are the prime sex educators.

When asked whether their parents had talked with them about nine separate topics on sexuality—menstruation, female anatomy, male anatomy, intercourse, birth control, venereal disease, dating, marriage, and children—the most striking differences between women in the two groups involved the topics of dating, marriage, and children, for which the early-onset group had considerably lower percentages (see Table 5.2). The women disabled before adolescence also had lower percentages on the topics of venereal disease and birth control. Differences on the remaining four topics were minor.

These findings again suggest differences in parental expectations between the two groups. Parents of women disabled before adolescence might have doubted the need to talk about topics that they felt would not be relevant to their daughters' future role. They might also have been concerned about stirring up unrequitable longings and feelings of deprivation. Silence may have seemed preferable (Rousso 1981).

Along related lines of parental communication, the women disabled before adolescence were asked first whether their parents ever spoke with them about the cause and nature of their disability, and whether their parents ever spoke with them about the impact of their disability on their social and sexual lives. While seven out of ten of the women reported that their parents had spoken with them about their disabilities, only about one-fourth of the women reported conversations on the effect of disability on sexuality. Of these women, only one indicated that her parents had given her a positive message about her social potential given her disability.

When those women whose parents did not talk with them about the effect of disability on their sexuality were asked to explain the parental silence, some indicated that their parents did not discuss sex with anyone regardless of disability: "No one in the house ever discussed sex—our Catholic upbringing." Other women interpreted the silence to mean that either they already knew all they needed to know or that they would ask for help when they needed it. "My parents figured in time I'd experience a relationship where I'd confront this and it would be okay to ask or ask for help." However, many of the women interpreted the silence as a pessimistic statement about social possibilities. For example, "They simply did not think that sexuality was going to be part of my repertoire." Also, "By not talking about sexuality and dating with me but by talking to my sister, she implied that it was not for me."

When asked whether their parents had any fears about the emergence of their sexuality, slightly fewer women disabled before adolescence compared to women disabled after responded affirmatively. There were no differences in the kinds of fears that the parents of the two groups expressed; major fears included pregnancy and being taken advantage of. At the same time, more than half (sixteen) of the early-onset group and only two of the late-onset group described their parents as too protective, not specifically in the sexual arena but in general. These findings suggest that parents of women disabled before adolescence were by no means freer or more trusting of their daughters' capabilities in general but that they might have been somewhat less concerned about sexuality. This may be because they did not perceive their daughters as sexual.

When the women disabled before adolescence were asked what kinds of messages they got about the social and sexual potential of disabled people, almost half of those who answered indicated that they had gotten negative messages, and another quarter indicated that they had gotten mixed messages. Only one woman indicated that she had gotten a positive message. While peers and society were identified as the major sources of messages, parents were also a frequently mentioned source.

A number of women disabled before adolescence expressed appreciation for their parents' emphasis on school and career, noting that had they not been disabled, they probably would not have obtained such a good education or have gone so far in their careers. Indeed, comparing the women disabled before adolescence with those disabled after, the early-onset group did attain higher education levels and were more likely to be working full-time when they filled out the questionnaire. But they may have paid a price. Paul and Anna Ornstein (1985) comment on the potentially damaging psychological effects of parents recognizing some of their child's capabilities while disregarding others: "Parents may affirm selectively certain of the child's physical and intellectual attributes. But as far as the child is concerned, such arbitrary selective affirmation may be experienced as parental failure to validate other aspects of the developing self—that is, outright rejection of his or her total self" (p. 205). Even the appreciative women recognized that emphasis on educational strivings was based on an undermining assumption about their defectiveness as "real" women, that is, their incapacity to marry and have children. As one woman stated, "While I am grateful that my parents recognized my intellectual abilities and applauded me onward to get my Ph.D., it is distressing to think that their applause was partly grounded in their perception of me as a misfit."

Parental difficulty in recognizing and affirming the social and sexual potential of disabled daughters can be understood in terms of the individual dynamics of the parents and family, and in terms of broader societal values. For mothers in particular, affirmation of sexual potential and womanhood may require the mother's ability to see herself in her daughter and to be able to identify with her. As a result of their own dynamics and history, for some mothers the daughter's disability may loom too large and make the daughter seem too disparate; the mother may then have difficulty identifying and seek to keep her distance. For example, the disability may remind the mother of her own feelings of imperfection, and she may be reluctant to acknowledge that part of herself. Or, having a disabled child may seem like punishment for wrongdoing, a source of guilt safer dealt with from afar.

Fathers also play an important role in the confirmation of a female child's heterosexuality. For fathers to affirm their daughter's heterosexuality, they must be able to see in their daughters the potential to become the kind of woman they could choose as a mate. Again, as the result of feelings of inadequacy, guilt, or other dynamics, the father may have difficulty seeing his daughter in this light.

In addition, particular family needs may encourage members to keep the disabled daughter or sister an asexual child. This role may serve to give the mother an ongoing mothering function as the children grow older, to avoid conflict between the marital couple, or to address other family problems. Finally, parents may be concerned that should they foster a strong sense of heterosexuality in their disabled adolescent daughters, the daughters may be rejected, hurt, victimized, or abused. It may seem safer to disregard sexuality.

In understanding parental attitudes, however, the larger societal context must be considered. Some of the myths about disabled women have been cited already: that they are viewed as asexual and are seen as incapable of nurturing children and as likely to bear "defective" children. These stereotypes state that disabled women cannot fulfill traditional female role expectations. Parents of disabled daughters are likely to have internalized these myths to some degree. Thus, they may approach their daughter with a different set of standards and expectations.

Roskies (1972), in her study of parenting children disabled as the result of thalidomide, confirms some of the present findings on parental attitudes and expectations. She notes that parents of disabled children are much less likely to advocate for their children in the social arena in comparison to the educational and vocational areas:

The area of marriage and parenthood appears to constitute an exception to the mother's usual demands for social equity. More than in any other respect, in their expectations of marriage, the mothers of disabled children were prepared to accept that their children would remain deviant. Perhaps the difference in the mothers' expectations can be explained by the fact that they viewed marriage not only as a social relationship but a personal one. One can demand respect and equal opportunity far more easily from the society at large than one can demand love from an individual person. Moreover, to the degree that mothers tended to identify with prospective spouses, the difficulties loomed larger. As one mother expressed it, "How can I expect someone to marry X when I cannot marry someone like him." A mother could learn to love a child with missing arms or legs, but it appeared too difficult for her to imagine that a prospective husband or wife could do this too. (p. 176)

THE RELATIONSHIP BETWEEN HETEROSEXUAL INVOLVEMENT AND PARENTAL EXPECTATIONS

The findings thus far indicate that women disabled before adolescence had less adolescent involvement in the heterosexual arena than those disabled afterwards, and that parents of the women in the first group had lower heterosexual expectations than parents of the comparison group. Attention now focuses on the relationship between degree of heterosexual involvement and parental expectations.

Because a major goal of the study was to examine why some disabled adolescent women were socially successful while many others were not, the research hypothesis on this topic focused exclusively on the thirty-one women disabled before adolescence. An in-depth study of the women who had disabilities during adolescence seemed likely to produce the most fruitful results.

Nevertheless, some findings on the relationship between parental expectations and daughter's degree of heterosexual involvement for the whole sample of forty-three women are briefly considered. An attempt was made to examine this relationship by developing an index of parents' heterosexual expectations for their daughter, combining their expectations in three areas: having an active sociosexual life, getting married, having children. The forty-three women then were divided into two groups, depending on whether their parents' expectations were high (optimistic) or low (pessimistic), and the groups were compared on the average age of their first sociosexual encounters (first date, kiss, etc.) and their own evaluation of their degree of heterosexual involvement compared to peers (more active, less active, as active). Although the average age for the first events was slightly lower in four out of five event areas (except first steady relationship) for the high-parental-expectations group, the differences were not statistically significant. The women's ratings of themselves compared to peers also were not significantly different for the two groups.

This lack of significant results should not be interpreted to mean that parents are uninfluential; some other findings suggest the parental impact. The women's own heterosexual expectations for themselves were found to be positively correlated to their parents' expectations for them, to a statistically significant degree (at less than .05 level). This means that women who during adolescence were optimistic about their ability to have an active social life, marry, and have children when they got older were likely to have parents who were similarly optimistic, whereas women who were pessimistic about their heterosexual future were likely to have pessimistic parents. While statistically significant correlations do not prove cause and effect, developmental theory and logic suggest that this is likely, that parental attitudes do influence a daughter's attitudes. In turn, the daughter's expectations for herself may influence those of her parents, so the relationship may be one of mutual interaction and influence.

As further evidence of parental influence, when the women were asked to identify which factors were most influential in shaping the image of who they would become as adults, mothers were mentioned most frequently and fathers were in the top five (others included friends, teachers, and other nonfamilial adults). When asked about the direction of their parents' influence, the women responded in a manner reflecting the complexity of the parent-child relationship. One-fourth of the women said their mothers were a positive influence; another fourth indicated a negative influence; half said her influence was mixed. Findings were similar for fathers: ten women described him as a positive force; thirteen, as negative; and fifteen, mixed.

This complexity may help explain the lack of statistically significant findings in our analysis of the relationship between parental expectations and heterosexual involvement. Aside from lack of refinement in the questionnaire and the small sample size, which are definitely problems, there may be difficulties in the formulation. The statistics have attempted to examine whether expectations and degree of heterosexual involvement rise and fall together. The following discussion suggests that the answer may be that this is too simplistic a formulation.

For the thirty-one women disabled before adolescence, the primary research hypothesis was that positive expectations facilitated heterosexual involvement during adolescence, whereas pessimistic expectations hindered such involvement. The findings, however, reveal a more complex relationship. Positive expectations did facilitate heterosexual activities, but pessimistic expectations resulted in a range of responses, depending on a variety of factors.

The hypothesis was tested primarily through the clinical analysis of anecdotal material gathered in personal interviews with a small number of women and an even smaller number of their parents; these interviews offered extensive information on expectations, degree of involvement, and a host of factors about the parents, the women, and the environment. The written questionnaires by some of the women who were not interviewed also yielded rich anecdotal information. Secondarily, the questionnaire results were statistically analyzed, keeping in mind the various limitations of this approach.

The statistical findings mirrored those for the sample as a whole. The previously mentioned procedure of developing an index of parents' heterosexual expectations was followed, in which the women were divided into high- and low-expectations groups, and the two groups were compared on two measures of degree of heterosexual involvement: age of first sociosexual activity and degree of heterosexual involvement compared with that of peers. Again, there were no statistically significant findings, although the mean age of the first encounter for the high-expectations group was slightly lower on the same six out of seven activities.

From the anecdotal material it was possible to identify and organize some of the complexity in the relationship between parental expectations and degree of heterosexual involvement. In particular four categories of expectations and heterosexual involvement were identified.

1. *Parents viewed their disabled daughter as an intact woman, and the disabled woman was active in the heterosexual area.* Several women in the sample who were particularly socially and sexually successful during adolescence described themselves as having parents who viewed them as complete, intact women, disability and all. One women said, "My parents seemed to evaluate me and my sister using the same standard, considering our strengths and our failings; they were aware of my disability, my need to use crutches, and we talked about it, but they didn't seem preoccupied by it." Stated another women: "In childhood, I was led to believe that the same social performance was expected of me as of my cousins who had no disabilities. I was a social success in part because my mother expected me to succeed. In fact, she gave me no choice."

Interviews with the parents of these women seemed to confirm their perceptions. By and large, these parents tended to set similar expectations for their disabled and non-disabled daughters. To whatever extent these parents had lower social expectations for the disabled daughter, it was a reflection of their awareness of society's prejudices rather than their own personal statement about their daughter's social capabilities. Some of these parents seemed to feel that their daughter's disability would have no impact whatsoever on her social life. Other parents seemed aware of the physical barriers and the prejudices that might result from a disability, but they had faith in their daughter's social capabilities and sought to mediate the environment in order to minimize the barriers. Their strategies included moving the family to geographic locations more likely to be supportive of a disabled young woman; for example, to a location with a small high school, where the other students would interact with the young woman in the natural course of events, and thus would eventually see beyond her disability. Another strategy was for the parents to talk directly and effectively with their disabled daughters about social problems as they emerged, such as how do you flirt when you can't see, how do you talk with a boy about your disability, or how do you handle prejudicial remarks. To a lesser or greater degree, parents who explicitly dealt with disability barriers appeared to be viewing their daughters as intact women, but also *minority* women, in need of advocacy to deal with barriers and have the world affirm their womanhood.

Some of the typical characteristics of women and their families in this situation included an ability on the part of the mother to identify with the disabled daughter. One mother said, "When I was growing up, I wanted to complete college, work, marry, and have children. Both of my daughters [a disabled and a non-disabled daughter] were part of me, and I wanted for them the very same good things that I wanted for myself." It is difficult to generalize why some mothers can identify with their disabled daughters and others cannot, but one factor might be the mother's own definition of womanhood. Some of the mothers of women who fell into this first category had broader, nontraditional views of womanhood, definitions that encompassed, for example, a strong emphasis on work an education in one case, or being a lesbian mother in another; a broader definition of womanhood might more readily enable a mother to see the womanliness in a daughter who does not fit the societal (and often unreachable) norm.

Another characteristic of this group was a close relationship between the father and the disabled woman; indeed, a few of the women indicated that they felt closer to their fathers than to their mothers when growing up and that their involvement with their fathers offered the promise of successful involvement with men outside the home. The Landis and Bolles (1942) study also found a strong father-daughter tie in socially successful women.

In terms of concerns about the emergence of their daughters' sexuality, parents of the women in this group tended to show many of the concerns typical to parents of non-disabled adolescent women (for example, unwanted pregnancy or being taken advantage of) although their concerns did not seem intense. Several of these parents mentioned an additional concern—that their daughter would settle for a partner who was less attractive, competent, and intellectual than she was because prejudices would keep away men who were on a par with her. This concern seemed to give recognition to both the daughter's social capabilities and the prejudices she faced. One mother stated, "My daughter is an extremely enchanting, amazing young woman with tremendous social potential who may not find her way to a partner who is her equal because of people's attitudes."

Other characteristics of this group included the disabled adolescent women's living in a community that offered access to many different social groups, often because the parents made a deliberate choice to move there; and, finally, luck. At least two of the women indicated that they fortuitously fell into good relationships during their early adolescence and that these relationships fostered their self-esteem and helped overcome any doubts their parents might have had about their social potential.

2. *Parents viewed their disabled daughter as a "defective" woman, unable to meet typical social and sexual role expectations, and the disabled woman was active in the heterosexual arena during adolescence.* Disabled women in this group felt that their parents did not expect them to meet typical female role expectations; in particular, their parents did not expect them to marry and have children. One woman said, "My father told me that my disability was a liability when it came to getting married, and he offered to build me a house with the hope that that would perhaps enable me to catch a man; my mother told me, 'Put all your time into school—you'll never get a man.'" Another woman said, "My parents did not expect me to marry—my dad because he'd never marry 'an inferior person' so why would anyone else? My mom thought I'd never marry because I couldn't fulfill the nurturing role and because she was a martyr and felt I should be one too." In direct interviews, the parents of some of these women acknowledged that they had different expectations for their disabled and non-disabled daughters and that they tended to encourage education because they felt that marriage was not an option.

To understand the viewpoint of these parents, one must consider a variety of social, cultural, and psychodynamic factors. Several of these parents agreed with society's stereotypes about the limited potential of disabled people and could not see these as prejudice. This is in sharp contrast to the first group of parents, who acknowledged prejudice, fought against it, but never agreed with it as an accurate assessment of their daughter's potential.

Also, a number of the parents in this second group, particularly mothers, had traditional definitions of womanhood that focused on precisely those concrete skills that the disabled daughter could not perform, at least not in typical ways. For example, one mother emphasized nurturance through housecleaning, ironing, cooking, and feeding as essential for womanhood. She could not understand how her daughter, who was quadriplegic, could find a husband who could tolerate her not accomplishing these tasks and, in fact, would have to nurture her. Another mother, a highly religious Italian woman, felt that it was God's will that she take care of her seriously disabled daughter for as long as she lived, and she felt that it was against her religion and her culture to be fostering independence and encouraging her daughter to move out of the house, with or without a husband. For yet another mother, who had sacrificed her own educational pursuits for marriage, her disabled daughter represented the opportunity to experience career success vicariously.

Despite these discouraging parental attitudes, the women in this group managed to be socially active during their adolescence. What they report was a determination to prove their parents wrong. One woman stated:

When I became about 16 or 17, I pushed myself to have the very things my parents said I could not have. I was determined to prove I was a "normal" woman. I deliberately sought out the most handsome man to parade around. And although I did not consciously intend to do it, I became pregnant out of wedlock at 17, which was extremely affirming for me. One of my proud moments was parading around the supermarket with my belly sticking out for all to see that I was indeed a woman, and that my body worked like a normal woman's body.

Another woman similarly explained, "I was counterphobic. I had this terrible fear that my parents were right and as soon as I could, I began screwing around like mad to rebel against them and my own fear."

What factors enable some women to rebel rather than to internalize negative expectations? Often a combination of circumstances facilitates the rebellion. Similar to the first group, several of the women described close relationships with their fathers; some of the women who became disabled at age 5 or 6 reported strong positive relationships with their fathers predisability, and although the relationship often changed postdisability, the impact of those first few years was sustaining. Other women reported mixed messages from their fathers. While overtly the fathers told them that they could not make it socially in the outside world, at the same time these fathers remained very close to them, sometimes seductively so, providing the young women with the confidence to take on the social scene. Sometimes the presence of a sister, another family member, or a close friend or a group of friends helped the woman to challenge her parents' pessimistic assumptions about her. One woman noted that through her relationships with her girlfriends, she discovered that she had the capacity to give and to nurture, albeit not physically, and that if she could nurture her friends, perhaps she could nurture a husband and children as well.

A third factor appeared to be the nature of the community in which the disabled woman grew up, particularly in terms of architectural and attitudinal accessibility. The presence of curbcuts everywhere was significant for one woman, whereas the availability of a car was crucial for another, allowing both to explore the social arena despite parental prohibitions. The neighborhood's attitudes toward disability—or, more generally toward difference—could help or hinder the rebellion process. For example, in one community many of the residents were Holocaust survivors who had undergone trauma; they could understand the trauma of polio and receive a young woman with polio into their social environment. Finally, individual personality characteristics were significant. For example, several of the women described themselves as always having been rebellious, spunky, risk takers; they were determined not to let their parents' pessimism get them down.

3. *Parents viewed their disabled daughter as a "defective" woman, and the disabled woman had limited heterosexual involvement during adolescence.* Several women typified this situation of low parental expectations and limited involvement by the woman in social activities during adolescence. While the parental view of the daughter as defective was by no means the sole explanation for the limited social activity, or even the major one, it nonetheless was an important influence. Some of these women talked about their lack of self-confidence and low self-expectations as a major reason why they did not become more active in social activities. They held themselves responsible, sometimes describing themselves as "my own worst enemy." We know from clinical theory and research that self-esteem and self-confidence do not develop in a vacuum, but that the environment in general and parental attitudes in particular have a major impact.

Even assuming that the parents were not major causes of a daughter's low self-esteem, because the parents had serious doubts about her social potential, they were not in a position to challenge her negative assumptions and self-doubts. Stated one parent, "I knew my daughter was depressed because she felt she could not compete with the other girls for boys' attentions, and I felt bad for her, but what could I do? In her situation. I would feel the same; anyone with a disability would." This parent saw feelings of social inadequacy in her daughter as inevitable and biologically constructed, rather than as a socially constructed state, and thus did not seek either to help her or to get help for her.

In addition, parents who viewed their disabled daughters as defective women often did not recognize and acknowledge the existence of prejudice in the world toward people with disabilities, at least not when it came to the social arena. They were therefore less likely to select environments that would be socially supportive for their daughters, to advocate on their behalf when they were excluded from social activities, and to help them develop coping strategies to understand and deal with prejudice. As one woman stated, "When I would come home crying because I had not been invited to a party or because someone had teased me about my disability, instead of being outraged, my mother would tell me to spend more time practicing in front of the mirror to walk straight and look more 'normal' so that people would accept me; it was like blaming the victim."

What was striking in this group of women was the absence of any strong positive counterforce in their lives that would affirm their social and sexual potential. Either they internalized their parents' and society's negative perceptions of them or they waged an unsuccessful war against a host of barriers without the benefit of backup forces.

4. *Parents not only viewed their disabled daughter as "defective" but felt that sexuality was potentially dangerous for her; and the disabled woman had not only limited social involvement but also a particularly traumatic time in the heterosexual arena during adolescence.* This fourth situation is a variation of the third. Women in the previous category perceived their parents as having relatively few fears about the emergence of their sexuality because they did not perceive them as sexual people. In contrast, women in the present group described their parents as viewing sexuality for them as extremely dangerous; they received strong messages that men would use and abuse them, would take what they wanted sexually and then abandon them, would talk about their sexual conquests with them to the entire community or in other ways humiliate them. These women learned from their parents that they could be sex objects but, unlike non-disabled women, they would not be chosen as permanent partners or potential childbearers; this was another version of the defective woman theme. Most of the women in this group had sensory disabilities (that is, hearing or visual impairments) with otherwise physically intact bodies. Perhaps because they were close to the norm of beauty and attractiveness, parents could see these daughters as capable of giving sexual pleasure but not intact enough to fulfill feminine roles.

For several of these women, the consequences of such negative messages were devastating. Not only were their social and sexual lives in adolescence restricted by the typical range of barriers, but they actively avoided social situations out of fear of being abused. One deaf woman said, "I learned from my father and others that socializing, getting sexually involved, was a dangerous thing for deaf people to do. As a result, I built a wall around myself based on fear, fear of letting other people in, fear of being intimate." This woman described herself as resorting to drinking and ultimately becoming an alcoholic as a way to deal with her fears. Two women, one bisexual and the other lesbian, reported that they began to explore relationships with women as a preferable alternative to dealing with what they believed would be the inevitably destructive effects of relating to men. Clearly this was not the only factor encouraging their sexual preference for women, but it was one factor. As with the previous group, there was a lack of mitigating forces in these women's environments to counter the powerful negative parental messages.

Given the limited data upon which this study is based, it is difficult to generalize about the relative prevalence of these four kinds of relationships between parental expectations and disabled daughters' degree of heterosexual involvement during adolescence. Gross estimates suggest that from two-thirds to three-fourths of the thirty-one women in the sample disabled before adolescence fell into the third category, in which parents viewed their disabled daughters as defective women, and the daughters in turn had limited involvement in heterosexual activities; the remaining women were fairly evenly divided among the other three categories. What is most distressing is how few sets of parents—three to four at most—viewed their daughters as intact women clearly capable of meeting female role expectations.

SUMMARY AND CONCLUSIONS

This paper has considered the relationship between parental expectations and degree of heterosexual success during adolescence for women with physical and sensory disabilities. The research findings suggest that many parents have low heterosexual expectations for their disabled teenage daughters because they view them as unable to fulfill the typical female role of marriage and childrearing. While they may offer them strong encouragement and support in the educational and career arenas, such support is based on their underlying assumption that these daughters are defective women. In response, some disabled women rebel against their parents' assumptions and have active, satisfying social lives. For many other women, however, pessimistic parental expectations contribute to their limited social and sexual involvement and to their own feelings of inadequacy as women.

In contrast, some parents have positive social and sexual expectations for their disabled daughter; they see her as an intact woman, with her disability as one of her many characteristics. Such parental attitudes tend to facilitate disabled women's social success in adolescence; they foster high self-esteem and allow the woman to be able to rely on her parents to mediate an often difficult, prejudicial social environment.

These findings add to the growing body of literature that stresses the importance of the environmental influence, and more specifically the parental influence, on the development of women and men with disabilities. They speak against a biological, deterministic viewpoint because there has been no evidence that the fact of disability, type of disability, age of onset during childhood or any other biological givens (apart from the environmental response), explain degree of heterosexual involvement.

This research raises almost as many questions as it answers. We need to examine more fully the relationship between parental expectations and heterosexual involvement using a larger, more diverse sample and more sensitive data-gathering instruments. Some of the questions that need to be considered in further depth are these:

- What factors cause some parents to become overly focused on their daughter's disability and enable others to take a broader view, with disability as only one of her many features?
- Are certain kinds of disabilities more likely to elicit certain kinds of parental fears and concerns regarding sexuality? If so, why?
- Why and how is the father-daughter relationship an important factor in social success?
- What factors enable some disabled adolescent women to rebel against low parental expectations?
- Can the visible presence of role models (that is, highly socially successful disabled women) serve to alert parental expectations and facilitate the social success of disabled young women?
- Do disabled women have less *homosexual* involvement and interest during adolescence than non-disabled women?
- To what extent does degree of heterosexual success during adolescence have developmental significance for those disabled women aware of being lesbian or bisexual? For these women, how does the extent of parents' heterosexual expectations affect their degree of involvement in heterosexual and homosexual activities?

In addition, while the present research compared disabled and non-disabled adolescent women, it is equally important to compare disabled young women and disabled young men in the heterosexual arena. For example, given that disabled adult men tend to be more socially successful than disabled adult women (Fine and Asch 1981), are disabled adolescent men any more socially successful than their female counterparts? Also, given that definitions of manhood are much less based on physical appearance and perfection than are definitions of womanhood, are parents of disabled young men any more likely to see their sons as intact rather than defective and hence set more positive social expectations for them? In addition, for men sex is more readily recognized as a legitimate physical need than it is for women. Does this view encourage parents of disabled young men to become more active advocates for their sons in the social arena? Finally, it is necessary to consider whether young men are influenced by parental expectations to the same degree as young women. Some preliminary research comparing blind teenage men and women (Mayadas and Duehn 1976) suggests that male youth may be less subject to influence by adult expectations.

Disabled adolescent women have, indeed, been frustrated in their social and sexual lives. By not actively participating in heterosexual activities, they have experienced too often a sense of difference and have missed out on many of the joys and pleasures, as well as the pains, of budding sexuality. One mother in this study indicated that when the diagnosing doctor told her that her daughter had a disability, he also told her to "raise her like a normal girl." In view of our research findings, this would seem to be good advice, with a significant correction. Disabled girls and young women are not *like* normal girls; they *are* normal girls. Disability does not detract from normalcy. When parents are able to recognize this, they can help their disabled daughters to flourish socially and in other capacities. When they fail to recognize it, they become one more problem for the disabled young woman to take on.

Appendix

RESEARCH HYPOTHESIS
The research hypotheses of the study described in this chapter included the following:

1. *Women disabled before adolescence have less active heterosexual lives during adolescence than do women disabled after adolescence.* This follows from prior research findings.

2. *Parents of women disabled before adolescence have a different set of future expectations for their daughters than do parents of women disabled after adolescence.* In particular, it was hypothesized that parents of women disabled before adolescence had doubts about their daughter's ability to fulfill typical female roles and hence had lower expectations for their daughter in the heterosexual arena, the arena traditionally associated with womanhood, in comparison to parents of women who were not disabled during adolescence. It was also hypothesized that these same parents had higher expectations for their dis-

abled daughter in the education/career arena, not so much because these parents appreciated their daughter's career potential but because they believed that typical female options would not be open to them— they would have to work by default. In essence, parents of women disabled before adolescence were more likely to view their daughters as "defective" women and to alter their expectations accordingly.

3. *For women disabled before adolescence, positive parental expectations in the heterosexual arena facilitate the daughter's heterosexual involvement during adolescence, whereas pessimistic attitudes hinder such involvement.* This hypothesis was a beginning effort to generalize about the relationship between parental attitudes and disabled daughters' behaviors in the heterosexual arena. The designers of the study recognized its simplistic nature and anticipated that the findings might suggest more complex, realistic patterns, which in turn could be utilized for future research.

DESCRIPTION OF THE SAMPLE

As noted, forty-three women with physical and sensory disabilities were included in this study, thirty-one disabled before adolescence and twelve disabled after. Twenty-two of the forty-three women were attendees of a conference for young disabled women held in Minneapolis, Minnesota, sponsored by the Disability Rights Education and Defense Fund (DREDF), Berkeley, California; all of these women lived in the Minneapolis–St. Paul area. Another ten members of the sample were from the New York City area and were contacted through outreach to the coordination of disabled student services at Barnard College, New York City, and through personal contacts of the author. The remaining eleven women were contacted through an advertisement in the *Womyn's Braille Press* and through various informal national networks of disabled women; they lived in relatively large urban areas throughout the country. The geographic breakdown for the two groups in the sample is shown in Table A.

In terms of kinds of disabilities represented by the sample, the major categories were cerebral palsy; mobility impairments other than cerebral palsy, including muscular dystrophy, juvenile arthritis, dwarfism, spinal cord injury, and post-polio; brain and neurological impairments, such as seizure disorder, closed head injury, and learning disabilities; blindness; deafness; and other disabilities not elsewhere categorized, such as facial disfigurement. For the two groups in the sample, the breakdown by disability is shown in Table B.

Regarding the age of onset of disability, for the group disabled before

Table A

Location	Disabled before Adolescence	Disabled after Adolescence
Minneapolis–St. Paul	18	4
New York City	8	5
Other	5	3

Table B

Disability	Disabled before Adolescence	Disabled after Adolescence
Cerebral palsy	12	0
Other mobility impairments	8	6
Brain/neurological	1	4
Blindness	6	0
Deafness	2	0
Other	2	2

adolescence, twenty-one of the thirty-one were disabled at birth; the mean age of onset was 1.4 years. For the group disabled after adolescence, the mean age of onset was 20 years.

In terms of basic demographic data, the average age of the group disabled before adolescence was 32.9 years, whereas the average for the group disabled after adolescence was slightly younger: 31.3 years. The majority of members in both groups were white, heterosexual, and single (see Table C).

The majority of members in both groups had at least some college education, and a considerable number had continued their education beyond the bachelor degree. In terms of major work activities, most women in both groups were currently working full- or part-time (see Table D).

In describing living and educational circumstances during adolescence, the majority of women in both groups described themselves as living with their parents and siblings. The majority of both groups attended mainstream public high schools (See Table E).

In summary, then, a typical member of the group of women disabled before adolescence was in her early thirties; was disabled at birth with cerebral palsy; and was white, single, heterosexual, without children, and a resident of the Minneapolis–St. Paul area. She had completed postcollege training and held a full-time job. During her adolescence, she lived at home with her parents and siblings and at-

Table C

Characteristic	Disabled before Adolescence	Disabled after Adolescence
Ethnicity		
White	26	10
Black	2	1
Other	3	1
Sexual orientation		
Heterosexual	18	10
Lesbian	4	0
Bisexual	2	1
Uncertain	7	1
Marital status		
Single	22	8
Married	5	2
Divorced	2	1
Other	1	1
No answer	1	0
Have children		
Yes	4	2
No	27	10

Table D

Characteristic	Disabled before Adolescence	Disabled after Adolescence
Highest level of education completed		
Grade School	1	0
Some high school or high school diploma	5	0
Some college	4	4
College graduate	2	0
Postcollege	9	5
Still in school	7	2
Other	2	0
No answer	1	1
Main work now		
Full-time job	17	2
Part-time job	4	2
Full-time student	1	4
School and work	4	1
Volunteer	1	1
Unemployed	1	1
Other	0	1
No answer	3	0

Table E

Characteristic	Disabled before Adolescence	Disabled after Adolescence
Lived with during adolescence		
Parents and siblings	24	10
Nonrelatives	2	0
Boarding school	3	0
Institution	2	1
No answer	0	1
Type of high school attended		
Mainstream public	16	7
Public special ed.	2	0
Residential	4	1
Rehabilitation center	2	0
Mainstream and special ed.	3	0
Other	2	3
No answer	2	1

tended a mainstream public high school. Much of this description applies equally well to the typical member of the group of women disabled after adolescence, with these exceptions: members of this group were more likely to have had some kind of motor impairment other than cerebral palsy, having become disabled around the age of 20; they were more likely to have come from New York City than Minneapolis–St. Paul, and they were more likely to be full-time students than full-time workers.

DESCRIPTION OF THE DATA-GATHERING INSTRUMENTS
Two major instruments were used to gather data from this sample. The first was a questionnaire, "Social and Sexual Experiences of Disabled Women during Adolescence"; twenty-three of the thirty-one women disabled before adolescence and all twelve women disabled after adolescence were asked to fill this out and return it by mail. The remaining eight women disabled before adolescence were interviewed in person using the questionnaire as a guideline to obtain more in-depth material; these women were selected because they represented a range in degree and nature of social activity during adolescence.

The questionnaire asked the respondent retrospectively to consider her adolescence, particularly the middle adolescent years of 13 through 17, and to answer questions in a variety of areas. Major topics included (1) the extent and nature of her social life, where social life was defined as dating and other activities involving male partners toward whom the woman had a romantic/sexual interest; (2) comparison of her social life to that of her non-disabled peers; (3) sources and kinds of messages and information about sexuality; (4) her own interests, expectations, and aspirations in the heterosexual, educational, and vocational arenas; (5) her parents' expectations and aspirations for her in those same arenas; and (6) the extent and nature of parental communication with her on sociosexual issues.

The second major source of information was personal interviews with six parents of women in the sample disabled before adolescence; these four mothers and two fathers were parents of four of the eight women who also were interviewed in-depth. They were selected not only because of the diversity of their daughters' adolescent experiences but also because each parent had both a disabled and a non-disabled daughter, thereby facilitating comparisons. In a fashion similar to the questionnaire, the interviewees were asked to reflect on the social lives of their disabled and non-disabled daughters during their middle adolescence. Major topics included (1) a comparison of the social lives of the interviewee's two daughters during adolescence; (2) a comparison of the interviewee's heterosexual, educational, and vocational expectations and aspirations for the two daughters; (3) a comparison of the interviewee's handling of sex education and sexual issues for the two daughters; and (4) the interviewee's beliefs, feelings, and concerns about the impact of the disabled daughter's disability on her social life and the extent and nature of the parent-daughter communication about these concerns.

When considering the data obtained from the sample of women and parents, it is important to keep in mind the following limitations:

1. The sample size of forty-three women is small and was selected for its availability rather than its randomness or diversity; it was intended as a beginning, a way to generate hypotheses that could be tested more comprehensively with a fuller sample. Ethnic minorities, lesbians, and lower educational and socioeconomic groups are particularly underrepresented.
2. The subsample used as a comparison group—that of women disabled after adolescence—is particularly small, making statistical comparison problematic.
3. Because of the geographic distribution and the age of the women involved, few parents were available for direct interviews; thus, much of the parental information is based on daughters' perceptions rather than parents' own reflections.
4. The data instruments asked the respondents and interviewees to recall and report on the past, often a rather distant past, rather than to speak about the here and now. These recollections do not necessarily reflect an accurate account of adolescence, for they

may be colored by a variety of conscious and unconscious factors, including the disabled woman's current degree of social success, self-esteem, and relationship with her parents, as well as the counterpart issues for the parents.

References

Asch, A., and H. Rousso. 1985. Therapists with disabilities: Theoretical and clinical issues. *Psychiatry* 48(1):1–12.

Bardwick, J. M. 1971. *Psychology of women: A study of biocultural conflicts.* New York: Harper and Row.

Blos, P. 1962. *On Adolescence.* New York: Free Press.

Carrera, M. A. 1983. Some reflections on adolescent sexuality. *SIECUS Report* 11(4): 1–2.

Darling, R. 1979. *Families against society: A study of reactions to children with birth defects.* Beverly Hills, Calif.: Sage.

Duffy, Y. 1981. *All things are possible.* Ann Arbor: Garvin and Associates.

Fine, M., and A. Asch. 1981. Disabled women: Sexism without the pedestal. *Journal of Sociology and Social Welfare* 8(2).

Fox, G. L. 1980. The mother–adolescent daughter relationship as a sexual socialization structure: A research review. *Family Relations* 29:21–28.

Fox, G. L., and G. L. Inazu. 1980. Patterns and outcomes of mother-daughter communication about sexuality. *Journal of Social Issues* 36(1)7–29.

Goodman, E. 1983. The turmoil of teenage sexuality: Parents' mixed signals. *Ms.* 12(1):37–41.

Katz, P. A. 1979. The development of female identity. *Becoming female: Perspectives on development,* ed. C. B. Kopp. New York: Plenum Press.

Kris Study Group, Beres/Caldor section. 1971. The influence of early childhood illness and defect on analyzability. Paper presented at the New York Psychoanalytic Institute, September 14.

Landis, C., and M. M. Bolles. 1942. *Personality and sexuality of the physically handicapped woman.* New York: Hoeber.

Lussier, A. 1980. The physical handicap and the body ego. *International Journal of Psychoanalysis* 39:264–72.

Malmquist, C. P. 1985. *Handbook of adolescence.* New York: Aronson.

Mayadas, N. S., and W. D. Duehn. 1976. The impact of significant adults' expectations on the lifestyle of visually impaired children. *New Outlook* (September):286–90.

Ornstein, A., and P. Ornstein. 1985. Parenting as a function of the adult self. In *Parental influences in health and disease,* ed. J. Anthony and G. Pollock. Boston: Little, Brown.

Roskies, E. 1972. *Abnormality and normality: The mothering of thalidomide children.* Ithaca, N. Y.: Cornell University Press.

Rousso, H. 1981. Disabled people are sexual, too. *Exceptional Parent* (December): 21–25.

———. 1984. Disabled yet intact: Guidelines for work with congenitally physically disabled youngsters and their parents. *Child and Adolescent Social Work Journal* (1(4):254–69.

Thompson, S. 1984. The search for tomorrow: On feminism and the reconstruction of teen romance. In *Pleasure and danger: Exploring female sexuality*, ed. C. Vance. Boston: Routledge and Kegan, Paul.

Welbourne, A., S. Lifschitz, H. Selvin, and R. Green. 1983. A comparison of the sexual learning experiences of visually impaired and sighted women. *Journal of Visual Impairment and Blindness* 77(6):256–59.

Zellman, G. L. and J. D. Goodchilds. 1983. Becoming sexual in adolescence. In *Changing boundaries*, ed. E. Allegeir and N. McCornick. Palo Alto, Calif.: Mayfield.

6. Friendship and Fairness: How Disability Affects Friendship between Women

BERNICE FISHER and ROBERTA GALLER

A group of women sit around a low table drinking tea, eating cheese and crackers. We talk about friendship. Each of us views it somewhat differently. Judy defines a friend as "someone who is there for me around important things." Sara sees her friends as "people I do nice things for." Barbara emphasizes her own desire to be recognized: a friend is "someone who knows you from the inside." Karen reminds us that we need our friends to "celebrate" our accomplishments and our joys. Ruth and Diane begin to talk about the quality of their own friendship. Diane stresses reciprocity and notes that friendship also involves many everyday considerations—such as whether the other person lives close enough for the two to get together easily. Ruth speaks warmly of the interests that have drawn her and Diane together as good friends:

Having a lot of shared activities and things in our background that are similar helps a lot. There's a common vocabulary that we share, a minimum of explaining to do. When we talk about all sorts of things—especially having to do with our love for music or our work as therapists, or being Jewish—I know I'm being understood and that I'm understanding someone else.

Although we sometimes grasp for words to describe what friendship means in our lives, the women at this gathering enjoy telling each other of its importance. Our friendships are a testimony to our capacity to love and be loved, to our ability to share our passions and interests, our disappointments and difficulties. But at moments we are ill at ease. We have come together not only to talk about the meaning of our friendships, but about how the fact that some of us are disabled affects the quality of our friendships. Our caring and empathy and common interests have brought us together as friends. But a difference such as disability could, potentially, divide us.

Friendships between disabled and non-disabled women follow in a long tradition of friendships among women: friendships that often begin with (but do not always confine themselves to) women's common experience. Both popular literature and social research suggest that this common experience leads to a special sort of sympathetic understanding between women and is basic to women's friendships (Bell 1981; Bernikow 1980; Block 1980). The prevailing style of women's friendships has not come about by chance. Historically, the division of labor based on gender and the frequent segregation of women into a "separate sphere" have contributed to the pattern of women's friendships. Where most women have worked around the home in cooperation with women kin and neighbors, friendship has been the "natural" outcome of daily life. When women rebelled against the family structure, as they did increasingly in the late-eighteenth and early-nineteenth-century industrial societies, making alliances with friends became an important method of resisting patriarchal control. With industrialization, the movement of many (often single) women into cities created further opportunities for women to meet each other on their own turf. Women now could make friends in the workplace, in nonwork activities and mass entertainment, and through becoming involved in political and social causes. These settings gave women new worlds to share, new arenas for empathy, and new interests in common (Brain 1976; Faderman 1981; Lindsey 1981; Mavor [1971] 1983; Smith-Rosenberg 1980; Wolfe 1983).

However, the same conditions that brought women together in contemporary settings also created a tremendous diversity within these newly constituted worlds of women. Women with widely different backgrounds and life stories faced each other as strangers, strangers who might not know each other's language or the meaning of each other's lives. Where there was no particular pressure for women to become more intimate, an individual might pick and choose whether she wanted to make friends—to get to know the woman-stranger standing beside her on the assembly line or sitting beside her at the next office desk. In some contexts, however, women were actively encouraged to overcome their differences. This has been true particularly in the women's movement, especially the contemporary women's movement, with its strong emphasis on our common experience of oppression. To build a broad-based, radical movement, women have been urged to overcome all the socially defined differences that divide us, to work together toward our shared interest in liberation. In such a context, making friends with women who are "different" has been a logical outcome of the larger political commitment. Sometimes it also has been a test of political virtue, or a testimony to one's activist commit-ment (Dill 1983).

Given the strains built into the idea of a broad-reaching women's movement, the course of friendships among feminists from diverse backgrounds has been far from smooth. Despite the many difficulties, however, this feminist commitment also has prompted women to write about their friendships across socially imposed barriers: interracial friendships, friendships between lesbians and heterosexual women, friendships between disabled and non-disabled women (Campbell 1983; Fisher and Galler 1981; Nickerson and Smith 1984; Walton-Fischler and Newton 1976). In the course of these explorations, feminists have strug-gled to understand how our actual practice of friendship conforms or fails to conform to our ideal of what friendship should be, how the personal connects to the political, how friendships develop and grow in relation to political values that permeate our lives. This does not mean that women's friendships thrive only in a feminist context. It suggests, however, that even the most intimate aspects of our friendship have a basically political dimension. It suggests that our search for fairness, equality, or respect in our friendships mirrors the search for these values in the larger political order, and that understanding one helps us to understand the other (Kidder, Fagin, and Cohen 1981).

In the course of this essay, we would like to explore the possibility of friendship between differently situated women by considering a particular difference: that pertaining to physical disability. Our involve-ment with this topic comes out of our own friendship of thirty years. One of us, Roberta, is disabled from a childhood bout with polio. The other, Berenice, is non-disabled. Both of us have been politically active for significant portions of our lives. In recent years, the disability rights movement and women's movement have affected us both profoundly. These movements enabled us to talk about many things of great impor-tance to our individual lives and our friendship. Without that shared political experience, this chapter could not have been written.

Our friendship developed in the 1950s in a college atmosphere that stressed social rebellion. In a period of early marriage for women, we, as single women, saw ourselves as bravely independent. For Roberta, the creed of independence fit with the image of overcoming her handicap of escaping the stereotypes of the poster girl or of the pitifully dependent woman. Neither of us saw her orthopedic disability as a significant factor in our lives. In terms of the conservative, conformist atmosphere of the period, neither of us was "normal." We asserted our common difference with pride, touched with a shade of contempt.

In the earlier years of our friendship, we never spoke about

Roberta's disability. When we spent a year together as roommates (sharing with another woman a third-floor apartment), we never discussed what it meant for Roberta to climb the stairs. Our pattern, as a friend of ours put it, was one of "unspoken accommodation." Berenice automatically took the grocery bags when we came home from shopping. When we were walking down the street, she slowed her pace to match Roberta's (or if Berenice neglected to do so, Roberta quickened her own, and said nothing.) We shared many important things—experiences, thoughts, ideas—but we omitted others. During a long period of separation in which Roberta worked with the civil rights movement and Berenice continued in graduate school, disability played little overt role in either of our lives. When we encountered each other again—at a 1970 feminist demonstration—we were just beginning to discover the more fundamental ways in which being women made a difference. It was six or seven years before we began to understand that disability made a difference as well.

In the process of discussing our own relationship and in talking with the dozen or so women we consulted and interviewed for this paper, three major themes have stood out in trying to understand how disability affects friendship between women. The first theme is that of opportunity: the opportunity to get to know the other person, to test out whether friendship is possible. The second theme is that of reciprocity: the desire for reciprocity as part of a friendship ideal and the ways in which disability affects reciprocity. The third theme is that of responsibility: how disability raises certain special issues of responsibility in the ways friends relate to each other and how they, together, deal with the world. In exploring these themes, we have drawn to some extent on various kinds of research concerned with social relations. But, given the ways in which both disabled people and all women have been systematically excluded from most social research, we have drawn even more heavily on our own stories and on those of a small number of women with whom we spoke and informally interviewed for this paper.[1] Because the numbers have been small and the variety limited, we do not wish to offer hard and fast generalizations. Rather, we offer our analysis as a genuine exploration, one that we hope will invite modification and questioning.

OPPORTUNITY: GETTING TO KNOW EACH OTHER
Among the extensive studies on how people get to know each other, the works of Erving Goffman and Fred Davis still stand out as especially relevant and powerful accounts of the effect of disability on this process (Davis 1961; Goffman 1963). Goffman's well-known book, *Stigma*, of-

fers a complex theory of interaction, but its underlying message is relatively simple: disabled people carry an unfair share of the burden in social interactions with others, especially when disabled and non-disabled first meet. Although far more critical of the social context of interaction, recent researchers on disability rights have made the same point: as one disabled woman we interviewed put it: "You're going to have to go more than halfway to make friends" (Asch 1984; Weinberg 1983).

The reason that disabled people must go more than halfway lies in the obvious but painful fact that having a disability reduces one's opportunities to make friends. The degree of reduction depends on other factors, especially the extent to which the disability is visible in a given situation. Visible disability often causes the non-disabled to guard themselves or to withdraw entirely. They cannot imagine becoming friends with a disabled person. Indeed, many non-disabled people find it intolerable to spend even a short amount of time with someone with a disability. Disability is frightening in our society. It taps into our fears of ostracism, illness, and death. It plants a stigma not only on the person with the disability but on anyone who might be identified with it. (Thus, disabled people sometimes avoid each other to keep from being identified with disability or with a disability more harshly stigmatized than one's own.) Disability also implies that something has gone wrong—and that, if possible, if should be put right again. (Roberta has been approached on the street by people suggesting physical or spiritual "cures" for her disability.) For this reason, perhaps, women view disability with particular apprehension. Because women are assigned the rules of nurturer, helper, and healer, getting to know someone with a disability may *seem* to imply that the non-disabled woman must automatically become a caretaker. The opportunity to nurture someone who is disabled may, in fact, be welcomed by certain women. For others, however, friendship with a disabled person, and perhaps especially with a disabled woman, may appear only as an added burden (Asch 1984; Nestle 1981; Smith 1981).

Given this general pattern of avoidance, disabled people often go more than halfway by employing a strategy that Davis has called "Normalizing." Disabled people normalize relationships by getting the non-disabled person to go beyond their preoccupation with the disability (and the "fictional acceptance" that covers up that preoccupation) to the discovery of what they and the disabled person really have in common. Similar patterns of normalizing emerge when other oppressed people encounter those whose class, race, gender, or other privileges lead them to assumptions that make conversation difficult. Pam Fishman's striking study of interaction between women and men shows how women, like disabled people, carry a disproportionate burden of the interaction, moving conversation along, helping it to go smoothly and to the satisfaction of their male partners (Fishman 1978). Our discussions with disabled women suggested that being both a woman and disabled may well intensify the determination to make social interactions run smoothly.

Despite the fact that most of the women we talked with had a measure of feminist and disability consciousness, they rarely expressed resentment at carrying a disproportionate share of the burden of getting to know others. Diane, who has a wide network of friends and has been a leader in the development of disability consciousness, accepted nonetheless the idea that she would have to go out of her way to make friends. Her opportunities were radically reduced by her disability, she granted: "I don't pick my friends. They pick me." Emily, who noted how the disability movement had helped her to joke about the limits of non-disabled people, still placed a high value on making interactions run smoothly. If anything, the disability movement helped her do this, given her more refined strategies for handling others' reactions.

Some of the satisfaction expressed by disabled women in their ability to handle social interaction undoubtedly stems from the sense of control that members of oppressed groups can gain from the subtle handling of relations with more privileged people. Managing social interaction also has other advantages. For some disabled women, such management is a source of pride because of the way it can be used to validate their identity as women. Being granted such an identity, as feminists active in the disability rights movement have pointed out, does not come easily for most disabled women. Disabled women often face open or indirect suggestions that they are not really women (Asch and Sachs 1983, Campling 1981, Fine and Asch 1981). This attack on the humanity of disabled women, by implying that they can never achieve the "proper" gender identity, often affects the way in which disabled women present themselves to others. Karen, for instance, talked about using her nurturing abilities to foster relationships with women friends and male lovers: "I never really felt I was treated or got recognition or experienced myself as a woman." For this reason, she enjoyed being successful in some of the more traditional womanly ways. For other disabled women, however, friendships with other women did not offer a promising arena for such validation. A group of older disabled women we spoke with veered away from the topic of friendships with women: they wanted to tell us how successful some of them had been in catching husbands. Some younger disabled women showed discomfort with the notion that nurturance facilitated getting to know others. Diane stressed that she was perfectly able to be "nasty" when a non-disabled person infringed on her comfort or self-respect. Yet, Karen's sentiments seem to be common: being nurturing provided a way into relationships.

One other important aspect of managing interactions lies in the disabled woman's desire to protect herself. Karen noted how she used her social skills to fend off any confrontation—any response from others that would cause her pain. She added that these same skills were needed to fend off the "patronizing" gestures of other women who tried to take care of her. Disability activist Connie Panzarino writes of the same problem: how much energy disabled women must spend to ward off the inappropriate gestures that non-disabled women make toward them (Panzarino 1981). Sometimes, as Diane's remark about being nasty suggests, disabled women are forced to use their interactional skills to get rid of people, and get rid of them quickly—to push away or yell at someone who is about to do some serious damage by trying to "help."

In looking at the problem of people getting to know each other, social researchers often view life as a sort of cocktail party: we approach each other tentatively, with little information, and try to decide whether we are willing to form a greater bond (Wolff 1950). In fact, large parties often pose problems for the disabled. Roberta, whose orthopedic disability makes sitting more comfortable than standing or mingling, finds party situations frequently isolating. Diane talks about how painful she finds large parties these days (as opposed to when she went to them with a male lover), because people often walk by her, or just put a drink in her hand and scurry away. The metaphor of life as a party seems especially applicable when people have to spend enough time together to get to know "who" each other is, or when the conditions for getting to know the other are limited in certain ways. Thus, Margaret, a deaf teenager, explained how her disability cut her off from others in her high school: most of the social life takes place on the phone, and her classmates find it awkward to make a date with her through her mother or sister.

But for other disabled women, at other periods, the cocktail party metaphor seems of limited applicability. We were struck with how the family and neighborhood structures into which disabled women were born (whether or not they were disabled from birth), could provide a secure and validating environment in which to cultivate friendships. Roberta, who is Jewish and grew up in a predominantly Jewish neighborhood of a large city, lived in the same apartment building as some of her relatives, and went to the same school as the kids on her block. She grew up with a strong sense of belonging to a community and a family, both before and after she contracted polio. Indeed, her adamant refusal to attend a special school for disabled children stemmed not only from her rejection of a disability identity (having just learned arithmetic, she argued that she didn't want disability to be "my common denominator"), but from her sense of what she had to lose if she were separated from her neighborhood and neighborhood school. Emily, who was brought up in a small town, did not experience her disability as isolating her from other children. The friends from her neighborhood and neighborhood schools remained friends for life. She recently had lunch with a group of women friends she had known since childhood, and they compared how difficult all their lives had been.

Although community often offers a promising context for making friends, the kind of community will influence the kinds of friendships disabled women can make and the ease of making them. Beverly noted that although a disabling stroke strained some ties within her black community, she had become friends with a disabled woman in her building and had become closer to some people in her established friendship network. Esther and Mary talked about how their common experiences in special hospitals and schools fostered their friendship. Despite the way in which segregated institutions isolated them from non-disabled children, finding themselves in adjoining beds in a polio ward and attending the same special school had provided the basis for their lifelong bond. Like contiguity, family structure and history can affect the possibility of developing friendship in different ways. Diane commented on how the extra efforts of her parents to include friends in family activities prepared her for friendship to play an important role in her life. In contrast, Barbara recounted how Felicia had withdrawn from a developing friendship because it began to remind her of her relationship with her disabled mother. The question of how community and family intersect with the possibility of forming friendships between differently situated women is clearly a subtle one. It suggests the need to look in a more detailed way at the precise conditions, social and economic, as well as psychological, that make friendship possible (Fischer 1982; Lewittes and Mukherji 1985).

RECIPROCITY: BUILDING FRIENDSHIPS THROUGH GIVING
Even when the winds of chance, social structure, and history blow in the right direction for developing friendship, women friends face crucial issues where disability is concerned. One of these issues is reciprocity. Studies of how people build relationships often view reciprocity as a balance of contribution and benefit: both parties feel that their contri-

bution to the relationship is fairly balanced by what they get out of it (Burgess and Huston 1979; Lerner and Lerner 1981). Although this "marketplace" image of social life has been criticized on the grounds that love (or at least feelings of contentment) transcend such trade-offs, some desire for reciprocity seems to have played a part in the friendships of all the women we spoke to—as well as in our own.

Like any people building close relationships, disabled and nondisabled women need to figure out a balance between preserving autonomy and permitting reciprocity. This balance is not created in a social or historical vacuum. The definitions of what constitutes autonomy and reciprocity change with our other values. Many years ago, when we never mentioned Roberta's disability, autonomy involved denying the experience and meaning of physical pain and possibility of asking others for help or comfort. Reciprocity included those physical things we could both do: where Roberta's disability precluded her participation, we managed not to know it. Given both the women's rights and disability rights movements, as well as the sense of shared vulnerability that our aging has given us, we have redefined autonomy so that it can include greater dependence and interdependence. We have struggled to see reciprocity in a new light and have become less quick to judge what elements should or should not be a part of a balanced relationship.

In talking with both disabled and non-disabled women, two areas seem particularly important to the development of such a balance: that of physical help, and that of emotional reciprocity. These two areas seem closely related. The disabled women we talked with often alluded to a sort of unspoken bargain that they struck with their non-disabled friends. Recognizing that friendship requires a certain special accommodation (if not direct physical help) by non-disabled friends, the disabled women attempted to balance the scale by being especially attentive and supportive in the emotional sphere, being extragood listeners, comforters, and so forth. Such an attempt, however, needs to be understood in the context of the strong investment in physical autonomy that characterized the disabled women with whom we spoke. All of them resented being given help they did not need or want. Doris spoke with outrage at the complete strangers who would grab her wheelchair and begin pushing her down the street at high speed. Roberta recalled angrily how people would grab her cane arm to "assist" her, thus throwing her off balance. If women generally have a strong stake in maintaining bodily integrity (whether in defense against rape, sexual harassment, or a host of other assaults), disabled women have an additional stake in protecting their body space from invasion, their adulthood from being discredited by the assumption that decisions about their bodies belong to others.

In these terms, any interaction involving physical help is especially loaded. Diane, who granted that "I'm not going to get through the world if I don't ask for help," still preferred to hire people to do many jobs for her, rather than impose on people she knew. Doris and Viola (who is non-disabled) suggested that Viola's sensitivity and their mutual candor about dealing with Doris's physical needs helped make their friendship a strong one. But they also stressed that Doris was both independent and helpful herself: since she had gotten a car she had been able to help Viola transport her children and do many errands.

Despite such strategies for maintaining equilibrium, it is evident that many disabled women fear that they cannot balance the friendship scales if they reveal their actual physical situation. Thus, they take refuge in hiding their real physical needs and/or the costs of ignoring them (Duck 1983; Thomas 1982; Weinberg 1982). Barbara recounts how, after making her way to work through severe winter weather, she would sit alone in her office and cry from the pain in her legs. Alison, who was raised in a strict southern Baptist family, recalls how she always considered her disability a private matter, her "cross to bear." She was able to hide its cost to her by periodically withdrawing from her non-disabled friends, to recover from the exhaustion that keeping up with them entailed. She considered such periods of recuperation crucial to the ability to lead the life she had chosen, and she felt frustrated by friends who would not grant her such time by herself.

Some disabled women suspected their non-disabled friends of preferring that the needs and costs of disability remain hidden. Our own experience and our limited discussions with the non-disabled friends indicate conflicting responses. At times, when disabled friends state needs linked to their disability, their non-disabled friends view them as a burden. However, the reasons for which non-disabled women sometimes shy away from giving help may or may not relate to the fact of the disability. When Berenice is overtired and irritable, she can easily resent Roberta's request to help take down the garbage before going out to dinner. At her most irritable, she may not want to say, "I'm tired; why don't you get someone else to take down your garbage or take it down yourself, furgodsakes!" Disability plays a role in this scenario, but its core concerns the problem of helping out (with anything, for anyone) when one does not feel like it. Similarly, Sara reported her discomfort with Diane's request for help in choosing a table setting for a special dinner. For Diane, this was a practical request for assistance—a request she easily might have made had she not been blind. For Sara, it was an expectation that she employ those traditional "feminine" skills that she had always resisted learning. Diane, who carefully avoids asking friends to do many helping tasks, was distressed. Sara felt frustrated.

The issue of physical help becomes even more complex where the definition of physical ability itself is at stake—where friends disagree on what the disabled woman can do. Just as the definitions of ability and disability can change historically with different social conditions, so they may be tested and modified in the course of a relationship. Diane noted that whenever possible she liked to "help in a concrete way." Because her friends rarely suggested that she do so, she had to make the offers—over and over again. In one difficult incident with her friend Ruth, Diane offered to shop for the two of them while Ruth did other necessary errands. When Ruth hesitated to take Diane up on her offer, Diane became angry: shopping for food was something she did for herself all the time! Finally Ruth agreed to the sensibleness of the plan, regardless of her initial concerns. Another conflict about what Diane could do was not resolved so easily. It involved Ruth's reluctance to let Diane baby-sit with Ruth's young child. When Diane charged, and Ruth admitted, that she was afraid to allow Diane to care for the child, Diane countered, with some bitterness, that her own parents had trusted her with the care of her siblings when she was only 12. From Diane's point of view, the most difficult aspect of this incident was the implication that she could not take care of children and should not, therefore, become a mother. Such an implied judgment seemed a sort of betrayal, a lack of faith.

Ruth acknowledged that she sometimes underestimates Diane's actual ability, that she (Ruth) must still go through a "conscious mental process" to remind herself that Diane can do certain things. Now that Ruth's child is a little older, she is more comfortable with Diane's taking care of him for a few hours. Some of her fear persists, however. From Ruth's standpoint, the most important change in this area of tension comes from accepting this fear. Although it might be ideal not to feel this way, "I no longer judge myself so harshly." She characterized her fear as her own, not Diane's. Acknowledging that fear, said Ruth, did *not* imply that Diane should not have children.

While competing definitions of physical ability make reciprocity in practical matters more complicated, society's image of disability also affects the possibility of emotional reciprocity. Because society pictures disability as precluding or limiting participation in important areas of life, women friends must find a nonthreatening way to approach these topics, if the friendship is to include understanding and support. In fact, many disabled women find that they or their friends tend to shy away from those topics that touch on their potential differences, that such sensitive areas are censored out, rather than included in emotional interchange. Following a pattern often set by her parents and significant figures in her childhood, the disabled woman may view these topics as inappropriate, engaging in an unspoken agreement with her friends not to bring them up.

Censored areas often include sexuality, courting, and childbearing. Although certain disabled women were able, as children, to talk with their friends about sexuality, adolescence and dating sometimes ended these conversations. Karen recalled her hurt when her non-disabled best friend in high school hid the fact that she had a boyfriend. Her friend, Karen thought, had been afraid that her own success would stand in stark contrast to Karen's exclusion from dating. Alison remembered laughing at her mother when she encouraged dating: that was for girls, thought Alison, and she felt like "another species." Emily recounted how she also missed high school dating. She was not left out of the small-town social life, however. Her friends did many things in groups, and when they married they included her in the preparations and the discussions surrounding the event. "I was envious, but I was involved in the plans . . . like a vicarious pleasure. It makes you feel a part of things." Barbara, who rebelled against the very notion of such exclusion, had an active social life and somewhat precocious sexual experience. Like other teenagers at the time, she didn't talk about her sexual adventures. Also, unlike some other disabled women with whom we talked, her parents expected her to marry and have children.

If many disabled women we spoke with experienced the censoring of sexuality and childbearing, almost all of them reported some difficulty with making the disability itself a topic of conversation. Alison noted that her parents openly talked about the practical aspects of her disability, but never talked about its emotional impact on her. Emily, who had friends from childhood, described how the patterns of silence on this key topic continued when she grew up: she never mentioned her disability, "but that was my choice." Only Diane reported her frank and early discussions about the personal meaning of her disability, a frankness clearly supported by her parents' insistence on her right to a full life. In Diane's first close friendship at the age of 10, her girlfriend shared both Diane's pain at being teased by other children and her outrage at such treatment.

Although disability may not be discussed openly, its silent presence affects the possibility of emotional reciprocity. "I think because of being aware of my particular physical needs and having to ask for concessions and help, I don't ask emotionally," said Alison. "I compensate by being the Rock of Gibraltar in the emotional department. You can't feel like a basket case in every department." Beverly noted that after she had had her stroke, many of her friends disappeared, but others continued to call her . . . for advice. Diane grieved over the imbalance that seemed to mark her current friendships. She was willing to "give without strings," yet, after having given so much support to her friends, she still found herself lonely. This loneliness, she felt, was not due to her blindness but to the fact that many of her closest friends had married and were involved in a social life she did not share. Unlike the pain of being taunted as a child, which she had been able to talk about at that time with her best friend, she found the meaning of this adult loneliness harder to communicate. It was difficult, said Diane, to demand love as a right, even though, deep in her heart, she viewed it "as a matter of justice."

For Alison, at times, justice involved the refusal to accept the sort of trade-offs that friends proposed: one emotionally volatile friend had insisted that her own temper tantrums balanced out Alison's physical disability. But Alison also struggled long and hard to find a way of coping with her more even-tempered, non-disabled friends, who would become very anxious when she told them she was too tired to continue some activity. Alison viewed their insistence that if-she-couldn't-do-it they-shouldn't-do-it as a kind of "bullshit" that required her, as a disabled woman, to take on their unnecessary "guilt," giving her "the added burden of feeling like a burden."

If disabled women have had to struggle to tell their friends how their disability affects their lives—including how their friends' responses to that disability affect their friendship—non-disabled women often have equal difficulty articulating their feelings in this area. One major theme concerns the moral discomfort of non-disabled women with their own non-disabled status (Fisher 1984). Ruth felt that her own "existential guilt" interfered with being as open and honest as she wished to be with Diane. This feeling stemmed from being non-disabled and involved the sense that she should be taking some "special responsibility"; this was a responsibility against which she also rebelled. Sara, who is non-disabled, found herself confused about her own "entitlements" in her relationship with her disabled friend. It seemed reasonable and just for Diane to insist she be treated fairly—in life in general, as well as in her close relationships. Sara, however, was less clear about when *she* was entitled to make demands. Berenice tapped into some of these same feelings when she became involved with bodywork and dance improvisation. She wondered if she could share her experiences with Roberta, whether her joy at discovering how freely she could move was legitimate in the face of Roberta's movement limitations. When she finally broached the subject to Roberta, Roberta expressed her enthusiasm for Berenice's new activities, her own sadness and fears around movement, and the tentative hope that she, too, might find a way to move her body that would reaffirm its—and her—value.

This discussion of ours certainly could not have taken place without the support of both the women's movement and the disability rights movement, with their parallel affirmations of the value of our bodies. In talking with other women, we found that these far-reaching social movements had a deep, if often indirect, affect on the openness with which disability was treated and the possibility of including realities of disability in the emotional dimension of close relationships. Emily described the tremendous impact of the disability movement on her teaching and counseling work and her personal relationships, how, after a lifetime of silence about her disability, she was "dumbfounded" to find all those people talking openly about their own. Alison found herself becoming more and more interested in the meaning of her disability, in part through women friends and lovers who kept bringing disability literature to her attention, asking, in effect, what does this mean for you, for us?

Increased openness, however, does not always lead to greater intimacy and more genuine reciprocity. If a disabled woman and her friends have a long history of mutually denying the meaning of her disability, they are unlikely to receive the news with grace. Alison, whose walk is affected by having had polio, recalled that in her early feminist consciousness-raising group many women bemoaned their feelings about their fat or hairy legs, but they simply ignored her attempt to introduce her own disability as a topic. As Roberta's disability consciousness began to develop, she, too, found longtime friends denying that all this concerned her: "But, *you're* not disabled," they said.

Doris and Viola's account of their friendship points to the importance of political conditions in supporting openness and honesty about disability. These two women met as students at a university that is especially committed to equal access for disabled students. Dormitories and classrooms were arranged so that students with disabilities could participate as fully as possible. Viola, who had had no previous experience with disabled people, suddenly found herself in the midst of students in wheelchairs and with aids. "I kind of watched," she said, "and it didn't take me long to see they just wanted to be treated like people." She and Doris, who used a wheelchair, quickly became friends. Doris related how Viola never asked her those probing, hurtful questions that so many others had, how she seemed to sense naturally how they should act together. Their easy understanding also profited from the fact that they didn't hold back on their thoughts and feelings (Lessing 1981). "Do you know what I like about Vi?" Doris asked "She tells it like it is, and we tell each other like it is. . . ."

RESPONSIBILITY: FACING INJUSTICE TOGETHER
Although friendship is often viewed as a "free" relationship (in contrast to those that entail family obligations), both the literature of friendship and discussions with women friends reflect the theme of responsibility. Disabled women carry more responsibility in making friends. Nondisabled women may feel a special responsibility if a friend is disabled. Friendships between women, where at least one of them is disabled, are greatly affected by the ways in which the society itself takes—or fails to take—collective responsibility for including disabled people in its ongoing activities.

In one rare and useful discussion of the relationship between social policy and the possibility of intimacy for the disabled, Constantina Safilios-Rothschild argues that our society has developed a "right to intimate relations," almost a constitutional right, from which no one should be excluded (Safilios-Rothschild 1982). Her remedy for injustice in this realm is integration: when disabled people are fully admitted into all of society's activities, they will no longer be disadvantaged in, and excluded from, close relationships. Part of this argument relies on the marketplace image of intimacy: that, if people are to have intimate relationships, they must have something to contribute to these relationships. If they lack resources, they will be either ignored by potential partners or forced to strike a poor bargain. The argument also assumes that disabled people cannot really learn the social skills needed for intimacy in segregated environments, and that such a setting is, by definition, inferior—outside the society where the real accomplishments take place. Although Safilios-Rothschild grants the value of a disability rights movement in which disabled people may gather to exert pressure on the larger society, she sees this as an interim solution—a solution until society comes to its senses and lets the disabled in.

Many aspects of the integration argument fit with the viewpoint we have been developing here. Public policy clearly affects the conduct of friendships. (If we two want to go to the movies, access to public spaces affects us every inch of the way.) Our discussions with other women also suggest that access to resources affects the possibility of reciprocity in friendship. For example, if public transportation makes it very difficult for one friend to join in an activity they both want to pursue, then it is tempting for either or both of them to blame the woman with the given disability: she must somehow compensate for the fact that she is a "burden."

Our thinking and talking with other women about disability also suggests certain limits to the integration perspective. Despite the serious injustice done through exclusion from society's resources, disabled people are not merely "disadvantaged." Their experience lays the groundwork for a far-reaching critique of society, of society's very definitions of "ability" and "disability" (Hicks 1982, Krause 1982). Disabled people also bring this potential for criticizing society's values to intimate relationships, where, as we have seen, the meaning of disability itself may be called into question. As we have noted, friends do not spend all their time talking about such topics. But the very process of becoming friends brings up the meaning of social values such as justice, fairness, and reciprocity, to be struggled over and figured out in the course of our daily lives. Friendships do not simply mirror prevailing values in the public sphere. In themselves, as Minnich (1985) suggests, they constitute a public sphere of their own, in which old ways of relating can be challenged and new ways explored.

Just as discrimination and stigmatization raise issues about reciprocity in friendship, they also force us to look at the meaning of responsibility. If, out of the many ways of viewing responsibility, we look at it in terms of what responses we make to a given situation or to the actions of others, and what happens as a result of those responses, the links between reciprocity and responsibility become more evident (Niebhur 1963). In the context of friendship, our responses depend on what we want and need from the relationship as well as on our interpretation of what the other person wants and needs. In the attempt to equalize our contributions to the friendship, we may interpret the other's desires or needs in ways that do not fit with their realities: a disabled woman thinks that she must be more nurturant because the other will not tolerate her disability (or the social consequences of having a disabled friend) without such extra consideration. A non-disabled woman sees herself as responsible for helping or healing her disabled friend because the injustice her friend suffers as a disabled person reminds her (the non-disabled one) of all the unfairness and deprivation people suffer—including her own. Each of these instances involves a highly problematic "taking of responsibility," because in neither case does the given friend *check* to see whether she is responding to some demand or wish of her friend, or to something coming entirely from her own idea of things, her own hopes and fears.

It is not always easy in friendships to tell it like it is. We are filled with fears. We are afraid that with too much honesty, the non-disabled woman will reveal her fundamental lack of acceptance of her friend, or the disabled woman will reveal her resentment and anger at her friend's social privilege. There is no simple way around these fears, but, as the previous discussion suggests, many factors can help facilitate greater candor. The development of a movement for justice—such as the disability rights movement—supports both disabled and non-disabled people in greater openness about responses. The creation of structures that take access for granted (such as the university that Doris and Viola attended) makes disability an ordinary aspect of daily life. Finally, the friendship itself provides a structure that can support increased honesty about where we are and what we want. The love and affection that friends feel toward each other, the pleasure they reap from sharing their interests and passions, the desire they share to make the friendship long and rewarding—all these factors help friends to survive periods of tension, to accept fears, to traverse shame, to admit a sense of inadequacy.

The capacity of friends to share their responses to each other is a central part of friendship-building. But sharing is not always enough. In order for non-disabled (or differently disabled) friends to respond in fitting ways to friends with disabilities, specific information about the given disability is needed. Thus, one of the ways in which disabled people go more than halfway in friendships is to educate their friends. Education may not always be self-conscious (Berenice learned some important things about Roberta's capacity to balance by watching her deal with the subway). And, the disabled friend may not always have the time or energy or patience to engage in education (sometimes Roberta will just come out with a strong "no" when doing a thing in a certain way doesn't take her disability into account). Slowly but surely, however, the demands of daily living or the disruption of daily living require that friends reach some degree of common understanding of what the disability is about. The sighted friend learns how to hand her blind friend a set of keys: the sighted woman has learned to "think blind." The non-disabled friend automatically walks on her friend's left side: she knows her friend needs room to swing the cane. Such lessons are not easily learned, and some of the disabled women we spoke with expressed frustration over the long time it took some of their non-disabled friends to "catch on." Nevertheless, the lessons constitute an important element in making such friendship possible. The more that is known and understood, the easier it becomes for both friends to express preferences and needs. (Knowing concretely what will be involved in, for example, a trip with a disabled friend may help free the non-disabled friend to say, "Look, I'm not up to it at the moment.")

The social structure and social values that surround us strongly affect the ways in which friends work out the shape of their friendship. The reverse also holds. As friends evolve the sort of friendship they want and need, they begin to respond to society in a way that reflects the values of the friendship. This may take different forms. One is the self-conscious use of the non-disabled friend (or the less stigmatized disabled friend) as a mediator. This strategy is made possible by the non-disabled friend (or the one least disabled) being in the position of what Goffman calls "the wise": people who belong to the nonstigmatized world but understand the perspective of the stigmatized group (Goffman 1963). Being in such a position, the wise can use their knowledge to educate others and to act as liaisons between their stigmatized friends and the rest of the world. This position is an ambiguous one, however, open to misuse and misunderstanding. Structurally, the non-disabled woman is trapped between potential disloyalty to her friend and paying the full price for identifying with someone who is considered not quite human. Moreover, the friend who is disabled may, understandably, fear being left out or sold out by her non-disabled (or less severely disabled) friend when the going gets rough. This continuing tension provides a constant theme for the friendship, perhaps only rarely surfacing, but always there.

Some women friends we spoke with seemed to expect that, at times, non-disabled women would "represent" their disabled friends and/or take a mediating role in relation to a non-disabled society. Karen talked about how relieved she felt when Sara, with whom she was attending a conference, mentioned to someone they were to meet that Karen had a disability. Diane, on the other hand, saw much mediation as dangerous. When a job was at stake, the mere mention of your disability by your friend might result in your never being considered for the position. Sara was concerned: it seemed unfair not to tell the other person that your friend had a given disability. Diane protested behavior in which the apparent sensibilities of others were put before her own. Any attempt to "warn" others, any attempt to "protect" her from their reactions, amounted to cutting her off from some opportunity—including the opportunity to deal with prejudice and meanness. Although there seem to be many varieties of mediation explored in friendships between disabled and non-disabled women, the viability of such mediation clearly depends on the common understanding and agreement between the two friends about its meaning for their relations to the world.

Viola and Doris described how mediation enables them to get access to social events they want to attend. When they go out together, they try to find out about accessibility ahead of time, but if they go to a place with stairs, Viola goes into action. According to Doris, Viola says, "Come on, Dee, you can go in. They can carry you upstairs. And I don't know what she says, but they come down." Viola's technique is simple, she says. She goes up to the apartment and says, "I've got a friend in a wheelchair, and I want her to come up. *Who's* going to help?" What is so striking in this situation is the shared sense of entitlement. Both women stressed the importance of "having fun" to their friendship. Going to parties together is their right. Thus, both women are willing to see access as a collective responsibility for their larger circle of friends. Yet, neither Doris nor Viola see this solution as ideal. They prefer going places where access is not a problem, or, where they are able, to arrange the world to suit their own needs (Viola had made her house fully accessible to Doris).

Even where mediation is necessary or desirable, it may require a good deal of support from the disabled woman for her friend's efforts. Recently Berenice (who had gone to buy tickets for an event) got into a fight with someone at a box office because he would not give her the information about accessibility she needed to make a choice of seats for herself and Roberta. The argument was prolonged and unpleasant, and Berenice doubts that she would have seen it through if she hadn't been assured of Roberta's understanding and support. Later that day, when we discussed the incident, we were able to share our criticisms of the system (the largest cultural facility in New York City treating disabled people with contempt) and strategies for dealing with such situations.

Sometimes, however, mediation is neither appropriate nor possible. Often the two friends find themselves face-to-face with injustice or a lack of awareness that interferes directly with their mutual well-being. Regardless of who makes the overt response, it must be a shared response, coming out of a shared interpretation of the situation. Doris recounted to us a common occurrence: she and Viola had just eaten in a restaurant and they were waiting at the cashier to pay their bills. Doris, who uses a wheelchair, handed the cashier some money and the cashier handed the change to Viola (think of a woman trying to pay the bill when she has taken a man to lunch!). At this point, Viola refused to take the change and Doris began to point out to the cashier: "Don't you know that was *my* money? What if I didn't know that woman, and she just walked off with my change?" Doris herself frequently challenges prejudice in all phases of her life. (Comparing disability to the racism that both these black women have experienced, Doris put a sign on her office desk saying, "Being handicapped is an open-ended minority—anyone can join!") But an understanding friend helps take the sting out of the injustice and their friendship feeds the spirit of resistance.

Disabled women or their non-disabled friends do not always have the energy or courage to resist, however. Emily related how one vacation she took with a non-disabled friend turned out badly because her friend could not tolerate the stares that Emily's disability evoked. When Emily tried to discuss the problem, her friend withdrew. "She's one of the people," Emily remarked, "who still thinks the world is a Doris Day/ Rock Hudson movie. She wants no conflict, no negative feelings." One of Alison's friends had a similar experience with a different outcome. Alison was using a wheelchair so that she could participate in New York's annual Gay Pride march. When a friend commented that riding in the chair seemed a fine way to travel, Alison gave her a turn. The friend did not last long. "People are looking at me like I'm *pathetic*," she said. She preferred to walk.

Disabled women, too, have difficulty putting themselves up front, in exposing themselves to the additional harassment and pain that political visibility entails. Emily recalled how hesitant she was to become involved in the women's movement or in disability rights issues. Her mother had told her, "Don't make a big issue about being different: you're different enough to begin with." Yet, most of the friends she made as adults were people who, like herself, had made disability a professional area, whose work entailed a kind of collective responsibility to improve life for disabled people.

Although only some of the women we spoke with had become friends through their work on disability issues, the fact that they shared values on the rights of the disabled seemed to strengthen their ability to confront together the unjust treatment the disabled friend encountered. Where the nature of the responsibility was not clear, where friends had difficulty communicating, shared commitment to these values seemed to help them through those difficult periods and painful discussions that all friends must deal with as part of their ongoing relationships.

Such discussions, of course, do not always center on differences due to society's attitude toward disability. Many of the themes touched on in this chapter will be familiar even to non-disabled people who have never had a disabled friend. Many of the conditions that shape the lives of disabled women find parallels in oppression due to race, gender, class, and other factors. Many of the problems of making and maintaining friendships between nondisabled and disabled women find their counterpart in the problems of making friends in the face of other socially imposed distinctions. Disability raises its own special issues for relationships because of the particular categories it involves and the special aspects of our lives that it touches. Like our other experiences with oppression, it also prompts us to imagine a world in which friendships would come easily, in which they would grow directly from the needs of our hearts and our intellects rather than having to inch forward over a rough and hostile terrain.

Notes

Acknowledgment: We are deeply indebted to the many unnamed women who, by sharing with us their thoughts on friendship and disability, gave this paper its essence. We would also like to thank Hedva Lewittes, Stephanie Nickerson, and several anonymous critics for their comments on an earlier draft of the essay. We owe a special debt of gratitude to Harilyn Rousso for her help in the interviewing and her overall support of our project. We owe additional thanks to Mimi Erlich and Morris Golub of the New York Federation of the Handicapped for enabling Berenice and Harilyn to talk with members at one of the organizations' social evenings.

1. The names of the women who were interviewed (with the exception of our own and two who wish to be identified) have been changed. Our modest fieldwork included a group discussion, lasting for about three hours, and a dozen interviews (some individual, some in pairs or groups), lasting anywhere from twenty minutes to more than three hours.

References

Asch, A. 1984. Personal reflections. *American Psychologist* 39(5):551–52.

Asch, A. and L. Sachs. 1983. Lives without, Lives within: Autobiographies of blind women and men. *Journal of Visual Impairment and Blindness* (June):242–47.

Bell, R. R. 1981. *Worlds of friendship.* New York: Sage

Bernikow, L. 1980. *Among women.* New York: Harper and Row.

Block, J. D. 1980. *Friendship.* New York: Macmillan.

Brain, R. 1976. *Friends and lovers.* New York: Basic Books.

Burgess, R. L. and T. L. Huston, eds. 1979. *Social exchange in developing friendships.* New York: Academic Press

Campbell, B. M. 1983. Friendship in black and white. *Ms.* (August):44–46, 95.

Campling, J. *Images of ourselves: Women with disabilities talking.* London: Routledge and Kegan Paul.

Davis, F. 1961. Deviance disavowal: The management of strained interaction by the visibly handicapped. *Social Problems* 9(2):120–32.

Dill, B. T. 1983. Race, class and gender: Prospects for an all-American sisterhood. *Feminist Studies* 9 (Spring): 131–50.

Duck, S. 1983. *Friends for life: The psychology of close friendships.* New York: St. Martin's.

Faderman, L. 1981. *Surpassing the love of man: Romantic friendship and love* between women from the Renaissance to the present. New York: William Morrow.

Fine, M., and A. Asch. 1981. Disabled women: Sexism without the pedestal. *Journal of Sociology and Social Welfare* 7(21):233–48.

Fischer, C. S. 1982. *To dwell among friends: Personal networks in town and city.* Chicago: University of Chicago Press.

Fisher, B. 1984. Guilt and shame in the women's movement: The radical ideal of action and its meaning for feminist intellectuals. *Feminist Studies* 10(2):185–212.

Fisher, B., and R. Galler. 1981. A conversation between two friends about feminism and disability. *off our backs* 11(5):14–15.

Fishman, P. 1978. Interaction: The work women do. *Social Problems* 25(4):397–406.

Goffman, E. 1963. *Stigma: Notes on the management of a spoiled identity.* Englewood Cliffs, N. J.:Prentice Hall.

Hicks, J. S. 1982. Should Every Bus Kneel? In *Disabled people as second-class citizens*, ed. M. Y. Eisenberg, C. Griggins, and R. J. Duval. New York: Springer.

Kidder, L. H., M. A. Fagin, and E. Cohen. 1981. Giving and receiving: Social justice in close relationships. In *The justice motive in social behavior*, ed. M. J. and S. Lerner. New York: Plenum Press.

Krause, E. A. 1982. Social crisis and the future of the disabled. In *Disabled people as second class citizens*, ed. M. Eisenberg, C. Griggins, and R. Duval. New York: Springer.

Lerner, M. J., and S. Lerner, eds. 1981 *The justice motive in social behavior.* New York: Plenum Press.

Lessing, J. 1981. Disability from an able-bodied perspective. *off our backs* 11(5):20–21.

Lewittes, H., and B. R. Mukherji. 1985. The best friends of older black and white women. Unpublished manuscript. The study was supported by the State University of New York Research Foundation, University Awards Program, Summer 1983.

Lindsey, K. 1981. *Friends as family.* Boston: Beacon.

Mavor, E. 1983 (1971). *The ladies of llangollen: A study of romantic friendship.* Hammondsworth, England: Middlesex.

Minnich, E. K. 1985. Friendship between women: The act of feminist biography (a review essay). *Feminist Studies* 11(2):287–306.

Nestle, J. 1981. My lesbian illness support group. *off our backs* 11(5):8 .

Nickerson, S., and A. Smith. 1984. White women's views of their friendship with black women. Paper presented to the American Psychological Association, Toronto, August.

Niebhur, H. R. 1963. *The responsible self: An essay in Christian moral philosophy.* San Francisco: Harper and Row.

Panzarino, C. 1981. Interview in *off our backs* 11(5):4–5.

Safilios-Rothschild, C. 1982. Social and psychological parameters of friendship and intimacy for disabled people. In *Disabled people as second-class citizens*, eds. M. Eisenberg, C. Griggins, and R. Duval.

Smith, E. 1981. One reason why able-bodied women avoid disabled-bodied women. *off our backs* 11(5):11.

Smith-Rosenberg, C. 1980. The female world of love and ritual: Relationships between women in the 19th century. In *Women's experience in America: An historical anthology*, ed. E. Katz and A. Rapone. New Brunswick, N.J.: Transaction.

Thomas, D. 1982. *The experience of handicap*. London: Methune.

Walton-Fischler, S., and E. Newton. 1976. *Womanfriends: A soap opera*. New York: Feminist Press.

Weinberg, N. 1982. Growing up physically disabled: Factors in the evaluation of disability. *Rehabilitation Counseling Bulletin* 25(4):219–27.

———. 1983 Social equity and the physically disabled. *Social Work* 28(5)165–69.

Wolfe, L. 1983. Friendship in the city. *New York*, July 18, pp. 20–28.

Wolff, K., ed. 1950. *The sociology of George Simmell*. Glencoe, Ill: Free Press.

7. Disability and Ethnicity in Conflict: A Study in Transformation

MARILYNN J. PHILLIPS

Recent disability studies recognize the transformational character of the disability experience. For example, DeLoach and Greer (1981) describe the process of coming to terms with one's disability as a metamorphosis, whereas Vash (1981) discusses the spiritual, transcendental character of a process she considers to be outside the disability experience. In fact, the literature in disability studies has undergone many transformations, from the early scholarly writings centered in medical, rehabilitative, and psychopathological models to more recent efforts of sociologists and social psychologists to focus on the total interactional environment of individuals with disabilities. Especially in these later works the common theme is that disabled persons are not a homogeneous group, nor are they prone to any more personality or psychopathological disturbances than those in the "normal" population. Even in primarily scholarly studies there is also a recognition of the need for continued activism and advocacy to ensure that attitudinal and architectural barriers do not interfere with the disabled individual's personal and social growth.

In addition, more scholars who themselves have disabilities are engaging in disability research; for example, DeLoach, Greer, and Vash all have physical disabilities. Earlier scholarly work in this field was done for the most part by advocates for the disabled who themselves

This chapter is a version of Chapter 5 of the author's dissertation, "Oral Narratives of the Experience of Disability in American Culture," Department of Folklore and Folklife, University of Pennsylvania, 1984. © Marilynn J. Phillips. Reprinted by permission.

were not disabled. It is notable that while non-disabled scholars were analyzing others' experiences of disability, persons with disabilities were writing and publishing autobiographies, in many instances focusing on "overcoming" one's handicap. As Hahn (1982) points out, the great majority of these autobiographies were of less than literary quality and were written primarily as inspirational stories, often with a particular religious credo as the thesis. Perhaps such autobiographies function partially as catharses, and as catalysts for their authors' understanding of their disability-related experiences; or perhaps the American public responds more favorably to accounts that illustrate traditional American scenarios, such as overcoming adversity. A study of readers' tastes in this genre may offer a more informed understanding of cultural attitudes toward disability.

Whatever the reason, we seem to have come full circle, from inspirational autobiographies that nurture our cultural belief that success awaits those who try harder to scholarly works focusing on such concepts as metamorphosis and transcendental experience—on "disability as a growth experience" (Vash 1981:129). A danger in this new mode is that even scholars may resort to quasi-inspirational analyses of the experience of disability. The possibility of romanticizing is real, particularly in a cultural milieu in which the concept of the different is repugnant and normalization tends to be deified. DeLoach and Greer (1981) seem to understand the double bind. Vash (1981), whose excellent text is very pragmatic in its activist orientation, nevertheless also presents as the ultimate remedy for Americans with disabilities a solution totally removed from the cultural ethos: a non-Western spiritual transcendence of what she describes as the Western Cartesian "mind-body trap" (p. 132). In contrast to DeLoach and Greer's concept of metamorphosis and Vash's notion of spiritual transcendence, my analysis of the transformational process is based neither in normalization of the physique nor in psychological adjustment of the disabled person, nor in transcendence through the deification of disability. Instead, I document transformations that I believe are my informants' renegotiations of the American cultural ethos, a process of reframing and redefining that is for each person a uniquely creative response to the restrictions of physiological characteristics of the disability and the oppressions of negative social experiences (see Bateson 1972:184–93). From my research I conclude that the transformational process is dynamic; that individuals who evolve through the process often experience instances of regression; and that each individual's transformation is unique in that success is defined in personal terms.[1]

THE PROCESS OF UNFOLDING: SOME SCHOLARLY
CONCEPTIONS

"In grappling with the barriers, problems, and processes involved with coming to terms with a physical disability . . . the term metamorphosis came to mind" (DeLoach and Greer 1981:4). So begins an analysis of the process of unfolding perceived to be essential to an individual's adjustment to physical disability, an adjustment that ideally culminates in the individual's "stigma incorporation." This metamorphosis refers to an internal process rather than to an external one. DeLoach and Greer (1981) affirm that at the onset of disablement, the individual's self-state is negatively affected not only by physiological changes and dysfunctions but also by social stigmatization. A primary thesis of their text is the need for both professionals who work with disabled persons and disabled persons themselves to effect social change through social and political activism. Nevertheless, the primary focus of their concept of metamorphosis is on the disabled individual's process of psychological adjustment, which they perceive to involve three phases: (1) stigma isolation, which is the misperception that all stress is external, and more important, that all experiences are beyond one's control; (2) stigma recognition, which involves the exploration of strategies to self-manage and thereby to effect reduction of one's physiological and social stress; and (3) stigma incorporation, which involves the integration of all components of the self.

DeLoach and Greer have modified this final phase to apply to the experience of adjustment to disability, but they also acknowledge it to be a variation of Maslow's (1968) definition of self-actualization: "An episode, or a spurt in which the powers of the person come together . . . in which he is more integrated and less split, more open for experience, more idiosyncratic, more perfectly expressive . . . more ego-transcending, more independent of his lower needs" (p. 97). The external influences that DeLoach and Greer believe affect the process of metamorphosis, particularly whether or not the disabled individual achieves stigma incorporation, include age of the onset of the disablement, reactions of family and significant others, peer experiences, and the degree to which the difference is articulated (by self or others) in social interactions. They recognize the significance of the nature and degree of physiological dysfunction, but they subsume physical abilities and inabilities to the development of the individual's learned capacity to reduce disability-related stress, minimally use the ego-defense mechanism, maximally employ task-oriented strategies for confronting problems, and recognize "the stigmatizing condition as a characteristic (but not the primary characteristic) of the self-state" (DeLoach and Greer 1981:218–21).

Vash (1981) also follows a psychological orientation in her analysis of the adjustment to disability. She, too, incorporates the notion of self-actualization in her discussion of the process of transcending, which she defines as the gradual perception of one's disablement not as an insurmountable tragedy but as a "catalyst to psychological growth." What is distinctive about Vash's disaffection with the ideal of normalization is her perception that to be normal is, in some regard, to be unfulfilled and unpotentiated; for Vash, an individual's transcendence of disability also requires that the individual transcend normalization. She attributes to Jung a capturing of the essence of this disaffection with normality when he indicates "that to be normal is a splendid ideal for the unsuccessful, for all those who have not yet found an adaptation; but for people who have more ability than the average . . . restriction to the normal signifies the bed of Procrustes, unbearable boredom, infernal sterility, and hopelessness" (Jung 1929:124–25). Consequently, Vash is dissatisfied with theoretical models that advocate "normative adjustment under non-normative conditions." Such models include that proffered by Kerr (1977), who delineates five major stages in the process of adjusting to disability: shock, expectancy of recovery, mourning, defense, and adjustment. Vash's major disagreement with Kerr's model is that it culminates in an adjustment to, rather than a transcendence of, disability. Nevertheless, Vash, along with Kerr, allows for the disabled individual's employment of an ego-defense mechanism while evolving through his or her psychological unfolding. Vash affirms that denial, instead of being necessarily pathological or a sign of maladjustment, may be a phase essential to ego-survival, that it may have a multiform nature, including a function as escape from devaluation by society. Vash's conception of the achievement of a "basal level of transcending disability" by allowing the gradual fading of one's physiological reality into the background of one's consciousness is similar to DeLoach and Greer's notion that the disabled individual ideally comes to recognize that the "stigmatizing condition" is not a primary characteristic of the self-state. Significantly, Wright's (1960:124–25) counsel to practitioners to guide their disabled clients through a process of adjustment includes as a major component a comparable notion of the client's need to "learn to subordinate physique."

Vash's concept of transcendence involves three levels of acknowledgment: (1) a recognition of the fact of disability, its physiological realities and its social consequences, and to this level Vash attributes negative valence; (2) an acceptance of the implications of the disablement, to the extent that the individual accommodates to limitations and perceives the disability merely as causing inconveniences that can be mastered, and to this level Vash attributes neutral valence; and (3) an embracing of the experience of disability, in that the individual recognizes that "without the disability s/he would be different from what s/he is, and there is no desire to be different," and to this level Vash attributes positive valence, in that the disability now is seen by the individual as an opportunity or gift and as a catalyst for continued growth. At this last level, Vash's model seems to intersect with the social minority model, particularly in regard to her belief that disabled individuals must embrace their differences. Of course, where Vash most deviates from the social minority model is in her emphasis on spiritual growth and in her apparent disapproval of striving *merely* toward social assimilation. Vash remains unimpressed with what she calls the "maladaptive societal programming" effected by a society that is "security-, sensation-, and power-oriented." She suggests that the disabled individual can achieve transcendence through a reprogramming of his or her consciousness in order to learn to devalue the lower consciousness (body) and exalt the higher consciousness (mind and soul), a process that she believes to be accomplished best through spiritual philosophies (Vash 1981:134–38).

Perhaps anyone who attempts to comprehend a raison d'être for those who seem to be denied what our culture deems to be the fullness of living inevitably also must fail to resolve the inconsistencies within the American cultural ethos. Indeed, Moore (1975) postulates that in every cultural ethos a discrepancy exists between ideology and social reality; what is unique to each culture is "what people do" about the inconsistencies—not necessarily resolving them but possibly making orderly such contradictory notions by recognizing and then assigning each notion to a distinctive realm, rather than retreating from the contradictions, paradoxes, and double binds. Although I am impressed with DeLoach and Greer's work, and with Vash's, my reservation about their theoretical frameworks is what I perceive to be their preoccupation with resolving the dilemmas in absolute terms and attempting to discern a pattern of rehabilitation or habilitation—a process of unfolding—that can be applied universally to those who experience physical disablement. I choose to follow Moore's predication, to acknowledge that ideology and social reality are situated in different realms, although communities or individuals may reinterpret or redefine or even synthesize elements of one ethos with elements of a contradictory ethos.

In effect, Vash accomplishes such a synthesis in her analysis of denial as a "healthy defense" against ego disintegration, in that she combines an element from the realm of social reality (that disabled persons have "a devaluated status in society") with an element from an opposing cultural ideology (ego-survival of the oppressed, an inversion of the cultural notion of survival of the fittest); through this synthesis, denial provides a temporary resolution for such individuals until "they become able to relinquish the 'protection' that denial affords" (Vash 1981:127). DeLoach and Greer, and Vash, initially do perceive the distinction between the two realms, particularly in the strong advocacy for social activism and their conviction that social reality must be changed before most persons with disabilities can engage in either metamorphosis or transcendence. On issues of social reality, all three scholars are exceedingly pragmatic. On issues of ideology, however, all three retreat from the dilemmas inherent in the cultural ethos by cajoling disabled individuals to psychological (DeLoach and Greer) or spiritual (Vash) development *beyond* the cultural ethos.

The flaw in each theoretical framework is the dismissing or the disregarding of the weight that culture bears on those who are stigmatized and the extent to which the individual's coming to terms with a disability may necessitate first coming to terms with the inconsistencies in the cultural ethos. In fact, each individual's renegotiation, redefinition, and synthesis of elements of the cultural ethos may be idiosyncratic to personal circumstances. Consequently, the process will not be guided by a single theory or applied to a single component (body, mind, spirit) of personality. Yet, my position is not that culture should be exalted as if omnipotent, as if controlling individuals' fates through some immutable force. I would argue rather, that culture is that structure on which, as Geertz (1973) asserts, "lies a complex set of significant symbols [that individuals] transform into activity," and that this transformation is in itself the most creative of human endeavors. Geertz concludes that "our ideas, our values, our acts, even our emotions, are cultural products—products manufactured, indeed, out of tendencies, capacities, and dispositions with which we were born, but manufactured nonetheless. [And all] men are cultural artifacts" (pp. 50–51). This may be the ultimate contradiction: The individual as cultural artifact embodies nonetheless the power and the resources (physical, mental, and spiritual) to transform culture, particularly those expressions of culture by which she or he is governed.

A CASE STUDY IN TRANSFORMATION
This process of transformation is illustrated through the personal narrative of an informant here called Margaret Orlinski.[2] Although I hesitate to proffer a definitive schemata to apply universally to those

who have physical disabilities, it can be said that the narratives of several informants are patterned recountings of their experiences, and that these recountings are framed in accordance with the individual's perception of personal growth and development through disability-related experiences. Margaret Orlinski's development seems to pass through four stages: marginality, retreat, renegotiation, and emergence. The process described here is dynamic rather than static and does not preclude oscillation between and among the various stages. In the analysis of the personal narrative of Margaret Orlinski, her own frame for her transformational process was utilized.

Marginality is that first stage in which Margaret's self-image is most negatively affected by the social image of her devaluation as an individual with form and functional differences. Her marginality begins with recountings of the onset of her disablement and proceeds through accounts of reactions by family, peers, and ethnic and religious communities to her new physical condition and social status. During the second state, retreat, Margaret emotionally withdraws from all expressions of her ethnic tradition, most especially from dance, but also from what she calls the "Polish psyche." In the third stage, renegotiation, she combines elements from her new profession as a pianist (social reality) with her new conversion to Jungian philosophy (ideology) to create a synthesis that for her functions as a new ethnic marker. At the fourth state a new identity emerges, a symbolic fusion of a cultural marker of her ethnicity with the physiological limitations that characterize her disability.

Marginality: "Like Sticks with Like"
Margaret Orlinski was born in 1944 into a second-generation Polish-American family living in a small ethnic community on the outskirts of a metropolitan area. When she was 7 years old, Margaret contracted infantile paralysis. The polio left both legs partially paralyzed. At first she was institutionalized, separated from all interactions with her community. When she returned home her relationships with the community and its church became a series of interactions in which she was perceived, and came to perceive herself, to be a marginal member of the community. Her brother's depression and her parents' sense of guilt served further to distance her from the community. Even her interactions with peers changed, as school friends no longer regarded her as they had before. Now, young and old considered Margaret to be "unlike" themselves. Margaret recalled:

The Polio Foundation used to intimidate parents to send their children to these Homes: "There are other crippled people her age in this particular environment." Their philosophy was "like sticks with like." So, with great reluctance my parents signed me in. My mother was so upset that she had a breakdown. To her it was like selling her own child.

This first phase of social exile was to affirm for Margaret her new marginal status. She recounts her experiences in the Home for the Merciful Savior in a style not unlike that of a prisoner recollecting incarceration. Even when describing her eventual release from the home, she incorporates the prisoner's jargon: "I got 'sprung' in June of '54." The release required nine months of petitioning of the authorities by her frustrated parents, who repeatedly were rebuffed with the patterned response: "We know what's best for your child. She should develop with people of her own kind." Only when Margaret's parents threatened legal suit was Margaret "pardoned"; but she was not delivered from the sordid memories of unhappy and lonely months of isolation:

The parents were allowed to visit only once a week. Any letters that we wrote to them were opened. We could not write, "Mommy, the nurse did such and such [to me]." I remember a girl who was about 13 and she had her first period—terrified the hell out of me! Because I didn't know anything about that and I saw this bed full of blood, and I got really scared. They hit her. Because she didn't tell them before that she needed something—protection.

When Margaret rejoined her family, she was 8 years old and "wrecked" emotionally:

I could not communicate. I was just very much afraid of anybody. I remember locking myself in the bathroom and screaming! "People, get away from me! I don't want any help! I don't want anything!" Finally, it's dawning on me—what's happening to me? I'll never walk again! What am I going to do with myself?

The family, too, was damaged, if not completely at the brink of destruction. Margaret felt that somehow she was the cause of all their pain and worry. It was becoming apparent to her that despite the family's attempts to piece together the fragments of the shattered family unit, her "difference" would make such a repair impossible. Margaret's family had become, as one scholar (Knight 1972) has come to call such families, a "disabled family."

Perhaps it is the relationship to siblings that is most strained when one child seems to be singled out for punishment. For Margaret's only sibling, an older brother with whom she had been very close before her disablement, her paralysis evoked behavioral reactions similar to those described in the literature on death and dying (Kübler-Ross 1969): "When they told my brother I had polio, he ran upstairs crying. He was afraid I'd never come back." Even after some semblance of normality had been reestablished in the household, her brother's feelings of somehow having caused the illness, his wondering why it happened to her and not to him, and his trying to cope with the social and peer pressure of having a "different" sister affected their interaction. Her brother's emotional distancing was impossible for Margaret to reconcile: "He would come home and just wouldn't relate to me at all and I was upset. And I couldn't see why, why is he doing it? Why isn't he speaking to me?" Not until their adulthoods could they be candid with one another and talk about these painful childhood episodes: "I found out later when the relationship straightened out that he had been under enormous peer pressure. They leaned on him: 'Your sister's a cripple! Your sister's a cripple!' And he'd get so pissed off that he didn't know how to react."

Margaret experienced yet another kind of social exile when school opened the following September. Before her disablement, Margaret had been enrolled at St. Joseph's Catholic School. Her mother called the mother superior, hoping that Margaret could resume her education there or perhaps be tutored temporarily by the nuns at home: "They had a real bitch for a principal in those days, and she refused [both requests]. So my mother went to the public school district, and they sent a tutor." Margaret was to be tutored in this isolated situation for the next four years. Her contact with the outside world was minimal, only the once-a-week visit to the hospital for physical therapy and an occasional outing in the family car: "But we didn't get the car until later. We were not a rich family." She cut herself off from the relatively few visits from her former second-grade classmates after she decided their friendships were insincere:

One time they brought a puppet show over for me, on one afternoon after school. They asked me how I liked it, and I said, "Okay," quite quietly for I was shy and withdrawn by then. One of the kids said, "Gee, I thought you'd like it more! After all, we're *supposed* to visit the sick!" And I was devastated. It hit me suddenly. Is that the only reason he came? So I went through a self-imposed isolation period.

Her tutor represented the neutral stranger, the one with whom Margaret did not have to interact on any deep emotional level, the one who demanded only that she develop her mind. He was not like the doctors and nurses and physical therapists who demanded the constant and seemingly futile exercising of a body she had grown to despise: "I felt very incomplete for a long time. I didn't like my legs at all. They didn't do what I wanted them to do." The neutral stranger also brought her music: "We used to have an upright piano in the room and he saw it there once, and he said, 'Would you like me to teach you how to read notes?' So he taught me." Music would serve to reestablish Margaret's connection to her ethnic community and to affirm the integrity of her new physique.

Between the ages of 7 and 11, Margaret not only was immersed in the full range of emotions possible for a child of her age but also was catapulted into a grief and pain few adults can manage. At first, she made of herself little more than a bewildered, trapped animal, angry, enraged, encased first in an iron lung that was "too small for me. I hated it. I felt like I was in a coffin." Subsequently, she was exiled to the Home of the Merciful Savior. After her release from the home, she became consciously aware of her entrapment in a body over which she would never again exert control. Of course, it is primarily neurological deficiencies that limit an individual's control over paralyzed limbs; yet just as the personality may become introverted and passive in response to social and environmental forces, so, too, may an individual's physiology be affected adversely by cultural standards and societal expectations (see Allport 1958). In regard to both her psychological and physiological development, Margaret was influenced negatively by the social exiling resulting from her disablement.

Margaret gradually became withdrawn and introverted, by her own admission so shy that she would speak in barely audible whispers: "By this time I was more mild. I didn't throw tantrums. Instead, I became very passive. You could have burned my fingertips with cigarettes, and I wouldn't have protested." As stated by Barker, "Physique has a social significance to the individual in terms of the cultural mores within which he lives, for physique is one of the important criteria upon which social distinctions are based" (Barker et al. 1953:3). Margaret had sufficient motor ability to be ambulatory (with the aid of braces and crutches), so her exclusion from the community cannot be justified solely in terms of her physiological dysfunctions. It seemed to Margaret that only her different physique resulted in her cultural assignment to a new social status as a marginal person. This significance of her exclusion, particularly her separation from former classmates, was traumatizing. Beuf (1978) notes that "segregat[ion] conveys a message to the stigmatized child that he is unfit to learn shoulder to shoulder with other normal[s]." Margaret's social stigmatization not only was related to her functional limitations but also, and perhaps more so, to her different form. It was during this phase that Margaret self-fulfilled the prophecy of the polluted physique: "I gained a lot of weight. I ate to compensate—didn't like myself. My face, my hair, the whole thing. But mainly the legs." Margaret thus internalized the negative social image.

Indeed, this social image became Margaret's self-image; it became her primary identity (see Douglas 1973).

This primary identity of her "crippledness" haunted Margaret, for in virtually every social interaction her difference was articulated. As noted, Margaret's peers perceived her to be an invalid whom they might visit out of mercy. Also, Margaret's disability, in effect, was the reason for her brother's emotional distancing. Even her parents were grief-stricken. Indeed, the foundations had been laid for Margaret's increasing alienation from all social interactions. The thrill she felt when she was at last allowed to return to St. Joseph's dissipated when her disability was highlighted—whether through others' sympathy or their adulation. In addition, Margaret recognized that her relationship to her community was strained; Margaret not only was excluded from the important ethnic dance celebrations but also was perceived to be incapable of performing the expected and appropriate gender roles of marriage and motherhood. Perhaps defiantly, perhaps courageously, perhaps just to salvage what little remained of her self-esteem, Margaret retreated from all expressions of her ethnic tradition.

Retreat: "I'd Rather Be Crippled than Polish"
When Margaret was 12, her parents convinced the principal at St. Joseph's that Margaret was capable of returning to the Catholic school, which, in effect, functioned as the religious and social center for their ethnic community. Academically Margaret did well, but the social adjustment was more difficult. Margaret remembers that superficially she got along well with the other girls her age, except when it came to sharing stories and giggles about boys and dating. Whenever Margaret approached a group of girls gossiping in the hallways, suddenly there was a quick shifting of topics of conversation—from boys to books. Her interaction with boys was minimal: "Boys avoided me like the plague! They'd say 'Hi' or ask condescending questions like, 'Can I do this [for you]?' Very patronizing—earning points in heaven! It was kind of 'Stay away from her, don't really get close to her cause she is, after all, *that!*'" Margaret's most humiliating school experience occurred at her eighth-grade graduation ceremony:

I got this prize . . . for the "girl who struggled the most to achieve a Catholic education." It was a five-dollar bill in an envelope! And they said to me, there on the stage, "You don't have to stand up. Father such-and-such will hand you this prize." Then they applauded, and they stood up! I was so upset. All these people staring just at me, God! And clapping! Then he made this elaborate speech, about how I was just like Franklin Delano Roosevelt![3]

Other "prizes for being a cripple" followed, like the Polish community's Kosciusko Essay Content for the outstanding essay on this Polish-American hero of the American Revolutionary War: "Of course, my winning was *absolutely* fixed! They put my picture in the local paper, a full-blown shot showing my braces. And the article made a point of my 'crippledness.'" Margaret paused here and added, smiling, "At least this time I was worth twenty-five dollars!"

Firth (1973:369–72, 395–97; see also Mauss 1925) addresses the possibility of an underlying notion of reciprocity in all giving of gifts: "The implications of a gift are rarely exhausted by a single transfer [as] the notion of reciprocity is often near the surface." I contend that such prizes as Margaret received may have represented gifts of this order, perhaps the community's affirmation of a socially appropriate and socially prescribed relationship, that is, the haves giving to the have-nots. Or, perhaps, as Firth concludes, "All gifts [also] have both competitive and cooperative elements," and Margaret's ethnic community may have envisaged the gift as a symbolic statement of a moral position, as an expression of sympathy for Margaret's suffering. Nevertheless, as Firth also asserts, "Insofar as a gift in material terms is a one-way transfer, it creates an asymmetrical relationship socially [and functions as] a symbolic enhancement of the donor."

Since Margaret asserts that she neither earned nor deserved the awards, it may be that the community benefited more from these rituals than did Margaret (see Goffman 1959, 1967). Indeed, these rituals may have functioned not only to reaffirm the appropriate social reality relationship between "normal" members of the community and a marginal member but also to renegotiate discrepancies between opposing elements in the cultural ethos. On the one hand, the community treated Margaret with reverence: "I was called a saint. 'God loves her so much to have given her this cross to bear.' I heard that so many times. I felt an enormous amount of pressure to be perfect because I was 'one of God's favorites.'" On the other hand, this specialness made her different, and being different, in her community, was cause for Margaret's segregation from community activities.

It is ironic that while her community excluded Margaret from normal activities, they created specially substituted occasions for her display before the collective. At such events Margaret was adulated, but isolated. For First Holy Communion, ordinarily an event celebrating one's spiritual growth in the collective setting of one's age peers, Margaret not only was tutored separately but also received the sacrament not in the church, but in an individualized ceremony at her home. Although the event was not celebrated in the traditional manner, among age peers and in the church, nevertheless it was designated for collective celebration: "People flooded the living room with tears! Here's this little crippled, pathetic girl receiving Jesus for the first time! And so many people came that they even stood outdoors! The parish rejoiced!" Another illustration of the community's vacillation between sympathy and adulation for Margaret was their inconsistent attitude toward Margaret's physical differences. Margaret was conscious of their repugnance toward her deformed physique:

In many senses, I was considered ugly. I had a pretty face, but they would remark, "Oh, she's so pretty. It's a shame she's crippled!" Implying if my face were ugly too, then everything would match up! The only people who didn't marry were people who had religious vocations and people who were considered ugly . . . my "kind of person" didn't marry. I was not part of the mold. I didn't fit in. They would speak in whispers—I overheard them—about this "curse," this "visitation." They'd talk about "It." And they wondered what would they do about "that creature" in there? I went through a period when I was ashamed of being Polish.

Such experiences led gradually to Margaret's ultimate withdrawal from all community interactions. Her retreat had begun years before, little by little; then, as she blossomed into a young woman, her alienation peaked, particularly as she again became cognizant of the community's belief that "her kind of person" did not marry:

It climaxed in my [high school] senior year when two nuns came up to me during one of our many retreats and they said to me, in effect, "You're not going to get married anyway, 'cause somebody like you would not get married, so why don't you consider becoming a nun? There's an order in Philadelphia, a contemplative order of nuns who are disabled. You could be happy in your own community!"

It was at this point that Margaret terminated her social affiliation with her ethnic community; she also disavowed affiliation with the essence of her ethnicity, the "Polish psyche."

From early childhood she had participated in those community activities that were primarily melancholic, such as funerals: "They said the prayers, the rosary. *Droning.* The chanting and the response, all in Polish. Eerie!" After her disablement, she herself had become the community's reminder "that sad things happen in this life. People would come up to my mother and say, 'What a shame!' And the older women would cry. This Polish thing of crying at the drop of a hat. Some people would just look at me and cry." Yet, Margaret noted, "Polish people have this weird psyche. They go from one extreme to the other." It was especially in "manic" celebrations that Margaret didn't fit in. She remembers "the gay abandon. I just never felt that I belonged with these people. I don't fit in with 'normal' people, singing, dancing. I felt that there were these thousands of eyes staring. They weren't happy occasions for me."

She remembers having wanted to participate in the dancing: "When you see people dancing and moving their feet, and you don't have any feet to move, damnit, that's a mind blower! Because you want to be out there dancing and having a hell of a time!" She could remember dances where she alone was sitting down, and she "couldn't wait to come home." What was more distressing than not participating in the dancing, according to Margaret, was that the others made her feel uncomfortable, made her feel unwanted at joyful celebrations. Perhaps for Margaret, whose marginality was her primary social and self-identity, the most (and perhaps only) culturally appropriate participation involved melancholic occasions. In effect, her intrusion into happy occasions inadvertently may have functioned to elicit melancholy, to remind the community of the "sad things" in life: "Yes, it's better not to have to look at that little cripple in the chair. You don't want to think about anything sad."

It may not have been the Polish psyche from which Margaret retreated so much as from her community's (and perhaps her own) inability to resolve, or at least to renegotiate, a major inconsistency in their cultural ethos. For Margaret's ethnic community, her disability was an insurmountable tragedy. In order to survive emotionally, in order to relinquish "this guilt thing, that I was responsible somehow for my disability because I didn't pray hard enough," Margaret chose to reject Polish traditions and the community. Unlike other girls in her community, who were expected to get married and to rear families and not to go to college, Margaret enrolled at a university to study music, and only then did she feel free from the trap of her ethnicity:

And then I realized how dull those people were. Polio opened my eyes to the world. Otherwise I would have been dull, slipping right into my culture. There was no hope in that community unless you had some means of getting out, and polio was a catalyst, made me see things differently, made me want to do something—because I had no choice. [I discovered then that] I'd rather be crippled than Polish![4]

The discovery that her disability acted as a catalyst for growth, Margaret reiterates, "did not happen all at once." In fact, in contrast to Vash's notion of embracing one's differentness, Margaret's affirmation of the positive value of her disability, at least initially, was a frantic resolve to recoup her self-esteem and preserve her ego-identity as a unique individual. As Margaret herself acknowledges, "I had no choice." For years, according to Margaret as many as ten years, she had tried to fit in; she had performed her social roles; she had provided her community with a reason for her being. Finally, she said "the hell with it!" and determined to become her own person, even if she had to "go to the other side of the spectrum." Still, despite her rebellion against oppressive tradition, she felt inextricably connected to her ethnic roots. Margaret found a way to resolve her conflict, to make things right, to return to her own culture without further destruction to her own ego. While at the university studying piano Margaret combined music, an element from her ethnic tradition, with Jungian philosophy, an element of her chosen ideology, in a synthesis that symbolically represented the key, the renegotiation of inconsistencies inherent in her two opposing identities: her ethnicity and her disability.

Renegotiation: "I Can Dance with My Fingers"
Margaret gleaned from Jungian philosophy a personal ideology ("When I studied Jung, I understood that it was up to me to establish my own system to live by") that functioned as part of a new strategy by which she could come closer to her own roots. The other component, music, came to function symbolically as the cultural expression that would reestablish Margaret's connections to her ethnicity. Although Margaret had retreated even from the musical expressions of that ethnicity, primarily because she sensed others' distress that her presence at the manic celebrations interfered with their gay abandon, nevertheless she was adamant about someday fitting in. It was not so much that Margaret attempted to transcend her disability, but that she sought a way out of the conflict, "a way out that could make things right." Margaret explains her motivation for seeking such resolution:

The Polish are a very musical people. They sing all the time, sad songs, happy songs, all the time. A musical people. And I wanted to be a musical person. I wanted desperately to get back because I always felt on the outside looking in for all those years, and I was not a part of their music and that's one reason I worked so hard at piano, because I wanted it so desperately, to be "in" with [Polish people].

Margaret understood, however, that Polish music is marked primarily by dance; according to Margaret, "to be Polish is to be dancing." Dance, particularly as this ethnic community's primary cultural marker, may establish a relationship between the individual and the group, one that could be expressed in terms of either superiority to or unity with other members of the community (Martin 1930:701). This

Polish community's major criterion for dancing was not how well one could dance—according to Margaret, good and bad dancers equally were welcomed to participate—but whether one was perceived to be physiologically able to dance. Margaret came to perceive herself to be damaged physiologically, particularly in regard to the dysfunction of her legs, even to the extent that she would make references to them as if they no longer existed: "When you're in a class of society like I was, where legs were very important, if you don't have them, it puts you apart."

Only when Margaret began the serious study of piano did she discover a way to redefine this cultural marker of dance. One day during her instruction, her music professor at the university was struggling to communicate more precisely the character of a particular manual technique. Finally he used an expression that was to serve as the kind of metaphor that Burke (1957:256) describes to function as a "strategy for dealing with a situation." Margaret recalls that moment of recognition:

"You have to dance with your fingers!" I remember the first time he said that to me. I actually started up and I looked at him and he said, "Yes, the way you play this particular part [is] you have to dance with your fingers!" And I reveled in that! And I thought about that night and day, and I thought, God, I *can* dance! I can dance with my fingers—my own way!

Margaret's parents, good dancers who had participated enthusiastically in Polish celebrations and particularly in dances, avoided such functions after Margaret's disablement. Her brother, two years her senior, has never danced—not even at his own wedding. Knight (1972) considers such symbolic assuming of the affected child's disability to be an aspect of the disability itself, that is, when other members within the family constellation symbolically also are disabled by the social stigmatization assigned to one member. It is important, as well, to consider the additional influence of the small ethnic community of which the Orlinskis continued to be a part, a community that functioned as an extension of the family constellation. Margaret's relationship to this extended community was in some ways as intimate and as filled with yearning for acceptance as her relationship to her immediate family. Yet the traditions of the community apparently did not allow the Orlinskis "access to supportive subcultural role models and ideologies," an access that Darling (1979:79) proposes to be vital not only to the parents' and siblings' interactions with the disabled child but also to the development of the disabled child's social and self-perceptions. Therefore, not only the physical activity of their dancing but also the community's uneasiness about Margaret's attendance at dances reinforced Margaret's perception of her marginality. Margaret was well aware that her nonparticipation in dance contributed to her marginal social status within the community. "Dancing with her fingers" was her creative response to the conflict; through music she could participate joyfully, albeit symbolically, in her ethnicity.

Emergence: "Becoming the Person I Want to Be—through Music"
Margaret's emergence into this new identity, into this person she has always wanted to be, is firmly grounded in her love for music: "I think music *is* religion. It's a very spiritual thing." She also believes that music is "a symbolic thing" through which she continues to develop and grow. Metaphorically, music has given her access to her ethnic community and thus has permitted her to examine more closely her ethnic heritage:

I do a lot more Polish things now. Playing Polish pieces, reading Polish literature and Polish poetry helps you to understand the music. Nor am I as fearful of Polish dance music like Chopin. When I was growing up, I would refuse to play a dance piece. Now I feel it's okay.

It is not that on occasion Margaret does not muse about what life would have been were she not disabled; nor does it seem that she experiences her disability, as Vash (1981:132) might counsel, with positive regard; nor does she deify disability. Neither does she deify normalcy. It seems that any fantasy Margaret might have had to become "normal" has been subsumed to the new and stronger identity that has emerged from the specific process of transformation that is unique to Margaret—to her potential, to her needs, and to her desires.

CONCLUSIONS
Preliminary conclusions can be stated about some of the indicators that would suggest an individual's engaging in transformation. First, the most obvious variable pertains to the content and presentation of the narratives. My methodology involves eliciting information by means of an "open" interview in which some informants relate only informational details of their lives, while others both narrate informational details and analyze their perceptions of the meaning of these experiences.[5] Of course, it is among informants who choose to approach the interview in the latter manner that the transformational process is most in evidence. Without long-term participant-observation of these informants, however, it is difficult to ascertain if the more elaborated style of speaking is a major indicator of such transformation or merely a cultural variable related to the individual's ethnicity, gender, age, socio-

economic status. Second, among informants who tend to elaborate on their disability-related experiences, the majority have been influenced directly by recent activist movements, including the women's movement and the disability rights movement. It is plausible that their exposure to such collective consciousness-raising not only has resulted in heightened awareness of their social status but also has provided a model for self-analysis. Third, the individual's disability age (that is, the length of time since disability occurred) often, but not always, is a factor in cases in which the process of transformation is most apparent. Of course, those who have had more disability time and, presumably, more disability-related experiences could be expected to have engaged in longer reflection on the implications of their circumstances; however, those whose disabilities are relatively recent but also erratic and progressive (such as multiple sclerosis) sometimes have a heightened self-awareness that transcends that of their longer-disabled peers.

I am reluctant to propose the universality of any schemata by which individuals with disabilities engage in their unique processes of transformation. Although I believe that the process of transformation is held in common by many who have disabilities, the schemata by which each process unfolds is peculiar to each individual. Ultimately it is individuals who transform the expressions of culture into activity that functions for them, as for Margaret, as their "own system to live by." The *process* of transformation may be common among those who most endeavor to create out of their cultural ethos, out of their social and personal circumstances, a strategy not only for survival but also for growth and development. Nevertheless, it is my contention that both the *framing* of and the *focus* for each process of transformation are unique to the individual, and narratives that articulate the process of transformation are created by each individual in accordance with that person's potentials, needs, and desires. The cultural ethos necessarily serves as thematic continuity and pattern, in effect, as a link and a connection to tradition, among the various idiosyncratic renegotiations, redefinitions, and syntheses.

Margaret, for example, framed her narrative around four phases of development (marginality, retreat, renegotiation, and emergence) and focused on the meaning and importance of ethnicity to her social and self-identities; nevertheless, she manufactured her strategy out of elements from her cultural ethos, out of elements of the conflicting values of community and individuality. Another individual's narrative might be framed in accordance with different criteria for number of phases, chronology, and contents. Another's narrative might focus on an activity (for example, physiological normalization rather than ethnic affirmation) that has meaning for that individual alone. Nevertheless, however distinctive the framing and the focus are, invariably they are situated in, and influenced by, the cultural ethos of which that individual is a part.

Notes

1. The transformation process is dynamic, and occasional regression or retreat is essential to the continuation of the growth process. Therefore, I disagree with Vash's (1981:130) notion that regression necessarily is negative or a growth retardant.

2. All personal and place names have been changed to protect the anonymity of the informant. The folklore genre that is the core of this study is the personal experience narrative, which I consider to be the medium for the individual's spontaneous oral composition, thematically connected to the traditional cultural ethos, yet articulated in the contexts of personal events and the narrator's perception of such events. See Dégh and Vázsonyi (1974), Honko (1964), and Stahl (1983) for various definitions of the personal experience narrative.

3. See Looker (1933) for a treatment of Franklin Delano Roosevelt as the embodiment of the American cultural ethos of perseverance; see Alsop (1982) for a discussion of the personal anguish of Roosevelt in regard to his physical disability; see Gallagher (1985) for an analysis of Roosevelt's deficiencies as a role model for disabled persons.

4. Margaret recognized the pejorative meaning of "cripple," yet, significantly, she elected to use the term in referring to her rejection of her ethnicity.

5. I borrow the concept of elaborated narrative styles from Bernstein's (1964) discussion of elaborated versus restricted linguistic codes in terms of social structures. My notion of the personal experience narrative as a kind of spontaneous oral composition thematically linked to the traditional cultural ethos has been influenced by Lord (1978).

References

Allport, G. W. 1958. *The nature of prejudice.* Reading, Mass.: Addison-Wesley.

Alsop, J. 1982. Roosevelt remembered. *Smithsonian Magazine* (January):45ff.

Barker, R. G., et al. 1953. *Adjustments to physical handicap and illness: A survey of the social psychology of physique and disability.* New York: Social Science Research Council.

Bateson, G. 1972. *Steps to an ecology of mind.* New York: Ballantine.

Bernstein, B. 1964. Elaborated and restricted codes: Their social origins and some consequences. *American Anthropologist* 66(6):55–69.

Beuf, A. H. 1978. *Presentation to the working group on stigmatized children.* International Year of the Child Committee report. New York: United Nations.

Burke, K. 1957. *The philosophy of literary form.* New York: Vintage.

Darling, R. B. 1979. *Families against society: A study of reactions to children with birth defects.* Beverly Hills, Calif.: Sage.

Dégh, L., and A. Vázsonyi. 1974. The memorate and the proto memorate. *Journal of American Folklore* 87:225–39.

214 • Disabled Women in Relationships

DeLoach, C., and B. G. Greer. 1981. *Adjustment to severe physical disability: A metamorphosis.* New York: McGraw-Hill.

Douglas, M. 1973. *Natural symbols.* New York: Vintage.

Firth, R. 1973. *Symbols: Public and private.* Ithaca, N.Y.: Cornell University Press.

Gallagher, H. 1985. *FDR's splendid deception.* New York: Dodd, Mead.

Geertz, C. 1973. *The interpretation of cultures: Selected essays by Clifford Geertz.* New York: Basic Books.

Goffman, E. 1959. *The presentation of self in everyday life.* Garden City, N.Y.: Doubleday.

———. 1963. *Stigma: Notes on the management of spoiled identity.* Englewood Cliffs, N.J.: Prentice-Hall.

———. 1967. *Interaction ritual: Essays on face-to-face behavior.* Garden City, N.Y.: Doubleday.

Hahn, H. 1982. The "good parts" of autobiographies: Accounts of relationships between physically disabled and nondisabled persons. Paper presented at the annual meeting of the American Folklore Society, Minneapolis, October 13–17.

Honko, L. 1964. Memorate and the study of folk beliefs. *Journal of the Folklore Institute* 1:5–19.

Jung, C. G. 1929. The problems of modern psychotherapy. In *The collected works of C. G. Jung,* ed. Read et al., vol. 16, 1966.

Kerr, N. 1977. Understanding the process of adjustment to disability. In *Psychosocial aspects of disability,* ed. E. Stubbins. Baltimore: University Park Books.

Knight, S. 1972. Untitled independent study project, University of California, Davis.

Kübler-Ross, E. 1969. *On death and dying.* New York: Macmillan.

Looker, E. 1933. *The American way: Franklin Roosevelt in action.* New York: John Day.

Lord, A. B. 1978. *The singer of tales.* New York: Atheneum.

Martin, J. 1930. Dance. In *The encyclopedia of the social sciences,* vol. 4. New York: Macmillan.

Maslow, A. H. 1968. *Toward a psychology of being.* 2d ed. New York: Van Nostrand Reinhold.

Mauss, M. 1967 (1925). *The gift,* trans. I. Cunnison. New York: Norton.

Moore, S. F. 1975. Epilogue: Uncertainties in situations, indeterminacies in culture. In *Symbol and politics in communal ideology,* ed. S. F. Moore and B. Myerhoff. Ithaca, N.Y.: Cornell University Press.

Stahl, S. K. D. 1983. Personal experience stories. In *Handbook of American folklore,* ed. R. M. Dorson. Bloomington: Indiana University Press.

Vash, C. L. 1981. *The psychology of disability.* New York: Springer.

Wright, B. 1960. *Physical disability: A psychological approach.* New York: Harper and Row.

8. Never-Married Old Women and Disability: A Majority Experience

BARBARA LEVY SIMON

My eyes and legs, it's true, slow me down. But who in my Methuselah crowd doesn't have such problems? My cataracts and arthritis are an ever-present pain, but they're nothing to make a fuss about. At least I'm not six feet under like a lot of them are by my age. (A never-married woman, Philadelphia, February 1984)

Such relaxed and philosophical acceptance of the physical problems that often attend old age is characteristic of the fifty never-married women, 65 years old and older, whom I have studied.[1] Far from identifying their chronic illnesses and disabilities as unusual burdens or as badges of atypicality, these never-married women view cataracts, arthritis, diabetes, circulatory diseases, muscular degeneration, hearing loss, and dental problems as predictable, unexceptional difficulties that are part of the fabric of old age. Indeed, they understand disability to be a majority experience for old people. From the perspective of this diverse group of never-married old women, the disabilities that attend their old age are inevitabilities that, oddly enough, constitute a source of social integration, not isolation, in relation to women and men in their age cohort.

THE SAMPLE AND STUDY
In 1979, only 6.1 percent of women in the United States 65 years old and older were never married (U.S. Bureau of the Census 1980b). Therefore, it came as no surprise to discover that finding a reasonably representative sample of fifty never-married women, aged 65 or more, who would agree to be interviewed was no mean task. To secure a cross-class, cross-racial sample, I contacted staff people in senior citizen centers, community centers, churches and synagogues, social service agencies, and voluntary groups. Friends and colleagues from a broad range of occupa-

Table 8.1. CHARACTERISTICS OF WOMEN INTERVIEWED ($N = 50$)

Age[a]

65–69	70–74	75–79	80–84	85–89	90–94	95–99	100–104
7	11	18	8	2	1	1	2

Country of origin[b]

Native-born	Foreign born
44	6

Race

White	Black	Hispanic	Asian	Native American
30	12	5	2	1

Education[c]

Second Grade	Sixth Grade	Eighth Grade	Tenth Grade	Twelfth Grade	Bachelor's/ Nursing/ Normal school	Master's degree	Ph.D. or equivalent
3	2	5	3	11	15	6	5

Employment area

Domestic	Factory	Retail	Clerical	Technical	Professional	Managerial
6	8	2	13	1	17	3

Religion

Protestant	Catholic	Jewish	Buddhist	Agnostic/Atheist
25	17	5	1	2

[a] Age at time of interview.
[b] The native-born category includes four women born in Puerto Rico. The foreign-born category includes one woman from each of the following: China, Cuba, Germany, Italy, Jamaica, and Russia.
[c] Highest grade completed.

tions and parts of the Philadelphia area also suggested women to interview. Students at LaSalle University, where I taught during the three years of interviewing, 1982–1984, identified other possible subjects. To supplement these suggestions and to ensure demographic and geographic diversity, I placed notices requesting interviewees in selected urban and suburban neighborhood newspapers. In addition, each woman interviewed was asked for suggestions of other never-married women, 65 years old or older, who might be willing to join the research project. The composition of the final sample of fifty never-married women is shown in Table 8.1.

Taped interviews lasting four to eight hours (mean average, 5.3

hours) were conducted with each woman in the sample, usually in the interviewee's home or apartment. Open-ended questions were asked to elicit each woman's reflections on five general topics: (1) past and present relationship to her family of origin; (2) past and present friendships; (3) work lives; (4) retirement and aging experiences; and (5) single life. The overall purpose of the interviews was an exploratory one—to identify the meanings these fifty women derived from and ascribed to their families, friends, work, retirement, aging, and single status.

SUBJECTIVE IMPRESSIONS/OBJECTIVE CONDITIONS

The subjective impressions concerning the prevalence and predictability of disabilities and chronic illnesses in old age of these fifty interviewees correspond closely with the objective conditions revealed in statistical surveys of elderly people's health status. DeJong and Lifchez (1983) report that 46 percent of those who are 65 years old or older have chronic activity-limiting disability. Of all Americans 65 years old and older, 43.5 percent were arthritic in 1976, and 19.8 percent of elderly people in the United States had heart disease in 1972 (U.S. Bureau of the Census 1980a). Among men and women 65–74 years of age in 1972 in the United States, 28.5 percent had cataracts, while 85.4 percent of people in that age group had one or more serious eye conditions that required medical attention that year (U.S. Dept. of Health and Human Services 1983). Between 1971 and 1975, 66.8 percent of all Americans 65–74 years old were measurably hard of hearing (U.S. Dept. of Health, Education, and Welfare 1980). In that same five-year period, 34.2 percent of the population 65–74 years old had "definite hypertension" (U.S. Dept. of Health and Human Services 1981).

Statistical studies, then, support these never-married old women's observation that most people in old age have at least one disability and, therefore, that old age makes them more like their married and previously married peers than at any other time of adulthood in at least one dimension of their life. (Old age provides a second major piece of common ground between never-married women and those who have married: it makes widows out of 41.2 percent of U.S. women between 65 and 74 years of age and of 69.7 percent of women who are 75 years old or older, thereby elevating single status to a majority ranking by the time women are 75) (U.S. Bureau of the Census 1980b).

Ironically, disability in old age has served to *integrate* the never-married women I interviewed into the general population of people 65 years old and older. Chronic disease and disability have provided a painful and somewhat perverse bridge across the social chasm that separates married from never-married people in earlier stages of their life course. The physical ailments of old age create a set of physical experiences, a series of logistical and social obstacles to contend with, a vocabulary and cluster of referents, a topic of conversation, and a career as patient shared by the majority of married, widowed, divorced, separated, and never-married people who are 65 years old or older.

Every day when the weather permits, I stroll in the park. There I meet my friends from nearby apartment complexes. They show me pictures of their grandchildren. I, of course, don't have any, so I show them photos of my grandnieces and nephews. Then, after long quarrels about politics, we talk about our arthritis and bursitis. We all have it, you know, to some degree or other. So we commiserate with each other about those aches and pains that will be with us for the duration. (A never-married woman, Philadelphia, August 1982)

"Those aches and pains" connote a reduction in mobility and health that is experienced by a broad range of people in the United States both before and during their retirement years. Disability, then, is a given both physiologically and culturally, an unavoidable rite of passage, like retirement, for men and women who live past middle age. Unlike other key rites of passage—marriage, parenthood, and widowhood—disability in old age is all-inclusive. No group is left out.

DISABILITY IN OLD AGE: A SUBORDINATE STATUS

"Poor Sylvia," they used to say. "She had to stay home and take care of her folks. What a shame she never had a life of her own." They were wrong, of course. I've had a fine life of my own. But my neighbors and relatives and people at church don't see it that way. You see, to them, if you're not married, you don't have a life. (A never-married woman, Philadelphia, October 1983)

For most women who remain single, the attribute of their existence that distinguishes them in the public's conception from most other women is their never-married status.[2] Singlehood past 40 years of age becomes the characteristic that overrides all others in the minds of people who interact with never-married women over time. Her single condition, in Hughes' (1945) words, becomes her "master status," that attribute given highest priority in the ongoing determination of her place in the social pecking order. This master status becomes the central explanatory construct for interpreting and predicting all her attitudes and behaviors. According to Hughes, this master status is the one salient trait that is *formally* expected and that serves to distinguish those who are socially admissible from those who are not. Such a status subordinates all other attributes, relegating them to the netherworld of informally expected characteristics.

I was a fine pediatrician for forty-odd years, of which I am proud. But do you know what? At family gatherings and in the old neighborhood, they still see me as the one who didn't marry. Not as the first in the family to go to college. Not as one of the first Catholics admitted into the fancy medical school I attended. Not as a well-known physician in Philadelphia. No, just as Sally, the one who never got married. (A never-married woman, Philadelphia, January 1984)

For most of these fifty never-married old women, the disabilities encountered by many in old age are insignificant as sources of alienation or marginality when compared with thirty to forty years of "spinster status." The presence of a hip brace, a walker, or a hearing aid is overshadowed, in the public's eye, by the absence, even in old age, of the legitimating wedding ring or of a conversational reference to a husband, living or dead. Marital status, in short, upstages physical disability as the leading determinant of the social billing of the never-married woman over age 40.

LIFELONG DISABILITY: A MASTER STATUS

Being single has been the least of my troubles. It is epilepsy that has branded me for life. It is epilepsy that kept me from marrying, as I did not want to bring a child into the world with such a curse. It is epilepsy that kept me close to home when I really wanted to rove the world. It is epilepsy that caused me to keep for forty-one years a foolish job that a moron could have performed. I was afraid, you see, that no one else would employ me. Back in the dark ages, few would. (A never-married woman, Philadelphia, June 1984)

Disabilities that afflict girls and young women, in sharp contrast to those that women encounter in old age for the first time, frequently dominate identity formation and become the primary determinants of social and economic prospects. Four of the fifty women I interviewed endured lifelong disabilities. One had polio; another, cerebral palsy; a third, severe hemophilia; and a fourth, epilepsy. Each of these women viewed her physical disability as the sole reason for remaining single and as the major force in determining her life chances.

With none of the insouciance toward their own disability that the other women exhibited, these four discussed in detail the severe anguish and deprivation that their respective disabilities had brought them over the years. They experienced their disease or condition as that which had set them apart from the rest of humanity. Though the four expressed widely varying levels of acceptance of their disabled fate, they were in strong agreement concerning the centrality of disability in shaping their self-conception and in contaminating the treatment they received at the hands of the public, employers, and potential mates. The following reflection was representative of the four women's views of the impact of disability on their lives:

If you are not a cripple, you cannot possibly imagine the way the world reduces you to that condition. For a woman, especially, normality, acceptability, and marriageability depend upon looking whole. I have been in leg and arm braces since I was three. Boys never considered me fair game for dating, even though they liked me a lot to pal around with. Teachers never thought it possible that I might accomplish what others could do. Firms that I interviewed with approached me with fear and loathing.

I got through because I believed in my inner wholeness, even if my outside leaves a lot to be desired. But the world around me saw a woman without— without the use of her limbs, without womanliness, without a man, without children. My disease was the lead actor in my life. Everything else had a cameo role.

Unlike their single counterparts who had been healthy in youth and throughout most of adulthood, the women with lifelong disabilities found their physical conditions to be of major consequence. Not surprisingly, they saw disability as a minority experience that left them on the margins of social life.

THE GREATER CONTINUITY OF SINGLE LIFE

Never-married people, Gubrium (1976) found, do not tend to see old age as new or notably different from the past. He brings forward Peter Townsend's desolation hypothesis, the notion that negative evaluations of life arise from social discontinuity much more than from isolation, in order to explain his finding that never-married old people were the least likely in his sample of diverse elderly men and women to be dissatisfied with their quality of life in retirement (Gubrium 1974). The high level of satisfaction with life in old age of never-married people, he suggests, flows from the uninterrupted quality of their daily routines and lifestyles developed over time.

Continuity, though certainly not isolation, characterize the lives before and after age 65 of the women interviewed. These never-married women describe their old age, in their own various ways, as a portion of a continuous skein of their life. They emphasize the continuity of retirement years with earlier parts of their life much more than they focus on the discontinuity it has brought them. With two major exceptions, those of retirement and of the loss of loved ones to death, never-married women do not undergo the number of shifts in status and in the organization of daily life that most married women face: engagement, marriage, motherhood, the departure of children, and widowhood. Single women encounter fewer fits and starts in old age.

I don't understand the big deal some make about old age. Sure, I am 82 now and walk like a snail. But who cares? I have spent seventeen years in retirement. It took me two weeks to get the hang of organizing my days around something other than paid work. Then I was fine. I do everything I always did—see friends, do volunteer work, take walks, go to concerts, take care of my grandniece. Except now I do a little more—I can travel now and read more and do more volunteer work than I could when I worked. For me, retirement hasn't made much difference except that it's more diverse and relaxed than the working life. (A never-married woman, Philadelphia, July 1983)

Chronic and acute illness inevitably disrupts, at least at first, the lives of everyone who becomes sick or disabled. Yet never-married women in old age appear to incorporate such disruptions into their daily routines with relative ease and stoicism. Perhaps it is the absence of most major disruptions throughout their lives that makes this glide into old age possible. The dislocations accompanying disability are more manageable in an existence in which most other elements are steady and predictable. Or perhaps it is the practiced independence of single life that causes the never-married women I have studied to pay scant attention to their disabilities.

INDEPENDENT VETERANS OF MARGINALITY
Women 65 years old and older who never marry are accustomed to living independent and somewhat unorthodox lives. As members of a tiny minority in a generally coupled world, they have long grappled with the social judgments of society and the economic and social demands of singlehood. A woman who has reached retirement years without marrying has necessarily evolved a set of strategies, justifications, and contingency plans with which to contend with economic uncertainty, stigma, ill health, deaths of loved ones, and retirement. Self-reliance, planning, and indifference to the condescension of others have been essential components of survival for the single women in my study.

Lord, I learned early on that I wasn't pleasing to the world without a husband. By 35, I knew that I made some people very uncomfortable with my single ways. They just didn't know what to make of me.
  Yet after awhile, I learned to ignore the ones who wanted me to change into a wife. So long as I could earn my own keep, support my mother to boot, and put some dollars in the bank for old age, I knew I would be fine. A spinster has to forge her own way and ignore the comments some will make. If a woman can't stand the criticism, after all, she can always get married. (A never-married woman, Philadelphia, November 1983)

All three of the attributes noted in the quotation above—independence, foresightedness, and a thick-skinned outlook—serve these fifty never-married women in old age, when disabilities and illness emerge. These single women's habit of taking responsibility for their own social and economic existence prepares them to face the physical, emotional, and economic challenges posed by disability. The tendency of these never-married women to plan for vicissitudes, a tendency shaped by the realities of a one-income existence, leaves them better able to respond quickly to unforeseen illness than women who have relied on a husband to plan for the future or even than women who have jointly planned for the future with their husbands. Most important, the emotional callouses a never-married woman develops in response to the married world's stereotypes are highly functional in the face of the labels that are applied all too often to bearers of disabilities. In other words, the traits that enable a single woman to survive and thrive in a generally married, male-dominated world are the very qualities that assist her to bear with and manage old-age chronic illnesses and disabilities, and their attendant stigmata.

FRIENDSHIPS

Investing in multiple friendships concurrently and across time is another habit of the never-married women sampled that appears to help them manage chronic illness and disability in old age. In forty-eight of the fifty lives explored, the women have sustained deep and complex friendship networks over many decades. The most common pattern of friendship among these fifty single women is that of a core, dyadic bond with one other woman, who usually also is single. This central friendship is usually surrounded by two to five secondary, but emotionally significant, relationships. Weekly contact, at minimum, is maintained with each friend. Daily contact is usually kept with the central friend.

It is obvious that old and close friends are a major asset for anyone who has a disability or illness in old age. Friends provide emotional support, help with transportation, run errands, clean house, and do the shopping. They might even give or loan money in times of sickness. The never-married women in my sample who have become sick or disabled lean on their friends for all or most of these things; they also supply their friends with these invaluable supports. Their habit of building and keeping up friendships is an investment that pays never-married women back richly throughout life, particularly in times of sickness or infirmity.

EXPOSURE TO DISABILITIES

A final part of the explanation for never-married women's relative ease and competence in handling their own old-age disabilities stems from their past role as caregivers to aged parents. Of the fifty women interviewed, forty-two were the person in their family who was centrally responsible for caring for an ailing parent or parents.

The experience of nursing someone who is sick, dying, or disabled strips away, for most people, the mystery, horror, and disgust associated at least initially with morbidity and mortality. Direct, sustained contact with a sick or disabled relative reduces a caregiver's dissociated loathing for illness. One who tends a sick or disabled person in an ongoing way comes to understand the tangible, definable, and delimited nature of disease or disability. A caregiver for a sick relative usually reduces her or his objectification of that person and of that relative's disease through frequent and multiple glimpses of the multidimensionality and humanity of the patient. It is not surprising, therefore, that these never-married women, who are deeply experienced in caring for sick parents in the latter's old age, tend to take their own sickness and disability in stride. They have known before in an intimate manner the difficulties they might encounter later in their own lives.

My mother died a slow and painful death. I cared for her every day for eighteen months. I washed her and read to her and made her laugh. And then she went at 82. *C'est la vie.* So is it any wonder that my diabetes seems like a very little burden to bear in comparison? I just watch my diet, take the insulin, and see a doctor now and then. I can certainly live with that. (A never-married woman, Philadelphia, January 1984)

CONCLUSION

The sturdy grace with which these never-married women whom I interviewed endure old age's disabilities springs from the self-reliance, planning, and invulnerability to insult that single women develop necessarily. Their friendships, carefully tended for the most part, serve them well in times of their own sickness and disability. Their early exposure to sickness and death, due to culturally ascribed roles as caretakers of aged parents, also assist them in accepting their own limitations in old age. Partial or progressive infirmities come as no surprise to them.

Disability in old age, for the fifty never-married women interviewed, makes their lives more like those of women who have been married. The physical dimensions of aging, consequently and ironically, constitute a source of subjective and objective integration for never-married women into the ranks of aged women in general. Because the social value of all women in a sexist and capitalist society hinges on their capacity to measure up to male-defined concepts of beauty and utility, *all* women lose value as they lose youth, fertility, and mobility.

In Rubin's (1975) terms, the "political economy of sex" creates a "traffic in women" that leaves on the side of the highway and on the margins of the sexual marketplace those women who are past what men designate as the female prime. Married women in old age, in short, lose their men and much of their desirability to men. They are reduced to the same category inhabited by never-married women and disabled women all of their adult lives—that of women manqué. The aging process creates a large caste of women into which never-married women merge after decades of social segregation.

Notes

1. This article is based on data from in-depth interviews with fifty never-married women, 65 years old and older, who live in the Philadelphia and New York City areas. These interviews were part of a study, "Never-Married Old Women: Pathfinders for Aged Singles," funded in part by the National Institute on Aging Small Grant #1 R03 AG04694-01 (1984).
2. Two exceptions to this generalization are important to note. The never-married woman with a severe, highly visible disability throughout life is set apart from others by this obvious deviation from the physical norm. Her disabled appearance and condition constitute her "master status." In a similar way, a never-married woman of a racial minority is an exception. Her color overwhelms her marital status because, in a racist world, it is her most blatant "blemish."

References

DeJong, G., and R. Lifchez. 1983. Physical disability and public policy. *Scientific American* 248 (June): 40–49.

Gubrium, J. 1974. Marital desolation and the evaluation of everyday life in old age. *Journal of Marriage and the Family* 36 (February): 110, 107.

———. 1976. Being single in old age. In *Time, roles and self in old age*, ed. J. Gubrium. New York: Human Sciences Press.

Hughes, E. 1945. Dilemmas and contradictions of status. *American Journal of Sociology* 50 (March): 353–59.

Rubin, G. 1975. The traffic in women: Notes on the political economy of sex. In *Toward an anthropology of women*, ed. R. Reiter. New York: Monthly Review Press.

U.S. Bureau of the Census. 1980a. *Social Indicators III*, Table 2/17. Washington, D.C.: GPO, p. 101.

———. 1980b. *Current Population Reports*, Series P-20, no. 349. Marital status and living arrangements: March 1979. Washington, D.C.: GPO, pp. 2, 7.

U.S. Department of Health and Human Services. 1981. Public Health Service, National Center for Health Statistics, series 11, no. 221, Hypertension in adults 25–74 years of age, U.S., 1971–1975. Washington, D.C.: GPO, p. 57.

———. 1983. Public Health Service, National Center for Health Statistics, series

11, no. 228. Eye conditions and related need for medical care among persons 1–74 years of age: U.S., 1971–1972. Washington, D.C.: GPO, pp. 21, 23.

U.S. Department of Health, Education, and Welfare. 1980. Public Health Service, National Center for Health Statistics, series 11, no. 215, Basic data on hearing levels of adults 25–74 years, U.S., 1971–1975. Washington, D. C.: GPO, p. 3.

III:Policy and Politics

The preceding parts of this volume discuss relationships of disabled women to their bodies, to parents, to friends, and to the community— all relationships that they have had some opportunity to shape. This section—which explores the experiences of disabled women in institutional settings of rehabilitation and work, in federal welfare policy, the law, motherhood and childbearing, and in feminism—dramatically underscores how the lives of disabled women have been shaped by institutions and policies they have not controlled. The story here is necessarily grim. Throughout, however, the authors offer alternatives to the existing situation that promise something better for disabled women of the future.

Nancy Felipe Russo and Mary Jansen tell us how gender bias has interacted with the social service mentality to subvert the goals of the framers of the law and policy governing rehabilitation. Even more than disabled men, disabled women do not receive quality training for competitive employment. While not denying substantial employment problems for disabled men, the authors demonstrate how the economy generally and the specialized service system for disability in particular constrict the work opportunities and life chances for disabled women.

Since the creation of Social Security in the 1930s, the federal government has recognized its role as provider for those it defines as needy. Nancy Mudrick examines income support programs for women with disabilities who find themselves outside the work force and in poverty and considers how they assist or impede disabled women across racial groups. Mudrick demonstrates that while federal programs are inadequate for women without disabilities and for men with them, they impose even greater hardships on disabled women because of their underlying assumptions.

"The motherhood mandate" (Russo 1981) is at the core of woman's role—but only if both mother and child are non-disabled. Even more than being nurturers to men at home and at work, women have been expected to give unsparingly to children. Yet for women with disabilities who wish to mother, or for anyone considering bearing a child with a disabling condition, the medical profession, the media, and the

227

law communicate powerfully that motherhood is not acceptable. Joanna Weinberg discusses the law as a major institution that influences the possibilities of mothering for cognitively impaired women. In critiquing the polarized views of autonomy and paternalism and the denial of respect for disabled women's rights and needs, Weinberg offers a way to rethink legal theory and social work practice. By examining the law as applied to perhaps the least powerful and thus most vulnerable of women with disabilities, Weinberg illustrates one facet of the complex problem of disabled women seeking sanction for motherhood.

The final chapters pose important questions for feminism and offer guidelines for more inclusive feminist politics. Adrienne Asch and Michelle Fine continue the theme of the relationship of disability to motherhood and to the reproductive rights movement in tackling two salient questions: should all women have the right to decide to abort or to carry to term a fetus with a diagnosed impairment? Should disabled newborns have the right to receive medical treatment regardless of parental wishes? Advances in reproductive technology and in neonatal medicine cause feminists, disability rights advocates, and everyone concerned with creating a caring society to examine deeply cherished notions about the meaning of mothering, family autonomy, and the essence of being human.

Last of all comes an eloquent message about how disabled women and mothers of disabled children have much in common with and much to contribute to the women's movement. Marian Blackwell-Stratton, Mary Lou Breslin, Arlene Byrnne Mayerson, Susan Bailey (all from the Disability Rights Education and Defense Fund [DREDF], the leading civil rights organization for people with disabilities in the nation) have been in the forefront of the fight for justice for disabled people, disabled women in particular. Without minimizing tensions and problems in committing themselves to all these struggles for social progress, these disabled and non-disabled women nonetheless demonstrate a steadfast commitment to the advancement of women, of disabled people, and of disabled women.

9. Women, Work, and Disability: Opportunities and Challenges

NANCY FELIPE RUSSO and MARY A. JANSEN

The historic changes in women's work and family roles of the past two decades have profound implications for public policy. The trend toward women working outside the home in the 1950s escalated in the 1970s, with labor force participation increasing from one-third of adult women in 1950 to nearly two-thirds in 1982. The forty-eight million women workers in 1982 accounted for more than 43 percent of all workers. Labor force participation rates for women were similar across racial and ethnic groups.

At the same time the relationship between work and family roles has changed. While the number of working women has more than tripled since 1940, the number of working *mothers* has increased more than ten times. In March of 1982, 59 percent of all mothers and children under 18 years of age (18.7 million mothers) were in the labor force; for mothers of preschool children (7.4 million mothers) the figure was 50 percent.

Another dramatic change, which has particular implications for employment policy, is the rise in female-headed households. In 1982, nearly one in six families was maintained by a woman. Nearly three out of ten such families were maintained by black women. Forty-one percent of all black families are maintained by women, compared to 23 percent of Hispanic families and 13 percent of white families. The proportion of poor families headed by women reached 47 percent in 1981 (see Russo 1984 for a more complete summary of these trends).

Disabled women, however, have not participated in women's employment revolution. In 1982, 24 percent of females with work disability participated in the labor force, compared to 64 percent of females with no work disability (McNeil 1983). Although women's employment issues are now a visible item on the nation's policy agenda, the analyses of women's problems and the policies suggested to allevi-

229

ate them continue to assume that the woman (as well as her family members) is able-bodied. Until recently little attention has been paid to the disadvantaged employment status of women with disabilities. This chapter considers that status and discusses the opportunities and challenges for research, education, and rehabilitation strategies designed to ameliorate it.

RESEARCH ON WORK DISABILITY: METHODOLOGICAL ISSUES

A basic step towards understanding and ameliorating employment problems of disabled women is the establishment of a useful knowledge base. Behavioral research on employment issues of disabled women is rare (Oakes 1984).

In evaluating the available data on work disability, it is important to keep in mind that work disability is defined as an *outcome* of physical or mental impairment. Work disability is considered to be present if normal work activity is prevented or limited. This definition deemphasizes the physiological and focuses on the economic, sociological, and psychological aspects of disability. The demands of the work environment are as much, if not more, influential as type and level of actual physical impairment in defining work disability. Given the separate worlds of work for the sexes, it becomes difficult to interpret gender differences in the incidence of work disability when so many unmeasured medical and nonmedical factors that differ for the sexes are treated simultaneously.

Most demographic and social data on disabled women's employment come from employment surveys sponsored by the federal government since the mid-sixties. These provide detailed information on the economic, social, and health status of persons identified as having a work disability. They include surveys specifically focusing on work disability conducted by the Social Security Administration (SSA) in 1966, 1972, and 1978. In addition, work disability questions have been included in several major general-purpose surveys, including the 1967 Survey of Economic Opportunity, the 1970 census, the 1976 Survey of Income and Education, the 1980 census, and the 1981 and 1982 March Supplements to the Current Population Survey. These studies produce the data that are most relied upon in formulating public policy for persons with disabilities.

Large variations in estimates of prevalence of disability are found across these studies, ranging from a high of 17 percent in the 1966 and 1978 SSA surveys to a low of 8.5 percent in the 1980 census. That the variation in rate is not related to the year of the study suggests differences due to methodology. Higher disability estimates are found when surveys focus specifically on disability. It has been suggested that these higher estimates reflect the identification of larger numbers of people with relatively minor limitations. Rates of severe work disability show more stability across studies than do rates of total work disability. While this may be a partial explanation, there is little understanding of the factors that affect disability response levels (Haber and McNeil 1983). There is a need for behavioral scientists to work together with epidemiologists so that the questions used to define work disability are equally appropriate for assessing relevant factors in the life experiences and occupational worlds of disabled women and men.

In this context, discussions of gender differences found in a particular survey could be problematical, and statements about sex differences in work disability rates should be made with caution. Males are generally reported to have higher rates of work disability when disabled persons who are still able to work are included in the sample. Females are reported as having higher rates of disablity when only persons who are not at all able to work are considered. Our ability to assess the current employment status of disabled women is limited by the fact that the most recent survey to assess severe work disability was the 1976 Survey of Income and Education conducted by the Social Security Administration. That study reported 6.4 percent of females and 5.1 percent of males as completely unable to work that year (McNeil 1983).

Fortunately, it appears that variables related to disability rates are similar across studies. There is a high level of consistency across surveys in the relationship of disability to major social and economic variables, such as age, race, education, labor force participation, income, and marital status. Labor force participation of work-disabled females is substantially lower than that of disabled males, whatever definition of disability is used (Haber and McNeil 1983).

Since the 1982 Current Population Survey (CPS) is most recent, the discussion of disabled women will be based primarily on those data (McNeil 1983). Use of CPS data raises yet another methodological issue, however. The CPS uses both direct and indirect measures to identify individuals with work disabilities. Direct assessment of disability status is determined by the following questions:

1. Does anyone in this household have a health problem or disability which prevents them from working or which limits the kind or amount of work they can do?
2. Is there anyone in this household who has a service-connected disability or who ever retired or left a job for health reasons?

In addition, work disability is assumed if the respondents meet any of the following criteria:

1. Did not work in previous week because of long-term physical or mental illness or disability which prevents performance at any kind of work [based on response to "main activity last week" question on the basic CPS questionnaire];
2. Did not work at all in previous year because ill or disabled [based on response to "reason did not work last year" question];
3. Under 65 years of age and covered by Medicare;
4. Under 65 years of age and a recipient of Supplemental Security Income.

Of the 13.1 million persons between the ages of 16 and 64 years who were classified as having a work disability and who were not in institutions, about 79 percent were identified by the first direct item. The second direct item identified an additional 9 percent. The remainder were not identified as disabled by either of the direct items, but they did meet the indirect criteria. However, the proportions of women identified by each of the measures are not reported. The fact that the respondents are specifically asked about service-connected disabilities in question 2 may mean that the procedure identifies males with service-related disabilities that do not currently interfere with their ability to work.

Given these methodological issues, the discussion will include some gender comparisons, but our main focus will be on how conditions for women with work disabilities differ from those of other women.

WOMEN WITH WORK DISABILITIES: A PROFILE
Of the 13.1 million adults who qualified as work disabled by the criteria cited, 6.4 million (49 percent) were women. Disabled women are a substantial proportion of American women of working age: in 1982, of the 74.7 million American women aged 16 to 64 years, one of every twelve had a work disability (8.5 percent).

Minorities had higher rates of work disability, especially blacks. Sex and race/ethnicity interact, however. While white women were slightly less likely to have a work disability than white men (7.8 percent versus 9.0 percent), the opposite was true for black and Hispanic women. (Hispanics may be of any race.) For blacks, 13.9 percent of women reported a work disability, compared to 12.9 percent of men. For Hispanics the figures were 8.5 percent and 7.5 percent, respectively.

Thus, patterns of work disability varied among demographic, social, and economic groups. Age, education, income, and marital status were all related to likelihood of work disability, but the direction and extent of the relationship varied by race/ethnicity. Causal relationships are impossible to determine from the data, however, and this description of relationships should not be interpretated as implying causality. The purpose here is to highlight characteristics of the population of work-disabled women that have implications for education and rehabilitation strategies.

Keeping these cautions in mind, we find that even within the restricted age range of 16–64 considered here, women with work disabilities were, on the average, much older than non-disabled women; 61.5 percent of work-disabled women were between the ages of 45–64, whereas this was true for only 28.0 percent of non-disabled women. For black women, the effect of age was slightly less; 57.7 percent of disabled black women were between the ages of 45–64, compared to 30.0 percent of non-disabled black women.

The age structure of the current population of work-disabled women suggests that vocational and rehabilitation efforts must clearly reflect knowledge of and sensitivity to issues of middle-aged women. This is perhaps the most understudied age group (Schlossberg 1986). This structure also suggests that, even accounting for cohort effects, a large number of women become disabled after completing their education.

Education and disability are related in complex ways. Disabilities may make it difficult to attend and complete school—a situation especially true for the current disabled population. As late as the 1960s, an estimated one in every eight disabled children received no education at all. In that decade, more than half of all disabled children did not receive special instructional services (Corbett, Lea, and Zones 1981). The same factors that lead to low educational attainment also may lead to the increased likelihood of becoming disabled; for example, lack of access to preventive health care. It may be that less well-educated people and poorer people tend to obtain jobs involving physical labor. Such jobs may have higher risk for physical injury. Physical limitations, whether or not their origin is job related, may be more disabling in physically demanding work environments. For example, impaired mobility may not effect the work status of a psychotherapist, but it may be a major work disability for a waitress or a nurse. Whichever causal relationship is assumed, it can be argued that increasing educational opportunities is an important strategy for preventing work disability.

This strategy is especially important for women. Work-disabled women are five times as likely as other women to have less than an elementary level of education (17.4 percent versus 3.5 percent). Age is positively associated with work disability and negatively associated with education in the current U.S. population. The large increase in proportion of work-disabled over 45 years of age may not be found in future years. Older age, however, does not totally account for the relationship of disability and education. Between the ages of 25 and 44, 16.9 percent of work-disabled women have no more than an eighth-grade education, compared with 5.0 percent of other women.

The relationship of education to work disability is strongest for black women. For blacks aged 25–64 with fewer than eight years of education, 46.1 percent of women have a work disability, compared with 33.4 percent of men. For whites the figure is 29.4 percent for both men and women. The differing impact of education on work disability for black women compared to white women underscores the importance of incorporating special sensitivities to racial and ethnic issues for minority women in vocational education and rehabilitation programs.

Higher education strategies must supplement those of vocational education and rehabilitation. For women 25–64 years of age, work disability varies from 32.3 percent among people with less than an eighth-grade education to 8.1 percent among those with a high school education and 4.0 percent among college graduates. The interaction of race and education is seen in the figures for black women, which are 46.1 percent, 13.2 percent, and 3.5 percent, respectively. Causal relationships may be difficult to ascertain, but the convergence of disability rates for black and white college-educated women points to increasing educational opportunities in higher education as an additional strategy for preventing work disability of black females.

EMPLOYMENT, POVERTY, AND DISABILITY

Employment, poverty, and disability also are related in complex ways: people who would not be economically disadvantaged may become so when they are ill. Poor people are less likely to be educated, lack prenatal and postnatal care, are malnourished, and have inadequate access to preventive health services—all of which contribute to risk of chronic illness, physical and mental disability, and the inability to participate in the labor force.

For both males and females, a work disability was associated with lower earnings and unemployment. Having a work disability had a stronger negative impact on women's labor force participation than it did on men's. In March of 1982, 23.7 percent of work-disabled females were in the labor force, compared to 41.5 percent of work-disabled males. Comparable figures for other females and males were 64.3 percent and 88.8 percent. The employment picture for work-disabled women younger than age 45 differed dramatically from that of older disabled women in this population. More than one in three (35.5 percent) work-disabled women between the ages of 25 and 44 was either working or looking for work; the figure for work-disabled women between the ages of 45 and 64 was less than one in six (15.6 percent).

Work-disabled women in the labor force are much more likely to face unemployment than are other women. The unemployment rates for work-disabled women between the ages of 25 and 34 is 23.5 percent, compared with a rate of 8.4 percent for other women in that age range.

The unemployment rate is not directly related to educational level for work-disabled women in the same way that it is for other women, who are less likely to be unemployed the higher their educational level. The highest unemployment rate is found for women with less than an eighth-grade education (29.6 percent); the lowest rate is found for women who have some college (8.8 percent). When unemployment is concerned, there was little difference between women with an eighth-grade education and women with one to three years of high school (16.9 percent and 15.6 percent, respectively). The unemployment rate for women with a college degree was 11.7 percent.

In 1982, the average yearly earnings of females with a work disability were $5,835; other females had earnings of $8,470. For males, the figures were $13,863 and $17,481. For year-round, full-time workers, females with a work disability earned $11,979, compared to $13,071 for other women. For men the figures were $21,070 and $22,247, respectively. These figures clearly demonstrate how tied the status of work-disabled women is to the occupational structure. Even if women with work disabilities were able to obtain full-time employment, they still earned fifty-seven cents for every dollar earned by disabled men.

Women with a work disability are likely to be poor. Of all work-disabled women, 61.7 percent had an income from all sources of less than four thousand dollars a year; 24.2 percent had an income below the poverty level. This compares with 10.6 percent for other women. Approximately 56 percent of all disabled people below the poverty line are women.

The pattern of sex segregation in the work world is reflected in the employment patterns of disabled women. Compared to men, disabled women—like all women—are overrepresented as clerical and kindred workers and service workers (traditional occupations for females) and underrepresented as craft and kindred workers, and as managers and administrators (traditional occupations for males).

There are some differences between disabled women and other women. Women with a work disability were more likely than others to be self-employed (2.2 percent versus 1.0 percent) and less likely to be employed as "professional, technical, and kindred workers" (13.7 percent versus 18.0 percent) and "clerical and kindred workers" (25.4 percent versus 34.6 percent). In contrast, they were more likely than other women to be employed as transport operators (13.6 percent versus 9.1 percent) and service workers (28.8 percent versus 19.3 percent). Nearly one in seven disabled women were black (14.6 percent). Sex stereotyping had an effect on disabled women of both races; black women were also concentrated in traditionally female occupations. Thus, pay equity and comparable worth, which are the keys to increasing the economic status of currently employed women, are also critical for increasing the economic status of women with a work disability.

There were differences, however. White women with disabilities are more likely than black women to be clerical or sales workers (34.9 percent versus 21.9 percent); professional, technical, and kindred workers (15.1 percent versus 4.4 percent); and managers, officials, and proprietors (6.8 percent versus 3.7 percent). Black women are more likely than white women to be service workers (53.2 percent versus 24.8 percent).

Also contributing to the likelihood of poverty for disabled women is the fact that many of our economic policies have been tailored to the needs of working males. Women receive fewer and less generous benefits from such programs as disability insurance, workers' compensation, and vocational rehabilitation, where benefit eligibility is tied to participation in the labor force and where benefits correlate with earnings (Kutza 1983). Women who have intermittent patterns of labor force participation, lower wages, and recent entry into the labor force are most affected.

Disabled women are much less likely to be covered by pension and health plans than are disabled men; 24 percent of disabled females, compared with 41.6 percent of disabled males, were covered by both pension and health plans in 1981. Forty-six percent of disabled females, compared with 33.9 percent of disabled males, were not covered by either type of plan. For non-disabled women, 34.6 percent had both health and pension coverage, while 36.3 percent had none.

It is possible that some women are covered by a husband's policy. However, a large proportion of disabled women are likely to be single heads of households. In 1982, more than one woman in six (16.5 percent) with a work disability had never married. More than one out of three (36.0 percent) disabled women were divorced, separated, or never married. Slightly more than half (50.6 percent) of women with work disabilities were currently married. In contrast, six out of ten disabled men (60.6 percent) were married. Thus, the sex difference in coverage has important implications. In addition to implications for health and pension coverage, these figures suggest that the disadvantage of having a work disability is compounded by the lack of a family support system.

Cash transfer programs offer partial replacement of lost wages and basic support. Work-disabled individuals made up a disproportionate share of people participating in some of the major assistance programs. Of the 12.1 million working-age individuals who received food stamps in 1981, for example, approximately 23 percent were work disabled, and there were no significant differences in participation of work-disabled persons by sex or race. The work disability rate among Medicaid recipients was 37 percent. The higher rate of poverty among women in general is seen in the finding that of female Medicaid recipients, 33.3 percent were work disabled; for men, the figure was 44.9 percent.

EDUCATIONAL ISSUES FOR DISABLED WOMEN

The relationship between education and work disability points to the importance of education as a strategy for work-disability prevention. Although the numbers of men and women with disabilities are roughly equal, a larger percentage of disabled boys than disabled girls is identified for special education classes. In 1978–1979, males accounted for 51 percent of the students in elementary and secondary schools, but for 61.0 percent of the students in classes for the educably mentally retarded, 75 percent of the students in classes for learning disabled, and 67 percent of the participants in judgmental programs (Corbett, Zea, and Zones 1981).

While special education classes contain a larger number of male students, the IQ's of these male students are significantly higher than the IQ's of their female counterparts. These facts suggest that boys are more readily identified as needing special education. It has been suggested that educating developmentally disabled boys has been given a higher priority than educating developmentally disabled girls, who are not seen as requiring skills to function beyond the home. It has also been suggested that developmentally disabled girls, in keeping with their female socialization, exhibit passivity, dependence, and withdrawal. If teachers are not attuned to identifying girls for special education services, and developmentally disabled girls do not exhibit aggressive behaviors to call attention to themselves, many girls who could benefit from special education services will not receive them.

Differential identification can have detrimental effects for both sexes. Boys, who are more likely to be labeled as needing special educational services and as having come from special programs, may in fact be denied the benefits of regular educational programs. At the same time, girls who would benefit from specialized educational services may be denied access to educational programs that would maximize their learning capabilities.

Inequities in special education go beyond differential identification and placement of males and females in specialized educational programs. Many of the curriculum materials used in special education classes are those that are used in regular education classes. While some progress has been made, pictures of males and stories about them are more frequent in educational materials; when females are portrayed, they are usually portrayed in stereotypically female roles rather than in roles that will expand the thinking of students about a wider range of opportunities and potential (Klein 1985). Minority women are rarely portrayed, and persons with disabilities (male or female) are rarely represented in curriculum materials.

The lack of role models for disabled females is especially serious because stereotypes of dependency, passivity, and incompetence are applied to both women and disabled persons. The convergence of these stereotypes for disabled women requires active intervention if such women are to achieve their full potential. Otherwise, women with disabilities will continue to be channeled into dependency roles and traditionally female occupations that are of lower status and are underpaid. One area for intervention is teacher education textbooks, which have reflected the same sex-role stereotyping. These materials shape the attitudes, values, and beliefs that future teachers will pass on to their students (Sadker and Sadker 1980).

Sex segregation in vocational courses is a prelude to sex segregation in the work world. Looking at enrollment data in secondary school courses, in 1979 more girls than boys took home economics at a rate of five to one (22 percent versus 4.1 percent), while the ratio of boys to girls who took shop was greater than ten to one (34.6 percent versus 3.0 percent) (U.S. Dept. of Education 1981). Despite the fact that these problems exist at all levels within the educational system, they are most obvious in vocational education programs. In 1980, vocational education programs enrolled more women than men, but most women were enrolled in sales, office work, childcare, and health support areas, while men were concentrated in agricultural, industrial, technical, and trade programs (Grasso 1980).

The placement of vocational schools also can create barriers to access. Vocational schools are predominately located in small cities and suburbs (U.S. Comm. on Civil Rights 1983). In contrast, 62.5 percent of disabled women live inside central cities or outside of metropolitan areas; for black women with work disabilities, the figure is 85.5 percent. The goals of teachers and counselors also must be evaluated. Currently, the priority is job placement. Ensuring that jobs match qualifications in a sex-fair manner is a secondary priority—if it ever even enters the employment equation. A 1981 report by the National Institute of Education found that nearly 70 percent of females in secondary school vocational courses were in programs leading to below-average-wage occupations; fewer than 10 percent were enrolled in programs leading to the highest-paid jobs. One reviewer has concluded that jobs in which minorities and women have been trained in vocational schools are the lowest paid, the least skilled, and the least promising in terms of upward employment mobility (McClure 1979).

In 1976 Vocational Education Amendments provided a major impetus toward addressing the problem of sex discrimination and sex stereotyping in vocational education, and there has been some progress made. In 1971, 65 percent of all female students in vocational education programs chose traditional programs of nursing, secretarial, and food service work. In 1980 this figure had decreased to 52 percent. Clearly, there is a substantial way to go. In addition, increases in female enrollment in traditionally male programs have been small and in areas already considered mixed; that is, where the proportion of one sex is not more than 75 percent (League of Women Voters Education Fund 1982).

Like their non-disabled counterparts, disabled women are channeled into these traditional roles by school counselors who frequently hold traditional biases. These biases affect the vocational aptitude assessment, interest testing and interpretation, and career counseling. Within this framework it is easy to see how options for disabled women can become severely limited (Corbett, Lea, and Zones 1981). The effects of these biases and role stereotyping go beyond vocationally oriented programs; they exist in training opportunities for women with disabilities in areas such as independent living skills, social skills, and personal adjustment (Gillespie and Fink 1974). As a result, women with disabilities are tracked into more traditionally stereotyped roles at both work and home. Intervention strategies must address all facets of their lives, including the personal, social, and vocational areas.

Who will take responsibility for change? A study of vocational education programs by the League of Women Voters found that each group tended to blame other groups for sex segregation; that is, counselors blamed peers and parents, and teachers blamed counselors and administrators, etc. (League of Women Voters Education Fund 1982).

In summary, the same social and cultural sex biases that affect women in general also affect work-disabled women. Dependence, passivity, and nonassertive behavior traditionally are viewed as appropriate and desirable behaviors for all women, but their effects are even more detrimental for disabled women because they are also stereotypes of *persons* with disabilities. As Vash (1982) has pointed out, in addition to the usual kinds of job and career information, disabled girls and women need additional advice in dealing with the dual burden posed by gender and disability. These views are reinforced in the training disabled women receive throughout the educational system, including the counseling that channels them into traditionally female training programs and occupations. As a consequence, disabled women and girls are less likely to be afforded the opportunity to acquire skills that will bring access to the higher-paying, male-dominated occupations.

WOMEN AND VOCATIONAL REHABILITATION

Vocational rehabilitation efforts assume a greater importance given that a large proportion of women become disabled after completing their education. Like vocational education, vocational rehabilitation is meant to help people attain their employment goals. Like vocational education, vocational rehabilitation has not provided women with an equal opportunity to train for the higher-paying occupations. Vash (1982) reports that in 1976 rehabilitated women, compared to rehabilitated men, were more likely to be closed in nonwage-earning capacity (30.0 percent versus 4.0 percent); less likely to enter industrial occupations (12.0 percent versus 46.0 percent); and more likely to earn less than men ($63 versus $112 per week).

The persistence of sex segregation in the occupational structure suggests that vocational rehabilitation counselors face a major challenge in instituting changes in the employment status for females with disabilities. Disabled women in rehabilitation programs face the same sex-role stereotypes that have channeled able-bodied women into low-paying, traditionally female occupations, stereotypes that are magnified by the additional stereotypes surrounding people with disabilities.

Clearly, services provided to clients reflect the values, attitudes, and beliefs of the service providers. Rehabilitation counseling is deeply rooted in traditional theories and approaches to counseling and psychology, approaches that themselves have viewed women as inferior and as less capable than men (Brodsky and Hare-Mustin 1980; Carmen, Russo, and Miller 1981; Russo 1984; Sobel and Russo 1981). Thus, women who attempt to secure rehabilitation services are frequently confronted by rehabilitation counselors who believe that women are more suited for careers as caretakers (nurses, teachers, childcare workers) or as service providers (sales clerks, secretaries, social workers), and that disabled women are those that need to be taken care of and to receive those services (Atkins 1982).

Rehabilitation professionals must, themselves, better understand how sex bias and sex-role stereotyping affect the lives of disabled women. Rehabilitation professionals have been predominately white males; the ratio of males to females rises to four to one in administrative posts (Backer 1982). As Atkins (1982) points out, a middle-class white male's lack of exposure to discrimination can result in a limited ability to empathize with its consequences.

The differences in rehabilitation perspective become apparent when we look at the education and training services provided to men and women clients and at the outcomes of rehabilitation. First, fewer women than men with disabilities receive training services. When they do, it is typically for occupations that are traditionally female. The Rehabilitation Services Administration (1978) reported that fewer disabled women than men became gainfully employed following training, and women were seven times as likely as men to be rehabilitated as "homemakers" (30 percent for females versus 4 percent for males). In that survey, of those that became employed following rehabilitation, men were substantially more likely than women to enter industrial occupations (46 percent for men versus 4 percent for women). When weekly earnings were considered, 48 percent of females were in the lowest earnings category, compared to 34 percent of males. Even more striking is the fact that 24 percent of disabled men were found in the highest earnings category, compared to only 10 percent of disabled women.

As has been seen in the discussion of the relationship between employment status and earnings for disabled women, rehabilitation programs must address the effects of occupational segregation; otherwise the economic disadvantage of disabled women will persist. This disadvantage stems from more than higher unemployment and lower earnings associated with female-dominated occupations. Disabled women also have higher living costs and frequently must assume the financial burden of attendant care. In contrast, disabled men are much more likely to be living in a married relationship that provides for their needs (Oakes 1984). Despite a basic lack of financial resources, disabled women are encouraged by the rehabilitation process to remain financially dependent as homemakers or as workers in low-wage occupations.

In this context, it is crucial that rehabilitation professionals, themselves, receive training designed to provide strategies for increasing their ability to understand and be responsive to the needs of their female clients. The traditional sex-role stereotypes held by many rehabilitation counselors must change if disabled women are to assume more independent and viable roles as productive members of society.

FUTURE EMPLOYMENT OPPORTUNITIES

The future employment hopes of disabled women will be affected by which occupations expand in the next two decades. According to the U.S. Bureau of Labor Statistics (1983), an increase of 25.2 million jobs is expected for this period. It is also anticipated that there will be 2.8 million more individuals in the labor force than the projected number of available jobs. What do vocational education and rehabilitation programs need to do to help disabled women fairly compete for these opportunities?

First: Identify where the jobs will be. More than 74 percent will be in the service-producing industries, with more than one in three of such jobs in the services sector that includes professional, medical care, and business services. Nearly 26 percent of the new jobs will be in the construction and manufacturing industries. Both speed and size of occupational growth create the demand for workers that encourages equal opportunity in employment. The five occupations projected for the *fastest* growth between 1982 and 1995 are computer service technicians (expected to grow by 96.8 percent), legal assistants (94.3 percent), computer systems analysts (85.3), computer programmers (85.3 percent), and computer operators (76.9 percent). More than half of the occupations expected to have the most growth between 1982 and 1995 are in the computer or other technical health fields, fields that have been historically male-dominated. Economic security for disabled women is dependent on training them to work in skilled trades and high-technology fields where wages are higher and upward mobility is possible.

The largest proportion of the projected job growth will occur in only forty occupations. The majority of such occupations will require some kind of postsecondary training, but only 25 percent will require a college degree. Many jobs that do not require any postsecondary education are also projected to expand. The ten jobs with the largest projected growth are building custodians, cashiers, secretaries, general clerks, sales clerks, registered nurses, kindergarten and elementary teachers, truck drivers, and nursing aides and orderlies (U.S. Bureau of Labor Statistics 1983).

Many of the jobs listed are in fields that are traditionally female; thus, there are expanding opportunities in so-called women's fields. This situation is a mixed blessing for women: their chances for employment are better, but the jobs are in fields that are typically lower in status and underpaid. The expansion of women's fields also takes pressure off vocational education programs to integrate women into the more highly paid occupations. Whether or not the physical and mental limitations of women become work disabilities will depend on our commitment to promoting fair educational, vocational, and rehabilitation programs that prepare women to take advantage of all career opportunities. Whether the higher incidence of disability in women is related to physiology, traditional social roles, or emerging roles, the personal and economic consequences are substantial. They deserve increased attention.

References

Atkins, B. J. 1982. Vocational rehabilitation for women: Recommendations for the eighties. *Rehabilitation Literature* 43(7–8):208–12.

Backer, J. T. 1982. Women as leaders in the field of rehabilitation. *Journal of Rehabilitation* 48:9–12, 68–70.

Bowe, F. 1983. *Disabled women in America: A statistical portrait drawn from Census Bureau data.* President's Committee on Employment of the Handicapped. Washington, D.C.: GPO.

Brodsky, A., and R. Hare-Mustin, eds. 1980. *Women and psychotherapy: An assessment of research and practice.* New York: Guilford.

Brooks, N., and M. Deegan. 1983. Women and disability, the double handicap. *Journal of Sociology and Social Welfare* 8(2):229–32.

Carmen, E. M., N. F. Russo, and J. B. Miller. 1981. Inequality and mental health. *American Journal of Psychiatry* 138(10):1319–39.

Corbett, K., S. Lea, and J. S. Zones. 1981. *Equity issues in special education.* Berkeley, Calif.: Disability Rights Education and Defense Fund.

Gillespie, P. H., and A. H. Fink. 1974. The influence of sexism on the education of handicapped children. *Exceptional Children* 41(3):155–62.

Grasso, J. T. 1980. The effects of school curriculum on young women. In National Commission for Employment Policy, *Educational sex equity and occupational stereotyping.* Special Report no. 38.

Haber, L. D., and J. McNeil. 1983. *Methodological questions in the estimation of disability preference.* Bureau of the Census. Washington, D.C.: GPO.

Klein, S., ed. 1985. *Handbook for achieving sex equity through education.* Baltimore: Johns Hopkins University Press.

Kutza, E. 1983. Benefits for the disabled: How beneficial for women? *Journal of Sociology and Social Welfare* 8(2).

League of Women Voters Education Fund. 1982. *Achieving sex equity in vocational education.* Washington, D.C.: League of Women Voters Education Fund.

McClure, P. 1979. Race and sex compliance issues in vocational education. In

The planning papers for the vocational education study no. 1. U.S. Department of Health, Education and Welfare, National Institute of Education. Washington, D.C.: GPO.

McNeil, J. 1983. *Labor force status and other characteristics of persons with a work disability: 1982.* U.S. Department of Commerce, Bureau of the Census. Washington, D.C.: GPO.

National Institute of Education. 1981. *The vocational education study: The final report.* Washington, D.C.: GPO.

Oakes, R. 1984. Physical disability in women: From liability to capability. Paper presented at the annual meeting of the Society of Behavioral Medicine, Philadelphia.

Rehabilitation Services Administration. 1978. Selected program-related characteristics of men and women rehabilitated in fiscal year 1976. *Rehabilitation Services Administration Information Memorandum.* Washington, D.C.: GPO.

Russo, N. F. 1984. Women in the mental health delivery system: Implications for policy, research and practice. In *Women and mental health policy,* ed. L. Walker. Beverly Hills, Calif.: Sage.

Sadker, M., and D. Sadker. 1980. Sexism in teacher education tests. *Harvard Education Review* 50:36–46.

Schlossberg, N. K. 1986. Midlife. In *Every woman's emotional well-being,* ed. C. Tavris. Garden City, N. Y.: Doubleday.

Sobel, S., and N. Russo, eds. 1981. Sex roles, equality and mental health. *Professional Psychology* 12(1).

U.S. Bureau of Labor Statistics. 1983. *Monthly Labor Review* (November). Washington, D.C.: GPO.

U.S. Commission on Civil Rights. 1983. A growing crisis: Disadvantaged women and their children. Washington, D.C.: GPO.

U.S. Department of Education. 1981. *The condition of education.* National Center for Health Statistics. Washington, D.C.: GPO, p. 92.

Vash, C. L. 1982. Women and employment. In *Women and rehabilitation of disabled persons,* ed. L. G. Perlman and K. C. Arneson. Alexandria, Va.: National Rehabilitation Association.

10. Disabled Women and Public Policies for Income Support

NANCY R. MUDRICK

Among the complex network of government programs that offer income support in the United States is a set that provides benefits to disabled persons. In general, disabled women receive less from these public income support programs than do disabled men, despite their often greater economic need. Part of this difference can be attributed to the poor fit between women's work patterns and the structure of these programs, and part of the problem lies in the assumptions about men's and women's economic and family roles that form the foundation of U.S. public income transfer programs. Finally, differences between the ways impaired women and men view themselves and are viewed by society may account for some of the gender differences in the receipt of transfer program benefits.

Because women make up a disproportionate share of those severely disabled in mid-life (Mudrick 1983a; Verbrugge 1976), it is appropriate to consider how well the structure of income support programs meets their social and economic needs in comparison to those of men. The extent to which these programs serve disabled women somewhat less than disabled men will be examined. Finally, changes in income transfer programs that would aid disabled women will be identified. The data presented in this analysis of income status and public income support of disabled women come primarily from the Social Security Administration's 1978 Survey of Disability and Work. This survey interviewed a nationally representative sample of 11,739 disabled and non-disabled men and women about labor force behavior, health, impairments, and income (for more technical details, see Bye and Schechter 1982). Some of the tables and estimates that follow are derived from the published data from this survey; the remainder are from the author's own manipulation of the data.

245

TRANSFER PROGRAMS AND DEFINITIONS OF DISABILITY

Income support programs for the disabled are part of a set of public cash benefit programs called income transfer programs. The term "income transfer" is used because the tax-based financing of benefits results in the transfer of income from one segment of the population to another. The transfer programs that serve only disabled individuals define disability in terms of the impact of impairments on the ability to work in paid employment. To establish eligibility, these programs adhere to a distinction between "impairment" and "disability" that often is blurred in the everyday use of these terms. First elaborated by Nagi (1969), the distinction between impairment and disability recently has been modified and codified by the World Health Organization (1980) in its *International Classification of Impairments, Disabilities, and Handicaps*. The definitions employed there are stated below:

Impairment is any loss or abnormality of psychological, physiological, or anatomical structure or function.

Disability . . . is any restriction or lack (resulting from an impairment) of ability to perform an activity in the manner or within the range considered normal for a human being.

Handicap . . . is a disadvantage for a given individual, resulting from an impairment or a disability, that limits or prevents the fulfillment of a role that is normal (depending on age, sex, and social and cultural factors) for that individual. (pp. 27–29)

The above definitions imply that the existence of a chronic health condition or impairment does not automatically cause one to be disabled. To be disabled by an impairment requires that it affect one's normal activities. Moreover, to be handicapped requires that the impairment or difficulty limit an individual's normal roles. Because "handicapped" and "disabled" do not specify medical conditions, but the response to such conditions, it is possible for a given impairment to disable or handicap one person, and not another. Because this distinction may result in individuals who work full-time and who have severe impairment, such as paraplegia or deafness, from being considered disabled, there have been objections to the use of this definition of disability (Asch 1984; Hahn 1982). Those who disagree with this construct point out that it defines only *work* disability and that a definition tied to work behavior ignores the significant and sometimes costly special arrangements impaired persons must make in order to maintain employment. Furthermore, other public measures (the 1973 Rehabilitation Act and PL 94-142) use a different and broader definition of disability. Despite these criticisms of the work disability/impairment distinction, this terminology is utilized here because these definitions are at the core of the disability transfer program eligibility criteria and the data on the disabled cited in this chapter.

Disability-related public income transfer programs aim either to replace wages lost due to the onset of disabling impairment or to provide basic income support to needy disabled individuals. Programs to replace wages are known as social insurance programs; they include Social Security Disability Insurance (DI), Workers Compensation, and Veterans Compensation. The programs that provide income support to the needy who are disabled and not attached to the labor force are called public assistance programs; they include the Supplemental Security Income program (SSI), and Aid to Families with Dependent Children (AFDC).

As has been noted in other contexts, the U.S. system of transfer benefits is a patchwork of programs legislated individually in response to particular needs and constituencies (Lurie 1975). For the disabled this means that there is no income support program for which eligibility is based only on the nature and severity of impairment. In order to receive disability-related benefits, the individual must not only meet the medical criteria, but have been in the military, worked for an extended period in employment covered by social security or a public employee benefit program, been injured on the job, or have a poverty-level income. Furthermore, the size of disability-related benefits is tied to these criteria, not to the economic need and costs of living associated with the severity of an individual's impairment. For example, the size of Workers Compensation, Social Security, and Government Employee's Disability benefits is related to the amount of wage loss associated with disability. Supplemental Security Income, AFDC, and some veteran's benefits vary in response to other sources of family income.

This structure of income support programs reflects two conflicting desires: to support those needy who cannot be self-supporting and to maintain the work ethic by offering publicly financed benefits only to those who have spent a substantial period in the paid labor force. These opposing values are evident when the characteristics of the programs to aid the needy and the programs to replace wages are contrasted. The programs for the needy require means tests for eligibility and provide low benefits, and beneficiaries often feel stigmatized as welfare recipients. Wage replacement programs are more like insurance: they use past employment as the basis for eligibility and offer higher benefits, and beneficiaries feel no stigma for receipt of payments they consider insurance benefits.

The most adequate income protection and support comes from the social insurance programs in which eligibility is based on employment or military experience. Those whose activities are not in these spheres—principally women—are more vulnerable to poverty. The extent to which disabled women are eligible for and utilize the benefits from public transfer programs appears to be related primarily to factors other than the severity of their impairments and health limitations. Women without military service or employment do receive public transfers; usually, however, it is because of their relationship to other eligible individuals such as retired or deceased husbands or needy, fatherless children. These requirements result in a devaluation of the work women perform both in the home and in the labor market because they encourage the view that women derive income protection through family relationships, not as compensation for work performed. There has been no serious effort to examine the life patterns of women and develop income protection to fit their needs.

The root of this system of public transfer programs is the 1935 Social Security Act, which aimed to assist an "ideal type" family—that is, a married couple with children in which the man, as household head, was in paid employment full-time every year until death or retirement, and the woman stayed home and cared for the house and children. Fifty years later, most families in the United States do not conform to this image. In more than 50 percent of all families with children, women are also in the labor force; in older households the proportion is much higher. Furthermore, a substantial proportion of women head their own households after marriages that end in separation or divorce. Because family size is smaller than in the past, women may have as many as twenty years after the youngest child has left before they are eligible for retirement benefits as wives.

Women who are disabled and who desire to be beneficiaries of income support programs face disadvantages because these programs are insensitive to the circumstances of both women and disabled persons. In consequence, a smaller proportion of women than men are eligible for disability benefits, fewer women who may be eligible for disability transfers apply for them, a smaller proportion of women than men receive benefits, and the average benefit received by women is smaller than that received by men. These differences can be traced to different perceptions of disability among men and women and to sex-role-related differences in the life patterns of men and women.

PERCEPTIONS OF DISABILITY

The impairments that most often disable adult women and men are diseases of the musculoskeletal system, the circulation system, and the digestive system (Lando, Cutler, and Gamber 1982). The incidence of all impairments increases with age, as does the number of impairments experienced by a single individual. While there are small differences between men and women in the types of disabling impairments by age, there are no clear trends to suggest that women experience a radically different set of impairments.

However, because different roles are normative for men and women, there appear to be differences in the extent to which men and women define themselves as disabled. These role differences also may affect the degree to which public transfer programs identify men and women with impairments as disabled.

A limit in the ability to earn a living wage is usually sufficient for a man to be considered disabled and for him to consider himself disabled. Because the normative role for prime age men is that of worker in the paid labor force, a man who cannot maintain paid employment is considered disabled, even if following the onset of impairment he helps to maintain his home. On the other hand, women may be considered disabled, and consider themselves disabled, only if impairment limits both the ability to work in paid employment and the ability to work in the home fulfilling the duties of mother or wife (Mudrick 1983a).

Table 10.1 reports data from the 1978 Survey of Disability and Work that illustrate these differences in perceptions of disability. This table shows how disabled men and women answered the question, "What were you doing most of last week—working, keeping house, going to school, or something else?" Although all the data on the table are from *disabled* persons (see definition stated earlier), the majority of women across all age groups state they were keeping house. In contrast, men who were not employed were more likely to state they were unable to work or were retired. Even disabled women who had been in the labor force were less likely than disabled men to report they were unable to work or were retired. Nineteen percent of disabled men, but only 7 percent of disabled women who have had some labor force attachment, reported they were unable to work. Among these groups, 2 percent of the men and 57 percent of the women reported their main activity was keeping house. Whether these disabled women are mainly engaged in keeping house because they have chosen this activity over employment or because impairments prevent employment is not clear. However, it appears that men and women at home with equal levels of impairment

Table 10.1. MAJOR ACTIVITY LAST WEEK, DISABLED WOMEN AND MEN:
PERCENTAGE DISTRIBUTION[a]

	Age in years							
	18–34		35–49		50–59		60–64	
Activity	M	W	M	W	M	W	M	W
Working	57.1	19.5	57.5	23.4	44.6	17.8	27.2	3.9
With job, not at work	6.5	5.5	4.3	5.3	3.2	0.7	5.7	0.7
Looking for work	1.2	0.8	1.9	0.2	1.5	1.2	0.4	0.0
Keeping house	0.9	53.4	2.1	52.6	2.1	60.8	5.4	69.9
Going to school	0.4	3.4	0.0	0.0	0.0	0.2	0.0	0.0
Unable to work	9.8	4.4	17.9	4.2	21.7	6.5	28.2	17.7
Illness	2.1	2.4	7.9	1.7	4.3	5.6	1.8	3.0
Volunteer work	0.3	0.4	1.5	0.0	1.3	0.2	0.1	0.0
Retired	0.0	0.0	1.1	0.1	9.8	0.4	18.9	1.4
Other	21.7	10.2	5.9	12.5	11.3	6.6	12.4	3.4
Total	100.0	100.0	100.1	100.0	99.8	100.0	100.1	100.0

[a] Percentages based upon weighted data.

Source: 1978 Survey of Disability and Work. Author's calculation.

define their activities differently; men state they are unable to work and women state they are keeping house. One consequence of this difference in self-perception may be that men are more likely than women to apply for and be awarded disability transfer benefits.

DISABILITY-RELATED TRANSFER PROGRAMS
Of all the cash transfer programs serving the disabled, the two major programs are Disability Insurance (DI) and Supplemental Security Income (SSI). Disability Insurance supports disabled workers with coverage under the Social Security programs. SSI supports low-income disabled children and adults who have no labor force experience or too little experience to be eligible for DI. While both of these programs now are administered by the Social Security Administration, they are distinct in their eligibility criteria and benefit structures. The programs that serve smaller numbers of disabled persons are AFDC, veteran's pensions, and Workers Compensation.

Social Security Disability Insurance
The Disability Insurance program is one of the trust fund programs under the Social Security Act. Eligibility is based upon years of work in Social Security–covered employment and satisfaction of the criteria for

disability (has a medically determinable impairment that prevents employment and is expected to last at least one year). The size of the benefit is calculated in the same manner as Social Security retirement benefits (based on prior wages). The worker's benefit may be increased to provide for spouses and dependent children, but nonwage income is not considered in establishing the benefit level. The average monthly cash benefit (without dependents' benefits) was $488 in 1986. Benefits are terminated when a beneficiary works for more than nine months at a job paying in excess of a specified amount (approximately $300 a month), because that work constitutes "substantial gainful activity." Benefits also will be terminated if the beneficiary is deemed by the medical criteria to be no longer disabled or refuses vocational rehabilitation if it is offered. After receiving DI for two years, beneficiaries become eligible for hospitalization and outpatient physician coverage under Medicare.

Supplemental Security Income
The Supplemental Security Income (SSI) program provides income support to needy aged and disabled individuals. This program defines disability in the same manner as the DI program. It differs from DI in that the size of the benefit varies with the recipient's income from all sources; income or assets larger than the eligibility standard render ineligible those who meet the disability criteria. Medical care is provided SSI recipients through Medicaid, a public assistance program. Program benefits consist of a basic federal benefit, which is uniform across the states, and an optional state supplemental benefit. Thus, total benefits under SSI vary by state of residence. In 1985 the maximum federal SSI benefit was $325 a month for individuals and $488 a month for couples in which both members were eligible for SSI. As with DI, SSI recipients must participate in vocational rehabilitation if offered, or be dropped from the program.

Other Transfer Programs
Four additional transfer programs serve smaller proportions of the disabled. Government employees may receive wage replacement for disability under the new Federal Employees' Retirement System. Veterans may receive disability-related income support either as a disability pension (for those with service-connected disabilities) or as a means-tested payment (for veterans whose disabilities are not service connected). Low-income families with dependent children in which a parent is disabled may receive assistance from the AFDC program, which

---

DIANE

Diane has cerebral palsy, which in her case includes a moderate level of mental retardation. She is 42 and unmarried, and she lives independently in a supervised group home. She works regularly at her sheltered workshop job and maintains contact with her parents, relatives, and friends. The money she earns is supplemented by Supplemental Security Income and aid from her parents. Diane's work at the workshop is productive, but it does not afford her any "credits" toward Disability Insurance or Social Security retirement. Her parents, now in their late seventies, worry that Diane will be forced into poverty when they die. SSI is likely to be Diane's only source of income as she ages.

---

pays a monthly benefit based upon family size and the amount of income from other sources. Benefits for a family of a given size vary by state, and there is wide state-by-state variation. In 1986 the average family benefit under AFDC was $354 (Sherman 1987). Families supported by AFDC because the household head is disabled constitute a small percentage (about 6 percent) of all AFDC families; in 1977, approximately forty-six thousand families were supported by AFDC because the father was disabled. Most families on AFDC are poor, female-headed families with minor children (U.S. Dept. of Health and Human Services 1980). Although disability was not the reason for AFDC support, in an additional 203 thousand AFDC households the mother was disabled. Finally, workers injured on the job may receive a Workers Compensation benefit. Benefits in this program (which also varies by state) are tied to the amount of wage loss experienced by the worker, and they may be received as a lump sum settlement or as a monthly payment for a specified period.

Although these programs are available to different groups of persons with impairments—veterans, government employees, workers, low-income persons—their benefits overlap. Veterans and government workers also may have Social Security coverage; those with Social Security benefits may meet the SSI need standard; and a poor family may receive support for dependents from AFDC while the disabled father receives SSI. Analysis of the overlaps among disability benefit programs has shown that not only are some people beneficiaries of several programs, but a sizable number of apparently eligible individuals are beneficiaries of none (Johnson 1979).

TRANSFER PROGRAMS AND THE INCOMES OF DISABLED WOMEN

Disabled women and men have different patterns of eligibility for and utilization of public transfer programs. Women are primarily beneficiaries of the means-tested public assistance programs AFDC and SSI, whereas disabled men receive transfers from the non-means-tested social insurance programs—Disability Insurance, Workers Compensation, and veteran's pensions. Although the eligibility criteria of these disability-related income support programs do not explicitly differentiate applicants by gender, assumptions underlying the social insurance and public assistance programs affect the receipt of program benefits: nearly 60 percent of disabled social insurance beneficiaries are men, and more than 60 percent of disabled public assistance beneficiaries are women. Because the social insurance benefits are usually larger than the public assistance benefits, disabled men and women also receive different levels of support.

The availability and size of income transfer benefits is an important issue for disabled women because they have lower incomes and a higher risk of poverty than do disabled men (Burdette and Frohlich 1977). In 1978 there were 2.3 million poor disabled women (Lando, Cutler, and Gamber 1982). Unmarried, black, or poorly educated disabled women are especially at risk of poverty (Luft 1979; Mudrick 1983b). Tables 10.2–10.4 make evident the disadvantaged economic status of disabled women. In 1977 the majority of previously married disabled women had total incomes of less than six thousand dollars (Table 10.2), with the incomes of black women lower than the incomes of white women. Forty percent of unmarried, disabled women had incomes at or below the poverty line, in contrast to 17 percent of unmarried disabled men (Lando, Cutler, and Gamber 1982). This proportion translates into 1.6 million single disabled women in poverty. A much smaller proportion (9 percent) of married disabled women were in poverty in 1977, just as fewer married women in general were in poverty.

Income also differs between white and black disabled women (Table 10.3). The median income of black disabled women in 1977 was on average 67 percent of that of disabled white women. Previously married disabled black women had the lowest median income, $4,223. It appears that these women (approximately 807 thousand persons), experience a triple discrimination—race, sex, and handicap.

With such low annual incomes, it is not surprising that a large proportion of disabled women are in need of or depend upon public transfer program income. The composition of the annual money in-

Table 10.2. IMPACT OF DISABILITY ON INCOME OF WOMEN: PERCENTAGE
DISTRIBUTION

Total Family Income, 1977	Married		Previously Married[a]		Never Married	
	All women	Disabled women	All women	Disabled women	All women	Disabled women
Less than $3,000	1.5	1.9	15.1	26.4	13.5	20.9
$3,000–5,999	5.5	12.4	25.0	35.3	11.5	22.6
$6,000–9,999	9.2	14.9	25.9	17.7	15.2	18.2
$10,000–14,999	19.2	24.2	14.7	11.5	15.6	12.7
$15,000–19,999	20.2	17.1	12.0	4.0	12.9	7.4
$20,000–29,999	25.1	17.5	3.9	1.6	18.7	12.1
More than $30,000	15.1	8.5	1.1	0.8	9.8	4.2
Not reported	4.4	3.7	2.3	2.8	2.8	1.9
	100.2	100.2	100.0	100.1	100.0	100.0
Median income	$18,641	$14,321	$7,522	$5,005	$13,130	$7,426

[a]Previously married women are widowed, separated, or divorced.

Source: 1978 Survey of Disability and Work. Derived from pp. 307–8. Lando, Cutler, and Gamber (1982).

comes of women (Table 10.4) shows a greater reliance upon transfer income by disabled women, especially unmarried disabled women. Altogether, public transfers average 30.4 percent of the income of unmarried disabled women and 9.1 percent of the incomes of married disabled women. In light of the very low incomes of disabled women and their high incidence of poverty, the utilization of transfers shown in Table 10.4 is surprisingly low. Earnings of other household members account for a larger share of income for all women, even unmarried disabled women.

TREATMENT OF DISABLED WOMEN BY INCOME TRANSFER PROGRAMS
The ability of disabled women to utilize public income transfer programs is affected by two assumptions: first, that women who are full-time homemakers produce no goods or services that must be replaced if they become disabled, and second, that a stringent recency-of-work test for Disability Insurance is a fair way of measuring the work attachment of both men and women. In addition to these assumptions, some specific provisions of disability transfer programs also affect women differently than men. The general outcome of these factors is that women receive fewer and smaller DI benefits, women constitute a dispropor-

tionate share of the disabled SSI beneficiaries, and many disabled women receive no transfer benefits.

Disabled Homemakers

Women who are full-time homemakers have virtually no access to social insurance benefits should they become too impaired to work. Social Security Disability Insurance was created with the needs of men and their families in mind. Disability Insurance was to replace a portion of wages lost by men too disabled to maintain paid employment, with additional monies for their wives and children. Given the premise that DI beneficiaries would largely be men with continuous labor force participation, the eligibility criteria for DI require a minimum number of consecutive quarters of social security contributions. As a result, housewives have no independent entitlement to DI benefits. Although both disabled and non-disabled wives may receive DI benefits as the dependent of a disabled husband, disabled homemakers have no DI entitlement of their own.

Although household production is not a wage-paying activity, it is work of value to the household (S. Berk 1980). Households that lose through death or disability the services of the member responsible for household production must purchase many of those services in the market. Despite this acknowledgment, there is no consensus regarding how to value household work (R. Berk 1980; Gauger and Walker 1980). It has been argued that without a clear indication of wage value, an appropriate wage replacement benefit cannot be calculated. Without that, there can be no benefit at all. A related concern is that it is difficult to determine when a woman who is a homemaker is disabled (Van de Water 1982). The indicator used by DI is the ability to maintain employ-

Table 10.3. PERCENT DISABLED AMONG MARRIED AND UNMARRIED WOMEN, BY RACE

Marital Status	White	Black
Married	17.87	20.78
Previously married	26.73	38.44
Never married	9.46	14.45
Median Income		
Married	$14,810	$9,110
Previously married	5,375	4,223
Never married	7,916	4,742

Source: 1978 Survey of Disability and Work. Derived from pp. 39–40, Lando, Cutler, and Gamber (1982).

256 · Policy and Politics

Table 10.4. SHARES OF 1977 FAMILY INCOME OF DISABLED AND NON-DISABLED WOMEN, BY MARITAL STATUS

	Married		Unmarried[a]	
Income Source	Disabled	Not Disabled	Disabled	Not Disabled
Earnings	78.9	88.6	53.4	79.7
Own earnings	9.7	18.1	20.9	34.7
Husband's	63.2	66.8	—	—
Other family	5.9	3.7	32.5	45.0
Assets	3.3	3.0	4.4	3.7
SSDI	1.4	0.0	6.6	0.1
Other Social Security	3.8	1.4	7.3	3.1
SSI	0.4	0.1	4.1	0.2
Other Public Income Transfers[b]	3.5	1.4	12.4	3.3
Other pensions	5.6	2.3	4.4	3.9
Other	1.5	.5	2.6	1.0
Not reported	1.8	2.8	4.9	5.2
	100.2[c]	100.1	100.1	100.2

[a] Unmarried women are never-married, divorced, separated, or widowed.
[b] Veteran's benefits, Unemployment Compensation, Workers Compensation, AFDC, Railroad Retirement, other public assistance.
[c] Columns do not total 100 percent due to rounding errors.

Source: *1978 Survey of Disability and Work.* Derived from p. 395, Lando, Cutler, and Gamber (1982).

ment and earn more than three hundred dollars a month. This indicator cannot be used for a disabled homemaker who was not paid wages for her work (Johnson and Burfield 1982).

The only social insurance benefit available to disabled homemakers is the Social Security Survivor's benefit for disabled widows or widowers aged 50–59. To be eligible, widows must meet disability criteria that are more stringent than those applied to DI applicants. This benefit is financed from the Old Age Survivors Trust Fund (not DI), and its size is based upon the deceased husband's earnings record. In the same manner as non-disabled widows who may claim their Survivor's benefits between ages 60 and 64, a disabled widow's benefit is reduced below full benefit that would have been received had the claim been postponed to age 65. The penalty for accepting the disabled widow's benefit (approximately 29 percent of the original amount) is permanent; a reduced Survivor's benefit is paid even after the woman passes the normal retirement age of 65.

Women's Work Attachment

Although women now are employed in increasing numbers and more women are working continuously, a substantial proportion of women are not continuously in the labor force. Despite rapid gains over the past thirty years, the average number of years women spend in the labor force over their lifetimes is less than for men (U.S. Dept. of Labor 1983). Many women work intermittently, taking time out of the labor force to bear and care for young children, to facilitate a husband's job change, and to care for an ailing family member. In contrast, men spend approximately 72 percent of their lives in the labor force. These differences in the work patterns of women and men account for some of the differences in men's and women's use of public transfer programs.

The impact of differences between men's and women's patterns of labor force participation is evident in their receipt of Social Security Disability Insurance. Eligibility for DI is based not only upon a determination that an impairment is long-term or permanent and prevents substantial gainful activity, but also on a record of employment for the requisite number of quarters in a job covered by Social Security. For persons over age 31, this means that twenty of the last forty quarters must be in covered employment. Given the sometimes intermittent character of women's work histories, even in mid-life, some working women may not meet these criteria. Women who enter the labor force in mid-life after taking time out to rear children are not entitled to any wage replacement benefits until they have been working for at least five years. In 1972, while approximately 14 percent of adult women reported theselves disabled, only 5 percent received Disability Insurance as disabled workers (Mudrick 1983b).

The DI benefits of women are 33 percent lower than men's (Muller 1980) for two gender-related reasons. First, because DI benefits are based upon prior wages, those with higher wages when employed have higher benefits when disabled (this is true even though the DI benefit formula

---

ELLEN

Ellen and her husband still live in their rural home, although their six children are all grown. Ellen, 45, was not employed while her children were small. Her husband, 48, works but does not earn a great deal. They are considering divorcing. Ellen is obese and bothered by high blood pressure, although she does not view herself as someone who is disabled. With no job experience or skills, the jobs open to Ellen are mostly physical (janitor, waitress), which her health limitations rule out. If Ellen divorces her husband, it is unclear how she will support herself until he retires and she becomes eligible for Social Security as his ex-wife.

Table 10.5. PERCENTAGE OF DISABLED WOMEN AND MEN WHO HAVE APPLIED
FOR OR RECEIVED DISABILITY TRANSFERS[a]

Program Participation	Women	Men
Ever applied for SSDI		
Yes	25.9	34.2
No	74.1	65.8
Ever received SSDI (of those who have applied)		
Yes	55.0	67.5
No	45.0	32.5
Ever applied for SSI		
Yes	10.6	9.5
No	89.4	90.5
Percent by marital status who received no transfer income		
Married	53.9	49.9
Widowed	15.7	37.5
Divorced/separated	34.0	40.0
Never married	23.8	40.5

[a] Percentages based on weighted survey data.

Source: 1978 Survey of Disability and Work. Author's calculation.

is weighted to return a higher proportion of predisability wages to low-wage workers). Women's wages are 59 percent of men's, and a large part of this difference can be attributed to wage and employment discrimination against women (Barrett 1979). This discrimination is perpetuated by the wage-based determination of DI benefits. A second reason for lower benefits in DI also relates to women's patterns of labor force participation. When women take more than five years out of the labor force for childrearing, those years are averaged into the benefit calculation formula as zeros, thereby reducing the benefit size. As a result, the size of the DI benefit of relatively well-paid woman with ten years out of the labor force for childrearing will be comparable to the benefit of someone whose wage rate was much lower. Women accepted into the DI program prior to 1981, for whom the benefit formula yields a low benefit, receive a minimum benefit. Newly entitled beneficiaries have no minimum benefit; their benefits are whatever the formula yields.

Data in Table 10.5 show that a smaller proportion of women than men who report themselves disabled apply for Social Security Disability Insurance, and of those who have applied, a smaller proportion are granted benefits. The reasons women most often give for not applying for DI are that they can work; they believe their health is not severe enough; they don't need the money; and they feel they have a poor chance of acceptance. To this, the differences in self-perceptions of disability (Table 10.1) could probably be added. In addition to these approximately 5.5 million disabled women who know about DI but do not apply for it, another 3.1 million disabled women are unaware of Disability Insurance. What percentage of these 8.6 million disabled women would ultimately receive DI if they applied is not clear. However, if even one-half of them applied, that would represent more than a doubling of the three million women aged 35–64 who had ever applied for DI by 1978. This is in sharp contrast to the nearly two million men who were *current* DI beneficiaries in 1978.

Other Transfer Program Provisions
Disabled women who have never been employed or who have insufficient quarters of coverage to qualify for DI may receive income support through SSI. The stringent income and asset tests of this public welfare program mean that only poor women living alone (that is, unmarried) are likely to be eligible. A slightly higher percentage of disabled women have ever applied for SSI than disabled men (see Table 10.5). This is probably because of the lower incomes of women and their decreased rates of eligibility for DI. Since SSI is income-tested and DI is not, it is possible for a woman to receive a small DI benefit and an additional amount from SSI.

With all sources of transfer income combined, more disabled women receive income support benefits than men. However, there are proportionately fewer women than men on DI and slightly more women than men who are disabled SSI beneficiaries. In addition, a substantial proportion of disabled women are supported by non-disability transfer programs. Most of the discussion has focused on the Disability Insurance program and how it treats women because DI is the biggest disability income support program in the United States and the one that pays the largest benefits. The invisibility of many disabled women explains in part why AFDC and dependents' social insurance benefits support disabled women to nearly the same extent as those programs intended explicitly to aid persons with disabling impairments. Since AFDC is a public assistance program rather than a social insurance program, it is accompanied by often demeaning bureaucratic procedures and a means test. Furthermore, continued eligibility for AFDC is based on characteristics (the presence of a minor child) other than that of continuing disability.

The social insurance benefits that frequently support disabled women are also related to characteristics other than continuing disability. Disabled widows under age 50 with children at home may receive survivor's benefits; young widows without children at home receive no benefits, even if impairments continue to prevent employment.

Despite the greater reliance of women on public transfers, approximately five million of them receive no public income support. Undoubtedly, not all these women would be found sufficiently disabled to qualify for transfers, nor would all five million be likely to desire to be participants in public transfer programs. Nonetheless, approximately 54 percent of married disabled women and 26 percent of unmarried disabled women receive no public transfer benefits. Given the high rates of poverty among unmarried disabled women, it seems likely that some portion of these women are in need of income.

ROSA

Rosa reentered the labor market as a secretary when she was 45 and her youngest child was in high school. In a recent automobile accident, Rosa, now 56, broke her leg in two places and dislocated her shoulder. Although her bones have healed, Rosa still has difficulty climbing stairs; her shoulder and arm remain painful and her ability to raise, lower, and twist her arm is limited. Because of these limitations, Rosa reluctantly quit her paid job and returned to her old job as a homemaker. This has been financially difficult for her and her husband because they needed her income to maintain their modest standard of living. No one has advised Rosa that she is probably eligible for Disability Insurance. Rosa believes she is ineligible for benefits because her injury did not occur on the job. Besides, she argues, she has a job as a housewife.

THE FUTURE

The future of income support for disabled women seems likely to be influenced by conflicting trends. On the one hand are the recent and continuing efforts at the federal level to restrict eligibility and benefits in the disability transfer programs and increase the work activity of beneficiaries. These efforts have included abrupt termination of benefits following mandated reviews of continuing eligibility, a "cap" on DI benefits, and an administrative "tightening" of eligibility criteria. New measures to encourage employment have also been instituted. On the other side is an increasingly vocal disability rights movement and an established women's movement, both of which are using the media and the courts and Congress to obtain equal treatment for their constituencies. These efforts have included obtaining an injunction to prohibit further disability review terminations, pursuing cases of discrimination under the 1964 Civil Rights and 1973 Rehabilitation Acts, and effectively lobbying Congress for legislation to amend transfer program provisions and administration.

The efforts to restrict program benefits, while not aimed specifically at reducing benefits for women, may nonetheless restrict their benefits proportionately more. For example, prior to 1981 all DI beneficiaries were entitled to a minimum benefit that was higher than the lowest benefit amount derived from the basic formula, a provision aimed at low-wage workers. In 1981 the minimum benefit was abolished for all new beneficiaries. Because women's wages generally are low, they may have been disproportionately affected.

In addition to the recent modifications described above, a number of additional restrictions in the eligibility criteria for DI and SSI have been discussed. One proposed change is to increase the quarters of covered employment required for DI eligibility. This would require even more years of continuous labor force activity. Because women, more than men, have intermittent patterns of labor force participation, this proposal would adversely affect the eligibility of women.

Another proposal would alter the quarters-of-coverage standard to one that simultaneously requires six of the past 13 quarters and thirty of the past forty quarters of covered employment for eligibility. These standards would adversely affect women who are recent entrants to the labor force when the onset of disability occurs, as well as women with an intermittent pattern of labor force participation. A congressional study concluded that under this plan a woman taking twenty-one months out of the labor force to bear or rear a child would need to work steadily for seven years to regain DI coverage (U.S. House of Representatives 1981). This proposal might also result in the ineligibility of individuals who withdraw from the labor force before their impairments are severe enough to meet the DI medical criteria. Those who withdraw under these conditions may end up with insufficient quarters of recent employment.

Yet another proposal is to alter the definition of disability so that qualified impairments must be expected to last at least twenty-four months instead of the current twelve months (U.S. House of Representatives 1981). Related to this is the proposal to increase the waiting period before DI benefits can be received from five to six months. These changes would require that eligible disabled persons be able to support themselves an extra month and that those with disabilities of less than two years duration find an alternative source of income for the period in which they are disabled. Unmarried women may find it especially difficult to find income for periods of temporary disability. Because women are often in the secondary labor market, they are not likely to be eligible for private, work-related pensions.

Some recent amendments to disability transfer programs may actually aid disabled women. Among these are the Social Security Disability Amendments of 1980 and the 1986 Employment Opportunities for Disabled Americans Act. The 1980 disability amendments require that health care (Medicare and Medicaid) benefits and eligibility for DI and SSI be maintained for two years after a recipient ceases to receive cash payments because of employment (U.S. Dept. of Health and Human Services 1981). These provisions lower the risk of trying to maintain employment; if the effort should fail, cash and health care benefits are immediately restored. Also included in the 1980 amendments is a measure to increase work incentives by excluding from consideration the costs of attendant care services, medical devices, equipment prostheses, and similar items needed to maintain employment when applying earnings or income tests. The absence of these measures had been labeled a "sizable impediment" to work (U.S. Dept. of Health and Human Services 1981).

The 1986 Employment Opportunities Act made permanent measures similar to the temporary SSI work incentives in the 1980 legislation (Rocklin and Mattson 1987). Under this act, severely impaired SSI beneficiaries who obtain employment do not risk termination of all cash benefits and medical coverage. Instead, benefits are reduced as the individual's earnings reach a "reasonable equivalent of benefits." Reinstatement of SSI benefits also is made easier for those recently terminated under these work incentive provisions. Although DI was not included in this legislation, continued experimentation with rules to increase work incentives under DI was authorized. These efforts would seem especially important to unmarried women, for whom employment may have seemed too risky when it meant total loss of public income support and health benefits.

Proposed additions to income support programs that also would aid disabled women have been discussed as part of a larger effort to provide more equitable retirement benefits for women (see Burkhauser and Holden 1982 and U.S. Dept. of Health, Education, and Welfare 1979). None have, as yet, been legislated. These additions would address the program inadequacies discussed above and would provide protection against income loss due to disability for homemakers and women with intermittent patterns of labor force participation (U.S. Dept. of Health, Education, and Welfare 1979). Among the program alternatives that would accomplish this, three that have been carefully examined are Earnings Sharing, Double-Decker, and Homemaker Credits (Johnson and Burfield 1982). Under Earnings Sharing one-half of the total earnings of both members of a couple is credited to the Social Security account of each. Thus, married women employed full-time in the home obtain entitlement to Social Security benefits in their own right. If a woman should become divorced, her account goes with her and is incremented thereafter by her own earnings. The second option, called Double-Decker, has two tiers. The first tier is a basic transfer benefit whose size is not tied to wages; the second tier is a wage replacement benefit that is added to the first tier for those with sufficient labor force experience. Under this plan disabled homemakers could be eligible for the lower-tier benefit. Finally, Homemaker Credits provide full-time homemakers with their own entitlement to income support benefits by the payment of additional monies to the Social Security system on their behalf. If a homemaker enters the labor force, her Social Security tax payments would be added to her record of payments made while a homemaker; thus, women would have disability protection as long as they continued contributing to the system, without regard to whether they were in or out of the paid labor force.

While some of these alternatives have been favorably reviewed with respect to retirement benefits, a major stumbling block to efforts to include disability coverage has been concern about the cost of providing disability benefits to housewives (Johnson and Burfield 1982; Van de Water 1982). Two issues have been prominent: the first concerns whether it is sensible and necessary to compensate families for the loss of household production. Currently DI and SSI offer support to the "work" disabled, which is interpreted as individuals whose disability prevents paid employment. Providing disability benefits to compensate for losses of household production would alter the traditional rationale for disability income support. The second objection stems from the difficulties associated with determining when a homemaker is disabled. In the absence of a money wage loss, what sorts of reductions in household production demonstrate disability and at what dollar level should they be compensated? Some also fear that the possibility of disability transfers for homemakers will encourage women to declare themselves disabled as a means of increasing household income (Johnson and Burfield 1982). Other countries, notably Israel and the United Kingdom, do offer benefits to disabled homemakers (Zeitzer 1983). It should be possible to learn from their experiences and design a system for supporting homemakers and women with intermittent patterns of work experience who become disabled.

If a system of income support were to be devised in a manner to meet the needs of disabled women, what should it strive to do? First, women should be eligible on the basis of the severity of their impairment, not their roles as wives or mothers. Second, the system should not penalize women in eligibility or benefit size for spending years out of the labor force in the socially sanctioned activities of homemaking and childcare. At the very least, it must be flexible enough to provide benefits to women whose life patterns include alternating between household and labor market employment. Third, disability transfer income must be available to aid disabled homemakers. This can be seen not only as assistance for women, but for their households as well.

LOUISE

Louise is a black woman, age 51, who lives in Detroit. She is a widow with a grown son who lives far away. Although Louise has worked intermittently on a factory assembly line, she can no longer perform the tasks required because of arthritis and chronic back pain. Louise is worried about income. Her own work history is too intermittent for her to be eligible for Disability Insurance on her own. She may be eligible for Social Security as a disabled widow: however, the definition of disability that will be applied to her is a rigid one and if she accepts the benefits, there will be a reduction in her Social Security income for the rest of her life. She could apply for Supplemental Security Income, but she hesitates to get involved with the welfare system. Although it leaves her very poor, Louise decides to try to support herself by babysitting. She hopes this will allow her a more comfortable retirement when she claims her Social Security at age 65.

A fundamental restructuring of disability transfer programs would be one way to accomplish these goals. Such a restructuring might also address issues pertinent to men, such as the rationale for tying disability benefit size to prior wages with no variation to account for the differing expenses of specific impairments. It is possible, however, to modify the existing programs so that some of the criteria just listed are present.

The provision of disability protection for women with intermittent or short periods of labor force experience can be accomplished easily within the existing Disability Insurance program. For example, the recency-of-work requirement could be eliminated or altered in such a way that years spent in childcare and homemaking would not cause a woman with a short or intermittent labor force experience to be ineligible for DI. If not eliminated altogether, perhaps all years in the labor force could be counted, whether continuous or not.

A second area in which income support programs might be modified to aid women is that of benefit size. This problem, too, can be remedied by excluding from the benefit calculation many more (or perhaps all) years in which a woman was engaged in full-time childrearing. Alternatively, it may be possible to compute a wage rate that could be entered in place of zeroes to represent the value of the work produced during those years. The effect of these proposals would be to raise the average size of women's benefits. These additional benefits would require additional funds from the DI trust fund that would have to be raised either through a higher Social Security tax or a reduction in benefits elsewhere in the system, or through the collection of contributions from women during the years they are out of the labor force.

Elimination of the permanent reduction in the size of disabled widow benefits is another program modification that would increase the standard of living of disabled women. The actuarial reduction of benefits is intended to encourage workers to remain in the labor force and yet allow those who truly wish to retire early to do so. While a similar reduction has been applied to disabled widows, the rationale is not equally applicable. Women who receive Social Security as disabled widows are women without much labor force attachment (otherwise they could collect DI as disabled workers). Reduced benefits are more likely to keep these women poor than to keep them in the labor force.

Perhaps the greatest challenge lies in changing the provision of benefits for homemakers. To do this within the existing system, a non–employment based definition of disability and an equitable way of financing those benefits must be developed. Despite the existence of income support programs for disabled homemakers in other nations, little effort has been made to design a program for the United States.

At a time when everyone is aware that resources are finite and that public expenditures need to be reduced, how can we justify adding benefits for woemn to transfer programs? One line of argument in support of this is the clear need of these women for income support; we support many other families, some of them less needy than these women. A more telling argument is based upon the contributions these women already make to the system as workers. The disability survey suggests that as many as 95 percent of women aged 35–64 in 1978 had been in the paid labor force at some point in their lives. Women are many times inelilgible for DI not because they have never worked and contributed to the system, but because their pattern of employment does not match the pattern of the eligibility criteria. The issue, then, is not one of providing women benefits for which they have made no contribution, but of modifying what appears to be an arbitrary standard so that the true contributions of women are counted. This issue, while especially pertinent to disabled homemakers, also applies to women who contribute to the social security system as workers but who receive benefits in retirement as wives.

CONCLUSION

Disabled women are frequently poor as a result of dual disadvantages. Not only are they disadvantaged with respect to wages and employment in a manner similar to all women, but they face additional difficulties as disabled persons. As earlier sections have pointed out, public income transfers are a crucial component of the very meager incomes upon which unmarried disabled women depend. Despite the crucial role of public income support, transfer benefits are frequently less accessible and smaller for disabled women than for disabled men.

One reason for the inadequacy of transfer benefits is the inappropriateness of the assumptions upon which these programs have been built. These assumptions are both inaccurate with respect to the structure of American families and insensitive to the needs of women whose lives have followed one of several normative patterns. Women who choose to be homemakers and conform to the traditional image of women's role obtain no protection against the economic effects of disabling impairments. Many of them need this protection because in mid-life they find themselves heading their own households. The message is that only those who have been participants in the labor force are worthy of income support when impairments become disabling. On the other hand, labor market work, because it is often intermittent and poorly paid, does not ensure income protection or adequate support benefits. Furthermore, women may get a sense that it is illegitimate to apply for disability transfer benefits as long as they are able to keep house—even if they would prefer to be employed.

Most people, disabled or otherwise, do not desire continued reliance on public transfer programs. Many impaired individuals do work. If antidiscrimination and barrier-free codes were more vigorously enforced, perhaps an even larger proportion of disabled persons would be employed. The intent of increasing the access of disabled women to public transfer programs is not to discourage independence and increase dependency. However, disabled women deserve a level of support at least equal to that of men. Such support may provide them the opportunity to obtain vocational rehabilitation or further education, or to take care of their health. A reliable source of income, rehabilitation services, and better health care may make it possible for disabled women to try an independence that otherwise would be too risky or impossible.

References

Asch, A. 1984. The experience of disability: A challenge for psychology. *American Psychologist* 39 (May).

Barrett, N. S. 1979. Women in the job market: Occupations, earnings, and career opportunites. In *The subtle revolution*, ed. R. E. Smith. Washington, D.C.: Urban Institute.

Berk, R. A. 1980. The new home economics: An agenda for sociological research. In *Women and household labor*, ed. S. F. Berk. Beverly Hills: Sage.

Berk, S. F., ed. 1980. *Women and household labor*. Beverly Hills: Sage.

Burdette, M. E., and P. Frohlich. 1977. The effect of disability in unit income—1972 survey of disabled and non-disabled adults. *Disability survey '72: Disabled and non-disabled adults*. Report no. 9. Washington, D.C.: Office of Research and Statistics, Social Security Administration.

Burkhauser, R. V., and K. C. Holden, eds. 1982. *A challenge to social security: The changing roles of women and men in American society*. New York: Academic Press.

Bye, R., and E. Schechter. 1982. *A technical introduction to the 1978 survey of disability and work*. Washington, D.C.: Social Security Administration, Office of Policy.

Gauger, W. H., and K. E. Walker. 1980. *The dollar value of household work*. Information Bulletin no. 60 Rev. Ithaca, N.Y.: New York State College of Human Ecology, Cornell University.

Hahn, H. 1982. Disability and rehabilitation policy: Is paternalistic neglect really benign? *Public Administration Review* 42 (July/August).

Johnson, W. G. 1979. Disability, income support, and social insurance. In *Disability policies and government programs*, ed. E. Berkowitz. New York: Praeger.

Johnson, W. G., and W. B. Burfield. 1982. Disability insurance under proposed reforms. In *A challenge to social security: The changing roles of women and men*, ed. R. V. Burkhauser and K. C. Holden. New York: Academic Press.

Lando, M. E., R. B. Cutler, and E. Gamber. 1982. *1978 Survey of disability and work—data book*. Washington, D.C.: Office of Policy, Social Security Administration.

Luft, H. S. 1979. *Poverty and health*. Cambridge, Mass.: Ballinger.

Lurie, I. 1975. Integrating income maintenance programs: Problems and solutions. In *Integrating income maintenance programs*, ed. I. Lurie. New York: Academic Press.

Mudrick, N. R. 1983a. Disabled women. *Society* (March/April).

———.1983b. Income support programs for disabled women. *Social Service Review* 57 (March).

Muller, L. S. 1980. Receipt of multiple benefits by disabled-worker beneficiaries. *Social Security Bulletin* 43 (November).

Nagi, S. V. 1969. *Disability and rehabilitation*. Columbus: Ohio State University Press.

Rocklin, R. G., and D. R. Mattson. 1987. The employment opportunities for disabled Americans act: Legislative history and summary of provisions. *Social Security Bulletin* 50 (March).

Sherman, S. R. 1987. Fast facts about social security, 1987. *Social Security Bulletin* 50 (May).

U.S. Department of Health and Human Services. 1980. *1977 Recipient characteristics study,* pt. 1, *Demographic and program statistics.* Washington, D.C.: GPO.

———. 1981. Social security disability amendments of 1980: Legislative history and summary of provisions. *Social Security Bulletin* 44 (April).

U.S. Department of Health, Education and Welfare. 1979. *Social security and the changing roles of men and women.* Washington, D.C.: GPO.

U.S. Department of Labor. 1983. *Women at work: A chartbook.* Washington, D.C.: GPO.

U.S. House of Representatives, Subcommittees on Social Security, Committee on Ways and Means. 1981. *Reagan administration disability proposals.* Committee Print WMCP:97-23. Washington, D.C.: GPO.

Van de Water, P. 1982. Disability insurance under proposed reforms: Discussion. In *A challenge to social security: The changing roles of women and men in American society,* ed. R. V. Burkhauser and K. C. Holder. New York: Academic Press.

Verbrugge, L. M. 1976. Females and illness: Recent trends in sex differences in the United States. *Journal of Health and Social Behavior* 17 (December).

World Health Organization. 1980. *International classification of impairments, disabilities and handicaps.* Geneva, Switzerland: WHO.

Zeitzer, I. R. 1983. Social security trends and developments in industrialized countries. *Social Security Bulletin* 46 (March).

11. Autonomy as a Different Voice: Women, Disabilities, and Decisions

JOANNA K. WEINBERG

This chapter examines the way in which the legal and medical systems affect the context of decision making for mentally disabled women. By explaining the ways in which legal and medical processes of decision making affect a small category of dependent persons, we can better understand how these institutions circumscribe the parameters of autonomy and choice making. A preliminary hypothesis of this analysis holds that existing societal mechanisms for making decisions involving dependent people—the rights-oriented legal adversary model and the traditional medical model of diagnosis, treatment, and cure—may not be effective to substantively improve the quality of life where the basic physical autonomy of day-to-day living is at issue.

Strong similarities characterize decision-making mechanisms that have been developed to address problems of dependent persons and those that legal and medical institutions have utilized to address decisions about women in the society. The procedural likeness reflects a similarity of attitudes regarding the definition of protection and dependence with regard to women and disabled people. Thus, a re-formulation of the concept of autonomy may be useful to both groups.

The world of the dependent person has been defined historically through the subjective impressions of others, and by reference to externalities of action and behavior, rights and duties. Recent years have witnessed efforts by courts and legislatures to develop procedural standards that objectively define decision making by re-creating the subjective world of a dependent individual, by ascertaining his or her "best interests" or actual will,[1] by authorizing advocates to speak for the disabled person, or by redefining the concept of informed consent to

269

better address the will of persons who are not considered competent to make decisions about their own welfare by traditional measures.

Legal and medical institutions utilize decision-making procedures that define autonomy by reference to action or inaction and perceptions by third parties about a person's *ability* to act. These models do not always respond adequately to issues that concern the internal or emotional quality of life, because they rely heavily on an exclusive view of autonomy that is limited by the constraints of the decision maker. Thus, while there has been close attention to externalities of behavior—protection of physical autonomy, legal or contractual rights, and even the need to interact within communities—there has been less focus on internal facets of autonomy—sexuality and the need for emotional relationships, redefinition of self-image, and psychodynamic development.

In both legal and medical spheres, traditional rules about how and when people make decisions and choices about themselves, their bodies, and their immediate social environment are in a state of flux. The deinstitutionalization movement in mental health and retardation redefined the parameters of physical autonomy for mentally disabled individuals, not only by removing walls but by subjecting the actions of all participants to intense scrutiny by the legal system, and by changing the boundaries of the medical model. The concomitant rights advocacy movement redefined the legal constraints on the behavior of both mentally disabled persons and their families, and service providers.[2] The ways in which issues such as informed consent, the right to refuse, demand, or withhold treatment, the right to die, and "least restrictive" treatment or habilitation have been addressed in both settings in recent years illustrate that the rules of the game have changed.[3]

At the same time, emerging discourse in the women's movement has profoundly altered accepted ideas about autonomy and choice. Historical attitudes toward women in the society parallel attitudes toward the physically or mentally dependent—both have been considered to be persons in need of protection and shelter, whose behavior and choices are defined by the mandates of others. Even apart from this metaphor, however, the modern women's movement has highlighted issues such as sexuality, social activity, and vocational patterns that explore the concept of autonomy in distinctive ways. Moreover, the legal, social, and medical frameworks for making decisions also have undergone rapid and dramatic changes, as "social" issues such as abortion, childbirth, and marriage and employment practices have replaced more directly political themes such as the right to vote. Consider, for instance, the *Roe v. Wade* standards for state involvement in abortion decisions,[4] or the changes in the management of conflicts over divorce and child custody (*U. Pa. Law Journal* 1984; Weitzman 1985).

The histories of women's issues and disabled-persons' issues have followed similar patterns in recent years. The progressive era codified a rationale for treatment of dependent persons—women as well as disabled—essentially paternalistic in nature, modeled on the ideal of benevolent protection separate from a "threatening" society. The women's rights and disability advocacy movements first developed in apposition to the protective model, making sharp distinctions between rights and duties, and creating legal rights and remedies without regard to the practicalities or acceptability of implementation. While recent studies suggest that the progressive "protective" strategies were concrete "claiming" strategies used by and not just imposed upon dependent persons, many of the remedies that emerged from these strategies allowed professionals to usurp control of the issues.[5]

The traditional understanding of autonomy remains incompatible with medical and legal definitions of dependence. Under these definitions, any person—woman, mentally disabled, juvenile—who is dependent cannot be autonomous. In contrast, a redefinition of autonomy is emerging based on a self-view rather than on the perceptions of others. In this redefinition, procedures for decision making attempt to re-create that self-view. Burt (1984) observes that

the newly adamant claims of handicapped people generally in public forums . . . are for rights to independence, to self-respect, and to self-sufficiency. But these claimed rights contain the implicit acknowledgement that handicapped people cannot vindicate their claims without others' assistance. This needed assistance may involve others' financial resources (as in tax support for special educational resources or for wheelchair ramps into public facilities); it may involve others' emotional resources (as in families' devotion or neighbors' tolerance for the appearance of handicapped people as residents in their community). It is thus paradoxical that handicapped people must depend on others' assistance in order to achieve their goal of independence from others. (p. 455)

Both for dependent persons and for women, issues involving sexuality and social freedom and/or activity have crystallized the difficulty of balancing autonomy and dependence and the pressing need for decision-making mechanisms that are workable. Some courts and legislatures have begun to develop procedures that re-create or restructure the world as it might be seen by the dependent person; in other words, procedures (mandated by the court) are used either to ascertain the wishes of the person or to create an equitable substitute for the wishes of the person.

New Jersey courts have led the country in attempts to address these issues. In *In the Matter of Lee Ann Grady*,[6] the court suggested a series of steps that courts should take in determining consent of a retarded woman to sterilization—steps that attempted to re-create the world from her perspective. The court developed a list of guidelines that must be applied in any sterilization application, which inquired into such areas as motivation (for the request), less restrictive alternatives, and the possibility of competing interests between the person making the request and the subject of the request. In the case *In the Matter of Claire Conroy*, involving removal of a feeding tube from an elderly woman with organic brain syndrome, the court again suggested a procedural mechanism by which medical care institutions and courts could explore the question of will and consent from the world of the incompetent patient.[7] These cases appear to be steps to design a mechanism through a legal system for making autonomy a more workable concept within medical or social service settings. Unfortunately, both decisions mandate such complex procedures that they are almost useless as precedents, an issue that will be explored more fully later in this chapter.

Decisions about sterilization, reproduction and parental custody have begun to develop along similar lines, focusing on procedures—such as informed consent and determinations of competence—to inform the substantive content. This approach might have the effect of reorienting a "rights" analysis by opening up the decision-making process to greater participation by more parties, and to closer scrutiny by the public. However, the disadvantage of this approach is the danger that decision making will become so rule-bound as to render it not workable in practice.

These cases involved decisions about dependent women, which marks a significant point for this inquiry. In her work on children's moral development, Gilligan (1982) has suggested that a contextual or communal "voice," which she characterizes as female, needs to be present in decision making. The examination in this chapter suggests that "proceduralization" of medical and legal settings reflects an attempt to provide that sort of context. It is therefore significant that the arena in which the greatest struggle has taken place to provide context for decision making involving disabled women remains that of emotions and intimate behavior. This chapter draws upon two sets of data—discussions with care providers and advocates for women in the community, and case law as sociological data—in order to inform my own conclusions about how processes of decision making for these issues might be deconstructed and reassessed.

MENTALLY DISABLED WOMEN IN THE COMMUNITY

Community, or mainstream, living has become widely accepted as an alternative to institutional treatment for the mentally disabled in the past twenty years. Most of the attention of the advocacy movements that brought about this restructuring of priorities focused on the disadvantages of institutional treatment and the advantages for disabled people of living in communities. D. Rothman (1971, 1980), in *The Discovery of the Asylum* and *Conscience and Convenience*, and Rothman and Rothman (1984), in *The Willowbrook Wars*, chronicled in detail the errors of omission and commission of institutional treatment of the mentally disabled; they, like most scholars and advocates of disabled people, joined with the medical and social service professions in welcoming deinstitutionalization as a necessary reform (see, for example, Ferleger and Boyd 1979; Gaylin, Glasser, and Rothman 1984; Herr 1983; Morse 1982). However, in practice, the ideal of deinstitutionalization has been somewhat illusory. The purpose of deinstitutionalization was to make an individual become an integral part of a local community, living in an autonomous manner. However, many disabled people cannot lead fully autonomous lives because of the physical, psychological, or social limitations of their disability. Therefore, the goal of community, mainstream, or home living more correctly should be to allow people to survive as autonomously as possible within the confines of that disability. Reconciling the limitations of a disability with the desired degree of autonomy proves difficult, a problem compounded for women with mental disabilities because of additional limitations on women's autonomy imposed by societal norms. This has been particularly true where autonomy means restructuring intimate behavior such as sexuality and reproductive activity, or social interaction requiring intimacy such as parenting.[8]

Autonomy in this context involves autonomy about making decisions. It does not require a total independence from other people. This distinction is critical because society tends to equate physiological or social autonomy with physical independence. One of the lessons that may be drawn from the conflict over rights and autonomy may be the acceptance of the model of interdependence as a norm for this society. As Burt (1984) notes in the sentence following the passage quoted earlier:

It is . . . paradoxical that handicapped people must depend on others' assistance in order to achieve their goal of independence from others. But . . . [they] resemble everyone who, in striving for independent autonomy, is nevertheless constrained by an inescapable economic and social network of interrelated dependencies—everyone, that is, in America today. (p. 455)

Autonomy in the context of mental disability represents a troubling concept, precisely because the standards for ascertaining this kind of disability are so hazy. Where a disability is physical, the extent of the disability may be knowable, in very much the same way by the disabled person as by the non-disabled. Mental disability, however, affects not only the life and thinking of the disabled person but also communication between that person and the non-disabled about the nature of the disability. In an effort to provide substitutes for that communication, the legal system and service professions have created fictional categories such as "substituted consent" and "best interests" tests, and vehicles such as guardians or conservators as alternative decision makers. Those substitutes, however, use a model of complete dependence as the operative norm. For many mentally disabled people, and especially for women, Burt's notion of interrelated dependencies may be more relevant to an understanding of autonomy.

Sexual Activity and Social Expression

The Context of Community
The goal of deinstitutionalization for the mentally disabled has been to provide an environment that resembles a "normal" home as closely as possible. Acquisition of life skills, those skills that need to be learned, is essential. However, training is often limited to the nuts-and-bolts aspects of home living—cooking, cleaning, personal hygienic care—while "normal" life also involves the development of social skills, including sexuality and the possibility of reproduction. In this respect, mentally disabled women in group homes or community living facilities are locked into a perpetual adolescence. For these women, like other women, social activity, including sexual activity, constitutes an important aspect of becoming an autonomous adult member of society. However, caretakers or families perceive social and sexual activity as threatening, worrying about consent and the possibility of abuse. It is true that mental disability may make the line between voluntary social or sexual activity and sexual abuse difficult to determine. Moreover, strong societal taboos are attached to sexual activity for disabled women, based in part on fears that they will give birth to children who will pass on genetic defects.[9] But this does not lessen the importance of such activity for the disabled person.

The arena of social or sexual activity highlights the limitations the disability places on the ability to become autonomous. In the Eriksonian model of child and adult development, the individual moves along a scale from dependence toward autonomy (Erikson 1950).[20] The dependence/independence conflict reaches its height during late adolescence, as issues of sexuality and intimate relationships with nonparental figures become significant. For mentally disabled women, whatever their age, the transition from dependence to an adult state takes place in a different manner, often in a different setting (from an institution to a community setting, for instance), and almost always at a later chronological age. Unlike the transition from childhood through adolescence to adulthood, a mentally disabled woman's transition reflects a more uncertain character. Because her disability may ultimately inhibit an adult lifestyle, the pseudo-adolescence may be long-lasting or even permanent. The "markers" that the society uses to signal the end of adolescence—completion of school, completion of the physical changes of puberty, "Sweet Sixteen" or a twenty-first birthday, and the rights to drive, drink, marry, make contracts—are usually ignored. No markers symbolize this transition for mentally disabled women.

More research needs to be done in this area, as the population of mentally disabled women in the community grows larger and spans a longer period of time. Service providers, clinicians, and disabled women are beginning to recognize the importance of social relationships and consensual sexual activity, the need for development of guidelines for consensual behavior that take into account these needs, and the reality that group home staff or parents are often overly protective of female residents. Without clear-cut guidelines that allow for legitimate sexual or social expression within the confines of an individual's disability, a repressive view of morality will likely govern their social relationships.

The Legal Framework
Women's sexuality and social activity have long been "protected" or "subordinate" (depending on one's perspective) and have been regulated by courts, legislatures, and social institutions. As far back as the Bible, and as recently as nineteenth-century British and American statutes, female sexuality has been treated by the law both as an aspect of life to be protected (or "saved") and as a resource, to be owned by men, that should not be wasted.[11] While these norms have shifted somewhat in recent years, away from the regulation of the activity itself, in the direction of regulation of the *consequences* of such activity—contraception and other means of preventing childbirth, abortion, termination of parental rights, custody and divorce—the concept of regulation has been only minimally undermined.

In 1873, the U.S. Supreme Court upheld the legal legitimacy of a "sexuality" distinction in a case holding constitutional the state of Illinois restriction of women practicing law. In the case, *Bradwell v. Illinois,* the court noted that

man is, or should be, woman's protector and defender. The natural and proper timidity and delicacy which belongs to the female sex evidently unfits it for many of the occupations of civil life. . . . The harmony, not to say identity, of interests and views which belong, or should belong, to the family institution is repugnant to the idea of a woman adopting a direct and independent career from that of her husband. (p. 130)[12]

While this line of reasoning seems unacceptable in today's social climate, courts still do not apply a "heightened scrutiny" test toward possible discrimination against women's activities as they have done in cases of racial or religious discrimination.[13] Where female sexuality or social life is even tangentially concerned, courts have been reluctant to apply even minimal scrutiny toward possibly discriminatory state activity.[14]

An uneasy balance between prohibitions of illegal discrimination and the legally sanctioned recognition of difference for the purposes of protection continues to play an important role in laws regulating the activities of women. The U.S. Supreme Court has refused to apply any heightened scrutiny of a state action, beyond mere rationality, to allegations of discrimination against the disabled, holding that the "rationality" test can legitimately turn on a state's interest in protection of the disabled.[15] The court has also refused to apply this test to allegations that the government discriminates against women by refusing to require them to register for selective service. Both of the cases involved in the rulings, *Rostker v. Goldberg* and *City of Cleburne, Texas, v. Cleburne Living Center,* contain language that echoes the paternalistic flavor of the 1873 *Bradwell* case. In both cases, the U.S. Supreme Court rejected the idea that fundamental rights of classes of people other than racial, religious, or ethnic minorities should be subject to a "strict scrutiny" under the Fourteenth Amendment to the Constitution.

Regulation of sexual activity of women whose autonomy is limited has found further support through regulation and sex segregation of the settings in which these women live, often institutional settings operating within a medical model. In that framework, institutional staff may perceive themselves as making decisions for a person in his or her best interests. Women in institutions are most likely to have been "protected" in such a manner. The deinstitutionalization of mentally disabled women into community settings has raised concerns among caregivers, guardians, and courts about protection, and again it has focused attention on regulating the *consequences* of sexual or social activity, rather than on examining the benefits or harm of the activity itself to the women.

The reproductive consequences of women's sexual activity have received more attention from the courts than have other aspects of sexuality and social life. During the nineteenth and early twentieth centuries, sterilization of the "unfit," including both women and men with mental retardation and other mental and physical disabilities, was a common practice.[16] Compulsory sterilization of institutionalized persons without their consent was upheld as a legitimate public health measure by the U.S. Supreme Court in 1927. In that case, *Buck v. Bell*,[17] Justice Holmes stated a premise that by today's standards seems appalling:

It is better for all the world, if instead of waiting to execute degenerate offspring for crime, or to let them starve for their imbecility, society can prevent those who are manifestly unfit from continuing their kind. The principle that sustains compulsory vaccination is broad enough to cover cutting the fallopian tubes. . . . Three generations of imbeciles is enough. (p. 200)

Although *Buck* has never been formally overruled by the U.S. Supreme Court, right-to-privacy cases such as *Skinner v. Oklahoma*, which declare sexual activity to be a fundamentally protected constitutional right, have limited its impact.[18] It is significant to point out that Justice Holmes spoke of fallopian tubes and the prevention of procreation by females, emphasizing that sterilization was aimed at the potential childbearer rather than the sperm donor. While most states have repealed their statutes authorizing sterilization without consent, courts usually permit sterilization where a woman has been declared to be incompetent and her guardian or custodian has petitioned that a court permit sterilization.

In many jurisdictions, in order for a sterilization order to be approved, the individual must consent or there must be some legally mandated substitute for consent. Substitute consent falls into two general categories: (1) a determination that sterilization is in the "best interest" of the person whose sterilization is sought; or (2) the fiction of imputed consent—substitution of a court's, legislature's, or custodian's judgment of what the decision of the person involved would be if he or she were capable of consent. These requirements are difficult to apply. A sterilization request will often be denied without an individual judicial hearing as to the "best interests" or imputed consent issue.

The law in this area has become less clear in recent years, more because of procedural uncertainty about the validity of third-party consent than because of any substantive recognition of the sexuality of mentally disabled women. In 1978, in *Stump v. Sparkman*, the U.S. Supreme Court held that courts had jurisdiction to rule on sterilization petitions of third-party guardians or custodians; therefore, the court refused to find damages in an action brought by a young woman, who had been sterilized as a teenager, against a state court that had issued a sterilization order based upon a petition filed by the woman's mother.[19] The woman, who was categorized in the court documents as somewhat retarded, did not even know she had been sterilized. She filed the suit after she married and found that she was unable to conceive a child.

Despite the Supreme Court's apparent approval of state authority in the area of sterilization, courts continue to be reluctant to impute consent in such cases. Thus, recent cases tend to turn on the question of whether a woman is sufficiently competent to consent to a sterilization request. In this area the more stringent requirements regarding informed consent have made both courts and legislatures tread with care. Moreover, available statistics suggest that nearly 90 percent of all mentally subnormal people are only "mildly retarded"; most of the remaining 10 percent either have serious genetic disabilities that render them incapable of reproduction, or they remain in settings so sheltered that the need for sterilization is not present (Friedman 1976; Price and Burt 1975; Wald 1976).

Recently the New Jersey Supreme Court suggested a process of substitute consent to a woman's sterilization. The parents of Lee Ann Grady, a woman with Down's syndrome, sought a sterilization order, arguing that because she lived in a community setting that was less restrictive than an institution, certain safeguards were necessary for her protection, and her autonomy in such a setting would be enhanced by sterilization.[20] In a decision that was significant for its assumption that process rather than context was the appropriate mechanism for recreating an essentially substantive and subjective decision, the court denied the Gradys' request. In its opinion, the court discussed in detail the parameters of individuals' rights to independent decision making. Concerned about substitute judgments, even for well-meant, best-interest purposes, the court held that the grounds for presuming consent to sterilization must be closely circumscribed, that concrete standards must be articulated by a court, in advance, and that care must be taken to separate the interests of the petitioner from those of the subject of the order because "the interests of the parents of a retarded person cannot be presumed to be identical to those of the child" (p. 475). The court then described the standards that must be applied by courts in making individual case-by-case decisions imputing consent to sterilization. *Only* the best interests of the incompetent person, and not the interests or convenience of society or the state, should be considered, and it is the duty of the court and not the parents or guardian to determine the need for sterilization. For purposes of determining consent, a guardian *ad litem* would have to be appointed for this proceeding, even if there was already a legal guardian. The court also described the standards by which competence was to be determined and the factors that would be considered in establishing the necessity for sterilization. The court concluded that those factors had not been met in this case, and that other, less restrictive alternatives had to be considered.

Imputed or implied informed consent has become an important issue in recent years as both technology and policy have increased the likelihood that severely disabled people will survive for extended and productive lives. The *Grady* case laid the groundwork for another case (the aforementioned *In the Matter of Claire Conroy*) regarding imputed consent to remove a feeding tube that was providing life support. The New Jersey Supreme Court again utilized a rigid procedural approach as the means for determining consent of an incompetent person. The court decided that the procedures would not have permitted consent to remove Claire Conroy's tube (although this decison was irrelevant, since she died while the appeal was pending). Once again, the emphasis on procedure effectively removed the substance from the issue; if it is procedurally nearly impossible to impute consent, then the underlying issue of the purpose of the consent need not be resolved in its practical context. The standards were recently revised and reassessed, again with a procedural focus, this time in the context of competent persons who choose to die rather than to undergo treatment for fatal and disabling conditions (*in Re Jobes*, A-108/109; *in Re Farrell*, A-76; *in Re Peter*, A-78, decided by N.J. Supreme Court, June 24, 1987).

The strict procedural approach has its origins in the concept that rules and procedures result in consistency and neutrality, and thus in fairness. This model of the legal process has been described as an "autonomous law" model (Nonet and Selznick 1976). Another underlying reason for utilizing strict procedure is the ambivalence of the legal system about issues involving personal autonomy, and the conflict over the individual's right to privacy (stemming from the Fourth Amendment) and the traditional common-law *parens patriae* role of the state and the family.

The lack of clear standards regarding consent or procedures for imputing consent to sterilization is a two-sided issue. Clearly a strong argument could be made that a mentally disabled woman's sexuality is demeaned by forced sterilization, which limits not only her ability to bear children but, arguably, other aspects of female sexuality such as those affected by hormonal and menstrual cycles. However, there also is support for the notion that sterilization removes some of the barriers to autonomy for a mentally disabled woman, that she might lead a more productive and more autonomous life free from the "worry" of contraception and childbirth.

The ease with which courts have developed procedures for imputing consent to sterilization to mentally disabled women may have more to do with legal and social attitudes about the protection and subjugation of women than it does with either eugenics or women's sexual freedom. Moreover, cases and statutes must be read in the context of cases in other areas that imply that women have particular need of protection in areas touching upon sexuality and social life. In 1981, for instance, the U.S. Supreme Court upheld a California statute subjecting men, but not women, to prosecution for statutory rape of any female younger than 18 years old.[21] That same year, in *Rostker v. Goldberg*, the U.S. Court upheld a male-only selective service registration statute, ostensibly on the grounds of deference to the prerogatives of Congress in military affairs; the ruling followed a detailed analysis of the appropriateness of Congress's decision to exclude women from the selective service registration requirement because that body had found that drafting women might "place unprecedented strains on family life."[22] In another case, the Supreme Court upheld (by a split decision) an opinion from the Third Circuit Court of Appeals that held that sex-segregated public high schools were constitutional.[23] The circuit court had found that segregation on the basis of sex in high schools was a legitimate basis for school board policy, and, in language reminiscent of the discredited "separate but equal" language of *Plessy v. Ferguson*, the court noted that the plaintiff's desire to attend a specific school was based on "its particular appeal to her," and not on a constitutionally protected right.[24]

A credible argument can be made that sterilization permits a woman to act more freely upon normal sexual or social instincts, without the potential burden or additional need for choice regarding abortion, custody, or other aspects of parenthood. In the *Grady* case, for instance, the parents sought to have their retarded daughter sterilized because they wished to place her in a sheltered workshop and group home setting. They had recognized her need for sexual and social development and felt that sterilization would remove limitations to that development. However, the real issue here is not so much the question of sterilization but the issue of choice. The New Jersey court felt that the interests of choice and autonomy required that less permanent and less intrusive means of contraception be explored before sterilization could be approved. The ability to make choices about sexual and reproductive control is an important aspect of (a woman's) sexuality, as is the "right" of the person or substitute consenter to opt for training or education about the appropriate use, for instance, of birth control pills or a diaphragm. At present, most contraceptive methods are directed at prevention of female pregnancy rather than at the ability of the male to inseminate; thus, decision making about contraceptive measures, at least for the present, has become a critical aspect of female sexuality, and one in which a woman's choice can be an affirmative statement. For women like Lee Ann Grady, consent, and indeed the issue of imputed informed consent, is a misleading formulation of the problem: no procedures, however carefully detailed, will ever *really* determine what Lee Ann's careful and intelligent choice would be. The important factor is that female sexuality should be evaluated on its own merits, as an issue separate from reproduction. As the New Jersey Supreme Court noted in *Grady:* "The fact is that the majority of the retarded population has the same basic need for love and sexual expression as the nonhandicapped."[25] Sexuality, however, like abortion and sterilization, is an aspect of personal privacy that is protected by the Constitution.[26]

Given the clear-cut pattern toward state regulation of female sexuality and social activity in general, the legal and caregiving systems have presumed that it is legitimate to regulate sexual activity where a woman is disabled, particularly where so-called "normal" autonomy is not achievable. This presumption, initiated by courts and medical settings, is reinforced by caretakers and guardians who rationalize their behavior by reference to "best interest"—which is what Lee Ann Grady's parents did. There is an irony here in the public image of autonomy for disabled persons. Autonomy for a disabled person is generally seen as ability to contribute to and enjoy a productive life in society—activities such as personal care, employment, education, and community involvement. This image, however, creates an androgynous concept of autonomy. Many disabled women feel that androgyny is reinforced throughout their lives through both overt and subtle messages; this, in fact, *is* one of the critical messages of this book. Disabled women may not be considered "normal" (that is, sexual or "marriageable") women, but they may become normal community members, educators, lawyers, or secretaries. So highlighting androgynous skills, the mainstreaming movement has achieved one goal at the expense of another.

One conclusion that may be drawn from the legal analysis is that autonomy can be limited under the guise of protection, and that this limitation of autonomy can effect a redefinition of sexual identity. A physical or mental disability makes so-called "normal" images of womanhood appear to be unobtainable. Because overt sexuality is not generally part of their experience of growing up, disabled women tend to develop images of themselves that highlight skills or intellectual or technical expertise. Ironically, as society in general has incorporated more androgynous images for women as a measure of gender equality, androgynous self-images for disabled women may stand in the way of the kind of sexual awareness that leads to autonomy and fulfillment within the society.

Custody and Parental Rights

Another area in which regulatory activity has both influenced and been affected by societal attitudes about mentally disabled women involves their parental rights and custody of children. In this area, too, the legal system is focused on a rights-oriented model of procedural justice, one that is ordered hierarchically. In turn this analysis has created conflicting claims: the right of a child (to a standard of care that is in her or his best interests); the right of a parent to custody of a child; and the obligations of the state to "protect" children as well as dependent adults under the doctrine of *parens patriae*. Because of increased regulation of and public concern about child neglect and abuse, courts and child welfare agencies today are more likely to intervene when a mother's parenting ability is questioned than they were in the past. Intervention is often for reasons that relate directly to the agency's perception of the mother's ability to function autonomously in society. While custody laws have changed so that fathers may obtain custody more easily, the initial primary responsibility for a child still rests most often with its mother. Statutes, case law, and social policy now address the ability of a custodial parent to parent effectively in a psychosocial sense as well as in a physical sense (Hertz 1979). This development has taken place in the context of emerging procedures mandating due process prior to any termination of parental rights. The procedures attempt to balance the due process of the parent with the right to a permanent determination of custody that is in the child's best interests (see, for example, Goldstein, Freud, Solnit 1979). What happens where the state is also concerned about the "best interests" of a disabled mother? Does the state have a conflict of interest when it has a dual *parens patriae* role? It is easy to see how well-intentioned intervention can thwart legitimate maternal rights.

Presently two standards are used in making custody determinations—parental fitness and the child's best interests. Because neither standard is well-developed, there is potential for conflict between the standards. If the best interests of the parent are also considered, the potential for conflict grows. This is particularly significant because it mirrors a conflict in judicial and legislative considerations of child welfare, and within child welfare agencies. Child welfare agencies now seem to intervene more readily in family situations where there is a possibility that a parent is unfit, and courts have supported removal of a child from the home even in cases where the "unfitness" seems more related to lifestyle than to abuse or neglect. (The number of examples is growing. Children have been removed from the custody of lesbian mothers and gay fathers, and from parents who live in communal settings or who spurn societal norms such as public schooling.)

At the same time, the child welfare system has finally recognized the importance of permanency planning for children. This presumes that long-term foster care is inadequate and that a child should remain with or be returned to his or her parents whenever possible. These theories also recognize the psychological importance of the child's own view of time, space, and relationships. This has resulted in a two-stage approach to child custody determinations that again forces courts or agencies to focus on procedure rather than substance. The first step is a determination of parental fitness. Once a determination of fitness is made, the "child's best interests" are considered for purposes of placement.[27]

When the custodial parent is a mentally disabled woman, however, she is initially presumed to be unfit. The process then focuses immediately on the second stage, the question of the child's best interests, and sidesteps the traditional "fitness" criteria. Because the issue is avoided, the custody decision is even more subjective, particularly when the mother's behavior deviates from society's norms. Some state regulations and statutes designate mental retardation or other mental disability as a key criterion for making a determination of child neglect. Several courts have upheld lower court orders in which a mother's low IQ was the basis for a finding of neglect. The statutes of sixteen states permit termination of parental rights on the ground of retardation alone (Gilhool and Gran 1984).[28]

This presumption harms mentally disabled parents in two ways. First it is not clear whether specific standards are used in determining unfitness, or whether the simple diagnosis of a disability or low I.Q. is sufficient before a parent's rights can be terminated. Second, public agencies may have a duty to provide a mentally disabled parent with parenting training. Most state statutes and regulations that mandate procedures for assessing parental fitness and determining custody *require* that child welfare agencies *must* provide meaningful rehabilitative services to improve parenting skills. This practice is clearly followed when a mother is not disabled. However, courts have approved termination of custody when the child welfare agency has refused rehabilitative services on the grounds that they would be "of no benefit," in effect equating the mental disability itself with a presumed inability to care for children (*Journal of Family Law* 1977–1978; *Stanford Law Review* 1979). Here, there seems to be no burden on the agencies to design rehabilitative (or habilitative) services for the client. Thus, mentally disabled women are often denied the social and emotional benefits of childrearing without a specific finding of incapacity, despite the fact that current research indicates that the mere existence of a mental disability does not render a parent unfit.[29]

This discussion about parenting has so far addressed the issue as it involves mentally disabled people without regard to gender. While statutes, regulations, and judicial opinions do not distinguish between mothers and fathers in their application of the standards, mothers still are most often the custodians of their children, despite changes in the presumption of maternal custody. An informal survey of court opinions terminating parental custody because of the mental disability of a parent reveals that almost all of the cases involved mentally disabled mothers.[30] Moreover, the qualities that have been emphasized as important for proving parental adequacy are traditionally "female" qualities— nurturing, housekeeping, ability to provide emotional support and physical and hygienic care—that ordinarily are associated with mothers. So ingrained is the notion that mentally disabled mothers do not have and cannot obtain such skills, that a child welfare agency's authority to invoke the system is rarely questioned. Thus, child welfare agencies have obtained custody immediately upon the birth of a child to a mentally retarded mother on the grounds of potential neglect, or without any evidence of neglect or inadequacy. Although in recent years courts have required a particularized showing of the likelihood of neglect, the terminology is fairly general—a showing that retardation renders a parent "unable to discharge her parental responsibilities" has been held to be sufficient.[31] Here, clearly, the child's best interests may not be the mother's best interests, and the state, in effect, is imposing its own subjective view.

As nontraditional arrangements for childrearing and custody gain support within the general population, additional support accumulates for non-nuclear custodial arrangements such as extended, non-biologically related families, group living, and shared custody; such arrangements might permit mentally disabled women to function effectively—autonomously—as parents. The irony of recent developments relating to sexuality and parenting is that while mentally disabled women are less likely to be sterilized, and thus more likely to bear children, they are more likely to lose custody of their children. The stringent due process tests applied to the issue of a person's competence to consent (to sterilization or abortion) are not used in considering a person's competence to be a parent.

Concern for the best interests of the child provides only a partial justification for this presumption. Like female sexuality, the idea of mothering invokes a notion of social interaction based upon behavioral norms that may not be the same for disabled and non-disabled persons; such norms mark mentally disabled mothers as both different and inadequate.

Recent court decisions in child neglect proceedings involving parents with *physical* disabilities forbid a presumption that a disability creates inadequacy: they require supporting evidence of neglect before parental ties can be severed.[32] The standards, however, are applied differentially for mentally disabled parents.

The child neglect statutes and regulations of most jurisdictions are based upon a principle of "least restrictive alternative"; that is, a child should not be removed from the home unless less restrictive alternatives have been tried and have not succeeded. This generally requires that states provide appropriate training in parenting and homemaker services to assist the parent; thus, the outcome of neglect proceedings may turn on the court's view of the quality or quantity of habilitative services that a state must provide. Beyond the quantity and quality issue, however, numerous questions are raised by a mother with a mental disability. Standards do not exist to measure the relationship between IQ and parental adequacy, nor do they provide for a means to measure improvement or training if services are not available to the mother or the family.

Sexual or Physical Abuse
Another issue that relates to sexual and social autonomy for mentally disabled women is the tenuous line between intimacy and abuse, particularly when a woman's social and communicative abilities are limited. Physical and sexual abuse of disabled or dependent people is a growing concern of legislatures, social agencies, and service providers. One of the major issues in the institutional due process and right-to-

treatment cases such as *Pennhurst* and *Willowbrook* was that the lack of adequate standards and staff within the large institutions created an atmosphere ripe for abuse.[33] The district court's opinion in the Pennhurst case contains graphic descriptions of abused residents and numerous instances of both physical and sexual abuse.[34] Abusers may be institutional staff as well as other residents. While the closer supervision of residents at home or in the smaller, more homelike atmosphere of the community or group homes may be less likely to produce abusive conditions, women in community facilities frequently are less able than their non-disabled counterparts to report instances of abuse. Also, the widespread distribution of the smaller group home facilities makes surveillance more difficult.

It is more difficult to report and prosecute suspected abuse when the victim has limited verbal or communication skills. Her testimony might not be admissible in court; like that of children, the uncorroborated testimony of a mentally disabled woman may not be acceptable without a separate determination of competence. Corroboration, especially of sexual abuse, may be extremely difficult to obtain, as recent research on sexual abuse of children has shown (Weisberg 1984). Moreover, mentally disabled women often have led fairly sheltered lives, and they need to develop social interactional skills. It may be difficult for a woman with limited social experience to distinguish between appropriate affectionate intimate behavior (sexual or other) and abusive behavior, especially on the part of a coresident, or a staff person to whom she relates as a parental or authority figure.

Existing protection-from-abuse statutes are minimally adequate, and they do not necessarily protect residents of group homes. For the most part, the statutes are addressed to abuse of *children*, either in their own homes or in custodial settings, and in many states these statutes apply only to children or to the elderly in nursing homes. Statutes protecting disabled or dependent people address primarily residents of large institutions. The Older Americans Act provides broad protections for the elderly in institutions and residential facilities; it applies to facilities where a majority of the residents are older than 65 (it also covers those residents under age 65 in such institutions).[35] But few protections exist for the growing population of mentally disabled women who are mainstreamed, or who live in small group facilities. This is yet another area in which the rights orientation has itself generated the potential for abuse; but the answer is not necessarily to back off from using rights as a vehicle to obtain autonomy but to design ways in which rights will be implemented in practice with an outcome that effectuates the autonomy sought.

IMPLEMENTATION OF RIGHTS AND SOCIAL POLICY

Procedure at the Margins

Women who are mentally disabled are caught in a paradoxical web of good intentions. As women they are defined by the dependent role fostered by society. As people who are mentally disabled, they also are labeled as dependent by a social, medical, and legal system that uses the label to circumscribe autonomy and create perpetual adolescence. In fact, in many ways such women *are* dependent on other people for certain skills, assistance, or routines that are not at issue for non-disabled people. However, it is erroneous and dangerous always to equate physical dependence with legal dependence, and to presume that dependence precludes autonomy. The "proceduralization" of issues such as autonomy and dependence in legal and medical/social service settings ignores critical elements of context that might otherwise allow these concepts to be balanced rather than to be measured in opposition to one another.

The legal system is structured as an adversary model, essentially polarized between the rights of one and the duties of another. When law or policy limit labeling as a form of discrimination and eliminate categorical distinctions based on race or religion as justification for differential treatment, as the civil rights movement has in many instances, the adversary process works well as a means of providing a legal definition of autonomy—to life, to work, to treatment or habilitation. However, recent Supreme Court decisions limit the rights orientation as it applies to claims of disabled people and to claims of women. The Court has refused to justify, for instance, strict scrutiny of laws or policies that discriminate against people on the basis of disability or sex. The rights model therefore may have less impact in those areas than was once believed.[36]

Court decisions do not automatically bring about autonomy; they often do no more than pronounce the existence of a *right* to autonomy. Implementation is critical in order to make the right effective, and to bring about autonomy in fact. The adversary model highlights competition; therefore, it may not be effective where implementation of a decision requires cooperation of formerly opposing forces. Many of the issues discussed in this chapter have as much to do with recognition of an interdependent community of interests or needs as they do with individual independence.

The dissonance between the rights of individuals and the needs and interest of communities carries particular relevance for decision making by, with, and for mentally disabled and dependent women who may be less than able, for many reasons, to have their rights vindicated in the traditional adversarial context. Their needs and rights may, in fact, come more under the category of communal interests or entitlements (care, shelter, love) than the adversary model has so far recognized. The issues discussed in the previous sections illustrate the ways in which the focus on legal procedures has affected the medical and social service systems that provide services and support for disabled people. The rigid procedures developed by courts and legislatures to address issues such as consent to treatment and competence to make decisions or to live in an autonomous manner have been difficult to implement in practical respects, such as in the case of *Lee Ann Grady*.

In recent years, criticism of existing psychological and moral decision-making models has focused on the hierarchical structure of such models. Gilligan (1982) has suggested that the normative model of making decisions (about moral dilemmas) reflects a hierarchical male model and that a "different voice" in decision making would focus more on context and community. This comparison has been extended to analysis of legal decision making as well (see, for example, Karst 1984; Menkel-Meadow 1986; Taub and Schneider 1982). The hierarchical model may be male-oriented; importantly it is also oriented around a fairly singular view of normality. That view equates physical or psychological independence with legal or psychological autonomy.

Gilligan's perspective is predicated upon a theory of moral development of individuals, and the "other voice" that she describes is formulated within the context of individuals' behavior. Gilligan's contrasting examples of Jake (an 11-year-old "hierarchically" oriented male) and Amy (an 11-year-old female who represents the "other voice") might be usefully extended to analysis of the procedures that circumscribe the lives of disabled women. Gilligan has suggested that, in the context of speculating about children's moral development, there are distinct voices present in individuals (which she labels "male" and "female," although she makes clear that they are not necessarily gender-linked). She postulates that the female voice tends to

see a world comprised of relationships rather than people standing alone, [with an] understanding of morality as arising from the recognition of relationships . . . [and a] belief in communication as the mode of conflict resolution. . . . [in other words] a network of relationships [and] an ethic of care. . . . For Amy, development would follow the inclusion of herself in an expanding network of connection and the discovery that separation can be protective and need not entail isolation. (Gilligan 1982: 159–60)

The contrasting examples of Amy and Jake, two children who participated in a rights and responsibility study that used the scale of moral development devised by Kohlberg (1981), suggest to Gilligan that the scale is based upon a male-oriented structure of decision making that is hierarchical and role-oriented, and therefore limited in scope. She suggests that the female voice, which emphasizes social interaction and individual contexts for decisions, is given less validity by society than the male voice, which is assertive, confrontational, and deductive. In this sense, while Gilligan does not address the issue directly, she appears to recognize that societal views of normality are directly related to the male model of individualistic autonomy. This provides further support for the notion that disabled women, who most need context, will always lose out to a proceduralized legal system.

In this chapter, I have tried to suggest that current conflicts over the way in which courts, legislatures, and medical/social service professionals handle issues involving intimate relationships of mentally disabled women are closely related to the conflict that Gilligan ties to concepts of male-model and female-model (self defined through separation and contrasted to self delineated through connection). The procedural posture adopted by the legal and medical systems in response to these conflicts seems to be an uneasy alliance of these models: the procedures maintain the hierarchy of the attempt to find an absolute truth, but they also open up the underlying issues to decision that, in Gilligan's words, arises "from the experience of connection and [are] conceived as a problem of inclusion rather than one of balancing claims" (p. 160). The cases and issues looked at suggest that "rights" provides only a partial answer, and that "interconnectedness" is critical for implementation of any practical decision-making mechanisms.

As a model for social policy-making, the "other voice" might produce procedures for decision making that are based upon interaction among diverse parties, and a mediative concept of autonomy in which the definition of individual rights incorporates a balancing of choices. One example might involve consent and competency determinations along a sliding scale of considerations that could be applied by interdisciplinary teams. Another example is what the New Jersey Supreme Court seems to have attempted in the *Lee Ann Grady* case and more recently in *Claire Conroy,* providing a group context for examining both the best interests of and the putative will of a person who cannot make that decision on her or his own. Karst (1984: 490–91) suggests that courts might adopt this view by weaving "into the fabric of justice . . . an ethic of care and responsibility . . . that an awareness of the claims of contextual justice can assist judges in their efforts to find creative judicial responses to the problems before them . . . [and that] the 'network' point of view informs a set of attitudes toward judicial review itself." How that "weaving" would take place within the already complex web of bureaucracy and procedure that presently governs the lives of disabled women poses new challenges.

An interactional model that would shift the implementation process away from a hierarchical procedural process might enable development of more desirable social intervention policies. Such policies would retain useful features of the law, social work, and medical models that exist at present, but would balance autonomy and interdependence in a way that better meets the current social needs of disabled persons in long-term care settings.

Restructuring Decision Making

Mentally disabled women face limitations imposed not only by their condition but also by a social and legal system that uses labels of dependency to circumscribe autonomy. Labels such as "competence" invoke procedures that limit both legal rights and an individual's ability to make decisions about his or her medical treatment. An adversary-modeled rights orientation has enabled many people to obtain legal recognition of their independent rights—to life, to work, to treatment or habilitation—but not necessarily to autonomous living. Implementation of those rights in a practical setting is necessary in order to make the rights effective, and to bring about substantive autonomy. Because the adversary model highlights competitiveness, it therefore may not be effective where implementation of legal rights requires cooperative planning; this is the case for many dependent people.

Theories of social work practice incorporate interactional techniques. Possible models derive from the social work literature of the early twentieth century, when social workers moved into the settlement houses and into communities to live and work with the populations—aged, dependent, poor, and disabled—who lived there. Others derive from community social work in the War on Poverty in the 1960s. The community social work/settlement house tradition suggests a decision-making model for social policies in which the concept of autonomy for individuals would be separate from the concept of independence, at least for the purpose of defining the relationship between individuals and government or professionals.

There has been a trend toward interactional forms of decision making within medical and legal settings, as well: the growth of hospital ethics committees and negotiated treatment planning that involve patients, families, and diverse professionals; and the increased use of mediation and negotiation as an alternative to formal legal process, particularly for community-centered conflicts such as landlord/tenant complaints or consumer complaints, or for family disputes such as divorce or custody.

The social work practice model described above has been criticized for being contextual and concerned with individualistic problem solving. Similar concerns have been voiced about legal procedures encouraging negotiation and mediation of individual conflicts without changing broader laws or policies, and without redefining rights for the people involved. Critics point to law reform litigation such as the welfare procedure cases (due process protections for denial of benefits, the overturning of the "man-in-the-house" rule) and tenant rights cases as having accomplished broad-scale reforms in policy-making at the state or federal level.

Because social work is concerned primarily with context and with community, and because it is centered around relationships rather than rules, it may provide a useful model for decision making when the goal of intervention is the preservation of autonomy as opposed to independence, or the application of equitable remedies when competing and equally deserving interests need to be balanced. Gilligan often uses examples drawn from legal practice or lawyers' behavior to illustrate her points about the "male dominance," or hierarchical moral development, theory and the conceptual problems it poses for women. In contrast to law, social work fits Gilligan's "female voice" model; it then becomes clear why law and social work are respectively considered male and female professions.

There is some concern that in order to achieve social equality for the individuals involved in such conflicts, who are generally poor and often dependent in some way, universally accepted procedures for decision making must be applied so that one set of facts can be compared with another. In this regard, decision-making models used to delineate rights may be different from the decision-making models for deciding upon and implementing remedies.

Formal procedures may be necessary in order to establish basic premises for individual rights and duties, based upon an ideal of equality, but where the issue is to find equitable ways of carrying out the mandates of those premises, informal processes may work best. Thus, in the legal system, complex or creative remedies ordered by courts have been most effective when they are arrived at through an interactional and negotiated process. However, the initial adversarial framework of litigation is necessary in order to define what the rights are.

As disputants, disabled persons are at the short end of the balance of power, with limitations that are political as well as physical. The medical model and its attendant legislative and administrative framework of benefits have fostered the imbalance by perpetuating the illusion of dependence. It is beginning to become apparent that an adversary model also fosters the imbalance of power by equating rights with independence, seeing self-determination as the ultimate remedy. When one is disabled, dependent, poor, or on a fixed income, closed out of the work force by "protective" government policies originally designed to provide concrete benefits, self-determination and independence may be no more than cruel illusions. The goal of autonomy may be counterproductive, inasmuch as the inability to achieve self-determination or independence may undercut the foundation of the rights claimed. What is left is a system that treats people by extremes: procedures are designed to avoid institutionalization unless self-determination is impossible and to incorporate strict safeguards to preserve independence. The procedures also prescribe the categories that fall outside these guidelines: "a danger to him-/ or herself or others," too dependent, too sick, too "incompetent" and poor to make decisions; outside the safeguards, the medical model predominates.

A viable model for decision making that depends on interactions among professionals and clients would be structured both by procedural guidelines and by specific, prenegotiated, substantive or ethical principles. It would incorporate decision-making procedures as a form of social policy for individuals within families or groups and as a model for decison making involving individuals in the social environment. Such a model seems to balance the needs of dependent or disabled people with their rights and to formulate an autonomous context for such individuals within the social environment, which would balance rights and equity.

This "voice," directed toward social policy-making, might produce a decision-making model based upon a mediated concept of autonomy in which the definition of individual rights incorporates a balancing of choices. An interactional model would shift the implementation process away from a hierarchical decision-making structure. This may, in turn, allow for development of social intervention policies that balance autonomy and dependence in a way that more appropriately meets current social needs.

Notes

1. Cf. Goldstein, Solnit, and Freud (1979) for development of the "best interest of the child" standard. *In the Matter of Claire Conroy*, 486 A. 2d. 1209 (N.J. Supreme Court, 1985), provides a judicial attempt to define how the actual will of a person who is comatose or otherwise noncompetent might be determined. The New Jersey Supreme Court has recently been in the forefront of

defining autonomy as a legal concept, ironically, however, in the context of establishing a "right to die."

2. *See*, e.g., D. Rothman (1980) and cases such as *Wyatt v. Aderholt*, 368 F. supp. 1382 (M.D. Ala. 1973) and 368 F. supp. 1383 (M.D. Ala. 1974), *New York Assn. for Retarded Children v. Carey*, 393 F. supp. 715 (E.D. N.Y. 1975) aff'd, 596 F. 2d 27 (2d Cir. 1979), cert. denied, 444 U.S. 836 (1979), *Pennhurst State School and Hospital v. Halderman*, 444 U.S. 1 (1981). See also Ferleger (1983).

3. For a discussion of informed consent and the law, see Roth, Lidz, and Meisel (1977) and Gaylin and Macklin (1982); on the right to refuse (or demand) treatment, see Hastings Center Report (1986); for a discussion of rights to treatment and habilitation, see the *Pennhurst* and *N.Y.A.R.C.* cases cited in note 2. See also President's Commission for the Study of Ethical Problems in Medicine and Biomedical and Behavioral Research (1982).

4. *Roe v. Wade*, 410 U.S. 113 (1973).

5. Even when groups initially lobby for protective legislation, there might be a loss of control over outcome—for instance, establishment of large-scale institutions for the disabled, or usurpation of prenatal and postnatal care by the medical profession. See S. Rothman (1983).

6. Compare *In the Matter of Lee Ann Grady*, 426 A. 2d 467 (1981), no. C-1917-78E (letter opinion, Aug. 3, 1981), and *Buck v. Bell*, 274 U.S. 200 (1927).

7. *In the Matter of Claire Conroy*, 486 A. 2d. 1209 (N.J. Supreme Court, 1985).

8. There are close parallels between the traditions of protection of dependent classes through social norms, and the codification and legitimation the legal system often has given to those norms, especially with regard to "intimate" behavior. It has been pointed out that many of the Supreme Court's decisions on sexual privacy seem to vindicate societal norms as to marriage, procreation, and sexuality. See, e.g., Karst (1980) and Dunlap (1981, 1982).

9. Eugenics, reserving the policy of sterilization to eliminate from the society "unfavorable" qualities such as retardation or "criminal tendencies," was popularized by Sir Francis Galton, a follower of Charles Darwin. See *Washburn Law Journal* (1984). See, generally, Milunsky and Annas (1976), and Herr (1983).

10. Other developmental models offer similar patterns of movement from a largely dependable status to an autonomous adult state. See Loevinger and Wessler (1970).

11. For a detailed discussion of biblical and early English custom and law on this subject, see Parker (1983).

12. *Bradwell v. Illinois*, 83 U.S. (16 Wall) 130 (1873).

13. See, e.g., the discussion of judicial decisions regarding sexuality and sexual expression in Dunlap (1982).

14. See also Karst's (1984) discussion of the development of constitutional doctrine relating to discrimination on the basis of sex, and *Harvard Law Review* (1981).

15. *Rostker v. Goldberg*, 448 U.S. 1306 (1981): *City of Cleburne, Texas, v. Cleburne Living Center*, 105 S. Ct. 3249 (1985). In *Cleburne*, the court rejected altogether any claim that disabled persons had a "fundamental" right not to be objects of discrimination, as that term has been applied to protection of the rights of racial and religious minorities.

16. Eighteen states have permissive sterilization statutes, although courts

294 • Policy and Politics

have increasingly been inclined to interpret such statutes narrowly. Most courts now require individualized judicial orders for sterilization, regardless of the existence of a statute. See, e.g., *Washburn Law Journal* (1984).

17. *Buck v. Bell,* 274 U.S. 200 (1927).

18. *Skinner v. Oklahoma,* 316 U.S. 535 (1942).

19. *Stump v. Sparkman,* 935 U.S. 349 (1978).

20. *In Re Grady,* 85 N.J. 235, 426 A. 2d 467 (1981).

21. *Michael M. v. Superior Court,* 450 U.S. 464 (1981).

22. *Rostker v. Goldberg,* 453 U.S. 57 (1981).

23. *Vorcheimer v. School District of Philadelphia,* 532 F. 2d 880, (3rd Cir. 1976), aff'd, 430 U.S. 703 (1977). This issue was subsequently raised in a Pennsylvania state court action involving another student; in that case the total court found that the *state* constitution *did* prohibit sex-segregated public high schools. (*Newberg v. School District of Philadelphia,* Phila. County Civil Division, No. 5822, August Term, 1982). The School Board did not appeal that decision, and the school (Central High School) subsequently admitted women.

24. *Vorcheimer* at 882, 888; See *Plessy v. Ferguson,* 163 U.S. 567 (1896).

25. *In Re Grady,* 426 A. 2d 467 (N.J. Supreme Court 1981).

26. *Griswold v. Connecticut,* 381 U.S. 479 (1965); *Roe v. Wade,* 410 U.S. 113 (1973). The present Supreme Court continues to be troubled by the potential for conflict over privacy and personhood, at least where female sexuality and, specifically, abortion are involved. However, during its 1985–1986 term, the Court decided two cases that raise the issue of state regulation of abortion. *Thornburgh v. American College of Obstetricians and Gynecologists,* 106 S. Ct. 2169 (1986), involving a challenge to the Pennsylvania Abortion Control Act, and *Diamond v. Charles,* 106 S. Ct. 1697 (1986), involving a challenge to the Illinois abortion statute. In both cases the Court struck down restrictive state legislation, but by extremely slim majorities.

27. See also *In Re Jeannie Q,* 31 Cal. App. 3rd 709 (2d Dist. Ct. App. 1973); *In Re Orlando F,* 40 N.Y. 2d 103 (1976); *In Re Jeannie Q,* 107 Cal. Rptr. 646 (2d Dist. 1973).

28. See also Herr (1983), Ch. 6, on lack of due process on postinstitutionalization.

29. *In Re Orlando F.* 351 N.E. 2d 711 (1976); *In Re Geiger,* 331 A. 2d, 1972 (1975). See Katz, Howe, and McGrath (1975); see also Gilhool and Gran (1984).

30. The author examined the judicial opinions cited in her research for this chapter. More than 95 percent of the opinions (more than 100 opinions, in more than twenty different state courts) involved challenges to a mentally disabled mother's custody of a child.

31. See, e.g., *Journal of Family Law,* (1977–1978). The Supreme Court's recent refusal to afford disabled persons the same protected status under the Constitution as racial minorities or even the lesser protection afforded to women makes it unlikely that this will change. *City of Cleburne, Texas, v. Cleburne Living Center,* 105 S. Ct. 3249 (1985).

32. *Stanford Law Review* (1979); *In Re Jeannie Q,* 107 Cal. Rptr. 646 (2 Dist. 1973); *In Re Jeannie Q,* 31 Cal. App. 3rd 709 (2d Dist. Ct. App. 1973).

33. *Pennhurst State School and Hospital v. Halderman,* 444 U.S. 1 (1981); *New York Assn. for Retarded Children v. Carey* (the *Willowbrook* case), 393 F. supp. 715 (E.D. N.Y. 1975), aff'd, 596 F. 2d 27 (2d Cir. 1978), cert. denied 444 U.S. 836 (1979). See also Rothman and Rothman (1984).

34. *Halderman vs. Pennhurst State School and Hospital*, 446 F. supp. 1295 (E.D. Pa. 1979) at 1302–10.
35. See also *Mental Disability Law Reporter* (1983).
36. *City of Cleburne, Texas, v. Cleburne Living Center.* See f.n. 26 for a discussion of current legal doctrine in the abortion context.

References

Burt, R. 1984. Constitutional law and the teaching of parables. *Yale Law Journal* 93:455.

Dunlap, M. 1981. Where the person ends, does the government begin? *Lincoln Law Review* 12:47.

———. 1982. Toward recognition of "a right to be sexual." *Women's Rights Law Review* 7:245.

Erikson, E. 1950. *Childhood and society.* New York: Norton.

Ferleger, D. 1983. Anti-institutionalization and the Supreme Court. *Rutgers Law Journal* 14:595.

Ferleger, D., and T. Boyd. 1979. Anti-institutionalization: The promise of the *Pennhurst* case. *Stanford Law Review* 31:717.

Friedman, P. 1976. *The rights of the mentally retarded person.* New York: Free Press.

Gaylin, W., I. Glasser, and D. Rothman. 1984. *Doing good: The limits of benevolence.* New York: Harper and Row.

Gaylin, W., and R. Macklin, eds. 1982. *Who speaks for the child?* New York: Plenum Press.

Gilhool, T., and J. Gran. 1984. Legal rights of disabled parents. Unpublished manuscript. Public Interest Law Center of Philadelphia.

Gilligan, C. 1982. *In a different voice.* Cambridge, Mass.: Harvard University Press.

Goldstein, J., A. Solnit, and A. Freud. 1979. *Beyond the best interests of the child.* New York: Free Press.

Harvard Law Review. 1981. Toward a redefinition of sexual equality. Note. 95:487.

Hastings Center Report. 1986. For the handicapped, rights but no welcome. 16. By George Will, p. 5.

Herr, S. 1983. *Rights and advocacy for retarded people.* Lexington, Mass.: Lexington Books.

Hertz, R. 1979. Retarded persons in neglect proceedings: The erroneous assumption of parental inadequacy. *Stanford Law Review* 31:785.

Journal of Family Law. 1977–1978. The law and the problem parent: Custody and parental rights of homosexual, mentally retarded, mentally ill and incarcerated people. Note. 16:797.

Karst, K. 1980. The freedom of intimate association. *Yale Law Review* 89:624.

———. 1984. A woman's constitution. *Duke Law Journal* 447.

Katz, S., R. Howe, and M. McGrath. 1975. Child neglect in America. *Family Law Quarterly* 9:1.

Kohlberg, L. 1981. *The philosophy of moral development.* New York: Harper and Row.

Loevinger, J., and R. Wessler. 1970. *Measuring ego development.* San Francisco: Jossey-Bass.

Menkel-Meadow, C. 1986. Portia in a different voice. *Berkeley Women's Law Journal.*

Mental Disability Law Report. 1983. State laws and regulations serving elderly persons and disabled adults. 7:158.

Milunsky, A., and G. Annas. 1976. *Genetics and the law.* New York: Plenum Press.

Morse, S. 1982. A preference for liberty: The case against involuntary commitment of the mentally disordered. *California Law Review* 70:54.

Nonet, P., and P. Selznick. 1976. *Law and society in transition.* New York: Octagon Books.

Parker, G. 1983. Legal recognition of sexual activity and the protection of females. *Osgood Hall Law Journal* 21:187.

President's Commission for the Study of Ethical Problems in Medicine and Biomedical and Behavioral Research. 1982. *Making health care decisions,* vol. 1. Washington, D.C.: GPO.

Price, R., and R. Burt. 1975. Sterilization, state action, and the concept of consent. *Law and Psychiatry Review* 1:57.

Roth, D., T. Lidz, and H. Meisel. 1977. Toward a model of the legal doctrine of informed consent. *American Journal of Psychiatry* 134.

Rothman, D. 1971. *The discovery of the asylum.* Boston: Little, Brown.

———. 1980. *Conscience and convenience.* Boston: Little, Brown.

Rothman, D., and S. Rothman. 1984. *The Willowbrook wars.* New York: Harper and Row.

Rothman, S. 1983. Women's clinics or doctors' offices: The Shepard-Towner Act. In *Social history and social policy,* ed. D. Rothman and S. Wheeler. New York: Free Press.

South Dakota Law Review. 1980. Involuntary sterilization of the mentally retarded: Blessing or burden? *Comment* 25:55.

Stanford Law Review. 1979. Retarded persons in neglect proceedings: The erroneous assumption of parental inadequacy. Note. 31:785.

Taub, N., and E. Schneider 1982. Perspectives on critical legal theory and woman's subordinates. In *The politics of law,* ed. D. Kairys. New York: Pantheon.

Unger, R. 1983. Critical legal studies. *Harvard Law Review* 96:561.

University of Pennsylvania Law Journal. 1984. Law: Rethinking sex and the Constitution. 132:955.

Wald, P. 1974–75. State intervention on behalf of "neglected" children: A search for realistic standards. *Stanford Law Review* 27:985.

———. 1976. Basic personal and civil rights. In *The mentally retarded citizen and the law.* New York: Free Press.

Washburn Law Journal. 1984. Procreation: A choice for the mentally retarded. 23:1359.

Weisberg, D. 1984. The "discovery" of sexual abuse: Experts' role in legal policy formulation. *University of California Davis Law Review* 18:1.

Weitzman, L. J. 1985. *The divorce revolution.* New York: Free Press.

12. Shared Dreams: A Left Perspective on Disability Rights and Reproductive Rights

ADRIENNE ASCH and MICHELLE FINE

Women have the right to abortion for any reason they deem appropriate. Newborns with disabilities have the right to medical treatment whether or not their parent(s) wishes them to be treated. Both rights are unequivocal, consistent, and currently protected by statute. Both sets of rights are, however, under severe attack—the former from the right and the latter from the left. And together they have been juxtaposed as a contradiction. We argue here that both sets of rights are essential to preserve and are compatible from a leftist, feminist perspective. In fact, this compatibility forces us to struggle with the reality that in each case, with women's right to abortion and disabled infants' right to treatment, the institutions and services that translate these rights into realities are currently denied appropriate levels of financial and social support—often rendering these rights hollow and irrelevant for those who most need them.

Rights of women to abortion and of newborns with disabilities to medical treatment are, in fact, separate rights that have been linked by the Right in an antifeminist and allegedly "pro-family" position, and by the Left out of ignorance of the meaning and politics of disability. In this chapter we review some of the recent controversies over disability rights as it relates to women's right to abortion, amniocentesis, and more generally a left politic. To make our argument, we cover three topics: (1) the bias against people with disabilities inherent in most of the reasons offered for nontreatment of infants with disabilities; (2) the bias against women and a woman's right to control her own body

This chapter appeared originally in *Radical America* 18(4):51–58.

inherent in the arguments against amniocentesis and abortion of fetuses with disabilities; and (3) the continuing problematic nature of the distinction between a fetus residing in the body of a woman and a newborn infant, as it relates to the question, Whose body is it anyway? Because the only voices from the Left—including feminist organizations—that have spoken for the rights of disabled newborns to treatment have been those publicly identified with the disability rights movement, we turn first to the issues of infants with disabilities. Unfortunately, these voices have been relatively ignored thus far and must be given serious weight in this debate.

RIGHTS OF NEWBORNS

In our earlier writing on this subject,[1] we challenged the prevailing assumption in the reproductive rights movement that any woman *would* have an abortion if she were diagnosed as carrying a fetus with a disaibility. We urged that the reproductive rights movement and other feminists not presume nor prescribe any reason (for example, "the tragedy of the 'defective fetus,' ") for an abortion. Just as we would not advocate the "tragedy of a female fetus" as a legitimate reason for an abortion—although many of us abhor the use of abortion for sex selection—activists cannot continue to exploit the disabled fetus as the good or compelling reason to keep abortion safe, legal, and funded. On the basis of women's rights alone, abortion must be safe, legal, and funded—not to rid our society of some of its "defective" members.

Recently the controversy has emerged in all its complexity: Baby Jane Doe, an infant born on Long Island with a series of disabling conditions including spina bifida and microencephaly, was denied an operation by her physician and parents acting jointly. Earlier, a Bloomington, Indiana, boy was born with a diagnosis of Down's syndrome and an esophagus unattached to his stomach. Routinely an infant's open esophagus is corrected by surgery, but Baby Doe's parents decided against surgery based on the diagnosis of his mental retardation. Despite some dozen offers of couples to adopt him, Baby Doe died at six days old of starvation. Even more recently and less well known, an infant boy was born in Illinois with a heart problem, and a "hand like a claw." His father, a well-known veterinarian, was handed the baby in the delivery room. On seeing the child he threw it to the floor, killing him. The community has rallied around this man, claiming that everyone has a psychological threshold beyond which he or she is not responsible. For him it was the presumed tragedy of having a disabled child.

The reasons used to justify denial of medical treatment to these infants have been the reasons given by people who believe that living with a disability is either not worth living, too costly to the family, or too costly to the rest of nondisabled society. But no one ever questions the use of costly treatments to ameliorate or cure all sorts of neonatal medical problems if those procedures result in a perfect, "normal" child. The question arises only when no amount of medical treatment will relieve all of an infant's medical or mental problems, and that infant will remain throughout its life as a person with some level of disability. At that point, leftists and feminists have, for the most part, joined in the arguments that such treatment wastes limited societal resources, harms non-disabled parents and siblings, harms society, and does not benefit the child. All these arguments arise from confusing what is inherent in disability with the problems imposed on disabled people by a discriminating society—one without national health insurance, adequate financial and social supports for persons with disabilities, one which prizes profit over human needs and persists in discriminating at the level of medical treatment, education and employment opportunities, and housing.

Unacknowledged by those who would deny treatment is this discrimination against people with disabilities. Such prejudice is found throughout the population and thus it is no surprise, although it is dismaying to see people who decry discrimination on the basis of race, ethnicity, gender, sexual orientation, or social class urging that public policy embody their fears, terrors, revulsion, and ignorance of disability and people with disabilities. Millions of citizens with biological limitations would assert that their main obstacles to fulfilling lives stem not from these limitations but from a society that stresses mental and physical perfection and rugged individualism, that often rejects, isolates and segregates them, assuming that disabled people are unpleasant, unhappy, helpless, hopeless, and burdensome.

Such stereotypes lead inevitably to the first of three major arguments given for nontreatment: that the child's quality of life will be intolerable. We ask: Intolerable to whom? How do we know? And, if that child's quality of life is less than someone else's, how much do we as a society contribute to its impoverishment by denying needed health care, education, independent living, rehabilitation, and social supports to ensure a better life? We do not know what the lives of any children will be when they are born. People who decide that Down's syndrome or spina bifida automatically renders children or adults "vegetables" or "better off dead" simply know nothing about the lives of such people today—much less what those lives could be in a more inclusive, person-oriented society.

Persons with Down's syndrome or spina bifida represent a broad range of potential. Many lead intellectually, economically, socially, and sexually fulfilling lives. Others don't. We don't know how they would live in a society that did not systematically deprive children of opportunity if they do not meet norms of appearance, intelligence, and autonomy. Some parents who gave their children with Down's syndrome cosmetic surgery have found that their children's social and intellectual skills improved once they no longer carried the stigma of the "Mongoloid" appearance. We cannot separate the essence of disability from the social construction of disability, and we must continue to struggle to ensure a life free of the kinds of oppressions we have described so that disability can refer to the physical or mental limitation alone.

Others who recommend against treatment contend that even if the child could have a "meaningful" life, its presence would unduly burden or deprive non-disabled family members. Some feminists hav argued that deinstitutionalizing disabled people and saving disabled newborns constitute yet another means by the Right to keep women in their homes, bearing the "double burden" of the pathetic disabled child. Women, it is argued, are oppressed by deinstitutionalization and medical treatment to ensure life for infants with disabilities, and siblings will resent the attention and emotional and financial resources given to the disabled child.

Such argument is based on the assumption that disabled children contribute nothing to family life, which even in today's society can be denied by thousands of parents and siblings who attest to the pleasures as well as the problems of living with disabled people. Moreover, it blames the disabled child and suggests eliminating that child, rather than blaming society for causing problems of inadequate resources for all. In the United States, it is, often, quite expensive to care for a child with a disability. But sometimes it is not. When it is, we must struggle politically for funded medical, social and caretaking public programs. We can neither locate the problem inside the child with the disability nor the solution with the individual mother of that child. In Sweden, national health care and a full range of social services enable parents of disabled children to easily partake in infant stimulation programs, integrated daycare and schools, respite care and a host of other services that contribute to their lives and their children's lives. Adult relationships do not founder; siblings without disabilities are not neglected. A supportive context diminishes the alleged negative impact—which we contend is massively overestimated—of having a child with a disability. We would also argue, however, that a parent unable or unwilling today to care for a child with a disability be offered the option of placing the child up for adoption or in foster care temporarily, and we would agitate for adoption agencies to recruit actively and to aggressively support adults interested in adopting or providing foster care for a child with a disability.

We come to the last argument against treating newborns with disabilities: society's resources are limited already and should thus not be spent on people who cannot measure up to the standards of what we think people should be. Obviously this argument rests on our first point—that disabled people cannot have a valuable existence. It also takes as given that society's resources are limited rather than misallocated. We know that under current political arrangements, military spending grossly overshadows spending for social programs. Saying that we should not treat disabled children because resources are scarce, existing services inadequate, and futures uncertain is like saying that poor people and black people should not have children because society is hostile to poverty and deeply racist. No progressive would accept that. Nor should it be accepted where children with disabilities are concerned. We should all fight to transform social arrangements and allocation of resources so that needs are better met for all of us.

Progressives should fight not against deinstitutionalizing disabled people, as some have, and not against treatment for Baby Janes, as many have, but for community-based residential centers, independent living policies, educational and employment opportunities, and the civil rights of all disabled children and adults. All these arguments against treatment rest on the assumption that disabled people are less than human. It is the assumption that should be questioned, not the rights of these children and adults to the societal goods to which the non-disabled members of the community are entitled.

If we believe, as we do, that all children with disabilities deserve treatment regardless of parental wishes, how can we support a woman's unquestioned right to an abortion if that abortion may stem from learning that a fetus being carried has a disability? We do so because we believe that abortion of a fetus and killing an infant are fundamentally different acts.

Women's Right to Abortion

Women have won the right to abortion as a part of the right to control their bodies. As a society we have decided that women are not simply vessels to reproduce the species. While a fetus resides within her, a woman must retain the right to decide what happens to her body and her life. Otherwise we ask that women bear not just unwanted children but also unnecessary physical and psychic burdens of sexual acts that men do not. Since we have decided that each heterosexual act need not be linked in mind or fact to reproduction, we must permit women to decide what becomes of their bodies and lives during a pregnancy.

When a woman decides that she wants to abort, rather than carry to term, a fetus with Down's syndrome, this represents a statement about how she perceives such a child would affect her life and what she wants from rearing a child. Every woman has the right to make this decision in whatever way she needs, but the more information she has, the better her decision can be. Genetic counselors, physicians, and all others involved with assisting women during amniocentesis should gain and provide far more and very different information about life with disabilities than is customarily available. Given proper information about how disabled children and adults live, many women might not choose to abort. And many will still choose to abort. While a fetus resides within her, a woman has the right to decide about her body and her life and to terminate a pregnancy for this or any other reason.

May we argue that a woman has a right to abort a fetus diagnosed with Down's syndrome but also that an infant with Down's syndrome has a right to treatment despite her or his parent's desires? Yes, we can and do. We must recognize the crucial "line" separating the fetus—residing in the body of her mother—and the infant, viable outside the womb. The fetus depends on the mother for sustenance and nourishment. We argue that the "line" of birth makes an enormous difference. Once that living being survives outside the mother, that mother cannot eliminate it because it does not meet her physical and mental specifications. As a society, our constitution accepts personhood as starting at birth. We cannot simply decide that "defective" persons are not really persons and not entitled to all the care and protection we grant other citizens.

The existing laws against murder, the recently passed child abuse amendments of 1984, as well as the provisions of Section 504 of the Rehabilitation Act, prohibit institutions and parents from withholding treatment to persons merely because those persons have disabilities.[2] If parents and doctors would use the disability of a newborn as a reason to withhold treatment and nourishment, and if such treatment and nourishment would permit life for that infant—not a dying infant but an infant with a disability—the social collective and not the individual parent(s) bears the responsibility for that infant's protection. Parents do not today have unlimited rights over their children. Children are not their property. As state and federal laws now protect children from abuse of their parents and as courts have intervened to insist upon medical care and education for minor children when their parents oppose these for religious reasons, the federal government can appropriately intervene to protect newborns from being killed because their parents and doctors find them inconvenient, distasteful, and/or burdensome.

Some will say that the government should not intervene in this private family matter—contending that parents are suffering a tragedy, that they are already going through a terrible time, and that they should be left alone. Socialist feminists have learned to be wary of such privacy-of-the-family arguments, aware that the family as we've known it has long been abusive to women and children. Grief-stricken, shocked, and anxious parents who may seek to end the lives of their "imperfect" infants should be counseled, educated, and told that the child will receive treatment whether or not the parent(s) agrees. We should work toward a policy in which the government picks up the medical expenses associated with such treatment; that parents be given extensive information about what it means to have a disability, have access to disability rights organizations and parents' groups, and be assured of informed consent, in which they are informed that should they wish they can put their infant up for adoption or foster care. Parents therefore may be removed *if they so desire* from responsibility, at which point the state acts to protect the infants. If nontreatment is contemplated when treatment would benefit the child, it should be rendered nonetheless. If state intervention is necessary to ensure it, then we should opt for state intervention. We already opt for state intervention in all manner of other situations where one person's or group's rights are infringed upon by another. Denial of treatment means denial of life, the most basic right of all.

This argument for treatment of newborns is not the same as that of the Reagan administration nor the Right to Life Movement. Unlike these supporters of the disabled, who care about them only when they are in the intensive care nursery and who slash budgets for needed educational programs for them and try to deny them civil rights to education, housing, and employment once out of the nursery, we believe that the government has major responsibility for assisting disabled children and their families throughout life. Not only does the government have the obligation to absorb the medical and social service expenses that children with disabilities entail. It has the obligation to provide parents with extensive information about life with a disability. In addition, the government must assist parents in finding alternative homes for children if parents do not feel prepared to raise them.

Such information about disabilities must include that provided by parents of similarly disabled children and that obtained through contact

Figure 12.1.
Trends in Abortion Attitudes (1962–1982)

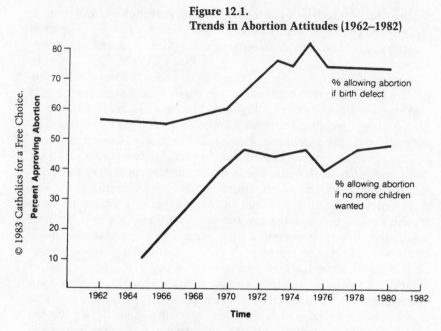

with advocacy groups of disabled adults. It cannot merely consist of medical, diagnostic, or prognostic information without including facts of the social meaning of disability and the ways people manage it in today's world. Disabled adults are among the most important advocates for disabled children, and they must participate in any decisions about the lives and policies affecting the lives of these children.

Like feminism, the disability rights movement entails a commitment to self-determination and a shared sense of community, recognizing that the one is meaningless without a sense of the other. Thus, as disabled adults increasingly advocate the rights of children with disabilities, they seek to ally with feminists and others on the Left to grapple with remaining questions posed. In short, they seek to put forward a shared dream of a just and inclusive society.

When disability rights groups and the American Academy of Pediatrics put forward a statement on the rights of newborns to treatment in November 1983, no known progressive or feminist groups signed the document. We urge that all of us on the Left rethink positions taken out of deep-seated terror and repugnance of disability and out of almost equally deep-seated—but in this case knee-jerk—opposition to the Right's attack on women and the pro-choice movement. We have conceded the issue of disability to the Right. We can and must commit ourselves to the lives of newborns with disabilities while protecting our hard-won gains as women.

New political contradictions will emerge in this struggle: for example, how to mobilize against physicians and medical researchers who systematically prolong the lives of dying infants in order to afford expensive equipment, research laboratories, and sophisticated technology at the expense of the pain and finances of the parent(s) involved; how to deal with late abortions, viable disabled infants who survive abortion procedures or could be kept alive with new technological interventions; or how to deal with infant disabilities that may arise because a woman refused some form of medical intervention during delivery (for example, a woman recently refused a cesarian section recommended because of an active vaginal herpes sore, producing a now blind infant). Such questions can not halt us but must be incorporated into our political struggles as contradictions always have been.[3] Indeed, if we can create a society that supports the newborn with a disability, perhaps the most defenseless of all citizens, we can create a society humane and just for us all.

Notes

1. Michelle Fine and Adrienne Asch, *Reproductive Rights Newsletter*, November 1982.

2. In *Bowen v. American Hospital Association* et al., 106 S.Ct. 2101 (1986), the U.S. Supreme Court ruled that Section 504 of the Rehabilitation Act did not apply to instances in which parents and physicians agreed on the particular course of medical treatment or nontreatment. The Court reasoned that because Section 504 applied to the conduct of institutions, the statute did not cover situations in which hospitals acceded to parental wishes. The Court indicated, however, that if a hospital regularly brings proceedings when parents refuse "medically necessary" treatment, but fails to do so in the case of a severely disabled child, such inaction by that hospital would appear to constitute illegal discrimination.

3. For a detailed feminist discussion of emerging issues in reproductive technology, see S. Cohen and N. Taub, *Reproductive laws for the 1990s* (Clifton, N.J.: Humana Press, forthcoming). See, in particular, A. Asch, "Reproductive technologies and disability," for a full-scale treatment of how these emerging issues affect the disabled population.

13. Smashing Icons: Disabled Women and the Disability and Women's Movements

MARIAN BLACKWELL-STRATTON,
MARY LOU BRESLIN,
ARLENE BYRNNE MAYERSON,
and SUSAN BAILEY

When Miss America, a vibrant, glowing image on the television screen, first walks down the stage runway, crying, laughing, nervously clutching a bouquet of roses, millions of women sigh in envy. This woman embodies a collective faith—that beauty, determined by youth and specific physical proportions, guarantees fun, happiness, money, success, and sexual desirability. To be Miss America, says the emcee, is every girl's dream.

But when the 5-year-old child in the Jerry Lewis Telethon walks slowly across the stage in her braces and crutches, no one envies her, although she, too, embodies another collective faith. She represents our belief in both technology and beauty. She, too, can have the rewards of beauty—but only when she is cured. The emcee reminds us that the child is a victim, the victim of a terrible tragedy that we can offset only by giving money.

These two images, the beauty queen and the poster child, could not be further apart. They represent the extremes, the outside limits of physical attributes. A woman viewer can perhaps take pleasure in imagining that she is close to the beauty queen and remote from the crippled child. To the viewer who is both a woman and disabled, however, it is impossible to escape the reproach of either image. How can she fight against the admonishment, seen not only on television but in every advertising medium, that a perfect body is essential for happiness?

More importantly, how can she assert herself against the belief that a disabled person is like an eternal poster child: cute, but not sexy; always the cared for, never the caring? Unlike the non-disabled woman, who has societally sanctioned roles as mother and wife (restrictive though they be), the disabled woman has no adult roles. Neither mother nor wife nor worker shall she be. This sense of rolelessness is reinforced by a public assumption that disabled women are inappropriate as mothers or sexual beings (International Rehabilitation Review 1977). Statistics reveal that disabled women are less likely to be married, more likely to marry later, and more likely to be divorced than are non-disabled women (Franklin 1977). In comparison to disabled men, disabled women are more likely to have a marriage in which the partner is absent, either through separation, divorce, or widowhood. Few disabled women are wage earners. Fewer than one-fourth of all disabled women are even in the labor force (Bowe 1984).

The effect of this rolelessness is that the disabled woman lives as a kind of social nomad. There is no place in society she can call her own. Her dual status as woman and disabled person endows her with a perspective that at times differs from those of both non-disabled women and disabled men. Quite naturally, this different perspective influences her formulation of political concerns and priorities. For the disabled feminist, neither the disability nor the women's movement fully addresses her concerns. In the disability movement the disabled feminist has to contend with sexism. In the feminist movement she must contend with colleagues who do not understand her disability-based political concerns. In response to this predicament, she far too often opts out of the political process altogether. As both disabled women and feminists, the authors believe that we must educate both movements in the issues specifically affecting disabled women, especially since the women's movement has shown a previous willingness to learn about the issues affecting other women of dual identities such as women of color, working-class women, lesbians, and survivors of incest.

This chapter shows how the following issues—parenting a disabled child, abortion/Baby Doe, education, voting rights, and employment—specifically affect disabled women, and how the women's movement can work with the disability rights movement. While the specific aim is to show how disabled women's issues can be integrated within the women's movement, the larger purpose is to describe the bonds that exist between the two movements. Topics are framed in the context of the attitudes and images that comprise society's perceptions of women and disabled people. By tracing common history and images throughout a discussion of differing approaches to political issues, activists in both movements may gain a deeper understanding of how and why the other has selected its political priorities.

CRACKED MIRRORS: BEAUTY PAGEANT AND TELETHON

When the feminist and the disability rights activist view their political agendas in the context of society's past and present attitudes of prejudice, they may discover that the most dissimilar of society's icons—the tall, elegant beauty queen and the cute, awkward, crippled child—have in fact much to say to each other. These TV images appear in the context of a programming format that invariably clues the viewer to society's perceptions of women and disabled people. The beauty pageant, for instance, is a contest: the women compete against each other for the favor of the judges. The competition separates women, encouraging them to compare themselves against all others. Rarely do the contestants perform together in the talent section of the pageant. Subtly but surely, society discourages women's friendship. In advertising, for example, women are usually pictured with a man, a child, or simply with the product to be sold. Only occasionally are they seen with other women; when they are, their attention is almost always directed to a man or the product. The women's movement, quite rightly, has recognized that it must challenge society's contention that women should be competitive with each other, for trust in other women is the key element of concerted political action.

But what about the poster child? While television bombards women with images of themselves as sex objects, disabled children are seldom seen on series, specials, or commercials. Once a year, the telethon saturates the screen with images of disabled children for twenty-four to forty-eight hours. After that, the disabled child, like the disabled adult, is "out of sight, out of mind." This programming format contributes to the popularly held notion that disabled and non-disabled children should be separate: an idea that translates easily into segregated schools for disabled kids, resulting in an absence of disabled children from every aspect of community life. Thus, while the beauty pageant format tries to separate women from each other, the telethon format separates disabled children from everybody.

More insidiously still, the message of the telethon is also that of separation. The telethon portrays disabled people as victims who need only to be cured, reinforcing the belief that disabled people can never fit into society unless they are cured. Quite wrongly, the telethon suggests that cures are the only acceptable solution to the exclusion of disabled people—and that society has no current obligation to accommodate those disabled people labeled "incurable." To a telethon supporter, a disabled person's inability to go to the second floor of a building is not due to the lack of an elevator or a wheelchair ramp; it is the result of the individual's sad "condition." By portraying disabled children as victims of a tragic fate, telethon organizers depend on the sympathy a crippled child engenders in the telethon viewer, knowing that pity will encourage the viewer to give money. But money alone, without efforts to eliminate the existing physical and attitudinal barriers that keep disabled people separate, is merely a salve for society's conscience.

Both disabled people and the parents of disabled children have strongly criticized the false images telethons generate and perpetuate. Disability rights advocates who themselves were poster children now view that experience in the context of a disability civil rights perspective, speaking out against telethons because they contribute so significantly to the public's negative perception of disabled people. Disability rights advocates have thus paralleled the efforts of feminists who have attacked beauty pageants for their commercial exploitation of women's bodies. To view pageants and telethons in terms of their exploitation of women and disabled children binds the women's and disability movements in a fundamental way. We are both exploited for grossly commercial purposes and for deeply rooted motives that reach far back into history. When we as disabled women and feminists can see a part of the other in the "mirror" of the telethon/beauty pageant, we will have come a long way in understanding the overlapping goals of our respective movements. But we must also remember: beauty pageants and telethons are liked cracked mirrors. Everything we see in them is distorted. The closer we get, the more we can see how the images and programming format skew our perceptions. Yet a step backwards also can be instructive. If the feminist steps back and views the telethon, for instance, from an historical and political perspective, then she will see the program to accurately reflect a centuries-old tradition of prejudice toward and exclusion of disabled people.

The nature and history of prejudice towards disabled people was recently documented in an amicus brief for the U.S. Supreme Court case *Consolidated Rail Corp. v. Darrone:*[1]

Disabled people throughout history have been regarded as incomplete human beings—"defectives." In early societies this view of disabled people resulted in persecution, neglect, and death. These practices gradually gave way to the more humanitarian belief that disabled people should be given care and protection. Persecution was largely replaced by pity, but the exclusion and segregation of disabled people remained unchallenged. Over the years, the false belief that disabled people were incompetent and dependent upon charity, custodial care, and protection became firmly imbedded in the public consciousness. The invisibility of disabled Americans was simply taken for granted and the innate biological and physical "inferiority" of disabled people was considered self-evident. (p. 1248)

For a woman staring into the telethon mirror, the assumptions about a disabled person's "self-evident" physical inferiority closely parallel those arguments once used to deny women an education and the right to vote. The particular argument contended that a woman's small stature and lesser muscle strength obviously proved that women were physically and mentally inferior to men.[2] This "innate inferiority" theory served to justify the exclusion of women from all aspects of society. Looking deeper into the telethon mirror, the feminist will see that "disability" implies much more than mere physical limitation:

For the individual who does have a physical or mental limitation the social consequences of this limitation bear no relationship to the disabling condition. For example, being paralyzed means far more than being unable to walk—it has meant being excluded from public school, being denied employment opportunities, and being deemed an "unfit" parent. These injustices co-exist in an atmosphere of charity and concern for disabled people. (*Con. Rail v. Darrone*, p. 13)

The dominant attitude of "charitable concern," which guided disability policy for decades, underwent a profound and historic shift in the 1970s. On the federal level, two landmark laws were enacted that set the stage for disabled children and adults to lead more meaningful, integrated, and independent lives: the Education for All Handicapped Children Act, also known as PL 94-142, enacted in 1976, and Section 504 of the 1973 Rehabilitation Act.[3] PL 94-142 requires that all disabled children, regardless of the nature or severity of their disability, receive a free, appropriate public education with non-disabled children to the maximum extent possible. Section 504 bars discrimination on the basis of disability in federally funded programs; a 1974 amendment to the rehabilitation act provided a comprehensive definition of disability, which takes into account society's stigmatizing views of certain types of disabilities.[4] For example, a burned person may have facial scars but be lacking in any impairment that limits a life activity. If a federally funded employer refuses to hire such a person out of fears that clients will be uncomfortable with the scars, the scarred individual is protected under the law and can file a discrimination complaint.

These laws were passed in a climate of changing legal mandates affecting not only disabled people but also women and racial minorities, who paved the way in the 1960s with the passage of the Civil Rights

Act. Title VI of the act prohibits racial discrimination in all programs receiving federal funds; Title VII prohibits employment discrimination against women and minorities, extending provisions to all employers engaging in interstate commerce, not merely those who receive federal funds. Women further benefited from the changing times by scoring two more significant victories in the seventies. The Supreme Court decision *Roe v. Wade* upheld a woman's right to abortion, and the passage of Title IX of the Education Amendments of 1972 prohibited sex discrimination in educational institutions receiving federal funds.[5]

Title VI of the Civil Rights Act and Title IX of the Education Amendments are the legal antecedents of Section 504. Section 504 is patterned after and has antidiscrimination language almost identical to both statutes.[6] This similarity in language attests to the federal government's recognition that disabled people as a group have been subject to discrimination and deserve the same basic civil rights protections that have been given to minorities and women. Yet despite the passage of laws guaranteeing the rights of disabled people, society persists in its view that disabled people are inferior beings.

The feminist before the mirror—who now has a firm grasp of the historical roots of prejudice towards disabled people and a specific understanding of the rolelessness of disabled women in society—must see fully one more aspect of a disabled woman's life if she is to integrate disabled women's issues into her political work. She must understand how the dual status of being both disabled and female affects the disabled woman's political concerns and priorities. A disabled woman formulates her political priorities from a unique identity, one that forces her to evaluate her political goals and choices differently from her non-disabled sisters. For instance, a disabled woman may be drawn to issues that affect her primarily because of her identity as a disabled individual, and secondarily because of her gender. Disabled people have been denied, and in some cases are still denied, equal voting access due to physical barriers and restrictive laws.

Secondly, a disabled women's dual status as both disabled and female influences her approach to political issues. Often, non-disabled and disabled women will agree on the larger issue but differ on either the solution to or the formulation of the specific problem. Say, for example, that both groups are protesting violence against women. The non-disabled women will organize a march to persuade the city council to allocate more money for street lighting. The disabled women, in contrast, will organize a different protest to persuade the para-transit bus company to operate wheelchair-accessible buses at night. The disabled woman has limited access to evening activities. What access she does have will be increased and made safer if she spends less time on the street. While the solution of better street lighting certainly benefits the disabled women, unless her higher priority of night transportation is addressed, it is unlikely that the march organizers will get any disabled women to participate.

In another example, a meeting may be called to protest police harassment of prostitutes. The disabled woman agrees that police harassment is an issue, but her concern may be directed toward police behavior that assumes any woman with slurred speech is drunk, ignoring the possibility that she may have a speech impairment. Or the disabled woman's concern may be with an officer's patronizing attitude that a disabled woman out alone should be escorted home "for her own good." While both disabled and non-disabled woman agree on the theme, the specifics of the issue differ.

Finally, the disabled woman determines her political priorities on the basis of "double" discrimination. This doubling of the discrimination factor can be seen in education, where sex discrimination combined with the segregation of disabled children has had a devastating effect on the education of disabled girls. The attempts of educators to remedy sexist curriculum materials never reach the disabled girl, because those nonsexist materials never get to the special classes in the segregated school. In employment, the double discrimination effect can be seen in the relative wage amounts of disabled women. Disabled women make less, on the average, than either non-disabled women or disabled men (Bowe 1984).

It should be clear by now that cracked mirrors, though occasionally useful, are more often dangerous, for they perpetuate stereotypes and divide women whose stronger political image is a united one. To both the politically minded disabled woman and to the activist feminist, the benefits of coalition work between the women's movement and the disability rights movement must be obvious. Disabled women represent 8.5 percent of all working-age women in the United States (Bowe 1984). The women's movement, by incorporating disability issues in its political agenda, moves a step closer to its goal of including all women in its movement. The disability rights movement, in turn, by aligning itself with the women's movement, gains a valuable ally in its struggle for the full participation of disabled people within all aspects of society.

What may be less obvious, however, is that the political ties between the two movements can be effected best by yet a third group of women: the mothers of disabled children. Like disabled women, they must cope with issues that link them to both movements. In all of the following areas—abortion/Baby Doe, education, voting, and employment—the mother of a disabled child has a stake because of her disabled child. Early in her child's life the mother of a disabled child will begin battling for her child's educational rights. Later, when the child is grown, the mother will be looking for needed services and civil rights laws that will enable her son or daughter to achieve an independent adulthood. The women's movement can give the parent of a disabled child support as a mother; it can also remedy her childcare needs by linking them with the childcare needs of all mothers. The disability rights movement can give her support as an advocate for her child.

For feminists, the inclusion of mothers of disabled children into the women's movement can serve as a bridge to the issues of the disability rights movement. Both feminists and mothers of disabled children have the same relationship to the disability rights movement: they have vital interests in seeing movement goals realized, but they will always be a little apart from it simply because they themselves are not disabled. This is not to say that feminists and mothers of disabled children have secondary roles in the disability rights movement; it merely means that their relationship to the movement is different from that of a disabled person.

NEW VISIONS: MOVEMENT ISSUES, COALITION EFFORTS

Parenting a Disabled Child: A Feminist Issue
In recent years the women's movement, recognizing that mothers, too, are working women, has given priority to such issues as childcare in setting working agendas. However, the childcare needs of mothers of disabled children are virtually invisible in the development of consciousness and policy. It is estimated that 10 percent of children under the age of 21 are disabled (Gliedman and Roth 1980). Almost one-fourth of all disabled children are raised by single parents. Among disabled children under age 17, 23 percent are living with only one parent, compared to only 16 percent of non-disabled children (Czajka 1984).

The reality of the lives of mothers of disabled children radically extends the traditionally perceived boundaries of motherhood. Mothers of disabled children must become not only experts in education and medicine; they must also become advocates and organizers in order to ensure the most basic rights and services for their children. The need to become an advocate and organizer is especially true for the mother who tries to secure an appropriate education for her disabled child. This process is inherently politicizing. It forces women to deal with the system. It is assertiveness-training boot camp.

The experience of these women is of critical importance to the women's movement, for mothers of disabled children have all the issues of other mothers and more. The women's movement cannot ignore these women. As with all disabled people, families with disabled children too often become isolated—out of sight and out of mind. Not only do these women need the support of the women's movement, they also have much to contribute to it.

Before these mothers can be integrated into the women's movement, however, their needs must be addressed. One important need is childcare/caretaking. While all mothers expect their infants and small children to be dependent, they also know that the dependence will lessen as the child grows up; changing diapers, feeding, and dressing last only so long.[7] Some parents of disabled children can, of course, look forward to the same progression. For others, however, primary daily caretaking does not end with early childhood. Parents of severely disabled children often must dress, feed, bathe, lift, transport, and groom their children until the parents die or the child leaves home. This is not only incredibly time-consuming but also is emotionally and physically draining. Changing diapers for two or three years is different from changing diapers for twenty-one.

If the parent cannot find adequate childcare services, her child must be institutionalized. Not only is institutionalization damaging to the child, it is many times more expensive than providing decent in-home services, which could enable the family to stay intact. In-home care for a severely disabled child costs approximately seven thousand dollars per year, compared to thirty-eight thousand dollars annually to institutionalize that child (U.S. Congress 1985). Nevertheless, public policy penalizes parents who choose to keep their severely disabled children at home. There are virtually no support services available. As bad as the childcare situation is for all mothers and children, it is worse for severely handicapped children. Generic services in the community for preschool children either lack access or simply refuse to admit severely disabled children. Mothers of young, school-age children often rely on neighborhood teenagers to baby-sit after school hours, but this option is generally unavailable for mothers of severely disabled children. Moreover, the need for care and supervision of severely disabled children extends beyond the age for non-disabled children. Even a highly assertive self-directing 16-year-old quadriplegic may still need some assistance in using a bathroom.

Childcare services have been given top priority by the women's movement. In promoting this cause, the women's movement has exposed the nation to the needs of nontraditional families—single mothers, working mothers, poor mothers, and minority mothers. More attention needs to be given to mothers of disabled children—mothers who might often also be single, working, minority, and poor.

The lack of childcare/caretaking services is only the first problem facing mothers of disabled children. The second most pressing issue is securing an appropriate education for her disabled child. It is here that the mother's advocacy skills are tested to the extreme. As important as an education is for any child, it is only within the past ten years that disabled children have had a legal right to receive a public education. In 1975, Congress passed the Education for All Handicapped Children Act (referred to as the EHA, or PL 94-142). This law was enacted in response to a long history of segregation and outright exclusion of disabled children from school.

The EHA is landmark legislation not only because it recognizes the right of every disabled child to a free, appropriate education in the least restrictive environment, but also because it gives parents a key role in educational planning and the ability to challenge school district decisions through a comprehensive system of due-process protections. However, as with all laws, the EHA is not self-executing, and theory and reality are often quite different. School administrators, trained to see themselves as professional experts with ultimate knowledge of what is best for the child, have not always welcomed the new role of parents. Special-education systems have been established around this "professional expertise" and its authority; parents who have been taught that the school knows best and who have relied on the advice of professionals since their child's birth also may have trouble assuming authority. Mothers have the additional burden of being women within a largely male-dominated hierarchical system.

In order for a mother to assure an appropriate education for her child, she must learn the skills to interact in this realm of professionalism and bureaucracy. She must not only develop the knowledge to evaluate educational and medical advice but she must also learn to advocate, negotiate, and organize.

As with any entrenched system, there is a vested interest in the status quo, and there is too much work and too little time. The child of an inactive mother will get what is available, which is not always what the child needs. In order to assure that the needs of the child will be addressed, mothers must learn to confront and manipulate the system. Thousands of "ordinary housewives" have become activists through the experience of having a disabled child, and the supermom syndrome has been imposed through necessity: in addition to providing daily care, rearing other children, running a home, and often having a job, mothers of disabled children also must constantly fight for services and for an appropriate education for their children.

Through the years, mothers of disabled children have learned (as have women in the women's movement) that individual efforts alone are not enough to effect systemic change. In addition to becoming experts in education, medicine, transportation, recreation, equipment, and so on, mothers of disabled children also have become potent community organizers. All across the country mothers have organized into parent groups, which press for positions before school boards and community councils and lobby for legislation in state capitols.

These women are part of the women's movement, yet neither they nor the women's movement may know it. These women have developed skills and strategies that could help reform all education. This is a resource that should be tapped. Here are women who have developed leadership in the context of working as part of a community. These women should be seen as role models—not idealized as valiant heroes in the face of tragedy, but hailed as women who have learned to take charge and make change.

Unfortunately, the vast majority of mothers of disabled children still do not know their rights and have not been given the support they need to confront the system. These women, too, must be a concern to the women's movement. These women are isolated; the women's movement should reach out to bring them in.

The Abortion/Baby Doe Controversy: A Disability Perspective

Just as the mothers of disabled children have a different perspective when considering parenting issues, so, too, do disabled women have a different perspective when examining abortion rights and the Baby Doe controversy. The disabled woman is concerned not only with abortion rights but also with the right to be free from involuntary sterilization. Further, the Baby Doe controversy involves the disabled woman both as a parent or potential parent and as a disability rights advocate.

The disabled woman's concern with the right to be free from involuntary sterilization stems from an important difference in the social roles of disabled and non-disabled women. In the past, feminists have struggled with being cast only in the limited role of mothers. As a U.S. Supreme Court case justifying the enactment of protective work legislation for women stated, "And as healthy mothers are essential to vigorous offspring, the physical well being of women becomes an object of public interest and care in order to preserve the strength and vigor of the race."[8]

Thus, the perception that women are weaker than men and are to be seen primarily as mothers has sometimes resulted in protective legislation. Disabled women, however, have never been considered fit as mothers. One psychologist comments, "Historically, child custody suits almost always have ended with custody being awarded to the non-disabled parent, regardless of whether affection or socio-economic advantages could have been offered by the disabled parent" (Vash 1981:115). The presumed inferiority of the disabled person has been translated frequently into social policy that condones the involuntary sterilization of mentally retarded boys and girls. In 1930, for example, twenty-eight states had sterilization statutes on the books (Burgdorf and Burgdorf 1977). In light of this history, it is imperative that reproductive rights activists advocate social policy that accounts for the right of all women to decide whether or not to have a child.

The second issue, the Baby Doe controversy, is a hotly contested debate involving the right of a parent to withhold life-sustaining medical treatment from a severely disabled infant. In "Baby Doe" situations, the infant is born with a severe disability and needs medical attention to survive. If given, the medical treatment will prolong the life of the child, but it will not lessen the child's disability. An example is that of an infant with Down's syndrome. She or he has a permanent mental impairment that may range from mild to severe. Let us say that shortly after birth the infant develops a blood infection and needs medical treatment to save its life. But the treatment, which may be very expensive, will not lessen the infant's mental impairment. These parents decide they would rather withhold treatment, thus pitting their right to privacy in making decisions regarding the welfare of their child against the right of the disabled child to live. Part of the parents' rationale for withholding medical treatment relies on the telethon "disability as tragedy" theory. Applied in this context, that argument says that a disabled infant imposes such an emotional and financial burden on the family that the state has no right to prohibit the parents from relieving themselves of the burden. Viewed from the parents' perspective, the argument appears compelling; take away the blinders imposed by the "disability as tragedy" theory, however, and the Baby Doe issue becomes a clear-cut case of civil rights. Viewed from a civil rights context, a disabled infant should not receive a different standard of medical care solely because of her or his disability. If a non-disabled infant developed a blood infection, there would be no question of a right to life-sustaining medical treatment.

In a recent case involving the validity of regulations prohibiting discriminatory treatment of disabled newborns, two public-interest law firms representing disability rights and women's rights (The Disability Rights, Education and Defense Fund and the Women's Defense Fund), filed a joint friend-of-the-court brief. It argued that the civil rights protections that apply to disabled adults also should apply to disabled infants, noting that the outdated stereotypes once used to exclude women and minorities from medical care (society's perception that women and minorities are "subhuman," "sick," or "inferior") are now used to limit a disabled infant's right to medical care.[9]

The cooperation between the women's movement and the disability rights movement in the Baby Doe controversy illustrates how effectively coalition work can function when viewed in the context of civil rights.

FLEXING MUSCLES:
THE STRUGGLE FOR CIVIL RIGHTS

In the past one hundred years, the women's movement has been fairly successful in gaining for women many of the civil rights that other Americans took for granted. These rights, including the right of equal opportunity for education, equal access to the ballot box, and equal opportunity for employment, form the basis for political power in this country. No movement for self-determination of its people can succeed unless it has achieved three goals: an educated leadership that provides role models for an educated and politically informed citizenry; equal access to the voting booth so that politicians perceive the group as a voting bloc whose needs must be addressed; and economic power, based on the jobs of the constituency, allowing movement strategies such as boycotts, class-action lawsuits, and campaign contributions to sympathetic politicians to be implemented. More basically, everyone needs jobs to survive. When movement goals include employment rights, the movement directly benefits constituents.

The women's movements have produced the unrestricted right to vote since 1920, strong federal employment protections since 1964, and protection from discrimination in education since 1972.[10] For the disability rights movement, successes have been much more recent. The first disability civil rights statute, Section 504 of the Rehabilitation Act, wasn't passed until 1973. Implementing regulations were not signed until 1977.[11] The Equal Access to Voting Rights Act was passed in 1984.[12]

Disabled women's struggles for education, voting rights, and employment force them to fight the sexism and disability discrimination inherent in all of society's institutions. In all three issues, the work done by the disability movement and women's movement provides fertile ground for coalition work.

The Right to an Education

The disabled woman's struggle for an education is plagued by double stereotyping and a lack of role models. One disabled woman in six has had fewer than eight years of formal education, as compared to only one out of every twenty-eight non-disabled women. Only 16 percent of all disabled women are likely to report some college education, compared with 31 percent of all non-disabled women (Bowe 1984). One way to show the devastating effect of the lack of role models for disabled women is to contrast the disabled woman's plight with the successful efforts of non-disabled women to obtain higher education and to show the positive effects of role models on nineteenth-century feminists.

One hundred years ago society believed the sole purpose of educating women was to serve men better. Rousseau (1908) stated:

The whole education of women ought to be relative to men. To please them, to be useful to them, to make themselves loved and honored by them, to educate them when young, to care for them when grown, to counsel them, to console them and to make life sweet and agreeable to them—these are the duties of women at all times and what should be taught them from their infancy. (p. 263)

Early education for women in the United States consisted of embroidery, French, singing, and playing the harpsichord (Flexner 1973).

Feminists believed that education was the first step toward solving the problems of women's inequality. But women who wanted to learn something more than domestic skills had to start their own schools. The first school for women, Troy Female Seminary, opened its doors in New York State in 1821. The school endeavored to teach the natural, as well as the domestic, sciences. Mount Holyoke, the first college for women, opened in 1837. Gradually, women were allowed into state-supported colleges, although their curriculum differed from that of the men (Clinton 1984).

In the 1870s there were still many obstacles. Women were thought to be biologically unable to compete with men because a study showed that the average man's brain weighed forty-nine grams and the average woman's brain weighed forty-four grams (Clinton 1984). Even more damaging was the notion that a woman who pursued a college education would become disabled. A best-selling book in 1873, *Sex in Education*, stated that "identical education of the two sexes is a crime before God and humanity, that physiology protests against, and experience weeps over" (Clarke 1873: 127). The author maintained that "amenor-rhoea, menorrhagia, dysmenorrhea, hysteria, anemia, chorea and the like" resulted from college education for women (p. 48).

Despite male opposition, some women did obtain an education—but the only way they could put it to use was by teaching small children. This was seen as an extension of motherhood, and was, there-fore, acceptable. It was not acceptable for women to teach high school, or to become school administrators. And a woman certainly was not allowed to teach at a university. A woman who was intelligent and wanted to teach at a college could teach only at one of the women's colleges, and she often had to go to a European university to obtain a Ph.D.

The visible presence of women professors in female universities—for example, two-thirds of the faculty at Smith were women (Clinton 1984)—first created role models for the young women of the generation after the Civil War. The educated middle-class women who emerged from these women's colleges provided the constituency and leadership for the feminist movement. A woman who was reminded of Rousseau's dictum on the education of women could point to M. Carey Thomas, the dean of Bryn Mawr; or to Belva Lockwood, the first woman admit-ted to practice law before the U.S. Supreme Court; or to Alice Freeman Palmer, who combined marriage and academics (Clinton 1984). She could respond to a comment on her small brain by mentioning Martha Mitchell, who discovered a comet; Margaret Maltby, the first American woman to do original work in physics; or Elizabeth Blackwell, the first woman doctor. As for the notion that education would make her sick, she could note that all the college professors she had seen appeared to be in fine health.

But for disabled women, the situation was far different. Non-dis-abled women could justify some amount of learning as a necessity in order to educate their children and to be pleasing to men. Disabled women were not seen as being able to take care of men, nor were they seen as competent to have or to care for children. They could not fit the Rousseauistic ideal of a nurturer. Also, the biological arguments that impeded women also applied to disabled women.

On the other hand, a disabled woman's education was vital to achieving any kind of independence. As one woman put it, "We can't do manual labor, so we have to cultivate our minds. The more disabled you are, the more you need a good education" (Matthews 1983: 46). How-ever, disabled children, when they were educated, were educated in special, segregated schools. Blind and deaf children, for example, were educated in large state residential facilities where they were taught braille and lipreading (Burgdorf and Burgdorf 1975). The education disabled children received in these segregated schools was vastly inferior to that in public elementary schools. After all, the belief went, if a disabled girl would never have to carry the burdens of motherhood or wifehood, why should education provide anything more than the survival skills necessary to prevent the child from becoming a beggar or a criminal?

The disabled woman who aspired to a higher education (assuming she received some education at a special school and had learned to read and write, or was educated at home) had no role models save one: Helen Keller. Her achievement was so singular as to be the exception that proves the rule. Twenty female college professors together show that a woman can be a professor; one educated disabled woman alone seems only to show how difficult it is. The typical disabled woman had no role models, no one to support her ambitions, and no school that would modify a physically inaccessible campus to admit her. The impetus for higher education that derived from female role models and a supportive community of educated women did not extend to the woman with a disability.

The difference is clear. Non-disabled women in the nineteenth century were struggling for the right to go to college. Disabled women barely were able to achieve an elementary education. In the 1970s the situation appeared to change when Congress passed amendments to the education act. Title IX prohibited discrimination on the basis of sex in all activities that received federal funding. This law affected all levels of education but has had most effect on the inclusion of women in higher education. In 1973, Section 504 of the Rehabilitation Act, using language similar to that in Title IX, prohibited all federally funded programs from discriminating against disabled people. The 504 regulations, enacted to specify an institution's obligation under the law, stated that disabled people had the right to an equal opportunity to participate in all school programs and activities, even if that meant making a building accessible to wheelchairs, or providing readers and equipment for blind students. It seemed that disabled girls and women, by the end of the seventies, had laws in place protecting them from both sex and disability discrimination in their attempts to secure an education.

In 1983, however, the Supreme Court ruled on a case that severely restricted the discrimination protections of women and disabled people. In Grove City v. Bell, the court narrowed the definition of recipient to include only the department that received federal financial assistance.[13] Previous to this decision any federal money a university received obligated every department of the university to comply with the requirements of Title IX. This case referred specifically to Title IX, but because the court interpreted language common to both statutes, the implications for disabled people are just as restrictive. Thus, it is now conceivable that within a university, an anthropology department that directly receives a federal grant cannot discriminate against women or disabled people in its policies or practices, whereas the chemistry department, if it receives no direct federal assistance, is under no such obligation.

The Grove City decision sparked a coalition effort between disability and women's groups. Recognizing that the similar language of Title IX and Section 504 meant that an attack on one was an attack on all, both groups have actively supported legislation designed to overturn the Supreme Court decision. Called the Civil Rights Restoration Act of 1985, this legislative effort marks the first time disability and women's groups have worked together in passing legislation. Though the bill did not survive the legislative session, it has been reintroduced in subsequent sessions, and the continuing coalition effort to get this bill passed will no doubt pave the way for more joint efforts.

The successful strategies to achieve educational equity for disabled and non-disabled women have much in common. As we have seen, role models are as important to disabled girls as to non-disabled girls. Authors of sex-equity materials need to include positive images of disabled women. And yet—those images will not help disabled girls if they remain in segregated classrooms, isolated from other students. This is where women's groups, parent groups, and disability organizations need to work together to ensure the mainstreaming of disabled children into regular classrooms whenever possible.

The battle to learn for disabled and non-disabled children begins at the kindergarten door. Only when the disability and women's movements work together at all levels of education—primary, secondary, and post-secondary—can there be a chance for educational equity for every child.

The Right to Vote
The nineteenth-century feminists who strove to educate themselves soon looked to the ballot box as a way of acquiring political self-determination.

It took women seventy-two years to get the vote. From 1848, the year women resolved to "secure themselves their sacred right to the elective franchise,"[14] to 1920, the year ratification of the Nineteenth Amendment affirmed their right to vote, women battled stereotypes that they were biologically inferior to men, eternally childlike, and mentally unfit.[15]

Today, women's right to vote is unquestioned, yet a woman who is disabled still may be denied this basic right. If she has a mental disability she may be subject to state laws that prohibit her from voting.[16] If she is physically disabled she may face architectural and communication barriers that limit her right.

Laws denying mentally disabled people the right to vote are based on the premise that it is in the state's interest to exclude from voting those individuals unable to make a rational decision. Each state has the power to determine its voter qualifications. All but ten states have some statute restricting the rights of mentally disabled people from voting. The problem with many of these statutes is that they unfairly generalize about the ability of certain classes of people labeled "mentally disabled" to make rational decisions. The assumption of these laws is that an individual judged to be mentally disabled within the meaning of the statute is totally incapacitated for all purposes, including voting. For example, take guardianship. Twenty-four states disqualify from voting those individuals placed under guardianship. However, the criteria for placing someone under guardianship is merely that the individual is incapable of handling his or her financial affairs. It is possible that an individual may not be able to save money or balance a checkbook, but may be able to decide rationally which candidate to support. The inability to handle money does not imply that the individual is incompetent in every area of life.[17]

A similar argument may be made against the laws that prohibit voting by anyone adjudged "insane."[18] While there may be certain individuals within that classification who should not vote, the law risks excluding those who are capable of voting. One psychiatric study of "insane" individuals in institutions concluded that most had the ability to comprehend the act of voting (Klein and Grossman 1968).

The stereotypes underlying these laws—that *all* individuals under guardianship are incompetent to vote, and *all* individuals labeled insane are similarly unfit to vote—must be examined. If the decision to deny an individual the right to vote is to be based on an inability to make rational decisions, that judgment should be made on a case-by-case basis and not as the result of an individual's mental disability classification.

Another problem with laws denying mentally disabled people the right to vote is the often vague definition of mental capacity in the statutes. Several states deny the right to vote to persons considered idiots. Idiocy has been interpreted broadly to mean "mental feebleness."[19]

In the beginning of the twentieth century, an attempt to define and identify "feeblemindedness" was developed in the form of an IQ test. In

1912 Henry Goddard administered his intelligence test to immigrants. The results showed that 83 percent of the Jews, 80 percent of the Hungarians, 79 percent of the Italians, and 87 percent of the Russians tested were "feeble-minded" (Goddard 1913). Because the test was given in English to largely non-English speaking people, it is easy to see why so many people failed it.

While individuals labeled mentally disabled have had to contend with laws that unfairly stereotype their abilities, physically disabled people have had their right to vote restricted by physical and communications barriers. These barriers affect those who are blind, deaf, and orthopedically disabled. They include architecturally inaccessible sites, voting machines that are impossible to use without assistance, ballots that are not in braille or in language that a learning-disabled person can understand. The right to privacy is denied when a disabled person is barred from choosing her own assistant to help operate an inaccessible voting machine or to read the ballot. In some states, disabled people may vote by absentee ballot. However, this method prevents disabled people from considering and reacting to last-minute political developments because absentee ballots must be mailed several days in advance of an election.

Advocates tried for years to pass legislation mandating accessible voting sites. In 1984, the Equal Access to Voting Rights Act (PL 98-435) was passed, mandating either accessible precinct polling places or accessible alternative polling places. Paper ballots must be provided for those unable to operate a voting machine, and blind people are able to have a person of their choice assist them. The law, however, only applies to federal elections. Each state will have to pass similar legislation to secure the rights of disabled individuals in state and municipal elections.

Unlike their non-disabled counterparts, who secured the right to vote in every election without restriction, disabled women still must look to each state to determine their status as voting citizens. Legal and physical barriers that make it difficult for disabled women to vote discourage involvement in the political process. The women's movement can do much to encourage the political involvement of disabled women by working on voter access issues. This is yet another area where the women's and disability rights movements can effectively combine forces. For example, women's groups can do voter outreach to disabled women. That means having fact sheets and issue papers in braille and on tape. Voter outreach extends to registration: women's groups need to visit nursing homes, state hospitals, and mental hospitals to register women to vote. Later, they must be ready to defend their newly registered voters from challenges of unfitness by state officials. Also, women's groups that support candidates for office should know their candidate's position on removing restrictions on the voting rights of disabled people. Finally, political clubs should lobby state voting officials to identify accessible polling places within the materials the state mails to voters. The clubs also can survey accessible voting places in precincts and encourage officials to provide as many accessible places as possible.

Employment Rights

In the analysis of employment discrimination, those flickering images of the beauty queen and the poster child return to haunt us. The intelligent, professional, career-seeking woman still is plagued by the constraints of the beauty queen image. She faces career stagnation and frustration caused by the closed male mentor, or "old boy," network. To those men who still wield power, the career woman too often is merely an elegant, dispensable ornament, not to be taken seriously. Viewed this way, she is almost never considered an integral part of a management team.

Ornament though she be, the beauty queen fares better than the poster child. Disabled people, and disabled women especially, are not considered able to work. Their inability to work is seen as a natural result of their disabling condition. Only 23.5 percent of disabled women are in the labor force. Of this percentage, 15.5 percent are unemployed. Compare those figures to the employment percentages of non-disabled women. Sixty-four percent of non-disabled women are in the labor force; thier unemployment rate is 7.5 percent (Bowe 1984). That the high unemployment rate among disabled women can be attributed partially to disability discrimination can be seen from surveys reflecting employers' attitudes towards disabled people. In one study, employers were asked to rank various groups in terms of which ones they would be most likely to hire. The list included physically and mentally disabled groups, minority groups, student militants, prison parolees, senior citizens, and "neutral" groups such as whites and Canadians. The study showed that physically disabled groups ranked lower than all minority groups, senior citizens, student militants, and prison parolees, but higher than all mentally disabled groups (Colbert, Kalish, and Chang 1973). In another study, employers were found more likely to hire a prison parolee or a formal mental patient than a person with epilepsy (Triandis and Patterson 1963). In a third study, 50 percent of the employers queried said they would never consider hiring a blind or mentally retarded person for any type of job (Williams 1972).

Disabled women, unlike disabled men, must contend with yet another aspect of societal stereotyping. This is the effect of a disabled woman's rolelessness. Non-disabled women, by virtue of their roles as mothers and nurturers, traditionally have been limited to job categories such as teaching and nursing. The disabled woman has been denied even these opportunities. While feminists struggle to enter nontraditional jobs, to a disabled woman every job is a nontraditional job.

Take teaching as an example. In the late sixties in New York City, a woman in a wheelchair was denied a license to teach in the city's schools on the ground that "being confined to a wheelchair as a result of poliomyelitis, she was physically and mentally unsuited for teaching." As a result of a lawsuit by the woman, the board of education reversed itself and granted the plaintiff a license and a teaching position. In another example, a blind English teacher was denied a job with the Philadelphia School District because she was certified as having a "chronic or acute physical defect." The court found this stereotyping unconstitutional.[20]

Thus, a disabled woman seeking employment risks discrimination twice: once by virtue of her gender, again by virtue of her disability. This double dose of discrimination is reflected strikingly in the economic disparity of disabled women compared to disabled men, or to non-disabled women. Almost 30 percent of all disabled women have incomes that fall below the poverty line. Compare this figure to 20 percent of all disabled men and 10 percent of all non-disabled women who have incomes below the poverty line. Non-disabled women earn 58 percent of what non-disabled males earn; disabled women earn only 51 percent (Bowe 1984).

These statistics are in part the result of employer policies that operate to systemically exclude women or disabled people from jobs. Two of these practices are the Bona Fide Occupational Qualification (or BFOQ) and the use of blanket medical standards. A BFOQ often presumes that a job position can be performed only by a member of a specified sex. Often the assumption is based on the belief that women cannot lift heavy weights, cannot supervise men, or should not work late at night. In one case the Maryland Racing Commission denied a jockey's license to a woman, arguing that only men could be jockeys. This was ruled illegal. In another case the court ruled against prohibiting a woman from transferring to another position simply because company officials believed the job too "strenuous" for one of her sex.[21]

The assumption that only men can perform certain kinds of jobs finds a disability parallel in blanket medical standards. These medical standards merely reveal the presence of a disability rather than indicate any job-related limitation. Some employers, for example, exclude all applicants with a history of cancer. Others refuse to hire anyone who has lost leg (DREDF 1982). One employer fired a truck assembler when it was discovered he had only one kidney.[22] Others exclude from all job positions those with a history of epilepsy (DREDF 1982). Most of these blanket medical standards have been found illegal unless it can be shown that the medical standard is related to the essential requirements of the job.[23]

Existing statutes prohibit employment discrimination against both women and disabled people. However, women have broader employment protections. Title VII of the Civil Rights Act prohibits employment discrimination based on sex by all employers with fifteen or more employees. Disabled people's protections, for the most part covered under the 1973 Rehabilitation Act, are limited to employers who are federal contractors or recipients of federal funds.

The laws that prohibit discrimination based on sex and disability have as their larger purpose the inclusion and participation of women and disabled people in society. That means eliminating discriminatory practices and in some cases instituting affirmative-action programs to remedy past discrimination. However, the disabled job-seeker faces an additional barrier besides the attitudinal ones: she or he faces physical barriers. A disabled person who is qualified to perform a job still faces discrimination when the employer says, "Yes, you are qualified for the job, but your wheelchair cannot get into the office because of the two steps, so I won't hire you." Or the employer might say, "Sure, you can fill out the forms, but you cannot reach the shelf where the forms are stored, so I will not hire you." The disabled job-seeker, first victimized by prejudice, now is hindered by an inaccessible environment. The solution for this dilemma—to require employers to make "reasonable accommodations to the known physical or mental limitation of an otherwise qualified handicapped applicant or employee"—is the heart of Section 504.[24] The reasonable accommodation requirement means, in essence, that employers should try to adjust the job to the individual. That can entail such simple remedies as removing a physical barrier, providing a piece of equipment that will enable the person to do the job, or adjusting a work schedule. The qualified disabled person who could not get into the office because of two steps could be accommodated through a ramp. The woman who could not reach the forms could be accommodated by either moving the forms or by lowering the shelf.

The law requires employers only to make "reasonable" accommodations. Recent court decisions have been defining the parameters of what is reasonable. In *Nelson v. Thornburgh*, the court ruled that an employer had to provide readers for blind employees. In *Coleman v. Casey Board of Education*, a school district was ordered to allow a bus driver with only one leg to drive a bus modified with a hand clutch. Accommodations also are required for applicants. In *Stutt v. Freeman*, the court ruled that a dyslexic person who could not read a written examination for a heavy-equipment operator had to be accommodated by means of an oral test.[25]

The concept of reasonable accommodation to remedy employment discrimination is not unique to disability. In one case of sex discrimination, the court said that the refusal to hire a woman welder because there were no women's bathrooms was illegal. The judge then ordered the company to install a women's bathroom. In another sex discrimination case, one involving height requirements, the court ruled that if a woman worker's inability to reach the machinery was due to her height, a platform should be built to accommodate her.[26]

The reasonable accommodation argument also has sprung up in another women's rights issue, that of pregnancy leave. There are two schools of thought on this. One group says that a woman who becomes pregnant should be treated exactly the same as anyone else who has a temporarily disabling condition, and she should be subject to the standard leave policy of her company. In other words, if she has to be off work for six weeks following birth, but the company provides only a four-week leave policy, then the company can legally terminate her. The theory is that equal treatment in the workplace means equal opportunity to compete for the high-paying jobs that men have.

Women have been striving for equal treatment in the workplace from the time protection laws were enacted in the early twentieth century. The equal treatment argument flows from the nonaccepted notion that "protective" legislation undermines and restricts women's job opportunities. Some of this legislation has included weight-lifting limits; restrictions on the hours a woman could work; and mandatory, additional rest periods that were denied to men (Kanowitz 1969). Women have fought for many years to eliminate the paternalistic notion that as a class they cannot do certain kinds of labor. Having realized that protective legislation often prevents their access to skilled labor jobs, their rallying cry is equal treatment to compete for jobs (Williams 1982).

The second school of thought opposes this logic as it relates to the issue of pregnancy leave. Feminists of this school say that in the area of pregnancy leave, equal treatment of the sexes results in inequality for women. A company that applies a four-week leave policy to all workers has a disproportionate impact on women. Many pregnant women require more than four weeks leave and therefore face almost certain termination—a hardship that no man has to bear. They argue that an adequate leave policy—one that allows a pregnant woman time to deal with pregnancy, delivery, and recovery from childbearing—should not be viewed as an additional benefit that borders on protective legislation. In fact, they argue, an adequate leave time merely equalizes the outcomes for women in the job market. It removes a barrier to continued employment that exists only for women. They further draw the analogy that just as a disabled person is entitled to reasonable accommodation to remove a unique barrier presented by her or his disability, so, too, should a woman be allowed adequate leave time to remove the barrier presented by her pregnancy (Krieger and Cooney 1983).

It is too early to tell which argument will win favor with the divided feminist community. The use of a primarily disability-based solution to a women's rights issue merely illustrates again the crossover of issues and answers from the women's movement and the disability rights movement.

CONCLUSION

The disability rights movement and the women's movement share common goals for their members: equality of opportunity and full participation in all aspects of society. This includes parenting, reproductive choice, education, voting, and employment. However, equal opportunity and full participation can exist only in a society that values the individual as part of the social collective. This new society will allow all women, disabled or non-disabled, to make life choices based on their needs. It will fit jobs to people instead of discarding people who don't fit jobs. It will recognize our right to control our bodies, to educate ourselves, and to value both work and motherhood. No longer will the images of beauty queen and poster child reflect a woman's or a disabled person's lesser status in society. In our new society, each individual will be able to live in a community tha mirrors her true self, undistorted by the icons of a past age.

Notes

1. *Consolidated Rail Corp. v Darrone,* 104 S.Ct. 1248 (1984). A brief submitted in support of the argument that Section 504 of the Rehabilitation Act covers employment discrimination. Amici's argument attempted to prove the existence of widespread discrimination against disabled people. The court agreed and held that Section 504 does cover employment.

2. One nineteenth-century judge remarked, "Man is or should be woman's protector and defender. The natural and proper timidity and delicacy which belongs to the female sex evidently unfits it for many of the occupations

of civil life." *Bradwell v. Illinois*, 83 U.S. (15 Wallace) 130 (1873). This opinion upheld the right of a state to deny a woman an application for a license to practice as an attorney.

3. Education for All Handicapped Children Act, PL 94-142, 89 stat. 773 (codified as amended at 20 USC 1400–1420 (1976 & supp. V 1981); Rehabilitation Act of 1973, PL 93-112, 504, 87 stat. 355 (codified as amended at 29 USC 794) (supp. V 1981).

4. Rehabilitation Act Amendments of 1974, PL 93-516, 88 stat. 1617.

5. Civil Rights Act of 1964, 601, PL 88-352, 78 stat. 252 (codified at 42 USC 2000d (1976); Title VII, 42 USC 2000e; *Roe v. Wade*, 93 S.Ct. 705 (1972); Education Amendments of 1972, 901(a), PL 93-318, 86 stat. 373 (codified at 20 USC 168(a) (1982).

6. Title VI reads: "No person in the United States shall, on the ground of race, color, or national origin, be excluded from participation in, be denied the benefits of, or be subjected to discrimination under any program or activity receiving Federal financial assistance."

Title IX reads: "No person in the United States shall, on the basis of sex, be excluded from participation in, be denied the benefits of, or be subjected to discrimination under any education program or activity receiving Federal financial assistance."

Section 504 reads: "No otherwise qualified handicapped individual in the United States shall, solely by reason of his handicap, be excluded from participation in, be denied the benefits of, or be subjected to discrimination under any program or activity receiving Federal financial assistance."

7. Reference throughout to mothers is not intended to dismiss the involvement of fathers. It simply recognizes that mothers are most often primary caretakers.

8. *Muller v. Oregon*, 208 U.S. 412 (1908).

9. Brief of Amici Curie for Petitioners, *Margaret M. Heckler v. American Hospital Association*, no. 84-1529 (2 Cir. 1985) cert. granted.

10. Voting rights: "The right of citizens of the United States to vote shall not be denied or abridged by the United States, or any state on account of sex" (U.S. const. amend. XIX); employment protection: Title VII of the 1964 Civil Rights Act. 42 USC 2000e; education rights: Title IX of the Education Amendments of 1972, 20 USC 1681.

11. 42 fed. reg. 22,676 (1977), found at 34 CFR 104 and 45 CFR 84.

12. Equal Access to Voting Rights Act, PL 98-435.

13. *Grove City v. Bell*, 103 S.Ct. 1181 (1983).

14. Declaration of Sentiments and Resolutions Adopted by the Seneca Falls Convention, July 19–20, 1848.

15. One example from a nineteenth-century religious figure: "We do not believe women . . . are fit to have their own head. . . . Without masculine direction or control, she is out of her element, and a social anomaly, sometimes a hideous monster" (see Gurko 1974).

16. The term "mental disability" used here is meant to be a generic reference to anyone suffering or presumed to be suffering from a mental health problem. It includes people who are labeled "mentally retarded" as well as those labeled "mentally ill."

17. Mental Disability and the Right to Vote, 88 *Yale Law Journal* 1644–46, 1651 (1979).

18. "Mental Disability and the Right to Vote," p. 1645.

19. In *Re South Charleston Beal Law Election*, 3 Ohio NP, NS 373 (1905), the court noted that definitions such as "insanity," "idiocy," "lunacy," "imbecility," and "feeblemindedness" are general terms and refer to manifestation in language or conduct of a disease or a defect of the brain.

20. *Heumann v. Board of Education of the City of New York*, 320 F. Supp. 623, 624 (S.D. N.Y. 1970); *Gurmankin v. Constanzo*, 411 F. supp. 982 (E.D. Pa. 1976) aff'd 556 F.2d 184 (3 Cir. 1977).

21. *In Re Kusner v. Maryland Racing Commission*, no. 37,044 Circuit Court, Prince George's County, Md. (1968); *Weeks v. Southern Bell Telegraph and Telephone Co.*, 408 F.2d 228 (5 Cir. 1969).

22. *Dairy Equipment Co. v. Wis. DILHR*, 95 Wis. 2d 319, 290 NW 2d 330 (1980).

23. "Once a Plaintiff shows an employer denied him employment because of physical condition, the burden of persuasion shifts to the Federal employer to show that the criteria used are job related and the Plaintiff could not safely and effectively perform the essentials of the job." *Treadwell v. Alexander*, 707 F. 2d 473 474 (11 Cir. 1983).

24. 34 CFR 104.12(a), 45 CFR 84.12(a) (1982).

25. *Nelson v. Thornburgh*, 567 S. supp. 369 (ED Pa. 1983), aff'd 732 F.2d 146 (3 Cir. 1984); *Coleman v. Casey Board of Education*, 510 F. supp. 310 (WD Ky. 1980); *Stutt v. Freeman*, 694 F. 2d 666 (11 Cir. 1983).

26. EEOC Dec. No. 70–558, Feb. 19, 1970; EEOC Dec. No. 71-1418.

References

Bowe, F. 1984. *Disabled women in America*. Washington, D.C.: President's Committee on Employment of the Handicapped.

Burgdorf, R., and M. Burgdorf. 1977. The wicked witch is almost dead: Buck v. Bell. *Temple Law Quarterly* 50:995.

Clarke, E. 1873. *Sex in education; or, A fair chance for the girls*. New York: Arno Press. Reprinted 1972.

Clinton, C. 1984. *The other civil war*. New York: Hill and Wang.

Colbert, Kalish, and Chang. 1973. Two psychological portals of entry for disadvantaged groups. *Rehabilitation Literature* 32(7):194.

Czajka, J. 1984. *Digest of data on persons with disabilities*. Washington, D.C.: Congressional Research Service, Library of Congress.

DREDF. 1982. *Medical standards project: Final report*. Disability Rights Education and Defense Fund and Employment Law Center, Berkeley, California.

Franklin, P. 1977. Impact of disability on the family structure. *Social Security Bulletin* 40(5):3–18.

Gliedman, J., and W. Roth. 1980. *The unexpected minority: Handicapped children in America*. New York: Harcourt Brace Jovanovich.

Goddard, H. H. 1913. The Binet tests in relation to immigration. *Journal of Psycho-Asthetics* 18:105.

Gurko, M. 1974. *The ladies of Seneca Falls: The birth of the women's rights movements*. New York: Schocken Books.

International Rehabilitation Review. 1977. February. Entire issue.

Kanowitz, L. 1969. *Women and the law: The unfinished revolution*. Albuquerque: University of New Mexico Press.

Klein, M., and S. A. Grossman. 1968. Voting competence and mental illness. *Proceedings of the 76th Annual Convention, American Psychological Association* 3:701.

Kreiger, L. J., and P. N. Cooney. 1983. The Miller-Wohl controversy: Equal treatment, positive action and the meaning of women's equality. *Golden Gate Law Review* 3 (Summer).

Matthews, G. F. 1983. *Voices from the shadows.* Toronto, Canada: Women's Educational Press.

Rousseau, J. 1908. *L'Emile; or, A treatise on education.* Ed. by W. H. Payne. New York and London: D. Appleton and Co.

Safilios-Rothschild, C. 1977. Discrimination against disabled women. *International Rehabilitation Review.* (February):4.

Triandis, H. C., and C. H. Patterson. 1963. Indices of employer prejudice toward disabled applicants. *Journal of Applied Psychology* 47:52.

U.S. Congress. 1985. *Families with disabled children: Issue for the 80s. Hearings before the Select Committee on Children, Youth and Families,* 99th Congr., 1st sess.

Vash, C. 1981. *The psychology of disability.* New York: Springer.

Williams, C. A. 1972. Is hiring the handicapped good business? *Journal of Rehabilitation* 38(2):30.

Williams, W. 1982. The equality crisis. Some reflections on culture, courts, and feminism. *Women's Rights Law Report* 7:175.

Epilogue: Research and Politics to Come

MICHELLE FINE and ADRIENNE ASCH

We take pride and delight in the articles assembled in this collection, yet we do not hesitate to note that there is much more to learn. We hope readers have been engaged by the collected writings to the degree that they will take up the questions we now pose.

Girls and women have a range of disabling conditions. While we have tried to give attention to those with more hidden, less body altering disabilities, this book and the field in general do best at telling about the experiences of those who, according to Goffman (1963),[1] are the most stigmatized—those least able to pass. These pages capture the experience of women with what are considered the most severe disabilities—mental retardation, physical and sensory impairments, and cancer, for example. We need much more information about women whose disabilities may be less immediately noticeable, but are of no less concern to their emotional, social, or economic lives. Or, because they have said less, can one conclude that such disabilities are less of an issue and that these women have less to tell?

Psychoanalytic writers speculate that growing up with a disability is more devastating than acquiring it later in life. Many of the authors and interviewees with disabilities represented in these pages are, indeed, girls and women who have lived most of their lives with impairments. This book has shown how their lives need not support the tragedy, devastation, and doom foretold for them; but what of the women disabled later on? The collections of disabled women's writings of the past five years have underrepresented this group. Social researchers who seek to study those who became disabled later in life usually locate such women through medical and rehabilitation facilities that provide services to newly disabled people. Thus, the literature has much about the immediate reaction to disability and rehabilitation and almost nothing about life two to ten years later, after women have left

333

the facilities and are trying to survive in their own communities. We need longitudinal studies and more reflective, less inspirational personal accounts. Researchers must work creatively to find people in their own settings, yet that task will remain difficult so long as society stigmatizes and penalizes women who acknowledge to the world that they function with impairments. What will these women tell us? Will they, too, report stigma, deprivation, efforts, and triumphs?

Other areas of disability studies remain untouched. For example, what is the experience of disabled women in relationships with women or men as partners? Does the partner's gender or disability make a difference? Is the pattern of disabled women's partnerships notably different from that of other women's? Who are these partners—are they the saints or the losers identified by the common wisdom? How much do they perceive themselves as nurturers and how much do they acknowledge receiving nurturance?

Women of color who have disabilities are also underrepresented in this volume. For some, disability is their primary self-definition; for others, it is not. How does race figure in a woman's experience of disability? How does it figure in cultural experiences of disability?

The complex relationship of social class, gender, and disability awaits more sophisticated analysis. How does being born into a working-class family affect disability? How is the onset of disability in later life shaped by and how does it shape adult economic circumstances? How do service systems narrow or exacerbate class differences among disabled women? These questions and more macroanalyses of these interactions warrant investigation.

While the vast number of disabled women are unemployed and underemployed, not all are. Studies of achieving women to date have been limited to those without known impairments. What can be learned about the theories of women's achievement by studying disabled women whose work affords them satisfaction, economic security, and some matter of status and prestige?

The non-disabled world assumes and acts on the assumption that disabled women make unfit mothers. Scores of disabled women lose custody of their children in divorce; others have children taken away from them by state social welfare agencies simply on grounds of their disabilities; still others report discrimination against them when they seek to become foster mothers or adoptive mothers. How have the women who have become mothers viewed their lives? We have scattered accounts, most suggesting that the essence of parenthood has less to do with specific physical or cognitive capacities and more to do with emotional ones.[2] Compared to the dire predictions, nothing in what disabled women have written supports the conclusion that they or their children suffer from their mothering; in fact, most state the reverse. What does this say about our notions of mothering for disabled and non-disabled women alike?

Throughout this country live girls and women with a host of disabilities. We know only of those we can find, of those who have been available, willing, or needful of sharing their experiences with us. Yet there are others; they live with disabilities ranging from mild to severe. Some are in institutions; some are imprisoned in homes not their own—run by parents, by philanthropy, or by the state. What of those who are happy with their lives, who are employed in or out of homes they enjoy, in partnership with women or men or happily alone, rearing their own or other people's children? If they say that disability has not influenced their lives, most social researchers counter that they are "denying," and their experience is discounted. We must communicate to them and to those who study people with disabilities that there is great value in learning how disabled persons make sense of their lives and relationships. Far from discounting them, we can learn from them.

At the outset, we said that gender has not figured into writings about disability. In the past five years, women with disabilities have begun to inject it. It is long overdue. Still, there remain questions for men with disabilities to answer. How much does disability complicate fulfillment of their lives? Leonard Kriegel is one of the few men who has explicitly tackled the topic, not necessarily to the satisfaction of disabled feminists.[3] Nonetheless, we ask that other disabled men be willing to talk about their gender. Also, we ask social researchers who look at gender to assiduously include disability in their work; do not exclude disabled women or men in the way that non-disabled women used to be excluded from social research—on grounds that they introduced "noise" into the findings. If disabled women and men truly are part of the world, as this book has sought to demonstrate, they deserve to be part of the world of theory and research about the meaning of gender.

Disabled women will not soon leave their place at the margins. When they do, they need not lose what they have gained from having lived there. Yet all of us—disabled and not—will gain more by modifying our theory, our practice, and our society to eliminate the need for boundaries that differentiate between mainstream and margins. This book stands as one step toward that goal. We await the work that will advance it.

336 • Epilogue

Notes

1. E. Goffman, *Stigma: Notes On the Management of Spoiled Identity* (Englewood Cliffs, N.J.: Prentice-Hall, 1963).

2. For writings about disabled women as mothers, see "The Lois Anderson Story," by Lois Anderson, pp. 275–79; "To Choose a Child," by Donna Hyler, pp. 280–83; "Parenting," by JoAnn LeMaistre, pp. 284–91, in S. Browne, D. Connors, N. Stern, eds., *With the Power of Each Breath* (Pittsburgh: Cleis Press, 1985); and S. Shaul, P. J. Dowling, and B. F. Laden, "Like Other Women: Perspectives of Mothers With Physical Disabilities," in M. J. Deegan and N. Brooks, eds., *Women and Disability: The Double Handicap* (New Brunswick, N.J.: Transaction, 1985), pp. 133–42.

3. Leonard Kriegel, *On Men and Manhood* (New York: Hawthorn Books, 1979).

About the Contributors and Index

About the Contributors

Adrienne Asch is a psychotherapist, activist, and scholar; has been on the staff of the New York State Division of Human Rights; and is completing a doctorate in social psychology at Teachers College, Columbia University. She is a member of the National Federation of the Blind, a member of the Board of Directors of the New York Civil Liberties Union, and Associate for Social Science and Policy with the New Jersey Bioethics Commission.

Susan Bailey has an M.A. in English from the University of New Orleans. She has taught at the University of California at Berkeley and is currently doing graduate work in chemistry at Mills College in Oakland, California.

Marian Blackwell-Stratton is a disability rights advocate and paralegal and has been associated with the legal, training, and technical assistance programs of the Disability Rights Education and Defense Fund since 1982. Blackwell-Stratton is a disabled woman and a feminist.

Mary Lou Breslin is acting director of the Disability Rights Education and Defense Fund. In this capacity she is spokeswoman for the rights of disabled children and adults, as well as program planner, administrator, and fund-raiser; she also is a disabled woman.

Shelly Chaiken is an associate professor of psychology at New York University. She works in the area of attitudes, social cognition, and health psychology.

Laura K. Clark is a staff psychologist with student health at Vanderbilt University and an adjunct member of the faculty at Western Kentucky University. Her research interests concern health psychology.

Michelle Fine is an associate professor of psychology in education and of women's studies at the University of Pennsylvania. Involved with concerns of public education, violence against women, and reproductive rights, her research and community-based work broadly address conceptions of and resistance to social injustice.

Berenice Fisher teaches women's studies and educational philosophy at New York University. As a feminist theorist and activist, she has written and worked on a wide range of women's issues. She became interested in disability rights through her friend and coauthor, Roberta Galler.

Gelya Frank is an assistant professor of occupational therapy and anthropology at the University of Southern California. With L. L. Langness she is author of *Lives: An Anthropological Approach to Biography* (Chandler and Sharp 1981). She is currently president of the Society for Humanistic Anthropology, a unit of the American Anthropology Association.

Roberta Galler is a psychoanalyst and psychotherapist in private practice in New York City. A longtime political and community activist, Galler is a frequent speaker and is the author of several articles on women and disability.

Adrienne Harris is an associate professor of psychology at Rutgers University and a psychoanalyst in private practice in New York City.

Mary A. Jansen is dean for professional affairs at the California School of Professional Psychology, Fresno. A former editor of *Rehabilitation Psychology*, she has worked in the areas of rehabilitation policy and international issues in rehabilitation and disability policy, particularly with respect to social security.

Deborah Kent has survived a previous incarnation as a social worker and now works as a free-lance writer. She writes novels for teenagers as well as articles and reviews, and she has a special interest in literary images of disabled people.

Arlene Byrnne Mayerson is directing attorney for the Disability Rights Education and Defense Fund. She is one of the nation's leading disability civil rights legal theorists, specializing in Section 504 of the 1973 Rehabilitation Act, and in PL 94-142, the Education for All Handicapped Children Act.

Beth E. Meyerowitz is an associate professor of psychology at Vanderbilt University and a clinical psychologist specializing in behavioral medicine. Her research has focused on investigating reactions to cancer and strategies for coping with the impact of the disease among patients, their families, and the general public.

Nancy R. Mudrick teaches research and social policy in the School of Social Work at Syracuse University. Her recent work has analyzed the extent to which public policy and programs for disability meet the needs of women, and differences between men and women in the nonmedical factors that influence whether impairments are experienced as disabling.

Marilynn J. Phillips is an associate professor of English at Morgan State University. She has an interdisciplinary background in history, literature, the history of ideas, and folklore; currently she holds a postdoctoral fellowship to document oral histories of former poster children.

Harilyn Rousso is a psychotherapist in private practice. She is also the founder and director of the Networking Project for Disabled Women and Girls, a national mentoring project sponsored by the YWCA/NYC for adolescent girls with disabilities; the coordinator of the Women and Disability Awareness Project, a New York City–based group involved in materials development and training; and an author, lecturer, and consultant on issues of disability and women, sexuality and mental health.

Nancy Felipe Russo is professor of psychology and director of women's studies at Arizona State University. She is interested in the impact of gender on the mental and physical development of women over the life cycle. Formerly on the editorial board of *Rehabilitation Psychology,* she continues to review articles for that journal in the area of sex roles and disability.

Barbara Levy Simon is an assistant professor at the Columbia University School of Social Work. Her book, *Never Married Women,* also published by Temple University Press, analyzes the successful social and economic strategies of women who remain single throughout their lives. She is currently doing research on aging processes among women at mid-life and older.

Joanna Kudisch Weinberg is a visiting scholar at the Center for Law and Society, University of California at Berkeley. She has researched legal issues pertaining to disadvantaged and disabled persons in the United States.

Dana Wideman is a graduate student in psychology at Rutgers University. She has worked as a family and marital therapist in Poland and the United States.

Index

Ability: testing, 239, 323, 324; to work, 5, 9, 10, 11, 230, 231
Abortion, 25, 270, 297, 301, 302, 307, 311, 312, 316
Adjustment: of a disabled person, 41, 42, 44, 47, 51, 72, 74, 76, 77, 78, 122, 195, 197, 198, 201, 221, 222; to a disabled person, 44, 74, 79, 84, 119, 188
Affirmative action, 327
Age, as a variable, 9, 10, 11, 72, 139, 144, 147, 148, 151, 153, 197, 211, 212, 215, 233, 234, 249, 313, 314, 333
Age distribution, 9, 233
Aging, 215, 224, 225
Aid to Families with Dependent Children, 247, 250, 251–53, 259
Art, 31, 90, 93, 103
Attachment, 118, 119, 120, 126, 127, 131
Attitudes, of non-disabled toward disabled persons, 15, 48, 140, 269, 307, 308
Attractiveness, 16, 25, 30, 60, 66, 74, 81, 83, 90, 104, 140, 157, 161, 223, 300, 306, 308
Attributions, of non-disabled toward disability, 16, 151; toward partners of disabled persons, 18
Autonomy, definitions, 270, 271, 274, 280, 287, 289, 290

Baby Doe controversy, 316–18
Barrett, Elisabeth, 90
Barriers to access: architectural, 5, 27, 53, 143, 159, 187, 309, 311, 323, 324, 327; attitudinal, 5, 8, 98, 142, 143, 145, 159, 309, 327; and child-

care, 314; institutional, 5, 8, 11, 12, 28, 238, 239, 259, 311, 314, 321; from medical professionals, 21, 28, 29, 74, 81, 82, 84, 118, 269, 287, 302; from rehabilitation system, 12, 21, 28, 60, 202, 240, 284, 287
Birth control, 9, 21, 149, 150, 281
Birth, of a disabled child, 9, 30, 45, 46, 119, 219, 297, 298, 307, 312, 316
Black women, 27, 229, 232, 233, 234, 236, 253, 262
Body image, 43, 47, 49, 57, 61, 65, 75, 77, 78, 80, 81, 83, 143, 204
Bona Fide Occupational Qualification, 326
Bowe, F., 1, 6, 11, 14
Bradwell v. Illinois, 276
Browning, Robert, 90, 102
Brownmiller, S., 17
Buck v. Bell, 277

Campling, J., 2, 177
Causes of disability: biological, 47, 70; environmental, 15, 72; society's beliefs about, 15, 16, 70, 94, 274, 319
Change, processes of, 71, 77, 78, 84, 197, 198, 211, 212, 221
Child abuse prevention act, 302, 317
Child Amputee Prosthetics Project, 45, 50, 51, 52, 54, 55, 56, 57, 66, 67
Chodorow, N., 5, 18, 19, 133, 135
City of Cleburne, Texas, v. Cleburne Living Center, 276
Civil Rights Act of 1964, 261, 309, 327
Civil Rights Restoration Act of 1985, 322
Communication, 16, 104, 156